Hotels & Motels

Valuations and Market Studies

Appraisal Institute
Professionals Providing
Real Estate Solutions

by Stephen Rushmore, MAI, and Erich Baum

Reviewers: Dianne G. Hays, MAI
David C. Lennhoff, MAI
Mark R. Linne, MAI
Michael S. MaRous, MAI, SRA
John A. Schwartz, MAI

*Vice President, Educational Programs
and Publications:* Larisa Phillips

*Director, Content Development &
Quality Assurance:* Margo Wright

Manager, Book Development: Stephanie Shea-Joyce

Editor: Mary Elizabeth Geraci

Supervisor, Book Design/Production: Michael Landis

Production Specialist: Lynne Mattick

For Educational Purposes Only

The material presented in this text has been reviewed by members of the Appraisal Institute, but the opinions and procedures set forth by the author are not necessarily endorsed as the only methodology consistent with proper appraisal practice. While a great deal of care has been taken to provide accurate and current information, neither the Appraisal Institute nor its editors and staff assume responsibility for the accuracy of the data contained herein. Further, the general principles and conclusions presented in this text are subject to local, state, and federal laws and regulations, court cases, and any revisions of the same. This publication is sold for educational purposes with the understanding that the publisher is not engaged in rendering legal, accounting, or other professional service.

Nondiscrimination Policy

The Appraisal Institute advocates equal opportunity and nondiscrimination in the appraisal profession and conducts its activities in accordance with applicable federal, state, and local laws.

Library of Congress Cataloging-in-Publication Data

Rushmore, Stephen.
    Hotels and motels—valuations and market studies / by Stephen Rushmore and Erich Baum.
        p. cm.
    Includes bibliographical references and index.
    ISBN 0-922154-70-8
        1. Hotels—Valuation—United States. 2. Motels—Valuation—United States. I. Baum, Erich. II. Title.
TX911.3.V34 R865 2001
647.9473'01'068—dc21

2001055336

Contents

List of Tables

Foreword

The Appraisal Institute is pleased to present *Hotels and Motels—Valuations and Market Studies* by Stephen Rushmore, MAI, and Erich Baum. This new text updates and expands on the 1992 *Hotels and Motels* book, the classic text on the valuation and analysis of lodging facilities.

Like the earlier work, this new text explores the history of the lodging industry and the fundamental supply and demand relationships that underlie hotel investments. A wealth of statistical data on recent trends in the lodging industry is provided and its use within the valuation process is demonstrated. Using case study examples, the authors take readers through each step in the analytical process, evaluating site and locational characteristics, quantifying lodging demand, evaluating competitive lodging supply, measuring property-specific characteristics, forecasting revenues and expenses, and estimating market value.

Hotels and Motels—Valuations and Market Studies offers sound theory, up-to-date information, and a sophisticated, systematic approach to help valuation professionals complete hotel market studies, feasibility forecasts, investment analyses, and valuations.

Brian A. Glanville, MAI
2001 President

Acknowledgments

I would like to acknowledge the hundreds of people I have known over the years in the hotel and real estate business who gave me the knowledge and experience to write a book of this magnitude. As always, I would like to thank my family and friends who provide constant support in my quest to visit every hotel within a 25-mile radius of any pleasure or vacation trip. Last but not least, I thank my wonderful wife, Judy, and my two children, Cindy and Stephen, Jr., who enjoy the hospitality industry as much as I do.

Stephen Rushmore

I'd like to thank my wife, Maureen Donnelly; my father, Robert Baum; my mother, Pamela Steele; and all HVS International colleagues past and present, particularly Suzanne Mellen. Special thanks to Steve Rushmore for offering me this opportunity, among many others.

Erich Baum

About the Authors

Stephen Rushmore, MAI, CRE, CHA

Stephen Rushmore is President and Founder of HVS International, a global hospitality consulting organization with offices in New York (Mineola), San Francisco, Miami, Boulder, Vancouver, Toronto, Sao Paulo, Buenos Aires, London, New Delhi, and Singapore. He directs the worldwide operation of this firm and is responsible for future office expansion and new product development. Mr. Rushmore has provided consultation services for more than 10,000 hotels throughout the world during his 30-year career and specializes in complex issues involving hotel feasibility, valuations, and financing. He was one of the creators of the Microtel concept and was instrumental in its initial public offering.

HVS International has provided consulting services for thousands of clients in all 50 states and more than 55 foreign countries. Its staff of more than 150 industry specialists offers a wide range of services, including market feasibility studies, valuations, strategic analysis, development planning, and litigation support. Through its divisions, HVS supplies unique hotel consulting expertise in the areas of executive search, environmental sustainability, food and beverage operation, gaming, technology, operations, asset management, interior design, and investment banking and counseling. HVS International is a primary source of comparable hotel sales information. Its databases contain information on more than 9,000 hotel transactions and thousands of financial statements. HVS is also one of the most comprehensive sources of hotel compensation data.

As a leading authority and prolific author on hotel feasibility studies and appraisals, Mr. Rushmore has written five texts and two seminars for the Appraisal Institute covering this subject. He has also authored three reference books on hotel investing and has published more than 300 articles. He writes a monthly column for *Hotels* magazine and is widely quoted by major business and professional publications. Mr. Rushmore lectures extensively on hotel trends and has taught hundreds of classes and seminars to more than 20,000 industry professionals. He is on the faculty of the Cornell Hotel School's professional development program.

Mr. Rushmore has a BS degree from the Cornell Hotel School and an MBA from the University of Buffalo. He holds an MAI designation from the Appraisal Institute, the CRE designation from the Counselors of Real Estate, and the CHA certification (certified hotel administrator) from the American Hotel and Lodging Association. Mr. Rushmore is a member of numerous hotel industry committees, including IREFAC, the NYU Hotel Investment Conference, and the Cornell European Investment Conference. In 1999 he was recognized by the New York chapter of the Cornell Hotel Society as "Hotelier of the Year."

In his free time, Mr. Rushmore enjoys skiing, biking, and sailing. He holds a commercial pilot's license with instrument and multi-engine ratings, collects hotel key tags, and is one of the foremost authorities on regional dining (www.roadfood.com).

Stephen Rushmore can be contacted at HVS International, 372 Willis Ave., Mineola, NY 11501
Phone: (516) 248-8828 x204 Fax: (516)742-3059
E-mail: srushmore@hvsinternational.com
Web: www.hvsinternational.com

Erich Baum

Erich Baum started his appraisal and consulting career under Suzanne Mellen in 1990 in HVS International's San Francisco office. He moved to Portsmouth, New Hampshire and began working for Steve Rushmore in 1996, continuing as an HVS employee. He has appraised or consulted on more than 200 hotels in 41 states and in Mexico and the Caribbean. A graduate of Cornell University's School of Hotel Administration, Baum also has a masters of arts degree in writing from the University of San Francisco. Mr. Baum is a state-certified appraiser in the State of California and has served as an expert witness in a number of courts of law.

In addition to serving as a contributing editor to the *Hotel Investments Handbook,* published in 1997, Mr. Baum has guest lectured on valuation issues at the University of Maryland. In his free time, Mr. Baum plays drums and pushes his daughter, Larkyn, on various swing sets throughout Portsmouth.

Erich Baum can be contacted at HVS International, 372 Willis Ave., Mineola, NY 11501
Phone: (516) 248-8828 x242 Fax: (516)742-3059 E-mail: ebaum@hvsinternational.com
Web: www.hvsinternational.com

Introduction

This book aims to present and explain contemporary procedures applied in the preparation of hotel market studies, financial forecasts and investment analyses, and valuations. As the hotel industry continues to change rapidly, the methodologies applied by hotel analysts have similarly evolved. This narrative will illustrate these new procedures using a case study, demonstrating the techniques that appraisers and consultants can use to arrive at sound conclusions and recommendations. Readers should note that the proposed hotel presented in the case study is hypothetical and the results of some of the mathematical calculations have been rounded.

The lodging industry has always tried to distinguish between hotels, motels, and motor hotels. In recent decades, motels have become more like hotels—multistory facilities with extensive food, beverage, and banquet facilities, convenient parking, efficient designs, and small public areas. The lodging industry has reached a point where the terms *hotel* and *motel* can be used interchangeably, and classifying statistics based on this terminology has become meaningless. Throughout this text, readers should assume that the words *hotel, motel, motor hotel, hostelry,* and *lodging facility* are synonymous.

Chapter 1 presents an overview of the hotel-motel industry. This historical background is relevant because economic trends tend to run in specific cycles. With an understanding of the historic changes in macro supply and demand, an appraiser is better able to forecast a hotel's future economic performance. New developments in lodging facilities also move in specific cycles, which reflect current travel patterns and modes of transportation as well as the preferences of patrons. The element of change is important because it often causes functional and external obsolescence and a rapid loss in property value.

All market studies and appraisals are based on the principle of supply and demand. In valuing a lodging facility, supply refers to the number and type of competitive transient accommodations located within a defined market area. Demand represents the total number of travelers expected to use these facilities. An appraiser initially evaluates local supply and demand relationships to determine how a proposed hostelry will fit into the market. Quantifying the total demand into measurable units and dividing these units among the competitive facilities establish the property's expected market share. This information is then converted into estimates of occupancy and average rate, which are used to project revenue.

Expense projections can be developed from comparable properties or published national averages. The data must be adjusted to reflect the individual characteristics of the subject property. When the projected revenue is combined with anticipated expenses, the resulting net income estimate represents the future economic benefits of the property. This estimate is converted into an opinion of value using the income capitalization approach.

Appraisers rely on three approaches (cost, sales comparison, and income capitalization) to estimate market value. The income capitalization approach, in which future benefits are discounted at an appropriate rate, is generally given the greatest weight in valuing income-producing properties such as hotels and motels. Various discounting techniques may be applied, depending on the assumed investment and income criteria.

Hotel appraisals must reflect the investment strategy and rationale of typical hotel and motel buyers and sellers. Because lodging facilities contain unusual elements such as business value, personal property, and many types of operating risks, familiarity with hotels and motels as investments is essential.

CHAPTER 1

Growth and Development of the Hotel-Motel Industry

Origins of the Lodging Industry

The hotels and motels we know today evolved from small, one-room, private dwellings that served merchants as early as 500 B.C. From this modest beginning, the hotel industry has come to play a vital role in the development of trade, commerce, and travel throughout the world.

The first record of innkeeping law is found in the Code of Hammurabi, who ruled Babylonia in approximately 2000 B.C. The code sets forth specific regulations for the operation of Babylonian taverns and inns, including corporal penalties for watering down beer. In this period, taverns and inns were prevalent throughout Greece, Italy, Egypt, and Asia. Greek taverns were frequently located near a temple for easy preparation and transportation of sacrificial animals. These establishments provided travelers with food, drink, and sometimes a bed. The Olympic Games, which began in Greece in 776 B.C., involved travel for both spectators and players, creating a demand for accommodations.

During the rise and fall of the Roman Empire, pleasure travel became possible due to good roads, stable government, economic prosperity, and increased leisure time. Educated, affluent Romans vacationed in Greece and toured Egypt. An excellent network of consular roads and post houses was developed to handle this increased travel demand.

After the fall of the Roman Empire in A.D. 476, travel and trade dropped significantly. The Middle Ages was a time of unstable politics and danger on the roads. Religious travelers were common, however, as the church increased its dominance. Religious orders provided accommodations for travelers in monasteries and in the hospices and inns they operated. Most trips during this period were pilgrimages to holy sites or journeys to fight in the Crusades, which began in A.D. 1095 and lasted approximately 200 years.

In the 13th century the innkeepers of Florence, Italy, formed the first hotel guild. Guild members interviewed visitors at the city gate, assigning foreigners to certain lodging facilities and local visitors to others. Most guild members did not own their hostelries; they rented them under three-year leases from the city.

A resurgence in lodging demand started in England during the Industrial Revolution (1760), when the British government arranged for mail to be delivered by coach. A national posting system was created and a network of posting inns was established to accommodate the young postboys and provide a change of horses. Travel by coach became fashionable and long coach trips gave rise to demand for overnight lodging and the development of the English inn. These lodging facilities, forerunners of the modern motel, were located on coach trails to provide refuge for weary travelers and protection from highwaymen. Accommodations in these inns typically consisted of single, unheated rooms with straw beds for the nobility and common sleeping areas on stone floors for their servants. Travelers and local townspeople alike enjoyed hearty food and drink.

The American counterpart of the English inn was the colonial inn and tavern. Such inns sprang up in seaport towns and along stagecoach roads and canals in the 1700s and 1800s. In addition to providing travelers with overnight accommodations, colonial inns were often public gathering places used for courts of law, town meetings, and school classes. Massachusetts recognized the importance of inns to statewide commerce and passed a law penalizing any town that did not provide this convenience.

The following description of a colonial inn illustrates how far American hostelries have come in 200 years:

> Accommodations often meant sleeping on the floor of the "long room," with one's feet turned toward the fireplace and one's head on a rolled-up coat, alongside a dozen or more other persons of both sexes. It meant a quick cold-water wash in an outdoor basin and gingerly use of a communal towel. A warning blast on the landlord's cow horn meant all hands to table, ready to tackle breakfast with fingers and knives.[1]

Over time the accommodations provided by colonial inns gradually improved in response to the needs of a mobile, restless society, and American innkeepers assumed their place as important community figures. Samuels Coles of Boston, who opened one of the first taverns in America, became a leading church member and a steward of Harvard University. Because inns functioned as centers of political and social activity, their owners and operators were community leaders.

---

1. Leslie Dorsey and Janice Devine, *Fare Thee Well* (New York: Crown Publishers, Inc. 1964), 4.

The First Hotels

The first hotel constructed in the United States was the 73-room City Hotel located at 115 Broadway in downtown New York City. Completed in 1794, the City Hotel was enormous compared to colonial inns and served as a model for similar establishments in Boston, Philadelphia, and Baltimore.

Boston's first hotel was the Exchange Coffee House (1806), which boasted seven stories and 200 rooms, many overlooking a five-story, domed interior courtyard (a forerunner of the atrium hotel). Philadelphia's first hotel, the Mansion House, was built in 1807. Baltimore followed, opening the Baltimore City Hotel in 1826. Each of these properties was larger and more lavish than its predecessor and became the focus of civic pride.

During the 1800s hotels moved westward and flourished in major American cities and towns. The Tremont House in Boston started a trend toward luxury accommodations by offering unheard-of services and amenities: private guestrooms, doors with locks, a washbowl with a water pitcher and free soap, bellboys, French cuisine, and an annunciator system that allowed the front desk to contact guests in their rooms.

Spurred by the success of the Tremont House, hotels nationwide attempted to outdo each other in size, luxury and inventiveness. In 1836 the Astor House in New York City installed steam-powered pumps to send water up above the first-floor level so that plumbing could be installed on upper floors. The New York Hotel, built in 1844, was the first hotel to provide private baths connected to some of its bedrooms, while the Buffalo Statler, built in 1908, included private baths in all of its guestrooms. In 1835 the American Hotel in New York City was the first to have gaslight throughout the building. Edison's electric light was first installed in the public areas of the Hotel Everett in 1882, and the Sagamore Hotel, which opened in 1883 on Lake George, New York, was the first to have electric lights throughout. In 1894 the Hotel Netherlands in New York City installed the first hotel telephone system. The Fifth Avenue Hotel in New York City was the first to have elevators, an innovation that later enabled hotels to be constructed as high-rise structures. The first fully air-conditioned hotel was the Detroit Statler.

As the number of hotels increased, many properties faced the prospect of rapid obsolescence and a consequent loss in value. The City Hotel, for example, became obsolete within 15 years due to competition and was converted into an office building 38 years later. The trend-setting Tremont House closed for major modernization after 20 years of operation and was considered a second-class property during the last two decades of its 65-year life. Today hostelries face similar problems due to constant changes in modes of transportation and customer preferences as well as competition from newer properties.

The hotels of the mid-1800s followed the railroads westward, and ornate, luxury properties were constructed at major rail centers: the Palmer House in Chicago

(1882), Brown Palace in Denver (1893), and the Palace in San Francisco (1875). Hotels became status symbols, and cities tried to outdo each other by building larger and more expensive facilities. In many cases the hotels developed far exceeded existing or potential markets.

In addition to luxurious city hotels, resort hotels were introduced as new rail lines enabled affluent Americans to travel on vacation. Spas, which were considered the first American resorts, were opened in Saratoga Springs, New York (Grand Union Hotel), and White Sulphur Springs, West Virginia (the Greenbrier). Other grand resort hotels built during the 1800s included the Hotel Del Coronado outside San Diego, California, the Ponce de Leon in St. Augustine, Florida, and the Broadmoor in Colorado Springs, Colorado.

Travelers who could not afford luxury accommodations usually were forced to stay at rundown roominghouses, which offered only minimal services and cleanliness. As rail transportation became affordable and more middle-class people began to travel, a new type of hostelry was needed to fill the gap between luxury hotels and roominghouses.

E. M. Statler recognized this demand and built the nation's first modern, commercial hotel in Buffalo, New York. When the Buffalo Statler opened in 1908, it offered many revolutionary conveniences: private baths, circulating ice water, full-length mirrors, overnight laundry, and free morning newspapers. Statler's slogan, "A room and a bath for a dollar and a half," put clean, comfortable transient accommodations within the reach of millions of Americans and increased the interest in travel among the middle class.

Prosperity, Decline, and Renewal

The economic prosperity of the 1920s produced one of the greatest hotel-building booms in America's history. Encouraged by rising occupancy rates, which exceeded 85% in 1920, hoteliers expanded existing properties and constructed hundreds of new and larger facilities. During this period the number of available hotel rooms in some cities doubled with the addition of large convention properties. Chicago's 3,000-room Hotel Stevens (now the Chicago Hilton) opened in 1927 and was the world's largest hotel for more than 35 years.

During the Roaring Twenties, hotel promoters set up shop in towns and cities throughout the United States and sold local residents on the idea that real estate was a sound and safe investment vehicle. Their sales pitch was not based on economic feasibility, but on civic pride and a chance to raise neighborhood or personal prestige. In some cases local merchants were promised patronage from hotel guests if they invested in the project. Seldom did an independent expert prepare a market study and appraisal; instead, the class, size and design of the facilities to be built were frequently determined by the amount of money that promoters could raise. In these "community-financed" hotel projects, real estate bonds for first and second mortgages were sold to members of the community. In many cases the financing structure involved high leverage and an inordinate amount of risk.

The financing fees and commissions promoters charged tended to be high and were usually paid as soon as the financing was in place. As a result, promoters had no vested interest in the hotel's performance.

Beginning in the mid-1920s, *Hotel Management* magazine, a trade publication now known as *Hotel and Motel Management,* published articles by several industry spokespersons warning against "over-hoteling." They urged professional hoteliers to tell the public the "real facts" about hotel occupancy levels and financial conditions to offset the exaggerated stories that had circulated earlier in the decade and contributed to overbuilding. To illustrate the extent of the problem, a national survey was conducted in 1928-1929 by an objective body, the Engineering-Economics Foundation. This postgraduate institution in Boston performed the research, quantifying hotel room supply, guest demand, occupancy levels, rates, and hotel failures from 1919 to 1928. They found that occupancy nationwide had dropped from 85.5% in 1920 to 67.6% in 1928. At the same time room rates appeared to be fairly constant, but the foundation claimed that additional services had to be provided to guests, which effectively lowered the rate achieved. The number of hotel failures also illustrated a downward trend, with 64 failures reported in 1924 and 112 in 1928.

During the Great Depression of the 1930s new construction ceased and more than 80% of the nation's hostelries were forced into foreclosure or receivership. By 1933 one-third of America was unemployed and the gross national product had dropped by nearly half. Commercial and leisure travel came to a virtual standstill, and the average national hotel occupancy fell to little more than 50%.

Although the depression forced many hoteliers out of business, it offered those with cash the opportunity to expand their holdings by purchasing distressed properties from receivers and lenders. Parties who had taken debt positions in the original financing structure found themselves owning a piece of the hotel after it was foreclosed. These parties included both institutional lenders and individual investors who had purchased mortgage bonds through public subscriptions in the 1920s. None of these investors knew much about hotel operations so all were eager to sell the properties or their shares to any willing buyer at greatly reduced prices. This created an exceptional opportunity for those who understood the hotel industry and had readily available cash or credit.

Typical purchase terms for failed hotels required a small cash down payment from the buyer. The lender, in turn, provided a restructured debt component for the balance of the purchase price. During the depression prominent appraisers warned investors not to value hotels based on the assumption that the prevailing low levels of income would continue into perpetuity; they projected future earnings to turn around within five years. For America's hotel industry, the depression lasted longer than expected due to the severe overbuilding that had preceded it and the lack of commercial and pleasure travel during the 1930s.

During the depression several hotel companies significantly expanded their holdings, which provided the impetus for the establishment of national hotel chains. Conrad Hilton began his lodging chain in 1919 with the acquisition of the 40-room Mobley Hotel in Cisco, Texas. During the 1920s he purchased and developed a total of eight hotels throughout Texas. Because his hotels were highly leveraged, Hilton lost three of his properties during the depression, but by 1935 profits from oil leases provided him with the cash he needed to satisfy his creditors and fund new purchases. Hilton took control of the Sir Francis Drake in San Francisco, the Town House Hotel and the Rosslyn Hotel in Los Angeles, and the Roosevelt and Plaza hotels in New York. In 1945 Hilton was able to acquire the Palmer House in Chicago for less than $20 million although it cost more than $25 million to build in 1929. That same year, Hilton acquired the Stevens Hotel in Chicago for about $8 million; that hotel was built in 1925 for $30 million. In 1942 Hilton bought the Waldorf-Astoria bonds for 4.5% of their original value.

Ernest Henderson founded the Sheraton hotel chain in 1937 with the purchase of the Stonehaven Hotel in Springfield, Massachusetts. Although he was inexperienced in hotel operations, he had cash and understood real estate and the use of leverage. Henderson took advantage of the depressed hotel prices of the 1930s and early 1940s and the readiness of sellers to negotiate. By 1941 his company had acquired four more hotels and was on its way to becoming one of the nation's largest lodging chains. Henderson believed in leveraging his cash position and acquiring hotels with a minimum amount of cash, sometimes negotiating with sellers to take back second mortgages in return for higher selling prices.

Leading hotel companies such as Hilton and Sheraton were able to overcome the fears of bankers and other lenders wary of independent developers and hotel investments in general. With fire sale prices and favorable financing terms, strong hotel companies with prominent names and proven track records were able to continue their expansions. In some cases the hotel chains guaranteed their mortgages by putting all of their hotel properties up as collateral. This strategy enabled them to borrow 60% to 70% of the property's fair market value.

America's hotel industry did not begin to recover until the early 1940s. By then the general economy had improved and the hotel room supply had been significantly reduced by closures. What really revived the hotel industry was the onset of World War II. The massive movement of defense industry workers, military personnel, and their families created an unprecedented demand for transient accommodations, and the national occupancy level soon exceeded 90%. Although most towns and cities needed more lodging facilities during this period, there was little new hotel construction because financing, materials, and labor were unavailable.

Lenders and investors, still wary of risk after the downswing of the depression, were reluctant to finance new hotels. In some areas the hotel room supply was actually reduced because hotels were converted into housing for American troops. Properties such as the Hotel Stevens in Chicago and the Greenbrier in West Virginia actually served as barracks during the 1940s.

Labor and material shortages during the war years made it difficult for hotels to maintain high standards of service. Guests often waited for hours in hotel lobbies only to find that no rooms were available. At one point New York City hotels had to limit each guest to a stay of three days.

The 1950s marked the beginning of a radical change in transportation. The railroad, which had served travelers for more than a century, began to lose customers to the more economical automobile and the faster airplane. The technology developed during the war helped produce a more affluent population that enjoyed shorter work weeks, more leisure time, and a new freedom to travel. The "mobile society" was born, and more people took advantage of the convenience of highways and airlines.

Sites directly across from downtown railway stations—once considered prime hotel locations—quickly became less desirable and economically obsolete. A more informal lifestyle was developing, and the traveling public seemed willing to sacrifice luxuries such as doormen, bellhops, valet parking, and evening turndown service in exchange for less expensive rooms.

The Birth of the Motel

A new type of highway-oriented lodging facility offering inexpensive, "no-frills" accommodations was needed to meet the needs of travelers. So, in 1950, the modern motel was born. Although the origins of the motel can be traced to the relatively primitive tourist cabins of the 1930s, the motels of the 1950s offered much better facilities.

Most early motels were one-story, wood-frame structures built on slabs with approximately 20 to 50 units. Their modest rooms had inexpensive furnishings, particle board walls and ceilings, tile floors, small baths, metal shower stalls, and radios. Few motels at this time provided food and beverage service or meeting rooms.

Motels were spartan compared to most hotels, but they became competitive because of their convenient highway locations, ample parking, and low rates. The motel market included vacation travelers (especially young families and senior citizens), salesmen, middle managers, and government employees. Operating statistics for the 1950s show steadily declining hotel occupancies but stable occupancy levels for motels. Because the number of motel rooms was increasing, motels were beginning to capture a transient market previously monopolized by hotels.

The first motels were radically different from hotels with respect to size, construction costs, land values, operating ratios, and management requirements. The distinction between a hotel and motel has lessened, however, due to a variety of factors:

- Motels began to grow with additions to existing properties and more total units constructed for new properties.
- Motels joined referral groups and franchises to obtain national images and greater exposure.
- Motels began offering more amenities, such as television, air-conditioning, carpeting, tile baths, telephones, swimming pools, restaurants, lounges, meeting and banquet rooms, and gift shops.
- Motels began providing more services, including 24-hour telephone switchboard and front desk attendants, nationwide telephone reservation systems, acceptance of credit cards, direct-dial guestroom phones, and morning wake-up calls.
- Improved building techniques were introduced, including the use of concrete and steel, pre-assembled units and high-rise construction.

By the mid-1960s, most new motels offered all the facilities and amenities typically available at hotels. At the same time, hotels were modifying their operations to compete with motels. The result was a gradual merging of the two types of properties into a new type of facility known as the motor hotel. Motor hotels combined the services and facilities of hotels with the convenience of motels.

Although independent motels and motor hotels flourished throughout the United States, their potential guests had little idea of what to expect when they pulled off the highway. Standards of service and quality varied and guests were frequently disappointed. Kemmons Wilson recognized this problem when traveling with his own family and saw it as an opportunity. In 1952 Wilson started a new era in the hospitality industry by founding Holiday Inns, one of the earliest motel chains. Holiday Inns offered guests a modern motel with standardized service, a recognized name, and moderate prices. Starting with four motels near Memphis, Tennessee, in the early 1950s, the Holiday Inns chain grew to more than 100 motels nationally by 1960. This tremendous growth was accomplished by selling franchises to individuals who would operate the properties as their own businesses. The first Holiday Inns franchise was sold in Clarksdale, Mississippi, for $500 and a flat fee of $.05 per occupied room. In return for these payments, the franchisee received the Holiday Inn name and logo, architectural plans, training and operation manuals, and national advertising. In 1964 Holiday Inns launched its Holidex I reservation system and a major benefit was added to the franchise package. Kemmons Wilson was overwhelmed with franchise applications.

During the 1950s the supply of motel rooms nationwide increased from 600,000 to 1,500,000. Several factors contributed to this boom. The first was the passage of the Interstate Highway Act in 1956, which laid out a map for the growth of highways and hence roadside motel sites. Travelers on interstate highways bypassed motels on state highways and these older lodging facilities rapidly succumbed to external obsolescence. A change in the income tax laws in 1954, which permitted real property owners to use an accelerated method of depreciation, also contributed to the increased motel supply and led to a period of readily available cash from "tax-based" hotel deals. In such deals, syndicators offered investors participation in hotels and the benefits of large depreciation and interest expense deductions to offset income in the investment's early years. Franchising was the third factor contributing to the increased supply of motel rooms during the 1950s. Developers' ability to benefit from the name recognition of motel franchises enticed many non-hoteliers into the business.

Lodging Chains

Several new lodging chains were established in the late 1950s and early 1960s. The Marriott Corporation, once known mostly for its food service business, entered the lodging industry in 1957 with its Twin Bridges Marriott Motor Hotel in Arlington, Virginia, outside of Washington, D.C. Marriott is now the largest hotel operator in the nation.

In 1957 the Pritzker family of Chicago diversified its holdings by entering the lodging industry with the purchase of the Hyatt House at the Los Angeles International Airport. Hyatt is now a leading operator of convention hotels. Hyatt hotels are best known for their spectacular atrium lobbies.

In 1954 the Howard Johnson Company, known for its restaurants, opened its first motor lodge. By 1959 the Howard Johnson name was already on 75 motor lodges, both company-owned and franchised. In the mid-1950s Marion Isbell and his associates began acquiring motor hotels in the Southwest. By 1962 they had formed the Ramada Inn chain.

In 1962 the Carlson Companies, founded by Curtis Carlson, acquired the Radisson Hotel in downtown Minneapolis to initiate that company's diversification into the hotel business. The company began purchasing and renovating inner-city hotels in the Midwest and operating them under the Radisson name.

International activity by American hotel companies became prevalent in the 1960s. Inter-Continental Hotels Corporation, a Pan American Airways' subsidiary established in the late 1940s with the opening of the Inter-Continental in Belem, Brazil, continued to develop hotels in Latin America. Hilton Hotels, which had been operating the Caribe Hilton in Puerto Rico since the late 1940s, established its Hilton International division in the 1960s, expanding its operations into Europe and South America.

A move toward vertical integration within the airline and lodging industry occurred during the 1960s as several large airlines acquired or merged with hotel companies. Trans World Airlines purchased Hilton International Corporation; United Airlines purchased the Western International chain (now Westin Hotels); and American Airlines purchased and developed its own hotels under the name Americana Hotels. Now, all of these relationships have been terminated, showing that the ownership synergy between the travel and lodging industries is not as strong as was once believed.

Arrival of the Budgets

As the motel evolved into the motor hotel, it began to lose one of its primary competitive advantages—its low price. By providing more facilities and services, motels were forced to charge higher rates. This created a void at the low end of the room-rate scale and precipitated the birth of the "budget motel."

Budget motels were introduced in the late 1960s and flourished during the building boom of the early 1970s. These hostelries offered accommodations at prices substantially lower than the prevailing rates of first-class motor hotel chains. To offer this discount, budget motels take advantage of lower initial investment costs, operating efficiencies, and high volume.

Lower Initial Investment Costs

The initial investment costs for budget motels are lower because these facilities have smaller guestrooms, minimal public space, lower land costs, and a simple, no-frills design. The quality of construction, however, is not reduced.

Guestrooms in budget motels average 250 square feet, while rooms in conventional motor hotels typically contain 335 square feet. Smaller rooms reduce construction costs and interior decorating expenditures and less land is needed to build a budget motel. Budget motels eliminate low-revenue public areas such as meeting and banquet rooms, large lobbies, extensive food and beverage facilities, and executive offices.

Because the size of the facilities is reduced, budget motels require approximately 1.6 acres per 100 rooms, compared to 2.5 acres per 100 rooms for conventional motels. Utilizing secondary locations such as land off an interchange or a short distance from the prime commercial/office area can sometimes create additional savings. Most people traveling on a budget are willing to drive a little farther for a better price.

Budget motels are planned for the efficient use of materials and space. Guestrooms are double-loaded (back-to-back) and constructed on concrete slabs with cinderblock walls between rooms. Modular construction has been used successfully in some areas. Landscaping and decoration are kept to a minimum.

Many budget motels are built with construction specifications and standards similar to those of conventional motor hotels. Operators realize that inferior materials and building techniques may produce initial savings but are a poor choice in the long run when repair and maintenance expenses are considered.

Operating Efficiencies

Compact facilities and fewer guest services contribute to operating efficiencies and result in lower expenses. With smaller guestrooms and reduced public space, budget motels require less cleaning and maintenance and can be more efficiently heated and lighted. Some budget chains use maintenance teams that work at several properties, performing routine repairs and preventive maintenance.

The elimination of bellmen, elaborate food and beverage facilities, room service, entertainment, the acceptance of credit cards, and other services reduces payroll and operating expenses. Major savings are realized on food and beverage service; in budget motels cafeteria and coffee shop service is typical. Often a budget hotel will lease land adjacent to a restaurant chain to avoid any involvement in the food service business.

Price, location, and value all generate high volume for budget motels, but travelers choose budget motels mostly because of their low prices. As with any product with an elastic demand curve, a reduction in price increases volume. Operating results substantiate this premise, indicating that budget motels typically operate at higher occupancy levels than surrounding conventional properties do. Many budget motels are purposely located next to higher-priced hostelries to attract price-conscious travelers.

Although budget motels economize in many areas, they still tend to provide clean, quality guestrooms. The rooms contain comfortable beds, full baths, color televisions, standard furnishings and fixtures, and cheerful drapes, bedspreads, and wall coverings.

From an investment or valuation perspective, budget motels are often vulnerable to increased expenses and decreased occupancies. Because of its lower price structure and similar fixed costs, a budget property generally has a higher breakeven occupancy level than a standard motel does. Appraisers must consider this risk when projecting income and expenses and determining a proper capitalization rate.

Budget hotels appeal to price-conscious travelers.

The 1970s Hotel Boom

In the 1970s, just as budget motels began to inundate the market, the entire lodging industry experienced the start of a construction boom reminiscent of the 1920s. Many factors contributed to this period of expansion and later led to its demise.

New construction was sparked by an enormous amount of financing made available by lenders, particularly real estate investment trusts (REITS). These high-leverage finance companies were created to allow small investors to participate in real estate mortgages and equities. Wall Street quickly accepted the concept, and soon billions of dollars were available to finance real estate projects. Many lenders became so overwhelmed with new money that their underwriting procedures broke down and some marginal developments were approved.

During the late 1960s and early 1970s, hotel companies began to expand their chains through franchising, which at the time was a source of new capital for hotel franchise companies and allowed them to grow and attract national recognition using the franchisee's financial investment in individual properties. Some franchisers, eager to demonstrate such sustained growth and recognition, used questionable marketing tactics to sell new franchises. Many of those selling franchises were compensated based on the number of franchises sold, so there was little incentive to discourage developers from investing in poor locations and overbuilt markets. Many lenders and hostelry developers were led to believe that being part of a national franchise would guarantee success.

The combination of readily available financing and the eagerness of hotel chains to sell franchises resulted in overbuilding and the development of many poorly located, undercapitalized hostelries managed by inexperienced owners. The lodging industry floundered, however, when inflation caused construction costs and interest rates to escalate; the 1974 energy crisis drastically reduced travel, and the accompanying recession curtailed business trips, conferences, and conventions.

Operators of marginal properties quickly fell behind in their mortgage payments, and lenders were forced to foreclose. As lenders became hostelry owners, they either organized workout departments headed by experienced hoteliers or got professional motel management companies to assume operational responsibilities. Sales data indicate that lenders looking for quick sales to remove non-performing hotel assets from their books had to lower their sales prices substantially to attract all-cash buyers. Lenders willing to hold onto foreclosed hotels and employ professional management to reposition and improve the properties' operations were generally able to recoup their original investments within three to five years as the hotel industry began to recover. However, even lenders who repositioned their properties had to take back favorable purchase-money financing to sell the properties because money from other sources was not available.

History has shown that, during economic downturns, hotel values do not fall in the same proportion that their declining incomes do. Sellers—particularly lenders who take back hotels through foreclosure—are not always willing to sell at substantially lower prices. Rather, they are more likely to wait out the downward cycle and dispose of their assets when the market starts to rebound. Appraisers, therefore, can best reflect market behavior by projecting a facility's net income to a stabilized level reflecting renewed market stability and applying the proper discounted cash flow procedure over this time period.

The end of the 1970s was a period of relative calm for the lodging industry. Because most lenders were recovering from the financial wounds inflicted on them by the 1975 recession, they had little interest in making hotel/motel mortgages. New construction was restrained, consisting primarily of additions to existing properties and the development of some large, downtown, convention-commercial hotels. The rebirth of center city hostelries was a direct result of fuel shortages and the availability of government financing for inner-city redevelopment projects. Highway-oriented properties, on the other hand, were hit by escalating gasoline prices and decreased car travel. Hence, these lodging facilities lost some of their appeal among investors and hotel companies.

Decreased building activity along with the normal retirement of older hostelries from the lodging market and an improving economy created a favorable supply and demand relationship and record-high occupancy levels in 1978 and 1979. Average room rates rose rapidly as hotel operators took advantage of the excess demand to recoup earlier losses and keep up with inflation.

The 1980s—A Decade of Change

During the 1980s America's lodging industry changed significantly. Another massive building boom took place, several new types of hotels were introduced, and hotel chains began to increase their product lines through segmentation. The industry began to focus on the global hotel market after foreign investors acquired several American hotel chains and individual properties. Use of the hotel management contract became the main means of operation for most publicly traded hotel companies.

After the decline in new hotel development during the late 1970s, the real estate environment appeared ready for a period of renewed hotel expansion. However, the Federal Reserve tightened the money supply in the 1980s, sending the prime interest rate up to record levels. Most of the projects that were in the preliminary planning stages but lacked sensible financing were put on hold.

Eventually, monetary and fiscal policies, along with falling energy prices, reduced the national rate of inflation. This produced a downtrend in hotel interest rates beginning in 1983 and suddenly massive amounts of capital were available for real estate investments. Hotel developers, effectively out of the market since the mid-1970s, rushed to create new projects. They were aided by several major real estate development incentives: favorable industry trends, readily available debt and equity financing, and unique income tax benefits designed to stimulate real estate growth.

Lodging industry trends during the early 1980s were favorable for new hotel development. Many markets showed relatively high occupancy levels, hotel room rates were able to keep up with inflationary price increases, and the travel industry was expected to boom as a result of a healthy economy. National demographics characterized by affluent baby boomers, two-income families, and more leisure time further fueled developers' optimism. As in the past, sellers of franchises were aggressively signing up new prospects using product segmentation to justify the saturation of a market with a common brand.

This time financing was readily available from the savings and loan industry. After recent deregulation, these banks were permitted to lend on commercial real estate such as hotels. Although savings and loans had experience in making real estate loans on single-family homes, most had little expertise with commercial properties, particularly hotels and motels. The result was almost identical to the real estate investment trust fiasco the decade before. Loan underwriting and administration was useless and sometimes nonexistent; the quantity of loans made seemed more important than the quality of the real estate and the integrity of the borrower; and short-term monies were often being used to finance long-term mortgages.

On the equity side, the money raised for hotel developments and acquisitions generally came from syndicated limited partnerships. Most of these ownership structures were devised to take full advantage of the generous tax benefits allowed for hotel real estate. Initially, the majority of hotel syndications were relatively small and the equity raised was less than $10 million. Later, however, Wall Street investors saw the opportunity to make huge fees from selling these equities, and pools of hotels were packaged and sold to investors in $100,000 units. Some of the larger packages attracted more than $100 million in equity. Everyone wanted to invest in hotels, particularly when the property was a prominent, trophy-type hotel or the sponsor organizing the partnership was a major hotel company. A number of the syndications sold out in minutes and some were even oversubscribed.

The favorable treatment provided by America's income tax regulations also contributed to hotel development during the 1980s. By carefully structuring hotel syndications to take advantage of available tax benefits, investors could virtually recoup their total cash outlay in the first year and reap additional benefits in the future regardless of the economic success of the underlying asset. Because there was little incentive to justify a transaction's economics (i.e., cash flow and reversionary benefits), many syndicators overpaid for premier trophy properties, took out excessive fees, and overloaded their hotels with debt.

Hotel franchisers also played an important role in this overbuilding through a new concept called segmentation. In order to show continuous growth, the hotel companies, which at the time catered to only one pricing segment, realized that they could create new products for other pricing segments and thereby offer two or more affiliations in the same market without directly competing against themselves. For example, Holiday Inns, a mid-priced lodging chain, went upscale and established Crowne Plaza and then ventured downscale with Hampton Inns. Marriott, which was known as a first-class operator, went downscale with Courtyard and downscale further with Fairfield Inn. In addition to adding new pricing segments, hotel companies created entirely new products (e.g., the all-suite hotel, the extended-stay facility, and the microtel). Hotel developers soon rushed to build new properties financed with plentiful amounts of available money and flagged with an assortment of franchises and new products.

A change in the tax law in 1986 eliminated many of the real estate tax benefits of hotels, but the overbuilding in most markets was either in progress or had already happened. By the end of the 1980s, the abuses of the savings and loans became apparent, but it was too late to reverse the overbuilding.

Up until 1990, the lodging industry in most areas of the country was facing massive overbuilding, which created a supply problem. Lodging demand was still strong and, although a recession seemed likely, most industry experts were hopeful that the economy would remain stable. Given this favorable economic scenario and the fact that little new development was anticipated for the first several years of the decade, some experts expected hotel occupancies to improve quickly and the lodging industry to fare better than it had during the 1970s. Unfortunately, the economy did go into a recession, which curtailed business, convention, and leisure travel and produced a downtrend in lodging demand.

The 1990s–Recession, Recovery, and Expansion

The national economy entered another recession in 1990. This, coupled with overbuilding and the Persian Gulf War in 1991, caused the national hotel occupancy rate to bottom out in the low 60% range. In some markets, occupancy rates dropped as low as 35%. The supply and demand imbalance was almost identical to the situation in the 1970s that led to numerous failures. Trailing closely behind this downward occupancy spiral were hotel room rates. Full-scale rate wars broke out in many markets as managers, seeing their patronage decline, attempted to test the elasticity of hotel demand. Since lower room rates rarely create additional new hotel demand and tend to redistribute the existing business among the area's facilities, this strategy produced only short-term revenue gains for some properties and eventually led to long-term profit declines for almost everyone.

Many hotels quickly fell behind with their highly leveraged debt service payments. This immediately led to a rash of foreclosures and bankruptcies. At the same time, the savings and loan industry floundered under the burden of non-performing loans; the Resolution Trust Corporation (RTC) was created to handle the crisis. Since savings and loans were prominent hotel lenders at the time, the RTC soon began to take over hundreds of defaulted hotel loans and actual properties as they acquired insolvent banks. Instead of holding onto these assets and waiting for values to recover, the RTC held massive auctions and disposed of hundreds of hotel properties at bargain prices. Those investors with the foresight to see a market turnaround made huge profits by buying low and selling high.

Many lenders opted to restructure their non-performing hotel loans rather than force their borrowers into bankruptcy. Combinations of principal reduction, interest rate adjustment and other types of forgiveness were structured to assist hotel owners in coping with excessive levels of debt service. Borrowers who were able to survive and get through these crisis years generally preserved some of their equity and tax benefits.

By 1993, new hotel construction had declined significantly. Lenders, trying to get out from under problematic hotel portfolios, curtailed all real estate lending and would not even consider hotel financing opportunities. The tax benefits associated with hotels had disintegrated, and passive investors left the hospitality market entirely. The slowdown in supply growth, coupled with an improving national economy emerging from recession, helped improve occupancy levels, which began to recover in 1992. As increases in lodging demand outpaced the growth in supply, occupancy levels continued to climb through 1995. The improvement led to the resumption of supply growth, but only for smaller limited-service hotels, generally financed by local banks. However, higher-rated economy and mid-scale properties soon became economically feasible (i.e., economic value exceeded development cost). These projects were more commonly financed with funds supplied by regional banks and Wall Street conduits that structured mortgage-backed securities to sell off pieces of the debt that were risk-rated by the rating agencies. During this period, the replacement costs for first-class and luxury hotels still exceeded the value of similar existing properties. As a result, little development took place in these two segments.

The re-emergence of Real Estate Investment Trusts (REITs) also influenced pricing trends and sales volume during the mid- to late 1990s. Given their structure, organizational purpose, and low capital cost, REITs were driven by the need to grow by acquiring assets. According to information provided by the Lodging Research Network, the number of hotels owned by REITs increased from 39 in 1993 to 970 in 1998, while the number of hotel rooms controlled by REITs increased from 6,643 in 1993 to 183,784 in the first quarter of 1998. As the REITs and other public companies, including C-Corps, pursued high-quality hotels, competition for these properties accelerated, placing upward pressure on hotel values. This rapid growth ended abruptly in mid-1998, when the stock market lurched downward in response to fears of a global recession, particularly in Asia. The fears proved to be unfounded and stability returned to the capital markets, but the relationship between stock prices of larger hotel companies and the perceived health of the lodging industry continued to create a sense of uncertainty. As the decade ended, the budget and economy segments of the lodging industry were most at risk, whereas the luxury segment was the safest category for investment. New construction in the luxury sector continued to be difficult to cost-justify, so additions to supply have been minimal. Furthermore, the barriers to entry and long development time required for hotels of this type are likely to delay overbuilding for a number of years.

Throughout the past decade, hotel values in the United States have fluctuated dramatically. During the late 1980s and early 1990s, values declined in most parts of the country. The downturn, which began in most markets in 1988, was largely attributable to lower operating incomes caused by an oversupply of new hotel rooms that were constructed during the mid-1980s. Overbuilding resulted in flat or declining average rates and occupancies, which caused revenues to fall. A number of other factors exacerbated the situation. The national recession caused a drop in demand in many markets during the early 1990s, and the Persian Gulf War created a virtual freeze on travel in the beginning of 1991, further limiting hotel demand. Operating costs continued to rise despite poor market conditions, resulting in a decline in the net operating income of many hotels throughout the nation. Because operating costs have a large fixed component, some lodging facilities experienced precipitous drops in net income.

As bottom-line profits eroded, many hotels were unable to meet debt service, and hundreds of properties entered foreclosure or bankruptcy. Lenders and government agencies soon became hotel owners. Because most financial institutions were preoccupied with their distressed real estate, little mortgage capital was available and the nation suffered from a well-publicized credit crunch. The property owners, who in most cases were lenders, financed a majority of the hotel transactions that occurred during the early 1990s.

In the early 1990s, the primary market participants were owner-operators with the expertise to turn under-performing properties around. Hotels were out of favor with passive investors as a result of the industry's poor operating performance and the uncertainty of future appreciation. The wide disparity in buyer and seller expectations also limited the number of transactions. Many sellers were unwilling to accept the fact that the market value of their hotel investments had declined below the cost of the project or the original investment. Moreover, many owners faced a significant tax burden upon sale, further reducing their willingness to settle for a price that was below the original acquisition cost.

As a result of these market forces, there was little sales activity involving large, high-quality hotels in the early 1990s. The primary difficulty was the lack of properties available for sale. Owners who were not forced to sell opted to wait for prices to recover. The few hotels that did enter the market during this period generally attracted 15 to 20 interested bidders, mostly consisting of owner-operators. As a result of the competition for these few assets, the prices of better-quality hotels escalated rapidly. In response, more sellers were encouraged to place their products on the market, and the number of hotels available for sale (and the number actually sold) began to rise in 1994. This trend continued to accelerate through the first half of 1998.

An indicator of this market trend is the number of hotel sales that have occurred during the past few years. HVS International tracks major hotel transactions of more than $10,000,000 annually. In 1992, major transactions numbered 70; a slightly lower level of 53 was registered in 1993. This total increased significantly, to 108 in 1994 and 147 in 1995. In 1996, the total number of major transactions soared to an estimated 227, then increased again to 280 in 1997. The wider availability of mortgage capital was a material factor influencing the increase in both market activity and prices. Initially, the number of lenders returning to the market was extremely limited and the underwriting criteria were fairly stringent: loan-to-value ratios were in the 60% to 70% range and amortization periods were shortened to 20 or 25 years. The qualification of the borrower was also a crucial consideration for most lenders.

In the mid-1990s, more lenders entered the hotel mortgage market. Although these institutions remained cautious, the greater availability of funds fostered competition, particularly for high-quality assets and well-qualified buyers. As a result, loan-to-value ratios returned to historical levels of 70% to 75%, and interest rates fell to the 8.0% to 9.5% range for most deals. Amortization periods remained in the 20- to 25-year range. The lingering influence of the downturn in the early 1990s is evident in the widespread practice of underwriting based on net income after the deduction of management fees and a reserve for replacement; these line items typically total 7% to 8% of gross revenues.

The market for hotel investments slowed in the third quarter of 1998 due to a reduction in both equity and debt capital available for real estate acquisitions. At that time, many hotel buyers and conduit lenders withdrew from the market due to a downturn in lodging REIT and C-Corp stock prices and the uncertainty of capital markets. The number of major hotel transactions slowed to 241 in 1998 and declined further in 1999 to 118. The market improved somewhat in the first quarter of 1999 as the international capital market stabilized. Transaction activity in the first half of 1999 was significantly below that of the first half of 1998 due to the virtual withdrawal of REITs from the market. By the third quarter of 1999, hotel transactions increased again as buyers and sellers adjusted to new pricing levels and took advantage of the relatively low cost of capital. Private equity capital and traditional debt from commercial banks and credit companies are expected to continue to fuel hotel transactions over the near term. Activity by conduit lenders and public lodging companies also resumed, albeit at a more moderate pace than that witnessed in 1997 and early 1998.

In 1998, moderate to high supply growth in the economy and mid-priced segments caused America's hotel occupancy level to decline. The decline of occupancy in several major American markets, coupled with an unstable global economy, has caused several major lenders to halt hotel financing in anticipation of another economic slowdown. Furthermore, as the number of high-quality, available assets and the amount of available financing diminish, sales activity is expected to slow and will likely result in the stabilization and decline of sale prices.

New Products and Concepts

In recent decades, several new lodging products were introduced, including the all-suite hotel, the extended-stay hotel, and the hard budget hotel. These facilities have gained wide acceptance among the traveling public. While the all-suite hotel and the hard budget hotel essentially absorbed existing demand from traditional hotel products, extended-stay properties actually created new transient lodging demand by attracting long-term travelers who had previously used apartments and residential hotels.

The all-suite hotel is based on the theory that certain types of commercial and leisure travelers do not use the meeting, banquet, restaurant and lounge facilities found in most full-service hotels. Using the space allotted for these facilities as guestrooms instead could create suites with separate living and sleeping areas. The key to the all-suite concept is to reallocate space in a manner that keeps the room rates of a suite similar to those of comparable, full-facility hotels. This creates a favorable price-value relationship for the guest who does not need all the facilities found in a full-service property. Most all-suite hotels also offer a free breakfast and an evening cocktail hour to attract patrons.

The all-suite hotel has been well received by individual commercial travelers and by some leisure travelers. In many markets such hotels are currently the occupancy leader with room rates on par with similar, full-facility hotels. Since they generally have limited food and beverage facilities, all-suite hotels are usually easier to operate and their profit margins are higher.

The extended-stay hotel is designed for the traveler who must stay in an area for five or more consecutive days. It differs from a standard hotel in that the rooms and amenities are oriented toward someone who wants a more residential atmosphere. The guestrooms in an extended-stay hotel have large living areas and full, eat-in kitchens; some have two separate sleeping areas, individual dining rooms, and separate baths. The exterior of such a hotel usually has a residential feel similar to that of a garden apartment complex, complete with recreational facilities and barbecue grills.

The high occupancy levels of the initial wave of extended-stay hotel development dramatically heightened interest in this segment, and the number of extended-stay hotel products continues to expand, breaking into sub-segments ranging from economy to first-class. The true depth of the extended-stay demand segment remains difficult to gauge, although managers of the lower-rated extended-stay products often find themselves competing with operators of conventional limited-service hotels, while higher-rated extended-stay products often compete as first-class, all-suite hotels. Generally, the hotels succeed, as the strong investment in the guestroom offerings presents a strong price-value perception for guests. Nevertheless, the operating efficiencies in the design and operating concept diminish as the length of a guest's stay shrinks.

The hard budget is the 1990s version of the budget hotel. Over the years the budget hotel concept has experienced what has been called "amenity creep." In an effort to increase room revenue and thus franchise fees, hotel franchise companies encourage franchisees to upgrade their properties by adding more amenities. This usually starts with simple additions such as a free morning newspaper and continental breakfast; later it may include extras like coffeemakers in guestrooms, free shampoo and other beauty supplies, fitness centers, turndown service, and so forth. Each of these amenities creates an expense that must be offset by an increase in revenue. In the end, amenity creep can turn a budget hotel into a mid-rate property or a mid-rate hotel into a first-class property.

Hard budget has taken the budget concept back to basics. Its guestrooms have been downsized to only 192 square feet. It offers none of the normal hotel amenities such as a restaurant, lounge, meeting space, or swimming pool. A hard budget is 10% to 20% less expensive to construct, requires less land, is easier to operate and maintain, and can undercut the room rates of comparable budget hotels by as much as 25%. The hard budget concept, which had its genesis with Statler's "room and a bath for a dollar and a half," illustrates the recurring cycles in the lodging industry.

Market Segmentation

Market segmentation, as a hotel industry phenomenon, originated in the 1980s and continued through the 1990s. Essentially, it represents an expansion strategy for hotel companies. When hotel chains such as Holiday Inns, Marriott, Hilton, and Sheraton were founded, they developed a standardized form of operation that was oriented toward a single class of traveler. For example, Holiday Inns were designed, operated, and priced to appeal to the mid-rate commercial and leisure traveler. Marriott went after more affluent, first-class guests by offering higher-quality facilities and services. Over the years these chains developed strong brand loyalty among these specific classes and types of travelers. As it became apparent that markets for the "core" brand of these hotel chains were essentially satisfied (e.g., most of the available hotel markets within the United States had a sufficient number of Holiday Inns to satisfy their mid-priced travelers), the hotel chains had to find a vehicle for expansion that would allow them to develop or franchise additional properties within their established market areas. The answer to this dilemma was to develop a new product and brand name to capture a different class of traveler.

Market segmentation allows hotel chains to expand without simply drawing a portion of the demand away from their core properties. For example, Holiday Inns implemented market segmentation by developing an upscale product with higher-quality finishes and decor, a higher level of service, and more amenities to attract first-class travelers. This brand of hotel was called the Holiday Inn Crowne Plaza (now known only as Crowne Plaza).

Holiday Inns also developed a downscale, budget-type product known as the Hampton Inn, which was designed to capture the more price-sensitive traveler. The Hampton Inn brand (which is now controlled by Hilton Hotel Corporation) offers a lower level of service than the standard Holiday Inn does. It has no restaurant, lounges, or meeting space and the size of its guestrooms and the quality of its decor and amenities are less than one would expect at a typical Holiday Inn. By offering three types of products, Holiday Inns significantly increased the size of its potential market. This allowed the chain to develop or franchise hundreds of additional hotels within its established market areas throughout the United States.

Marriott has demonstrated the benefits of market segmentation, leveraging the substantial goodwill and marketing power it has established through decades of consistent quality into nearly every possible hotel demand segment. Marriott has expanded by both segmenting and acquiring the rights to a variety of brands, including Residence Inn in the 1980s, and, in the 1990s, Ritz-Carlton and Renaissance. These strategic acquisitions have emerged as another common means for sustaining growth.

Strategic Acquisitions and Mergers

Earnings growth is critical to public companies, and hotel ownership increasingly became the province of publicly held companies in the 1990s. Whereas market segmentation continued to represent a viable approach to achieving earnings growth (along with property-by-property acquisition), a far more efficient means to this end was commonly practiced in the mid- to late 1990s in the form of strategic acquisitions and mergers. Starwood Hotels and Resorts and Patriot American Hospitality (now known as Wyndham International) were the most conspicuous companies. Starwood acquired the assets of hotel companies such as Sheraton, Westin, and HEI Hotels, while Patriot American amassed the assets of the Wyndham Hotel Corporation, Carnival Hotels & Resorts, Interstate Hotels, and Grand Heritage Hotels, among others. At the decade's end, the Promus Hotel Corporation, which controlled the Hampton Inn, Doubletree, Homewood Suites, Embassy Suites, and Red Lion brands merged with Hilton Hotel Corporation. A few key multi-brand hotel companies, marketed cooperatively for greater efficiency and economies of scale, now control most of the industry's most recognized brands in similar groups.

The outcome of this shift in the nature of hotel ownership is difficult to discern at this stage; however, hotel companies are now scrutinized and evaluated based on their ability to increase shareholder value, a shift away from the traditional primacy placed on day-to-day operations and basic property level performance. Through future years, the most successful hotel companies will likely maintain a property level perspective and prioritize on-site management while still increasing their earnings through brand leverage, greater economies of scale, and an increasingly global perspective.

Globalization of the hotel industry should intensify during the next decade. More American hotel companies may expand throughout the world and more foreign hotel chains will probably seek opportunities in the United States. From an appraisal point of view, a global knowledge of hotel trends and valuation techniques will be essential.

Management Contracts

A final factor that has majorly impacted America's hotel industry is the use of hotel management contracts, which emerged during the 1980s. Under this type of agreement a hotel company is paid for taking over a hotel's day-to-day operations. If the hotel company is a well-known chain, the management fee also includes the right to use the trade name. The hotel management company generally has little or no ownership interest in the hotel and is not responsible for funding any operating losses.

Management contracts are particularly appealing to public hotel companies, which, for accounting purposes, do not like to keep real estate assets such as hotels on their balance sheets. Progressive chains such as Marriott have created a strategy in which they develop or acquire a hotel, implement their management, and then sell the property to either an individual investor or a partnership but retain operational control through a long-term management contract. Due to the widespread use of the hotel management contracts and franchises, few hotels operating as part of a national chain are actually owned by that chain.

Learning from History

Many of the changes and trends that developed during the 1990s will continue to affect the United States lodging industry in the next decade. In the future, the lodging industry will have to adapt continuously to inevitable changes. Some of the factors that will impact the hotels and motels of the future are discussed below.

Faster Transportation

The jet airplane revolutionized long-distance travel by allowing people to cover more miles in shorter trips. As the speed of transportation increases, supersonic or orbital aircraft will make it possible to fly round-trip between New York and Tokyo and attend a business meeting all in one day. This would eliminate the need for any hotel accommodations.

Better Communications

Before long every home and office will be linked by a computer and video communication system. The need for face-to-face meetings will be greatly reduced when this technology becomes commonplace. Many business meetings, small conferences, training seminars, and conventions could take place without incurring travel and hotel expenses.

Globalization

Faster transportation and communications could hurt the lodging industry, but the inevitable globalization of businesses will create a need for business travel when face-to-face meetings are essential. Major business centers throughout the world will benefit from this trend.

Increased Pleasure Travel

As the number of affluent, two-income families has increased and transportation has become quicker, easier, and less expensive, the travel industry has seen an increase in pleasure travel. This trend is likely to continue, and resort areas will benefit from it most.

In addition, the preceding description of the hotel-motel industry in the United States identifies several important points that could affect the market value of lodging facilities.

1. The typical hostelry experiences a relatively high degree of functional and economic obsolescence. These factors tend to reduce a property's economic life, thereby decreasing the period during which an owner can fully recapture invested capital.

2. The growth of the lodging industry is influenced by developments in transportation. The first hostelries were located on coach trails; when the railroad came, hotels moved closer to passenger terminals. Later the automobile led to the creation of the motel, and the airplane generated demand for rooms at airport locations. A decline in a particular form of transportation can lead to the failure of associated lodging facilities.

3. The budget motel is the result of a cyclical phenomenon. The rooming house was America's first economical lodging facility. After the rooming house's popularity declined, Statler introduced the first full-facility hotel at an affordable price. In the 1950s the highway motel brought rates down for the mass travel market, and 20 years later the "revolutionary" budget motel was introduced. In the 1990s amenity creep made it possible to recreate the budget motel, this time called the hard budget.

4. Enormous amounts of financing were available in the late 1920s, the early 1970s, and the mid-1980s. Ready capital, coupled with factors such as income tax advantages, other government incentives, and an overheated economy, led to excessive overbuilding, and many properties were forced into bankruptcy or foreclosed soon after they opened. In these boom periods, hotel owners soon discovered what usually happens when a property is poorly conceived, under-capitalized, and mismanaged.

5. Distressed hotels have traditionally been valued by looking ahead to a time when recovery is expected and then projecting income and expense out until a stabilized level of occupancy is achieved. Discounted cash flow analysis is then applied to convert the projected income before debt service into an opinion of value. Using the actual net income of a distressed property would probably understate its market value because most sellers would wait for a recovery to occur unless they were forced to make an immediate sale.

6. The lodging industry has been characterized by change. Appraisers must stay abreast of current industry trends and developments to understand and cor-rectly reflect investors' motivations and behavior in this dynamic market.

Performing a Hotel Market Study and Valuation

CHAPTER *2*

What Is a Hotel Market Study and Valuation?

Each time a hotel is bought, sold, developed, financed, refinanced, syndicated, or assessed, parties to the transaction may require some type of market study and valuation to indicate its future financial performance. Over the years the lodging industry has used a variety of terms to describe the process of forecasting the revenue and expenses of a property and estimating its market value. These studies may be called *feasibility studies, market studies, market studies with financial projections, market demand studies, economic studies, economic feasibility studies, appraisals, valuations, economic valuations, economic market studies and appraisals, or market studies and valuations.*

Although the studies identified by these names will generally produce similar findings, in this text the term *market study and valuation* will be used to describe a six-step process.

1. Evaluate the hotel's site and locational characteristics.

2. Quantify lodging demand.

3. Evaluate competitive lodging supply.

4. Measure property-specific characteristics (for an existing hotel).

5. Forecast revenue and expenses.

6. Estimate market value.

Most appraisers are already experts at estimating market value, so this book will concentrate on the steps leading up to and including the forecasting of revenue and expenses. The valuation section will focus on the income capitalization approach and show how the cost and sales comparison approaches provide support for the final value conclusion. By following the procedures described in this book, appraisers will have the tools they need to perform various types of studies.

Phases in a Hotel Market Study and Valuation

When an appraiser is retained to perform a hotel market study and valuation, a four-phase process is used to accomplish the goals of the assignment. The phases are outlined here in a logical order, but some of the work required in the individual phases can proceed concurrently. The phases employed in performing a hotel market study and valuation are identified as follows:

Phase 1. Define the assignment

Phase 2. Data collection

Phase 3. Data analysis

Phase 4. Formulate conclusions

Each phase will be explained in order.

Phase 1. Define the Assignment

Before beginning any type of study, the appraiser must define the assignment. Some questions that should be considered when defining a hotel market study and valuation assignment are

- Where is the property located?
- Is the hotel existing or proposed?
- What facilities constitute the property (if it is existing)?
- What is the date of value?
- What is the purpose of the study?
- What property rights are to be appraised?
- Is there any excess land?
- Who will operate the hotel?
- What is the financial structure–debt and equity?

The answers to these questions are generally provided by the property owner or client and form the basis for defining the assignment.

Phase 2. Data Collection

Once the assignment has been defined, the appraiser begins to collect data. The collection process starts by determining exactly what type of data is required to complete the assignment. A data collection checklist is often employed to ensure that no essential information is overlooked. The appraiser must then determine where to look for each type of data. Typical data sources include

- Information provided by the property owner or client
- Primary market research conducted in the field by the appraiser
- Secondary research of in-house data and other secondary sources

The data collection process should be thorough, accurate, and all-inclusive. The results of the market study and valuation are only as accurate as the data collected.

Phase 3. Data Analysis

The appraiser evaluates and analyzes the collected data to form a basis for conclusions. Sophisticated analytical procedures are used to manipulate data so the appraiser can simulate, or model, actual market conditions. Three procedures employed in hotel data analysis are presented in this text: room night analysis, the fixed and variable income and expense forecasting model, and the mortgage equity valuation model.

Room Night Analysis

Room night analysis measures the current hotel demand in the area and forecasts future demand. The market share for the subject property is then calculated based on its competitive strength relative to other hotels in the area. With information on the subject's market share over the projection period and the forecast room night demand, the process can calculate the subject's probable percentage of occupancy.

Fixed and Variable Income and Expense Forecasting Model

The income and expenses for a lodging facility tend to fluctuate with changes in the sales volume and usage of the property. By identifying the portion of a revenue or expense item that is fixed and the portion that varies directly with volume or usage, the fixed and variable income and expense forecasting model provides a basis for forecasting a hotel's net income before debt service.

Mortgage Equity Valuation Model

Hotel investors typically make purchase decisions using a mortgage-equity technique in which the forecast net income before debt service and residual value are discounted to present value at a discount rate that reflects the cost of debt and equity capital.

In addition to the three analytical procedures described above, the appraiser evaluates data used in the cost and sales comparison approaches.

Phase 4. Formulate Conclusions

Based on Phase 3 analysis, the appraiser can formulate conclusions. In a typical market study and valuation, there are a series of intermediate conclusions that lead to the ultimate opinion of value. Some of these intermediate conclusions are listed on the following page.

Intermediate Conclusions

1. Suitability of the site for hotel use
2. Suitability of improvements and amenities (if the hotel is existing)
3. Surrounding neighborhood characteristics
4. Local economic and demographic conditions
5. Current level of room night demand subdivided by market segments
6. Expected future trends in lodging demand
7. Existing and projected competition
8. Subject's relative competitiveness and projected capture of room night demand
9. Subject's projected annual occupancy up to a stabilized level
10. Subject's projected room rates
11. Projected use of and revenues from food, beverage, and banquet facilities as well as other services and amenities
12. Projected operating and fixed expenses
13. Estimated net income before debt service for each year of the projection period
14. Income capitalization parameters such as mortgage interest and amortization rates, loan-to-value ratio, term, equity yield, terminal capitalization rate, and inflation rate
15. Opinion of value by the income capitalization approach
16. Opinion of value by the cost approach (if appropriate)
17. Opinion of value by the sales comparison approach (if appropriate)
18. Reconciliation of each approach and final estimate of market value

Note: These conclusions are referred to by number in the discussion of the data collection checklist on pages 34-59.

Assumptions

The four-phase process for performing a hotel market study and valuation will be thoroughly described in the following chapters. Readers should keep in mind that these procedures will speed up the data analysis process, but they do not take the place of accurate and complete data collection and experienced judgment in formulating conclusions.

Before proceeding, some assumptions made by the author must be set forth.

1. The term *hotel* is used throughout this text. However, the procedures described for a hotel market study and valuation are equally applicable to motels, motor inns, motor hotels, inns, conference centers, and resorts.

2. This book does not contain a complete discussion of macro supply and demand trends or the theory behind various valuation techniques. It is assumed that the reader is already familiar with these topics.

3. Case studies are used to illustrate the procedures and techniques described in this text. These examples concern an existing hotel with an operating history and a proposed hotel. With these assumptions in place, the four–phase process can be applied systematically. Phases 1 and 2 are described in detail in this chapter. The remaining phases in the process are covered in subsequent chapters.

Define the Assignment

Establishing a complete and clear definition of the assignment is the first phase in all hotel market studies and valuations. A clear definition is needed because a person cannot determine how to get somewhere until he or she has a specific destination. An appraiser must understand the client's needs before beginning data collection and analysis. A thorough definition is also needed to determine the amount of time and staff required to complete the assignment, which will determine the fee quoted.

Types of Data

To define the assignment, the appraiser assembles data that can be classified as either property-specific or assignment-specific. This information usually comes from the client or the property owner, if they are two different parties. Often much of this data is accumulated over the telephone. A sophisticated client may put together a formal request for proposals (RFPs), which sets forth detailed instructions and requirements for the assignment.

Property-Specific Data

Property-specific data relate to the vacant land, if the hotel is proposed, and the land and improvements if the hotel exists. Some property-specific data are essential in defining the assignment. For instance, the exact location of the property is needed. A survey is often helpful but a street address will suffice. A market study and valuation for a proposed hotel requires considerably more market research and data collection than a similar study of an existing hotel because the appraiser cannot examine the property's financial track record.

If the hotel exists, the appraiser should identify precisely which facilities are being studied. A minimum description of facilities would include room count, the number of restaurants and lounges, the square footage of meeting and banquet space, the amount of retail space, and a list of other facilities and amenities.

If the hotel is proposed or the site may contain excess land, the appraiser should obtain a description of the parcel. Size, frontage, access, visibility, and topography are important factors to consider in defining an assignment.

Excess land is surplus land that is not needed to accommodate a site's highest and best use. It refers to a part or section of the site that is not needed or used by the current hotel facilities or, alternately, land that could be used for an addition to the existing hotel or for another compatible use. The availability of proper zoning, access, visibility, and utilities must be considered in determining whether or not land can be deemed excess land.

Assignment-Specific Data

Assignment-specific data include general information and assumptions that the client provides, such as the purpose of the study, the property rights appraised, the date of value, and the property's financial structure and operator.

Purpose of the Study

To meet the client's needs, the appraiser must understand the study's purpose. A market study and valuation can serve many purposes, including the following:

- To develop an opinion of market value or investment value for potential hotel purchasers
- To estimate market value or investment value for potential hotel sellers
- To interest lenders in providing project financing
- To attract investors for equity syndications
- To resolve property tax disputes
- To establish value for bankruptcy and/or foreclosure
- To value property for condemnation proceedings
- To determine if a proposed hotel will be economically feasible
- To determine if present management is maximizing the value of the property
- To quantify the value of property expansion or renovation

Property Rights Appraised

The property rights appraised are the interests that will be transferred as of the date of value. In hotel appraisals, appraisers typically value the fee simple, leasehold, leased fee, management contract, limited partnership, corporate stock, and minority ownership. Each type of interest includes specific property rights and risks, which must be evaluated and reflected in the value opinion.

Date of Value

Every valuation is made as of a specific time. A retrospective value, current value, or prospective value may be estimated. Because the data collected must reflect market conditions on the effective date of value, the appraiser must know the client's assumed valuation date before beginning the assignment.

Financial Structure of the Property

Depending on the assignment's purpose, it may be necessary to examine the hotel's existing or contemplated financial structure, which usually encompasses both debt and equity components. This information is essential in developing an investment value opinion for a particular hotel investor because specific return requirements must be considered in the income capitalization approach.

Operator's Performance Abilities

When a hotel market study and valuation is performed and a hotel management company is assumed to be the property's long-term operator, the forecast of income and expense should reflect the anticipated performance abilities of that specific operator. Performance abilities typically refer to the company's capacity to operate the property in a manner that maximizes long-term revenues while minimizing long-term expenses.

The performance abilities of hotel management companies vary widely and can have a significant impact on future operating results. Therefore, the appraiser must determine at the outset whether the market study and valuation is to assume a generic, competent hotel management company or a specific operator. If a specific operator is assumed, the appraiser should request information pertaining to the operator's performance abilities. Helpful data would include financial statements, occupancy and average room rates for comparable properties, and information concerning the operator's experience in managing hotels of specific types, classes, and franchise affiliations in particular locations. Later chapters will cover procedures for evaluating this type of comparable operating data and using it to forecast future operating performance for the subject property.

Both property- and assignment-specific data are useful in defining an assignment accurately. Hotels are complex investments, so appraisers should keep in mind that each assignment is unique; additional information not specifically set forth here may be needed to fulfill the client's needs and expectations.

Data Collection

Data collection is Phase 2 of the hotel valuation process. The findings and recommendations contained in a hotel market study and valuation depend on the quality of the data gathered and used in the assignment.

The remainder of this chapter describes a process for collecting the data needed to develop a hotel market study and valuation. First, primary sources of data are explored; then specific types of required data are illustrated with instructions for their collection. Because the material is arranged in a step-by-step manner, it may not be immediately clear how certain types of data will be utilized in the analysis. As the process unfolds, however, the use and organization of data should become apparent.

Primary Sources of Data

Data for a hotel market study and valuation can be obtained from a wide variety of sources. The sources described below indicate where the appraiser should start looking for information. The three categories of hotel market study and valuation data are: client-supplied data, in-house data, and field data.

The client usually supplies property- or assignment-specific information. Client-supplied data include the information needed to define the assignment as well as additional materials such as plot plans, legal descriptions, architectural plans, financial statements, management contracts, franchise agreements, and budgets. The appraiser should request these data in the proposal contract. In fact, some appraisers begin their contractual work schedule when all the client-supplied data requested are actually received. The quality of data provided by the client is generally good; these data tend to be factual rather than subjective in nature.

Information that is accumulated and maintained by a hotel appraiser in the normal course of business (i.e., not for a specific assignment) is categorized as in-house data. In-house data include comparable sales of hotels, hotel directories, travel surveys, occupancy and average rate databases, financial operating statements, trade and professional journals, and economic and demographic databases. The quality of this type of data is generally good. The ability of an appraisal firm to accumulate a significant amount of meaningful in-house data tends to be directly related to the quantity of hotel assignments it performs.

Information that is not supplied by the client or found in the appraiser's in-house database must be collected from the field specifically for the assignment. Field data include site- and location-related descriptions, information on market area characteristics and the nature of local lodging demand, competitive property data, and economic and demographic trends. Field data are usually generated through primary research. Therefore, the quality of these data depends on the data-collecting techniques used and the skill of the appraiser performing the fieldwork. Collecting field data for a hotel assignment can be time-consuming. The work may take up to 10 days to complete, depending on the firm's familiarity with a specific market area and the nature of the assignment.

Data Collection Checklist

The following checklist illustrates the specific types of data that might be accumulated in performing a hotel market study and valuation. The list is not all-inclusive but does indicate most of the major data hotel appraisers use. Some of the data listed may not be appropriate for all studies.

The checklist is followed by detailed explanations of each data type. The numbers in parentheses refer to the intermediate conclusions listed in the description of Phase 4 of the valuation process on page 28. These references are provided to show how particular types of data contribute to the many conclusions that must be reached in a hotel market study and valuation.

FIGURE 2.1   **Data Collection Checklist**

Primary sources of data
    Client-supplied data
    In-house data
    Field data and key contacts
Property-specific information
    Land
    Access
    Visibility
    Utilities
    Improvements
- General description and building layout
- Lobby and entrance
- Guest rooms
- Corridors and elevator lobbies
- Food, beverage, and room service facilities
- Housekeeping
- Kitchen
- Meeting and banquet facilities
- Amenities
- Back-of-the-house layout
- Building systems
    - Vertical transportation systems
    - Heating, ventilation, and air–conditioning (HVAC)
    - Energy management systems
- Telephone
- Life safety systems
- Security and exterior lighting
- Miscellaneous

Area-specific data
    Neighborhood
    Assessed value and real estate and personal property taxes
    Zoning/building department
    Planning department
    Highway/transportation department
Economic and demographic data - trends
    Chambers of commerce/economic development agencies
    Newspapers
    Demand generators list
    Airport authority
    Convention center and visitors bureau
    Car rental agencies
    Competitive hotels
    Rooms, bed, or occupancy tax
    Hotel associations
    Competitive restaurants and lounges
    Liquor license laws
    Sales of competitive hotels
Other sources of data and information
    Commercial real estate firms, boards, etc.
    Local appraisers, counselors, bankers
    Photographs

Client-Supplied Data

The client should supply the following types of data:

- Date of market study and valuation (and opening date if hotel is proposed) (Conclusions 9-18)

- Interest appraised—i.e., fee simple, leasehold, leased fee, other value (12-18)

- Purpose of study (1-18)

- Balance sheets and profit and loss statements for past three years with supporting schedules (9-13)

   Financial statements should be prepared in accordance with the Uniform System of Accounts for Hotels.

- Development costs, including land, improvements, and furniture, fixtures, and equipment (16)

   Cost estimates are particularly important for proposed hotels.

- Monthly occupancy and average rate over two years (8-10)

   These data are most important for hotels with seasonal demand patterns.

- Copies or summaries of all leases, management contracts, franchise agreements, title reports, stock or partnership agreements, etc. (13-18)

   Leases include ground, property, furniture, and equipment leases.

- Architectural plans, floor layouts as built, plot plans, survey and legal description (1,2,16)

   If a hotel is proposed, a detailed estimate of the project's cost is essential.

- Operating budgets and projections (9-13)

   The owner or operator will usually prepare these items.

- Marketing plans (5-11)

   The subject's competitive position and proposed marketing orientation should be evaluated.

- Engineering reports (1,2,16)

   Reports should show current conditions and any need for capital improvements.

- Capital expenditures over the past three years and capital budget (cost) projections (1,2,8,16)

   Past expenditures will indicate the need for future capital expenditures.

- Real and personal property tax bills, assessments of other hotels in the market area, name of legal owner (12)

   Assessments of comparable hotels in the market area can be used to verify the fairness of the subject's assessed value or to develop an assessed value if the subject is proposed.

- Past appraisals and market studies (1-18)

   Studying the work of others can save time, but all findings should be verified.

- Purchase price, date, terms, contract, and closing statement for subject property if sold within the past five years (16-18)

    A previous sale price of the subject property can indicate its value.

- Agreement of sale, option, or listing for subject property (16-18)

    Although such data are not strong indicators of value, they can provide useful information.

- Financing documents and mortgage and equity data (14,15,18)

    Such information forms a basis for developing a capitalization rate if the data are recent.

- Union contracts (12)

    Contracts provide insight into labor rates and work rules. The appraiser should follow up to determine how effectively the unions control productivity.

- Franchise reports concerning occupancy, inspection, and reservations (2, 7, 8, 9, 10)

    Hotel franchise companies often provide owners with a wide variety of reports and surveys, including occupancy reports, inspection reports, and reservation reports. An occupancy report compares the occupancy and average rate of the subject with other hotels in the same franchise system; an inspection report records the results of periodic physical inspections made by the franchiser; and a reservation report documents the reservation activity generated by the franchiser's central reservation system. It sometimes includes a denial report, which indicates the number of guests turned away because the hotel was full. All franchise reports should be requested if the subject property is an existing, franchised hotel.

- Meeting planner's brochure and marketing packages (2, 8-11)

    All property-specific descriptive information should be reviewed before starting fieldwork. Data can also be collected during inspection of the property.

In-House Data

In-house data are gathered before fieldwork begins. Sources of such data are described below.

- Reports on past appraisals performed in the market area (1-18)

    Prior work in the market area forms a base of information that will be updated and refined during fieldwork.

- Personal contacts (1-18)

    Reviewing personal contacts in the market area can help identify individuals who could be helpful in performing the assignment.

- American Hotel and Lodging Association construction report (7)

    This monthly report describes proposed hotel projects throughout the United States.

- Publications—*Official Hotel and Resort Guide, Hotel Travel Index, Red Book, AAA Travel Guide, Mobil Travel Guide, Appraisal Institute Directory of Members, and Lodging DataBank* (1-18)

    Various publications on hotel properties and hotel sales data as well as directories of real estate professionals can be helpful in performing a hotel market study and valuation.

- *National Real Estate Investor* city data (3, 4)

    This is a valuable source of general data on real estate activity in major markets.

- *Sales and Marketing Management* database and *Survey of Buying Power* (4)

    These publications are sources of economic and demographic data.

- *Restaurant Business Restaurant Activity Index* (RAI) and *Restaurant Growth Index* (RGI) (11)

    Appraisers should consult these sources for restaurant supply and demand information.

- FAA terminal forecasts (4, 6)

    These forecasts provide estimates of airline enplanements for most commercial airports in the United States.

Field Data and Key Contacts

Field data are typically gathered at the subject property and in the surrounding market area. The individuals listed below are primary sources of data and information pertaining to an existing subject property.

- General manager
- Assistant/resident manager
- Director of marketing
- Director of sales
- Director of engineering
- Front desk manager
- Controller/accountant

Key contacts can provide introductions to other general managers and representatives of the local chamber of commerce, convention and visitors bureau, hotel association, etc. Hotel personnel can provide introductions to other data sources in the market area. Key contacts can also provide:

- A definition of primary market area in geographic terms (3-7)

    As a rule of thumb, a hotel market area is the area within 20 driving minutes of the subject property. Defining the market area tells the appraiser where to investigate both supply and demand.

- Demand generator analysis—industry type, location, map (4-6)

  When performing demand generator analysis, appraisers should identify which attractions create local transient hotel demand, plot them on a map, and investigate major generators within the market area.

- A list of major businesses and industries in the market area (4-6)

  Appraisers should list businesses to quantify commercial and meeting demand and forecast future growth trends.

- Information about major users of the subject property (2,4-11)

  Listing the primary users of the hotel and determining whether any users receive special, discounted rates is useful for conducting demand interviews.

- Data on major contract business—term, rate, number of room nights (2, 4-11)

  Contract business users such as airline crews typically rent rooms for a specific period of time at a set rate. Appraisers should understand the terms of any significant contract business.

- Competition analysis—competitive hotels, occupancy, average rate, and market segmentation (7-10)

  A marketing plan should contain detailed information about all the hotels that compete with the subject. This information is used to quantify area demand and determine the subject's relative competitiveness.

- Information about the mode of arrival and the transportation provided (1, 5-11)

  What modes of transportation do guests use to travel to the subject property? This information shows the importance of access and visibility and indicates the relative competitiveness of the subject.

- Market segmentation data (5-11)

  Appraisers should determine the types of travelers (e.g., commercial, meeting, leisure) as a percentage of the total usage and note any changes in the percentages that occur over the year. This information can be used to determine the suitability of the improvements and amenities and to project future hotel usage.

- An indication of the average length of stay (2, 9-11)

  How long does the average guest stay at the subject property? Appraisers should identify this information by market segment.

- Specific points of origin—feeder markets (5, 6)

  Where do the guests come from? Appraisers should identify this by market segment for both the subject and the market area.

- Details of seasonality—weekly, monthly, by segment (5-11)

  How does usage change over the year? Appraisers should identify this by market segment for both the subject and the market area.

- Quantification of unaccommodated demand by segment (5, 8, 9)

  Appraisers should quantify the amount of demand that cannot be accommodated because facilities are filled and identify for both the subject property and the market area. These data are important if new supply enters the hotel market.

- Double occupancy percentage (10, 11)

  Determining the average number of guests per room for each market segment affects the subject's room rates and usage.

- Indications of rate resistance, by segment (5, 8-10)

  Which market segments display rate resistance and at what rate level does this begin? This information influences future rate increases.

- Rack rate strategy—usage of yield management (5, 8-10)

  What type of yield management, or hotel pricing policy, does the subject use? How does it function? Appraisers should address these questions.

- Percentage of reservations from franchise (8-11)

  Appraisers should ascertain how effective the franchise identification is in generating room reservations. If the subject is proposed, the franchiser can sometimes provide estimates.

- Information about the amount of travel agent commissions (8-11)

  Appraisers should ask how much business is generated from travel agents.

- Information about unions (12)

  The number of hotels in the market area that are union-operated affects the labor component of operating expenses.

Property-Specific Information

Land

- Description of the size, topography, and shape of the land (1, 16)

  Data obtained from the plot plan or survey is important for evaluating access and visibility and the site's suitability for new improvements.

- Municipalities (3, 4, 12)

  Appraisers should determine the municipality in which the subject is located and identify other municipalities in the market area. This information is needed to research local economic, demographic, and municipal trends.

- Area or acreage (1, 2, 16)

  The site area found on the plot plan or survey determines the number of units for a proposed hotel and the amount of excess land for an existing hotel. Land value, which is calculated in the cost approach, is usually based on area.

- Excess land—salability, highest and best use (16, 18)

  If the subject site contains surplus land that could be used for expansion or another use, additional value may be present.

- Plot plan, survey (12)

    These documents are sources of land information.

- Frontages (1, 8-11)

    Frontage determines access and visibility.

- Adjoining uses (3, 8-11)

    Appraisers should inventory the land uses surrounding the subject property. Surrounding land uses can enhance or detract from the value of the subject property.

- Grade compared to surrounding roads, uses (1, 2, 16)

    Grade level can impact access, visibility, and development costs.

- Contours, slope, drainage (1, 2, 16)

    Topography affects development costs.

- Flood hazard insurance (12)

    If extra insurance is required, a hotel's fixed expenses increase.

- Soil tests—water table, percolation tests, flood zones, seismic activity, other engineering studies (1, 2, 16)

    These considerations can affect a proposed hotel's development costs.

- Air rights, subsurface rights, water rights (16, 18)

    Additional rights often enhance a property's value.

- Landscaping (1, 2, 8-12, 16)

    Landscaping can significantly influence a hotel's competitiveness.

- Easements, other restrictions (16, 18)

    Restrictions can increase or decrease a property's value.

Access

- North-south roads and east-west roads (1, 8-11)

    Appraisers should list immediate and nearby roads and highways and investigate both the immediate and secondary access for all modes of transportation.

- Modes of transportation (1, 8-11)

    Appraisers should determine how guests reach the subject property and consider that access may be accomplished by more than one mode of transportation.

- Direct access patterns (1, 8-11)

    Appraisers should describe the access to the subject property by the primary modes of transportation and describe adjacent and nearby highways, including the number of lanes, medians, turn restrictions, traffic signals, one-way streets, curb cuts, and limited-access roads.

- Future access (8-11)

  Appraisers should consider how access is likely to change in the future.

- Distance to major facilities (8-11)

  Appraisers should calculate the distance in miles and time to highways and interchanges, airports, mass transportation, convention centers, major demand generators, and competitive lodging facilities.

- Competition (8-11)

  Appraisers should compare the subject's access to that of the competition.

Visibility

- Evaluate visibility from nearby roadways (1, 8-11)

  Appraisers should consider how long the subject is visible to drivers and their ability to exit the highway after the subject becomes visible.

- Visibility from nearby demand generators (1, 8-11)

  Appraisers should see if the subject is visible from any demand generator.

- Visibility from nearby competitive hotels (1, 8-11)

  Appraisers should see if the subject is visible from any competitive hotels.

- Building height and depth (1, 2, 8-11)

  Appraisers should ask how the subject's building height and depth affects visibility.

- Slope of land (1, 8-11)

  Appraisers should know how the topography of the subject parcel affects visibility.

- Obstructions (1, 8-11)

  Appraisers should evaluate all obstructions to visibility—both existing and proposed.

- Signage—location, visibility, condition (1, 8-11)

  Appraisers should describe the subject's signage and evaluate its visibility. They should also ask if it can be improved.

- Views from the subject's guest rooms, food and beverage outlets, etc. (1, 8-11)

  Appraisers should evaluate visibility during the day and night and consider how it is likely to change in the future.

Utilities (2,12)

- Location, capacity, and provider

  Appraisers should investigate the availability and cost of these utilities:

  - Electricity: local rates, normal demand charges, quantity discounts, seasonal adjustments
  - Natural gas: local rates, quantity discounts, seasonal adjustments

- Oil: tank size, local prices, quantity discounts
- Water: potable, hot and chilled
- Steam
- Telephone
- Sewage
- Liquified petroleum gas (LPG), propane
- Trash removal
- Storm drainage

- Alternative sources
  If a utility is unavailable, appraisers should consider alternative sources. What will it cost to make it available?

Improvements (2, 8-12, 16, 18)

The following portion of the checklist is concerned with the subject improvements. During the property inspection, the appraiser focuses on the physical and functional characteristics of the hotel, giving special attention to:

- Age and condition of improvements as well as furniture, fixtures, and equipment
- Immediate and future need for upgrading and renovation
- Physical attributes of the property compared to the competition
  Appraisers should evaluate the facilities offered and their condition, class, and desirability.
- Functionality of the property's layout and design
  Appraisers should find out what impact the design has on service, maintenance, labor expenses, and security.
- Improvements' effects on future revenues, expenses, and profits

General Description and Building Layout

- Plans and physical description
  Appraisers should obtain all necessary information from the property owner.
- Year opened
- Description and date of expansions and renovations
- Number of structures
- Location of buildings on site
- Number of stories
- Building configuration—H, L, U, straight
- Total square footage

- Landscaping and sidewalks
- Exterior facade—architectural style, materials, balconies
- Future development plans, including project description and costs
- Current engineering reports
- ADA-compliant and adequate number of ADA-equipped rooms

Lobby and Entrance

- Porte cochere
- Valet parking stand
- Shuttle bus pickup and parking area
- Doors—automatic, airlock vestibule, bell stand
- Luggage storage
- Concierge desk
- Restrooms
- Phones—house and public
- Front desk
    - Visibility to incoming guests

Extravagant, decorative lobbies such as this—with high ceilings, ample space, and artistic detail—can attract guests and increase a hotel's desirability.

-   Elevator visibility

-   Reservation and registration systems

-   Location of executive offices

-   Lobby—decor, size, ceiling height

-   Lobby layout and circulation

-   Layout and circulation on other floors

Guest Rooms

-   Total rooms, broken down by type of room so all are accounted for

-   Number of connecting rooms

-   Walking distance from facilities

-   Size, ceiling height, terraces

-   Furnishings—when last replaced, typical furniture inventory

-   Refurbishment schedule

-   Amenities—extra phones, multi-line phones, voice mail, computers, shoeshine, cable TV, VCR, etc.

-   Doors—construction material, peephole, type of lock

-   Closets—size, type of doors

-   Wall material—plaster, drywall, concrete

-   Windows—material, operation, glazing

-   Sprinklers, smoke detectors, other life safety equipment

-   Rooms for the handicapped

-   No smoking rooms

-   Bathroom—lighting, amenities

-   ADA-equipped facilities

Corridors and Elevator Lobbies

-   Double-, single-loaded

-   Interior, exterior

-   Direction and width

-   Lighting type(s), sufficiency of light level

-   Ceiling height

-   Wall covering, wainscoting

-   Floor covering

-   Elevator lobby furnishings

-   Ice machine

- Soda and snack machines
- Maid, linen closets
- Life safety systems (smoke, fire, evacuation plan, location cards on all room doors)

Food, Beverage, and Room Service Facilities
- Seating capacities, meals served, and hours of operation
- Copies of menus
- Decor, theme, style, and quality of furnishings
- Bar
- Back-of-the-house access from kitchens
- Description of room service facilities
- Separate outside access, visibility of separate entrance
- Access to restrooms
- Entertainment policy
- Point-of-sale accounting system
- Number of meals served (covers) per meal period per outlet
- Average turnover per meal period per outlet
- Average check per meal period per outlet
- Estimate of in-house capture and outside capture per meal period
- Banquet space—square foot area and rental rates

Housekeeping
- Offices, storage, sorting areas
- Trash chute
- Linen chute
- Exhaust fan
- Washers
  - Manufacturer
  - Model number
  - Quantity
- Dryers
  - Manufacturer
  - Model number
  - Quantity
  - Fuel

- Guest laundry, contract
- Self-serve guest laundries

Kitchen(s)
- Location(s)
- Access and distance to receiving and storage areas, food and beverage outlets, meeting rooms
- Description, quality, quantity, configuration, and condition of equipment
- Adequacy of size and layout

Meeting and Banquet Facilities
- Size, name, and capacities of each meeting room, including floor plan and locations
- Mix and number of breakout rooms
- Decor
- Entrance, porte cochere
- Service and public corridors to and from meeting rooms
- Proximity to kitchen
- Adequacy of audiovisual equipment, furniture, and meeting support amenities
- Furniture storage area
- HVAC zone control

Amenities
- Swimming pool—shape, indoor or outdoor, type of enclosure, type of heating system
- Tennis courts—lighting
- Golf—number of holes and yards, annual rounds played, fees
- Jogging trails
- Type and inventory of health/exercise equipment—sauna, steam bath, whirlpool, massage, aerobics
- Description of spa
- Game rooms
- Facilities for horseback riding, ice skating, bowling, boating, sailing, fishing, water skiing, snorkeling, windsurfing, skiing, racquetball, squash, other sports
- Business services—computer, fax, typing, express mail, etc.

Back-of-the-House Layout
- Employee entrance, lockers, rest areas, cafeteria, access pattern
- Security—timekeeping, personnel, purchasing offices
- Receiving/loading dock—guest view, lift

- Storerooms
- Engineering—shops, paint, TV, locks, carpenter

Building Systems

- Structural support
- Foundation type
- Framing—steel, pre-cast concrete, reinforced concrete
- Walls—load-bearing, non-load-bearing
- Roof—age, condition, sloped or flat
- Roof material—asphalt shingle, built-up felt and tar, tar and gravel, slate, metal, clay tile
- Parking
  - Number of spaces
  - Indoor or outdoor
  - Valet service
  - Cost to guests
  - Percentage of use by others

Vertical Transportation Systems

- Passenger elevators
  - Number
  - Floors served
  - Manufacturer
  - Cable or hydraulic
  - Capacity
  - Feet per minute
  - Automatic or manned
  - Control system—mechanical or electrical relays, computerized load system
- Service elevators
  - Number
  - Floors served
  - Manufacturer
  - Cable or hydraulic
  - Capacity
  - Feet per minute
  - Control system—mechanical or electrical relays, computerized load system

- Escalators—number and floors served
- Dumbwaiters/freight lifts—number and floors served
- Stairs

Heating, Ventilation, and Air-Conditioning

- Type of heating system
  - Hot water, steam, electric
  - Fuel type
  - Two-, three-, or four-pipe, forced-air delivery
  - Simultaneous heating and cooling
- Boilers
  - Manufacturer
  - Model number
  - Age and condition
- Burners
  - Manufacturer
  - Model number
  - Age and condition
- Water heater
  - Manufacturer
  - Model number
  - Size of holding tank
  - Age and condition
- Resistance
  - Manufacturer
  - Model or capacity
  - Age and condition
- Heat exchanger
  - Manufacturer
  - Model or capacity
  - Age and condition
- Heat pump
  - Manufacturer
  - Model number
  - Capacity

- Age and condition
- Type of cooling system
  - Central/chilled water, heat pumps
- Chiller
  - Manufacturer
  - Model or capacity
  - Age and condition
- Cooling tower
  - Manufacturer
  - Model or capacity
  - Age and condition
- Zones
  - Guest rooms, meeting rooms, public space control

Energy Management Systems
- Type of system
  - Manufacturer
  - Model number
- Individual thermostats
  - Guest rooms
  - Meeting and public space

Telephone, Television, Entertainment, Internet
- Type of system
  - Manufacturer
  - Model number
- Type of call accounting
  - Least cost routing
- Other special functions

Life Safety Systems
- Smoke detectors—local or wired
- Heat detectors—local or wired
- Sprinkler system
- Fire extinguisher
- Pull stations
  - Control, communication system

- Manufacturer and model
- Annunciator panel—location
- Emergency lighting—battery backup
- Exit signage—battery backup
- Fire hoses
  - Fire pump manufacturer
  - Fire pump model
- Standpipes
- Kitchen range hood—CO_2 system/dry system
- Public address system
- Emergency generators and power
  - Manufacturer
  - Model number

Security and Exterior Lighting
- Electronic surveillance equipment
- Sodium, fluorescent, incandescent, spot, mercury, halogen bulbs
- Building signage

Miscellaneous
- Presence of asbestos
- Presence of urea-formaldehyde foam insulation
- Building inspection reports
- Health inspection reports
- Underground tanks
- Estimated deferred maintenance
- Estimated functional obsolescence

Area-Specific Data (3-12)

Neighborhood (3, 4, 6)

A neighborhood is a group of complementary land uses that are similarly affected by the operation of the forces that affect property value. The geographic boundaries of the subject's neighborhood are indicated by land use changes, transportation arteries/ bodies of water, and changes in elevation and topography.

- Neighborhood characteristics—residential, commercial, retail, or industrial use; rural, suburban, metropolitan, or CBD; age, condition, and economic trends
  Appraisers should define the characteristics of the neighborhood and describe how these characteristics could impact the subject's ability to generate revenues.

- Neighborhood buildings

  Appraisers should make an inventory of the improvements surrounding the subject property and consider the impacts they might have on the subject's revenue-generating ability. Investigating the following factors can help.

  - Types of building improvements
  - Style, size, density, vacancy levels, rental rates, and trends
  - Effective ages and maintenance or condition
  - New development and construction
  - Competitive facilities, particularly food and beverage
  - Immediate generators of visitation
  - Adverse conditions such as noise or other nuisances

- Future trends and potential changes in neighborhood characteristics

  Appraisers should ask what impact these changes will have on the subject property.

Assessed Value and Real Estate and Personal Property Taxes (12)

- Estimate of future property taxes for the subject

  Appraisers should evaluate local assessing practices and determine which jurisdictions levy real estate and personal property taxes.

- Current assessment of subject

  Appraisers should obtain the name, address, and phone number of the assessor and a tax map showing the subject acreage in square feet and length of boundaries. They should also research lot and block number, tax identification number, current assessed value of land, and building and assessment date.

- Basis for assessment—income, cost, sales comparison, change upon sale

  Appraisers should consider how the assessed value is calculated for land, improvements, and personal property.

- Date and frequency of assessment, fiscal year

- Five-year and current tax history

- Future trends in equalization rates, assessed values, and mill rates for the subject's taxing jurisdictions

- Comparable hotel parcel numbers and assessments of land and buildings

  Appraisers should obtain information on how comparable hotels in the area are assessed and determine what the assessed values of comparable hotels for land, improvements, and personal property on a per-room basis.

- Tax abatement

  If the subject property qualifies for or receives any form of tax abatement, the appraiser should ask how it is calculated and what impact it has on property tax liability.

- Special and future assessments

  When an appraiser investigates probable future changes in assessments including any special assessments and tax liabilities, the assessing department can sometimes provide information related to local hotel trends, including

  - Proposed hotels or hotels under construction

  - Land sales of hotel sites

  - Sales of hotels

  - Rates and occupancies of local hotels

  - Names of hotel owners

Zoning/Building Department (2-12)

- Jurisdiction covering the subject property and, when appropriate, adjacent jurisdictions

- Names, addresses, and phone numbers of all contacts

- Proposed hotel development in market

  - Names of developers, hotel companies, etc.

  - Estimated completion dates

- Hotels under construction

  - Status of each proposed hotel

  - Description of approval process

- Zoning of subject—historical and current

  Appraisers should obtain a zoning map and a copy of zoning regulations and investigate the following:

  - Conforming or nonconforming use of subject property

  - Height restrictions

  - Lot coverage, number of units, size restrictions, floor-area ratio

  - Setback restrictions

  - Parking requirements

  - Sign restrictions

  - Other restrictions

- Moratoriums on building, utilities
- Environmental impact study required for new development
- Zoning of surrounding land uses
- Future of neighborhood
- Floodplain and seismic areas
- Zoning trends for area
  - Potential/probability of zoning changes
  - Building permits—five-year history, number, and dollar value
- Ability to expand subject property

Planning Department (1-12)
- Jurisdictions encompassing the subject property and adjacent jurisdictions
- Occupancy and rates of existing hotels
- Proposed hotels, additions, expansions, or renovations
- Master (renewal) plan for development
- Pertinent documents
  - Land use map
  - Economic/demographic studies
  - Transportation studies
- Directions of growth—industrial, commercial, redevelopment
- Availability of public development or redevelopment funds/tax incentives for hotels

Highway/Transportation Department (3-11)
- Names, addresses, and phone numbers of all contacts
- Origination and destination studies
- Traffic flow/count maps
- Future changes in transportation—road improvements and traffic rerouting roadway changes such as left-turn lanes, lights, curb cuts, medians, turn restrictions, and additional lanes
- Historic and current traffic counts, toll receipts
- Proposed hotels or hotels under construction

Economic and Demographic Data—Trends
During fieldwork the appraiser collects economic and demographic data describing the local economy and population. Data from the past five to 10 years provides

a useful benchmark, but projected data are more useful for predicting future trends. Economic and demographic information is used to forecast changes in lodging demand and food and beverage usage over the projection period. Data an appraiser should collect include

- NAIC employment within the local market area
- Population—migration vs. births, peak vs. annual
- Population age distribution
- Income levels and effective buying income
- Retail sales
- Sales at eating and drinking establishments
- Office space occupancy levels, absorption trends
- Major businesses by employment sector, number of employees, ability to generate hotel demand
- Industrial space occupancy levels, absorption trends
- Unemployment trends
- Housing starts
- Building permits—number, dollar value
- Area maps
- Major generators of visitation room/bed tax data
- Visitor statistics, area attractions

Chambers of Commerce/Economic Development Agencies (3-12)

Local chambers of commerce and economic development agencies can often supply much of the economic and demographic data previously described. The following information should be sought:

- Names, addresses, and phone numbers of all contacts
- Area description—growth, economic and population trends, industries, demand generators
- Businesses entering and leaving area
- Area attractions—historical and projected visitation
- Introductions to area officials, hotel associations, etc.
- Occupancy and average rates at existing hotels, area-wide average
- Proposed hotels and hotels under construction
- Miscellaneous economic and demographic data

Newspapers (1-18)

- Advertising/research department
  - Economic and demographic data
- Real estate department
  - Articles on recently announced commercial/hotel projects
  - Stories on recent hotel or land sales

Demand Generators List (3-11)

The appraiser should develop a list of market area demand generators.

- Typical hotel demand generators
  - Major companies
  - Office and industrial parks
  - Scenic sites
  - Hospitals—local, regional, or national specialty
  - Military installations
  - Colleges
  - Amusement parks
  - Resort facilities
  - Government offices
  - Residential developments
  - Racetracks
  - Historic events
  - Historic attractions
  - Retail shopping
  - Theaters
  - Museums
  - World's and state fairs
  - Sports stadiums
  - Sporting events
  - Festivals
  - Shows
  - National and state parks
  - Courts of law
  - County seats and state capitals

- Information collected about each generator
  - Description
  - Proximity to subject
  - Type of visitors
  - Visitor counts, admission charges, recent changes
  - Origin of visitors
  - Accommodations required
  - Season of visitation
- New generators entering the market

Airport Authority (4-12)

If the market benefits from a nearby airport, data related to its usage should be obtained.

- Passenger and cargo traffic—past five years, projected, monthly fluctuations
- FAA terminal forecast of projected enplanements
- Airlines and number of flights
- Physical description of airport
- Airport expansion plans
- Cities served (origination)
- Restrictions on aircraft size, times of usage, number of days closed annually

Convention Center and Visitors Bureau (4-11)

A convention center can be a major generator of hotel demand. A visitors bureau often promotes convention centers and area attractions.

- Name, address, and phone number of all contacts
- Physical description of convention center—size, capacities, age, facilities
- Historic and projected number of conventions and delegates, seasonality
- Average expenditure per conventioneer
- Average length of stay, average convention size
- Future calendar, number of future events
- Marketing plan
- Promotion budget—past five years and projected, deficit funding
- Nature and type of events—local, state, regional, national
- Visitor statistics
- Hotel association
- Proposed hotels and hotels under construction

Car Rental Agencies (4-11)

- List of major companies renting cars
- Number of cars rented monthly, annually
- Average length of rentals
- Renter's points of origin

Competitive Hotels (5-11)

Such fieldwork is directed toward investigating competitive hotels. The data collected are used to quantify existing lodging demand and evaluate the relative competitiveness of area hotels.

- Name and address of competition
- Name of owner, management company, franchise
- Location and distance from subject and demand generators
- Access and visibility
- Year opened
- Number of rooms
- Various room types (e.g., king, double-double, ADA-equipped, etc.)
- Square footage
- Rates—high, medium, or low
- Type of construction
- Income-producing facilities
  - Names of restaurants, number of seats, types of service, hours of operation
  - Other food and beverage services
  - Banquet and meeting rooms
  - Amenities
- Interior or exterior corridors
- Condition and renovation plans
- Expansion plans
- Layout and functional utility
- Brochure description
- Published rates and special rates
- Occupancy and average rates, existing and historic trends
- Percentage of reservations from central reservation system
- Market segmentation (commercial, meeting, leisure)
- Usage of food and beverage facilities

- Seasonality of demand and usage and number of fill nights
- Major customers
- Frequent travel programs
- Special services provided
- Unionization of workers
- Proposed hotels and hotels under construction
- Additions and renovations of existing hotels
- Hotels for sale or recently sold in market area
- Photographs of properties

Rooms, Bed, or Occupancy Tax (4-10)

Many jurisdictions impose a rooms tax, which is typically based on a percentage of rooms revenue. Tax data are often available and show revenue trends for the market area as well as for individual properties.

- Definition of taxable properties, change in number of taxable rooms
- Method of tax computation
- Historical taxes per month, past five years, future projections
- Identification of tax by property—occupancy and rate if available
- Historical tax rates and changes in rates

Hotel Associations (5-11)

Some market areas have organized hotel associations, which can provide useful information.

- Name, address, and phone number of all contacts
- List of existing hotels, market segmentation, rates, occupancies
- Total room count—current and historical
- Taxes per room or bed
- Hotels recently withdrawn or added to supply
- Sales transactions involving hotels
- Proposed hotels or hotels under construction

Competitive Restaurants and Lounges (7-11)

The following information is sometimes helpful in analyzing the competitiveness of the subject's food and beverage facilities.

- Name and address of competing facility
- Number of seats
- Year opened

- Meals served, days open
- Affiliation
- Name of owner
- Renovation, expansion plans
- Seasonality—weekly, monthly
- Type of menu, service
- Type of patrons—age, income
- Decor/theme
- Entertainment policy
- Average check
- Covers, turnover
- Annual sales
- Reputation
- Location relative to subject property
- Condition

Liquor License Laws (2-11)

The availability of a liquor license for a proposed hotel and the ability to transfer the liquor license of an existing hotel can be important considerations.

- Acquisition, time, cost, limitations
- Restrictions
  - Ratio of liquor to food
  - Open to public
  - Required unit of sale
  - Minimum age
- Types of licenses

Sales of Competitive Hotels (17)

- Local data bases that accumulate information on property transfers
- Hospitality Market Data Exchange—a national clearinghouse of sales transactions involving hotels and motels

Commercial Real Estate Firms, Boards, Brokers, Developers, and Relocation Services (1-18)

- Apartments that accommodate extended-stay demand (less than six months)
- Inventory of commercial, office, industrial, and retail space, historic absorption, and anticipated growth

- New projects, expansions, renovations

  Useful data may include developer, location, size (in square feet), opening date, description of major committed tenants, projected occupancy, and tenant mix. Tenant mix by NAIC code and national vs. local company can indicate a hotel's ability to generate room nights.
- Geographic patterns of growth in office, industrial, retail, and residential space
- Source of tenants
- Sales transactions involving hotels
- Proposed hotels or hotels under construction

Local Appraisers, Counselors, Bankers (1-18)
- Land and hotel sales
- Occupancy and average rate
- Market segmentation
- Proposed hotels, additions, and expansions
- Economic and demographic data
- Land use, value, and property tax rate trends

Photographs
For a permanent record of site and neighborhood characteristics, the appraiser may want to take the following photographs:

- Access to and visibility of subject property
- Entrance and sign
- View of subject—four sides
- View from subject—four sides
- Traffic photos—all directions
- Interior photos—lobby, registration, rooms, food and beverage outlets, meeting space, recreational facilities, back-of-the-house
- Surrounding land uses
- Competitive hotels
- Significant demand generators

The preceding description of a data collection checklist is quite detailed. Appraisers should utilize a checklist such as this in a hotel market study and valuation to ensure that all data sources are contacted and all relevant information is collected. When performing fieldwork, it is wise to collect as much information as possible, even if it does not appear to be important. Returning to a market to collect overlooked information can be expensive and time-consuming.

Data Collection Techniques

Once the type and source of data have been defined, various techniques can be applied to collect data. Appraisers know that some types of data are readily available, while others must be carefully researched. Some data sources may willingly assist the collection efforts, while others may try to withhold accurate information in an attempt to influence the outcome. By using proven data-collecting techniques, however, appraisers can obtain the best information available and usually screen out any bias or self-interest.

Data collection can be accomplished by using a combination of techniques:

- Personal observation
- Review of published data
- Face-to-face and telephone interviews
- Written surveys

The order of this list reflects the reliability of the data collected by using each technique. For example, information derived from personal observation is highly reliable and an experienced appraiser will not be influenced by self-interest or bias. Published data and interviews are somewhat less reliable. Written responses are the most suspect because each respondent is an isolated, unknown party. By understanding the shortcomings of each technique, an appraiser can employ the techniques in a manner that will produce reliable results. Using the data collection checklist as a framework for the types of information needed for a hotel market study and valuation, all four data collecting techniques are illustrated.

Personal Observation

Personal observation is generally employed during fieldwork. The appraiser visits the site, the neighborhood, and the market area, inspects the subject property (if existing), competitive properties, and demand generators, and makes any other observations necessary to formulate the required conclusions.

1. Suitability of the site for hotel use
   a. Size
   b. Frontage
   c. Topography
   d. Excess land
   e. Landscaping
   f. Access
   g. Visibility
   h. Utilities
   i. Parking area

2. Suitability of improvements and amenities

   a. Building layout and design

   b. Age and condition

   c. Functionality

3. Desirability of the surrounding neighborhood

   a. Types of area land usage—i.e., retail, commercial, industrial

   b. Age and condition of nearby improvements

   c. New development underway

   d. Highway patterns

   e. Demand generators

4. Existing and projected competitive environment

   a. Competitive lodging facilities (existing and proposed)

     i.   Location, access, and visibility

     ii. Facilities and amenities

     iii. Age and condition

     iv. Chain affiliation

     v.   Competitiveness

   b. Competitive food, beverage, and banquet facilities

   c. Competitive amenities

5. Market sales of competitive hotels

Personal observation makes use of an appraiser's experience and expertise. Intermediate conclusions are formulated by comparing the observations and outcome of previous assignments with the observations made during the current assignment. Personal observation is the most reliable data collection technique because it is not influenced by external bias, which can slant the results derived from other techniques.

Published Data Sources

Published data include all information gathered by businesses and organizations that can be considered within the public domain—i.e., readily available to anyone either for free or for a price. This type of data is generally reliable and forms the basis for many important conclusions derived in hotel market studies and valuations. Some conclusions that can be supported by published data sources are outlined in Table 2.1 and explored in the following discussion.

Zoning Manuals

Published by local municipalities, zoning manuals describe the uses permitted under a jurisdiction's zoning regulations. Zoning manuals establish what can be

TABLE 2.1	Conclusions and Sources
Conclusions	**Published Data Sources**
Neighborhood characteristics	Zoning manuals, master plans
Local economic and demographic conditions	Economic and demographic data
Current room night demand by market segment	Directories of lodging facilities
Existing and projected competitive environment	Occupancy and average rate data
Expected future trends in lodging demand	Economic and demographic data
Projected usage and revenues from food, beverage, and banquet facilities, as well as other services and amenities	Hotel operating statistics
Projected operating and fixed expenses	Hotel operating statistics
Income capitalization parameters such as mortgage interest and amortization rates, loan-to-value ratio, term, equity yield, terminal capitalization rate, and inflation rate	Mortgage rate data
Opinion of value via cost approach	Construction cost data
Opinion of value via sales comparison approach	Hotel market sales data

constructed and set forth development restrictions such as site density, building height, setbacks, and site utilization. Hotel market studies and valuations often include a preliminary investigation of zoning to ensure that the subject property complies with zoning regulations and that the surrounding zoning uses will enhance the neighborhood and the subject's long-term economic viability. The property owner has the ultimate responsibility to see that the project is developed in accordance with local regulations.

Master Plans

Most municipalities have master plans that describe current and future land utilization policies. These plans are prepared periodically by local planning department staff and indicate how a municipality views development and real estate trends in the area.

Economic and Demographic Data

The term *economic and demographic data* refers to a wide range of statistics relating to historic and future economic trends as well as changes in population. This type of data may be provided by numerous sources, including econometric firms, government agencies, and professional journals.

Economic and demographic data are studied to estimate future changes in hotel demand. A hotel market study starts by estimating the current or base level of hotel demand employing a unit of demand known as a room night. The current level of demand is interesting, but more important is the future level of hotel demand in each projected year. This calculation establishes the estimated areawide occupancy. Economic and demographic data provide a basis for measuring future changes by imputing movement in hotel room night demand based on similar trends indicated by the data.

When selecting economic and demographic data for use in a hotel market study and valuation, the appraiser looks for statistics that are likely to reflect future variances in lodging demand. Because feasibility and value are tied to the present worth of future benefits, historic data trends are not important unless they suggest future events. Economic and demographic forecasts are far more meaningful because they represent a view of the future and can be programmed to account for probable changes in lodging demand.

Unfortunately, most published economic and demographic data merely provide a view of history; appraisers rarely have access to a large amount of data representing future economic expectations. During fieldwork, all relevant economic and demographic data should be accumulated and researched.

The data listed in Table 2.2 can be obtained for a reasonable cost and provides an excellent starting point for forecasting hotel demand trends. Most of these data focus on future projections, which are most useful to appraisers performing hotel market studies and valuations. Other economic and demographic data are gathered during fieldwork and from discussions and interviews with local officials and other knowledgeable individuals.

Sources of Economic and Demographic Data

Table 2.2 shows the type of economic and demographic information that is typically available and its likely source.

Table 2.3 lists information that is normally used in the economic market study and hotel appraisal. It also indicates likely data sources. The appraiser should keep in mind that the following data represent secondary research and, in some cases, the qualitative information associated with it may be subject to the bias of the organization providing the data.

Analyzing Economic and Demographic Data

Once the data are collected they must be organized into a workable format. Economic and demographic data are used to forecast trends in lodging demand, so the appraiser is interested in both the direction and rate of change. Table 2.4, using highway traffic counts as an example, illustrates a typical statistical analysis for a given demographic.

When evaluating trends in economic and demographic data, the appraiser is most interested in the direction and rate of change. If the data pertain to two consecutive years, the annual percent of change may be used; if the data span more than two years, the annual compounded percent of change should be calculated instead.

The annual compounded percent change calculations are used to project future changes in lodging demand. Because the unit of lodging demand—the room night—is a real number unaffected by factors such as inflation, all growth rates

| TABLE 2.2 | Economic and Demographic Data Available by Subscription |

Woods & Poole provides:

- Annual historical population data by county, state, and nation
- Future population projections by county, state, and nation
- Annual historical population age distribution by county, state, and nation
- Annual historical retail sales data by county, state, and nation
- Future retail sales projections by county, state, and nation
- Annual historical effective buying income (EBI) by county, state, and nation
- Future effective buying income (EBI) projections by county, state, and nation
- Annual historical eating and drinking place sales by county, state, and nation
- Historical population data by MSA, state, and nation
- Future population projections by MSA, state, and nation
- Future personal income data projections by wages and salaries, other labor income, proprietors' income, dividends-interest and rent, transfers to persons, income per capita, number of households, persons per household, mean household income by MSA, state, and nation. (The same data are available on a historical basis.)
- Historical population data by age group arranged by MSA, state, and nation
- Future projections of population data by age group arranged by MSA, state, and nation
- Future projections of employment by major categories such as: agriculture; mining; construction; manufacturing; transportation; communications; public utilities (TCPU); wholesale trade; retail trade; finance, insurance, and real estate (FIRE) services; federal civilian government; military; state and local government—arranged by MSA, state, and nation (The same data are available on a historical basis.)
- Future population projections by MSA, state, and nation

The Federal Aviation Administration (FAA) can provide:

- Future air carrier enplanements and operations projections made by specific airports (The same data are available annually on a historical basis.)

***Restaurant Business* magazine publishes:**

- Restaurant Activity Index (RAI) and Restaurant Growth Index (RGI), available annually on a historical basis

---

must be calculated in real terms, using constant dollars rather than inflated dollars. Table 2.5 illustrates this process.

Between 1995 and 1999, retail sales increased a total of 31% in current (inflated) dollars. Performing the same calculation with 1998 constant dollars shows a 19% increase. The real growth in retail sales over this period would be 19%. The difference between the 31% inflated dollar calculation and the 19% constant dollar calculation is 12%, which can be attributed to inflation, not to real growth in retail demand. The annual compounded percent of change in real terms over this period is 4.6%.

When economic and demographic data reflect dollar amounts at different times, the data should either be inflated or deflated to a standard, or constant dollar, year. The calculation requires a Consumer Price Index (CPI) adjustment. Table 2.6 shows the annual CPI between 1978 and 1999.

TABLE 2.3   Other Data Sources

Type of Data	Source	Type of Data	Source
Office space absorption	Real estate broker	Housing starts	Building department
	Chamber of commerce	Hotel rooms tax	Tax collector
Office vacancies	Real estate broker	Number of visitors to area	Convention and visitors
	Chamber of commerce	attractions	bureau
Office space under	Real estate broker	Businesses entering area	Chamber of commerce
development	Chamber of commerce		Economic development
	Building department		authority
Inventory of office space	Real estate broker	Businesses leaving area	Chamber of commerce
	Chamber of commerce		Economic development
Inventory of retail space	Real estate broker		authority
	Chamber of commerce	Convention center usage,	Convention and visitors
Inventory of industrial space	Real estate broker	number of groups, number	bureau
	Chamber of commerce	of attendees, types of events,	
Highway traffic counts	Highway department	expenditure per attendee,	
Origination and destination	Highway department	average length of stay,	
studies		headquarters of hotels,	
Major business by employment	Chamber of commerce	advertising budget	
sector and number of	Economic development	Assessed values	Assessor
employees	authority	Air cargo data	Federal Aviation
	Department of Labor		Administration
Unemployment percentages	Department of Labor		Airport authority
Building permits–number and	Building department	Tourist visitation	Tourism authority
value			Convention and visitors
			bureau

TABLE 2.4   Annual Average Daily Traffic (AADT) Counts

Year	Long Island Expressway	Percent Change From Previous Year
1994	28,950	–
1995	29,983	3.6%
1996	29,082	(3.0)
1997	31,568	8.5
1998	33,910	7.4

Annual compounded percent change from 1994: 4.13 %

TABLE 2.5   Retail Sales (in millions)

	Retail Sale (Current Dollars)	(1998 Dollars)	Percent Change Retail Sales from Previous Year
1995	$1,143,539	$1,223,076	–
1996	1,240,106	1,288,319	+ 5.3%
1997	1,326,962	1,347,631	+ 4.6
1998	1,410,385	1,410,385	+ 4.7
1999	1,492,920	1,460,660	+ 3.6

Annual compounded percent change from 1995: 4.6%

TABLE 2.6   Consumer Price Index

Year	CPI	Year	CPI	Year	CPI	Year	CPI
1978	65.2	1984	103.9	1990	130.7	1995	152.4
1979	72.6	1985	107.6	1991	136.2	1996	156.9
1980	82.4	1986	109.6	1992	140.3	1997	160.5
1981	90.9	1987	113.6	1993	144.5	1998	163.0
1982	96.5	1988	118.3	1994	148.2	1999	166.6
1983	99.6	1989	124.0				

The CPI adjustment required to make all dollar amounts reflect 1998 dollars is shown below.

Year	Retail Sales (Current Dollars)
1997	$1,326,962
1998	1,410,385
1999	1,492,920

Adjust 1997 current dollars to 1998 constant dollars as follows:

$$\frac{1998\ CPI}{1997\ CPI} = \frac{163.0}{160.5} \times \frac{\$1,326,962}{1} = \$1,347,631$$

Adjust 1999 current dollars to 1998 constant dollars as follows:

$$\frac{1998\ CPI}{1999\ CPI} = \frac{163.0}{166.6} \times \frac{\$1,492,920}{1} = \$1,460,660$$

Directories of Lodging Facilities

When using the buildup approach based on an analysis of lodging activity, the total number of rooms contained in the area's competitive hotels is a key factor in estimating the area's lodging demand. The size and types of lodging facilities operating in the market also influence the competitive environment. Before beginning fieldwork, an appraiser can identify most hotels in the area by using various directories of lodging facilities. These directories typically provide the hotel's name, address, telephone number, room count, facilities and amenities, and published room rates. Directories such as the *Mobil Travel Guide* and the *AAA Travel Guide* include a quality rating for each property, which can help in evaluating competitiveness.

The key to selecting directories of lodging facilities is to ensure that their information is current, that they cover the area thoroughly, and that they list each hotel's room count. Specialized directories may provide additional information such as descriptions of meeting and banquet rooms, the date the hotel opened, and the names of important contacts. The directories of lodging facilities listed below provide valuable information on current lodging supply.

Hotel & Travel Index
500 Plaza Drive
Secaucus, NJ 07096
(201) 902-2000
www.htihotelink.com

Official Meeting Facilities Guide
500 Plaza Drive
Secaucus, NJ 07096
(201) 902-2000
www.omfg.com

Mobil Travel Guide
Prentice-Hall
108 Wilmot Road, Suite 450
Deerfield, IL 60015
www.mobil.com/online_store/

AAA Tour Books
Complimentary to AAA members at local offices
www.aaa.com
(407) 444-7000

Smith Travel Research
105 Music Village Boulevard
Hendersonville, Tennessee 37075
www.str-online.com
(615) 824-8664

Occupancy and Average Rate Data

Information on the current occupancy and average room rate of each competitive hotel in the market area is vital in developing a hotel market study and valuation.

These facts serve as a basis for estimating existing lodging demand and the relative competitiveness of all the properties in the market. Since this type of property data is often confidential, few sources compile and publish this information. However, two publications, *Lodging 400* and *Texas Rooms Tax,* provide data from which appraisers can calculate occupancy and average room rates for individual hotels.

Each August *Lodging Hospitality* magazine publishes *Lodging 400,* the results of a survey ranking the top 400 hotels in the country on revenue performance. The issue contains tables identifying each hotel and pertinent information, such as room count, occupancy, information on total sales in various categories, and number of employees. With this information the appraiser can calculate the average room rate by dividing the guest room sales by the room count times the occupancy percentage times 365. Data from *Lodging 400* are accurate and provide a standard for the many areas of the country covered in the survey.

Texas Rooms Tax is another valuable data source. Many jurisdictions in the United States collect a hotel rooms tax based on a percentage of gross rooms revenue. In most jurisdictions this information is confidential and available only in aggregate form, but the State of Texas actually publishes hotel rooms tax information each month. A property's total revenue can be calculated if the rooms tax paid and the rooms tax percentage are known. If the average room rate can be estimated, the actual occupancy is then determined by division.

Occupancy and average rate data compiled on an aggregate, area-wide basis are often readily available. Local hotel associations, convention and visitors bureaus, accounting firms, assessing departments, and other government agencies record this information. Although area-wide occupancy and rate data are compiled for most major cities, obtaining this information depends on the cooperation of individual hotels. Sometimes the data supplied in response to these surveys are skewed upward or downward, depending on the biases of the participants.

Area-wide occupancy and average rate data should be used to substantiate information collected in the field about individual hotels. The room night analysis calculation presented later will demonstrate how to derive area-wide occupancy from the occupancy levels of hotels competing in the market. This calculated occupancy should be compared with published area-wide data. Any major variance indicates a potential error in one of the data sources that should be investigated. One source of occupancy and average rate data on an area-wide, aggregate basis is Smith Travel Research. They can be reached at (615) 824-8664.

Hotel Operating Statistics

A hotel market study and valuation aims to derive a forecast of revenues and expenses for the subject property. The forecast is based on a supply and demand analysis, which includes an estimate of the subject's occupancy and average room rate (rooms revenue) and a host of hotel operating statistics that support the forecast of other revenue sources and expenses. For existing hotels, the best source of operating statistics is the hotel's actual operating history. These data provide a standard that can easily be adjusted to project changes in occupancy levels and to evaluate the competence of management. The expected financial performance of proposed hotels can be based on the operating statistics of comparable properties. Comparability includes factors such as average room rate, room count, occupancy, ratio of food and beverage revenue to rooms revenue, type of facilities (convention, resort, all-suites, extended-stay), franchise affiliation, management, and geographic proximity. The degree of comparability between the hotels providing operating statistics and the subject property is an important consideration in evaluating the reliability of the projections developed.

When appraisers cannot find actual operating statistics from comparable properties, they must use the "data of last resort"—the national averages compiled by hotel accounting firms. Each year several accounting firms survey the financial statements of hundreds of hotels across the country. Using a computerized database program, the financial statements are sorted according to various characteristics (e.g., geographic location, size, occupancy) and averaged. The results are published in tabular form and provide several types of ratios, such as percentage of total revenue, percentage of rooms revenue, amount per available room, and amount per occupied room.

Hotel operating statistics derived from an existing subject property's actual financial results, from comparable hotels, or from a national average must be arranged in a format that facilitates the comparison of these data with the forecast assumptions for the subject property. This process will be described more fully in subsequent chapters.

Mortgage Rate Data

Investors typically purchase hotels based on a valuation approach that employs a mortgage-equity technique. The mortgage component of this technique represents the rates and terms lenders currently require on hotel mortgages. This information is plugged into a formula to derive capitalization and discount rates.

Data for the formula's mortgage component can be derived by surveying hotel lenders who actively make hotel loans. This method will work if the appraiser has a close relationship with lenders who will divulge confidential information accurately. However, the American Council of Life Insurance (www.acli.com) is a better source of data. This organization, which represents 20 large life insurance companies, collects and disseminates the rates and terms of mortgages actually originated by their members. Use of these data will be described later.

Construction Cost Data

The basis for the cost approach to value and an estimate of economic feasibility is a reliable estimate of the cost to produce a substitute property with equal utility.

The cost of replacing a hotel is estimated on either a cost-per-square-foot or a cost-per-room basis using data from a construction cost manual published by a recognized cost reporting service. When any type of hotel construction cost data is used the appraiser must verify that all components (e.g., improvements, furniture, fixtures, equipment, soft costs, pre-opening and working capital) are included in the final estimate. Complete hotel construction cost data can be obtained from Marshall & Swift at (www.marshallswift.com) on the Web, or by phone at (213) 683-9000.

Hotel Market Sales Data

In the sales comparison approach the appraiser compares recently sold, comparable properties with the subject property, adjusting their sale prices for differences such as market condition, time, age, location, construction, physical condition, layout, equipment, size, and external economic factors. Although hotel investors seldom rely on sales comparison as the sole indication of value, the approach can provide support for the value derived in the income capitalization approach.

Hotel sales data for the local market area should be accumulated during the fieldwork phase of the assignment. Other appraisers, the local assessor, and the hotel association are usually familiar with recent transfers and can provide valuable information.

Face-to-Face and Telephone Interviews

Much of the data and information collected during fieldwork is accumulated through interviews. Interviews may be conducted to gather non-confidential factual data such as the assessed value of the subject property, the names and phone numbers of local employees, zoning regulations, and the path of a new highway. Non-confidential factual interviews are easily conducted once the individual with the necessary knowledge or data has been identified. Factual data are often embodied in written documents or publications that can be easily acquired. Non-confidential factual data are usually accurate, particularly if they come from a recognized source such as a government agency, chamber of commerce, or university.

Subjective non-confidential data may also be obtained through interviews. This information is often more opinion than fact. The interviewer may ask: How will economic conditions change over the next five years? Will the proposed hotel ever be built? With which property will the subject compete? Why does this particular hotel have the highest occupancy rate in the market? If subjective data are to be meaningful, the source must have knowledge and expertise on which the appraiser can rely. Subjective data are more prone to error than factual data are; therefore, credible sources are essential.

Data perceived to be confidential is the most difficult type of data to elicit in an interview. Confidential information may relate to the occupancy, average rate, and market segmentation of competitive hotels or to the financial operating statistics and development plans for proposed hotels. The assignment's nature may affect the availability of data perceived to be confidential. For example, a competitive hotel is more likely to provide occupancy and average rate statistics to support a property tax appeal that could reduce real estate taxes than to assist a market study aimed at adding rooms to the market.

When confidential information is provided to the appraiser, it may be slanted in an attempt to influence the study's outcome. Hotel managers seldom are enthusiastic about additional competition; therefore, their responses to questions about future lodging trends and the success of their properties may not be entirely reliable.

Interview Techniques

Certain procedures can be useful in gathering confidential data. To illustrate, assume that an appraiser is researching the occupancy of competitive hotels for an assignment involving a proposed property.

To obtain relevant information, interviews are arranged with the general manager or high-ranking personnel of a competitive hotel— i.e., the assistant manager, front office manager, or director of sales. Because those interviewed might underestimate occupancies, the appraiser must be well prepared for the interview and should have collected accurate occupancy data from at least one hotel beforehand. This information can serve as a tool to evaluate the responses offered by the management of other lodging facilities.

For example, in performing the market study and valuation of the proposed hotel, the appraiser consults *Lodging 400,* published by *Lodging Hospitality* magazine, and discovers that the actual occupancy of a nearby Holiday Inn was 73% the previous year. This piece of data establishes a credible standard that can be useful in interviewing the hotel managers. After a series of introductory questions about the characteristics of the local market and the competitive environment, the appraiser asks the important question: "Would you mind telling me what your occupancy was last year?" The general manager being questioned might act surprised by such a question and may respond vaguely. He might answer like this: "You know, we have had several hotels open in the market and this has affected our operation negatively. My occupancy has dropped. I think we ended last year at about 65%." To check the accuracy of this figure, the appraiser immediately follows up with, "That low? What do you think the occupancy of the Holiday Inn is?"

Hotel managers regularly trade occupancy data with their nearby competitors, so it is not unusual for them to have this information readily available. In this case, if the general manager was truthful about the 65% occupancy, he will probably say that the Holiday Inn was operating at 73%. If, however, the occupancy estimate was biased downward—i.e., it was really 72%, but he told you 65%—the manager would probably make the same adjustment to the Holiday Inn estimate and respond "66%"

instead of "73%." Thus, the benchmark shows a downward bias of about seven percentage points, which could probably be applied to the 65% estimate, bringing it up to 72%. The appraiser also uses this procedure to verify the occupancies of all of the other competitive hotels in the market. The procedure can be used for other, competitive interviews as well as for interviews with employees of the chamber of commerce, visitors and convention bureau, assessor's office, the office building department, and so forth. Note that responses may be biased, depending on how the person being interviewed perceives the study and its likely effects.

When the results of the appraiser's interviews are organized on a spreadsheet, natural biases become apparent. By exercising good judgment the appraiser will be able to form a reliable estimate of each property's occupancy.

Although it may be difficult to obtain unbiased occupancy data from general managers, most of them will provide their average room rates and market segmentations. However, it is advisable to test their responses in these areas also if supporting data are available from other properties.

Written Surveys

The use of written surveys is another data–collection technique. Mailing mass quantities of questionnaires takes considerably less time than face-to-face or telephone interviews do. A written survey's success depends on several factors.

- The survey's subject matter must be compatible with this form of data collection.

- The survey should be simple so it can be completed in a short time.

- The survey must be mailed directly to individuals who fully understand its subject matter.

- Sufficient time must be available to develop, mail, and collect the survey responses.

Not all of the data needed to perform a hotel market study and appraisal can be collected using written surveys. Most confidential information, for example, must be obtained through face-to-face interviews. Economic and demographic data and statistics are generally available from published data sources. Written surveys work well when many data sources are available and the information to be collected is not considered confidential. Information obtained from demand generators fits these criteria.

A *demand generator* is anything that attracts overnight visitors who are likely to use a hotel's facilities into a market area. Demand generators include: airports, amusement parks, association headquarters, casinos, colleges and universities, convenient highway stopping points, county seats and state capitals, historic attractions and events, and other things.

One procedure for quantifying hotel room night demand is to survey a market's demand generators and estimate the number of visitors they attract over time who will use a hotel's facilities. This type of information is usually considered non-confidential and can be obtained easily with written surveys.

A written survey's design is crucial to obtaining an accurate response. Most people are bombarded with surveys and have little incentive or time to complete them, so a short, easy form is essential. The format shown in Figure 2.2 can be used to design a written survey to compare demand generator information.

In addition to designing a concise form that is easy to understand, the appraiser should include a self-addressed, stamped envelope with the survey so it can be returned quickly.

To increase the survey's response rate an appraiser should enclose a cover letter signed by someone known to the survey's recipients. Depending on the nature of the assignment this person could be the local mayor, another government official, the president of the chamber of commerce, a prominent business leader, or a local celebrity. The cover letter should also be brief, to the point, and should explain how the recipient will benefit by responding.

Pinpointing the person who is best equipped to answer the required questions is the key to a successful written survey. All correspondence should be directed to that person. "To Whom It May Concern" salutations seldom elicit a satisfactory response. Mailing lists from the local chamber of commerce are usually good starting points. Using this information as a base, a quick telephone survey can be conducted to obtain the names of the most appropriate respondents.

A relatively long lead-time is needed to develop, mail, receive, and evaluate written surveys, so appraisers should allow 30 to 40 days to use this data collection technique properly.

The main disadvantages of written surveys are the normally low response rate, the inability to follow up on specific questions, and a lack of data verification.

A written survey's response rate depends on many factors, including the form of the survey, the perceived benefits to the respondent, and the ability to direct the survey to the proper individuals. A 10% response rate is considered good; occasionally a survey will yield a 30% to 35% return. When developing a survey, appraisers should take this low rate of response into account so that enough forms are mailed to ensure a sufficient data sample.

Written surveys do not give the questioner an opportunity to follow up an answer with another question that could elicit an important response. Therefore, appraisers should review the responses to the survey and conduct telephone interviews of respondents who appear to have additional data that may be helpful.

Written surveys are often difficult to verify. During face-to-face interviews, the interviewer can evaluate the respondent's character and judge the accuracy of the data being provided. A person's intonation, body language, and general attitude convey a sense of whether the information being supplied is reliable. Users of written surveys do not have this advantage.

FIGURE 2.2 Hotel Survey Boilerplate

A new hotel is planned in your competitive market area. Responses to the following questions will help in assessing the type of lodging facility that will best serve the needs of your firm and other businesses in your area. While we realize that you may not have precise information regarding many of the following questions, we would appreciate your best estimates.

1. Name/Title _____

2. Company Name/ Department _____

3. Street Address _____

4. City, State, Zip _____

5. Telephone _____

6. What is the current number of employees? _____

7. What are the primary business activities at this location? _____

   in your firm? _____

   in your department? _____

8. Within the next year, is the number of employees in your firm/department projected to (please circle)

   Increase   Decrease   Remain the same

   By how much? _____   By how much? _____

9. What are the seasonal percentages of visitors to your firm/department requiring accommodations?

   Winter _____%   Spring _____%   Summer _____%   Fall _____%

10. What percentage of the visitors described above currently book their own accommodations? _____%

    have someone within the firm book their accommodations? _____%

    Please indicate the name, department and telephone number of the person within your firm responsible for booking accommodations: _____

    _____

    _____

11. Reasons for Overnight Stay

    (Please complete the following chart)

    (a) What percentage of people visiting your firm/department requiring overnight accommodations do so for the reasons indicated?

    (b) What is the average number of nights per visit?

    (c) On average, how many people stay in one hotel room per visit?

Reason for Overnight Stay	(a) Percent of Total Visitors	(b) Average Length of Stay	(c) No. of People per Room
Relocation			
Training			
Temporary Assignment			
Consulting			
Meeting/Conference			
Other			
Total	100%		

FIGURE 2.2   **Hotel Survey Boilerplate *(continued)***

12. Current Lodging Facilities Used

(Please complete the following chart)

Which lodging facilities does your firm currently use? (Please list in the order you would select them.)

Name of Lodging Facility	Room Rate Charged
1.	
2.	
3.	
4.	

13. Choosing a Lodging Facility ...

(a) Please rank the following six factors in order of importance in choosing a lodging facility.

(1 = Most Important and 6 = Least Important)

Factor	Rating		Factor	Rating
Price	_____		Convenience of Location	_____
Quality of Amenities	_____		Chain Affiliation	_____
Facilities Offered	_____		Other_____	_____

(b) Would the availability of a health club/fitness center be an important consideration in choosing a lodging facility?

14. Meeting and Banquet Facilities

Do you currently use meeting and/or banquet facilities at area hotels?
(Please circle whichever applies)

Meeting Facilities   Banquet Facilities   Neither

(If Meeting and/or Banquet Facilities are used, please complete the following chart)

	For Meetings	For Banquets
How frequently do you use these facilities?		
What is the average size of the group?		
What is the smallest size?		
What is the largest size?		
What percentage of attendees require overnight accommodations?		
What percentage occurs on weekends?		

15. Location

(a) Are you familiar with the location of our project? _____

(b) How would you rank the location of this hotel compared to the locations of the hotels you currently use?
(Please circle)

Better   About the same   Inferior

16. Given a choice between a full-service hotel (i.e., Marriott, Holiday Inn, Hilton) and a limited-service hotel (i.e., Days Inn, Red Roof Inn, Comfort Inn), which would you be more likely to choose in booking accommodations for overnight visitors? Why? _____

_____

_____

_____

CHAPTER 3

Demand for Transient Accommodations

In performing hotel-motel valuations and feasibility studies, appraisers are primarily interested in the micro, rather than the macro, aspects of demand. Micro demand for transient accommodations refers to the demand within a limited geographic area such as a town, city, or county. By quantifying the micro demand into measurable units such as room nights, half of the supply and demand equation is known. Macro demand is much broader in scope and takes into account national and international travel patterns. Although macro demand receives only limited attention in most appraisal reports, it is an important consideration because it often foreshadows changes in travel trends for micro areas.

Macro Demand

Four Categories of Data

Much of the macro data relating to travel in general and hotel demand in particular is compiled by government and industry organizations. This type of data can be divided into four categories based on its ability to reflect trends in hotel-motel demand.

Category 1 consists of information pertaining to the actual use of commercial accommodations. These data relate to the number of travelers actually using hotels and motels throughout the United States—a direct measure of lodging demand. They most clearly indicate the current status of the hotel industry because the data require little interpretation. Examples of Category 1 data would include a survey of the number of travelers using hotel accommodations during their trips and quantification of the occupied hotel rooms within a specific macro market over a certain period of time.

Category 2 information pertains to travel that may entail the use of commercial accommodations. This type of data does not directly reflect demand for transient accommodations; rather, it provides a basis for drawing inferences that could lead to supportable estimates. Examples of Category 2 data include information on the amount of airline travel, attendance at recreational attractions, and the number of travelers in general.

Category 3 data indicate the general condition of the national economy and describe the broad demographic trends that can indirectly impact the use of commercial accommodations. Like Category 2 data, this type of data does not directly reflect the demand for commercial accommodations; only indirect inferences can be drawn. Examples of Category 3 data include statistics on population growth and disposable income and various types of economic trend indicators.

Category 4 information details specific characteristics of transient travel demand (i.e., reasons for travel, types of accommodation selected, length of stay, and size of party). These data are used to evaluate the relative competitiveness of various types of hotels within a specific market.

The best type of data for quantifying hotel demand, evaluating historic trends, and formulating projections is Category 1 data. This type of data can be obtained nationally from government-administered sources charged with the task of tracking travel data of all sorts. On a regional or micro level, most appraisers develop their own information on the specific market areas surrounding their subject properties and then augment their findings with competitive data provided by Smith Travel Research. The procedures for quantifying hotel demand will be discussed later. Category 2 data are also readily available nationally but are sometimes difficult to obtain on the micro level.

Category 3 data covering most micro markets within the United States are available from many sources. Appraisers often use this type of data as a basis for forecasting future trends in hotel demand once a base level has been quantified through primary research techniques, which will be described in subsequent sections of this book. Category 4 data are available on a macro basis, but micro market data can rarely be obtained from public sources.

Most of the Category 1 and 2 data relating to macro hotel demand are compiled by the U.S. Travel Data Center, a department within the Travel Industry Association of America (TIA). This national, nonprofit center for travel research was established in 1973. Its goal is to advance the common interests of the travel industry and the public by encouraging, sponsoring, and conducting statistical, economic and scientific research concerning travel, the travel industry, and travel-related industries. To meet this objective the data center gathers, analyzes, publishes, and distributes the results of its research and cooperates with government agencies, private industry, and academic institutions with similar goals. As a result, the center has become the premier source for national travel research. Membership in the TIA is highly recommended for any appraiser who actively evaluates travel-related properties. For more information, contact TIA's Web site: www.tia.org.

Total Trips and Person Trips

The primary unit of travel demand used by the U.S. Travel Data Center is the "trip." Each trip unit represents the number of times a member or members of a household travel to a place at least 100 miles from home, one way, and then return. A "person-trip" is a unit of measure that accounts for the number of persons on a trip. If three persons from a household go together on one trip, their travel is counted as one trip and three person-trips. Therefore, the average party size can be calculated by dividing the number of trips by the number of person-trips. This type of Category 2 data, for the period 1987 to 1997 is set forth in Table 3.1.

Between 1987 and 1997, the number of trips increased at an average annual compounded percentage rate of 2.4%. This growth rate accelerated slightly to 2.8% between 1990 and 1997. The strongest rate of expansion was recorded in 1992, when trips increased by 9.8%, while 1997 also saw an above-average rate of expansion equal to 4.8%. As for person-trips, this indicator increased at an average annual compounded percentage rate of 3.5% between 1987 and 1997. The rate of growth accelerated again between 1990 and 1997, when travel volume increased at an average compounded rate of 4.0% per year. Since mid-1992 the national economy has been expanding, driving stronger rates of growth for the decade than have been recognized over the long term. Most industry experts tend to consider an annual growth rate of

TABLE 3.1	Person-Trips and Party Size Statistics				
Year	Total Trips (in millions)	Percent Change	Person-Trips (in millions)	Percent Change	Party Size (people)
1987	567.3	—	893.5	—	1.58
1988	584.9	3.1%	924.5	3.5%	1.58
1989	592.2	1.2	945.2	2.2	1.60
1990	589.4	(0.5)	956.0	1.1	1.62
1991	592.4	0.5	980.1	2.5	1.65
1992	650.7	9.8	1,063.0	8.5	1.63
1993	648.2	(0.4)	1,057.5	(0.5)	1.63
1994	665.3	2.6	1,139.1	7.7	1.71
1995	669.7	0.7	1,172.6	2.9	1.75
1996	682.8	2.0	1,161.2	(1.0)	1.70
1997	715.9	4.8	1,256.1	8.2	1.75
Annual Compounded Percent Change					
1987–1997		2.4%		3.5%	
1990–1997		2.8		4.0	
Source: U.S. Travel Data Center					

2% a reasonable benchmark for evaluating projected demand growth for a given market. Whenever an appraiser uses a higher demand growth rate, it must be recognized that such an estimate exceeds long-term national averages; thus, the applied growth rate should be justified by favorable local economic and demographic data.

Table 3.1 also illustrates the increasing trends in party size, where the average number of household members per trip has grown from 1.58 in 1987 to 1.75 in 1997. This dynamic resulted in rapid growth among person-trips relative to trips. Just as the rate of travel has increased since 1987, the size of traveling parties has also expanded.

Purpose of Trip

The U.S. Travel Data Center also reports total travel demand as categorized by the purpose of each trip. Table 3.2 shows trends in trip volume for four separate categories of travel, including business, pleasure, vacation, and weekend trips. Total trip volume is presented again for context. Because a given trip may have multiple purposes, the total of the four travel categories exceeds the number of total trips.

TABLE 3.2 National Travel Volume Segmented by Purpose of Trip

Year	Business Trips (in millions)	Percent Change	Pleasure Trips (in millions)	Percent Change	Vacation Trips (in millions)	Percent Change	Weekend Trips (in millions)	Percent Change	Total Trips (in millions)*	Percent Change
1982	119.7	–	291.2	–	–	–	–	–	479.0	–
1983	121.7	1.7%	291.0	(0.1)%	–	–	–	–	482.2	0.7%
1984	134.5	10.5	275.0	(5.5)	–	–	–	–	470.9	(2.3)
1985	156.6	16.4	301.2	9.5	–	–	–	–	497.8	5.7
1986	164.4	5.0	325.3	8.0	–	–	–	–	528.0	6.1
1987	185.0	12.5	348.6	7.2	285.0	–	–	–	567.3	7.4
1988	182.8	(1.2)	356.7	2.3	308.4	8.2%	–	–	584.9	3.1
1989	199.3	9.0	358.3	0.4	324.4	5.2	–	–	592.2	1.2
1990	182.8	(8.3)	361.1	0.8	328.7	1.3	263.7	–	589.4	(0.5)
1991	176.9	(3.2)	364.3	0.9	327.7	(0.3)	299.8	13.7%	592.4	0.5
1992	210.8	19.2	411.7	13.0	352.8	7.7	340.3	13.5	650.7	9.8
1993	210.4	(0.2)	413.4	0.4	352.2	(0.2)	330.0	(3.0)	648.2	(0.4)
1994	193.2	(8.2)	434.3	5.1	343.4	(2.5)	315.2	(4.5)	665.3	2.6
1995	207.8	7.6	413.0	(4.9)	349.7	1.8	317.5	0.7	669.7	0.7
1996	192.8	(7.2)	432.5	4.7	375.5	7.4	332.4	4.7	682.8	2.0
1997	207.4	7.6	443.2	2.5	388.6	3.5	353.5	6.3	715.9	4.8
Annual Compounded Percent Change										
1982–1997		3.7%		2.8%		–		–		2.7%
1987–1997		1.1		2.4		3.1		–		2.4
1990–1997		1.8		3.0		2.4%		4.3%		2.8

Source: U.S. Travel Data Center

* The total number of trips does not represent the sum of the preceding four columns; the definitions of the preceding categories may overlap.

Between 1982 and 1997, business trips increased at an average annual compounded percentage rate of 3.7%. Between 1990 and 1997, the rate of growth decelerated to 1.8% per year, while the year-to-year changes demonstrated significant volatility. Business travel volume decreased in 1990, 1991, 1993, 1994, and 1996. These declines were offset, however, by strong gains in 1992, 1995, and 1997.

Unlike the trends noted in business travel, pleasure travel volume accelerated in the 1990s. Whereas the rate of growth between 1982 and 1997 equated to 2.8%, the growth rate between 1990 and 1997 equated to 3.0%. Like business trips, the number of pleasure trips surged in 1992. The number of pleasure trips declined in 1995 but grew consistently over the historical period.

Vacation trip data were only available for the years between 1987 and 1997. Over this period the number of vacation trips increased at an average annual compounded percentage rate of 3.1%; the rate of growth decelerated slightly to 2.4% between 1990 and 1997. Data for weekend trips were only available for the years between 1990 and 1997, but they showed that weekend trips increased at an average annual compounded percentage rate of 4.3% over this period. The stronger rate of growth in weekend trips in recent years is tied to a national trend toward more frequent, yet shorter, vacations. Instead of taking extended vacations, Americans are taking more three-day weekends. Destination resorts near metropolitan centers have benefited from this change and commonly offer mini-vacations and weekend packages to capitalize on it.

Overall, these historical trends indicate that gains in pleasure-related trips (including vacations and weekend trips) outpaced gains in business trips, although trends for each variety of travel have been positive.

Hotel Trips

Table 3.3 sets forth historical trip volume statistics for travelers using hotels and motels during the years 1982 to 1997. These statistics, however, pertain only to trips involving hotel and motel usage. Because these statistics do not account for the trip's duration, the data do not necessarily correlate to hotel room nights occupied.

Between 1982 and 1997 trips involving hotel/motel stays increased at an average annual compounded percentage rate of 3.6%. The rate of growth, however, slowed to 2.0% between 1990 and 1997. Offsetting declines in 1994, 1995, and 1997, hotel/motel trips surged in 1992 and 1996.

Again, the number of hotel/motel trips does not necessarily correlate to hotel room nights occupied. In 1997 the number of hotel/motel trips declined slightly, by 0.1%, although the number of occupied room nights rose that year due to an increase in the average length of stay. Smith Travel Research (STR), the leading independent research firm serving the hotel industry, estimated the gain in 1997 occupied room nights to be roughly 3.0%. More extensive data provided by STR will be detailed later in this text.

TABLE 3.3	Trips Involving Hotel/Motel Usage					
Year	Hotel/Motel Trips (in millions)	Percent Change	Year	Hotel/Motel Trips (in millions)	Percent Change
1982	197.2	–	1992	325.8	11.9%
1983	206.3	4.6%	1993	329.5	1.1
1984	215.3	4.4	1994	318.5	(3.3)
1985	224.2	4.1	1995	316.4	(0.7)
1986	247.9	10.6	1996	334.0	5.6
1987	282.1	13.8	1997	333.6	(0.1)
1988	273.3	(3.1)	**Annual Compounded Percent Change**		
1989	290.5	6.3	1982–1997		3.6%
1990	291.0	0.2	1990–1997		2.0
1991	291.1	0.0			

Source: U.S. Travel Data Center

Additional characteristics associated with hotel/motel trips identified by the U.S. Travel Data Center are

- 79% of travelers had one overnight destination; the remaining 21% had multiple destinations.
- 66% of trips involved travelers arriving by car, truck, or recreational vehicle (RV); 31% arrived by air.
- 54% of the trips involved only one household member; 28% of the trips involved two household members.
- 54% of the trips were pleasure-related; business was identified as the main purpose of 42% of the trips.
- 53% of the trips were described as a vacation.
- The average length of the hotel/motel stay was 3.4 nights.
- 51% of the trips involved overnight weekend travel.
- For 24% of the trips, a travel agent was consulted; 20% of the trips were booked through a travel agent.
- A car was rented for 22% of the trips.
- 19% of the trips included a child.
- The average round-trip distance was 1,159 miles.

Characteristics of Trips

The U.S. Travel Data Center also compiles Category 4 data on trip characteristics. Table 3.4 shows the typical characteristics of different types of trips based on the

TABLE 3.4   Person-Trip Characteristics–1997

	Total	Business	Pleasure	Vacation	Weekend	Hotel	Age Distribution			
							<18	18–34	35–54	55+
Base (millions)	1,256.1	275.5	862.4	751.8	656.0	333.6	214.4	361.0	431.3	249.4
Type of Lodging										
Hotel or motel	45%	64%	39%	46%	47%	100%	40%	44%	51%	42%
Friends', relatives' homes	34	16	40	38	40	8	41	40	27	35
Camper, trailer, or RV	4	2	5	5	5	*	5	4	3	5
Owned cabin or condo	3	1	4	4	3	*	2	2	2	5
Rented cabin or condo	3	3	3	5	3	1	5	3	3	3
Other	5	3	4	5	5	1	3	5	5	5
No overnight stay	11	14	10	5	0	0	11	8	13	13
Average friends/ relatives (nights)	3.9	3.6	3.8	4.4	2.6	4.2	3.8	3.6	3.4	4.6
Average hotel/ motel (nights)	3.5	3.4	3.5	3.8	2.5	3.4	3.4	3.4	3.3	3.9
Main Purpose of Trip										
Pleasure travel (net)	71%	0%	100%	89%	78%	54%	83%	73%	62%	70%
Visit friends/relatives	36	0	51	41	41	17	44	39	27	37
Entertainment	24	0	34	33	25	28	26	22	24	24
Outdoor recreation	11	0	15	15	12	8	13	11	11	9
Business travel (net)	23	100	0	9	16	42	11	22	31	22
Business (unspecified)	14	60	0	1	7	30	4	14	21	12
Convention, seminar, meeting	2	9	0	1	2	4	1	2	3	3
Combined business/ pleasure	7	30	0	7	7	8	6	6	8	6
Personal business	*	1	0	*	0	*	*	*	*	1
Other	6	0	0	2	6	4	6	5	7	8
Vacation travel	60%	24%	75%	100%	66%	53%	69%	64%	53%	57%
Overnight weekend travel	52%	36%	58%	58%	100%	51%	57%	56%	52%	43%
Friday night	8	7	8	8	N/Av	9	8	8	8	7
Saturday night	10	7	11	10	N/Av	10	11	10	11	8
Both Friday and Saturday nights	34	22	39	40	N/Av	32	37	38	33	28

TABLE 3.4 **Person-Trip Characteristics—1997** *(continued)*

	Total	Business	Pleasure	Vacation	Weekend	Hotel	Age Distribution			
							<18	18–34	35–54	55+
Base (millions)	1,256.1	275.5	862.4	751.8	656.0	333.6	214.4	361.0	431.3	249.4
Round-Trip Distance										
200–299 miles	22%	18%	22%	18%	23%	15%	22%	19%	22%	21%
300–399 miles	15	14	16	15	18	12	18	16	15	14
400–599 miles	18	17	19	18	21	16	20	20	16	17
600–999 miles	14	15	14	15	14	16	12	14	16	13
1,000–1,999 miles	14	16	13	15	12	17	15	14	13	14
2,000 miles or more	12	15	10	13	8	17	9	11	12	15
Outside U.S.	5	5	6	6	4	7	3	5	5	6
Average round-trip distance (miles)	939	1,084	872	992	802	1,159	825	932	950	1,004
Primary Mode of Transportation										
Auto/truck/RV/ rental car	79%	65%	84%	80%	85%	66%	89%	79%	75%	78%
Airplane	18	33	13	17	13	31	9	17	23	18
Bus	1	1	1	1	1	2	1	2	1	2
Train	1	*	1	1	1	1	1	1	1	1
Other	1	*	1	1	*	*	*	1	1	2
Trip Duration										
No nights	12%	14%	10%	5%	0%	0%	11%	8%	13%	13%
One night	16	19	15	12	18	19	15	17	16	15
2 or 3 nights	39	36	41	40	58	43	38	42	40	33
4 to 9 nights	27	25	27	34	24	30	29	27	25	29
10 nights or more	7	6	7	9	0	8	7	6	6	10
Average duration (excludes 0 nights)	4.1	3.9	4.1	4.7	2.6	4.1	4.0	3.9	3.8	5.1
Average duration (includes 0 nights)	3.7	3.3	3.7	4.4	N/Av	N/Av	3.6	3.5	3.3	4.4
Number of Destinations										
No overnight destinations	12%	14%	10%	5%	0%	0%	11%	8%	13%	13%
One destination	75	72	77	79	91	79	75	81	74	70
Two destinations	9	8	9	10	7	14	10	8	9	10
Three or more destinations	4	6	4	6	2	7	4	3	4	7
Average number of nights per destination	3.2	3.0	3.0	3.4	2.3	2.9	3.1	3.0	2.9	3.6

TABLE 3.4   Person-Trip Characteristics–1997 *(continued)*

	Total	Business	Pleasure	Vacation	Weekend	Hotel	——Age Distribution——			
							<18	18–34	35–54	55+
Base (millions)	1,256.1	275.5	862.4	751.8	656.0	333.6	214.4	361.0	431.3	249.4
Census Region of Destination										
South Atlantic	19%	20%	20%	21%	18%	21%	19%	20%	22%	17%
Pacific	13	15	13	14	14	14	14	13	13	13
East North Central	13	13	13	12	14	12	14	14	14	12
West South Central	11	12	10	9	11	10	12	12	10	10
Mountain	11	11	10	11	10	12	10	9	10	12
Mid-Atlantic	9	9	10	9	10	8	8	11	8	10
West North Central	8	7	8	7	8	6	9	7	7	8
East South Central	7	6	7	6	7	6	7	6	6	8
New England	4	3	4	4	4	4	3	4	4	4
Outside U.S.	5	5	5	7	4	7	3	5	5	6
Number of Household Members on Trip										
One **	53%	71%	45%	46%	48%	54%	2%	43%	34%	38%
Two	28	17	31	30	30	28	12	26	32	55
Three	11	7	13	13	12	10	33	16	19	6
Four	6	3	8	8	8	6	37	12	11	1
Five or more	2	2	3	3	2	2	16	3	4	*
Average	1.8	1.5	1.9	1.9	1.9	1.8	3.5	2.1	2.2	1.7
Child from household on trip	21%	12%	25%	24%	23%	19%	100%	28%	35%	4%

*   Less than 0.5%

**   Includes those who travel alone or with someone from outside the household

Source: U.S. Travel Data Center

trip's purpose and the traveler's age. Note that each of the categories is analyzed based on person-trips, with the exception of the hotel category.

Weekend and pleasure travelers tend to cover the shortest distances in the course of their trips. Business and vacation travelers generally cover longer distances, and such trips are more likely to require use of a hotel. In addition, older travelers are more likely to travel farther than younger travelers. The average round-trip distances ranged from a low of 802 miles among weekend travelers to a high of 1,159 miles among travelers using a hotel.

In terms of the mode of transportation, each category of traveler is most likely to arrive via a car, truck, recreational vehicle (RV), or rental car; however, weekend and pleasure travelers and travelers younger than 18 are more likely than other travelers to use these modes of transportation. Air travel is most common for business travelers, travelers requiring a hotel, and travelers between the ages 35 and 54.

Travelers older than 55 posted the longest average trip length, with an average stay (excluding trips that require no overnight stay) of 5.1 nights. Vacationers posted a similarly high average trip length of 4.7 nights. Weekend travelers, who reported an average trip length of 2.6 nights, posted the lowest indication. Travelers using hotels and motels reported an average trip duration of 4.1 nights, equal to the average for all trips. As for the number of destinations per trip, vacationers, travelers using hotels, and travelers older than 55 were most likely to have multiple destinations.

Business travelers are the most likely to require a hotel or motel during their trips. Whereas 45% of all trips required hotels or motels in 1997, 64% of business trips required hotels or motels. Vacationers, weekend travelers, and travelers between ages 35 and 54 also used hotels and motels more often than average in 1997. The average length of the hotel stay equated to 3.4 nights in 1997, with the duration of the stays exceeding this average for pleasure travelers, vacationers, and travelers age 55 and older.

As for the purpose of travel, 71% of all travelers reported that their trip was for pleasure, whereas 23% of all travelers reported a business purpose. In contrast, of all those travelers who used hotel facilities on their trip, 54% had a pleasure-related purpose, while 42% had a business-related purpose. Otherwise, travelers aged 35 to 54 were more likely than other age groups to have a business-related trip.

Of all trips surveyed, 60% included a vacation component; categories for which this average was exceeded included pleasure travelers, vacationers, weekend travelers, and travelers under the age of 18 as well as travelers between ages 18 and 34. Overnight weekend travel was identified as a component of 52% of all trips, where an above average indication was noted in the following categories: pleasure, vacation, weekend, travelers under the age of 18, and travelers between ages 18 and 34.

Every category surveyed identified the South Atlantic as the most common region of destination, with vacationers, travelers using hotels, and travelers aged 35 to 54 noting particularly high visitation to the South Atlantic. Business travelers reported the highest ratio of total travel to the Pacific region.

In terms of the number of household members on the trip, 53% of all trips involved a single member of the household, while the ratio for business travel was 71%. The average number of household members for all trips was 1.8, with business-related trips reporting an average of 1.5 household members per trip. Trips involving a traveler under age 18 reported an average of 3.5 household members, whereas trips involving a traveler aged 55 or older reported an average of 1.7 household members. A child was included in 21% of all trips, while 19% of trips involving hotel facilities included a child.

Travel Trends by Gender

The U.S. Travel Data Center also analyzed travel characteristics as differentiated by gender. Table 3.5 identifies the results of this survey.

Differences in travel trends among males and females have narrowed significantly in recent years. As of 1997, the greatest disparities were realized in the share of business- and vacation-related person-trips. Less than 10 percentage points differentiated all other categories.

Month of Travel

Table 3.6 identifies month of travel statistics for 1996 and 1997. As indicated, travel is generally more concentrated in summer months. July and August represent peak national travel times. Travel volume declines significantly in January and February, but is generally consistent throughout the remainder of the year.

Payroll Employment

Another way to gauge hotel-motel demand is to look at the number of people employed in the hotel-motel industry. Table 3.7 identifies the total number of people employed in the nation's hotels and other lodging facilities between 1972 and 1998.

Between 1972 and 1998, employment levels in hotels and other lodging facilities increased at an average annual compounded percentage rate of 3.1%. The strongest rate of growth over this historical period was realized in the 1980s, when hotel employment increased at an average annual compounded percentage rate of 7.2%. Hotel supply increased dramatically throughout the 1980s, and a recession in the early 1990s contributed to the significantly slower rate of hotel employment growth between 1990 and 1998. As indicated, hotel employment levels declined in

TABLE 3.5	Comparison of Travel Characteristics by Gender–1997		
	% of Person-Trips		
Characteristic	**Men**	**Women**	**Difference**
Business trips	28%	17%	11 points
One person from household	37	28	9
Midweek travel	21	15	6
Hotel/motel use	48	43	5
Rental car use	15	10	5
Consulted travel agent	15	11	4
Travel by air	19	16	3
Vacation	55	65	(10)
Visiting friends/relatives	32	40	(8)
Child on trip	33	40	(7)
Overnight weekend	49	55	(6)

Source: U.S. Travel Data Center

TABLE 3.6	Month of Travel 1996 and 1997	
Month	**1996**	**1997**
January	6%	7%
February	6	6
March	8	8
April	9	8
May	9	8
June	9	8
July	10	11
August	9	10
September	9	9
October	9	9
November	7	8
December	9	8
Total	100%	100%

Source: U.S. Travel Data Center

TABLE 3.7	U.S. Employment - Hotels and Other Lodging Places				
Year	**Total Hotel Employment (in thousands)**	**Percent Change**	**Year**	**Total Hotel Employment (in thousands)**	**Percent Change**
1972	813.1	—	1988	1,540.1	5.2%
1973	854.2	5.1%	1989	1,595.8	3.6
1974	877.7	2.8	1990	1,631.1	2.2
1975	898.4	2.4	1991	1,589.4	(2.6)
1976	929.4	3.5	1992	1,576.4	(0.8)
1977	956.1	2.9	1993	1,595.7	1.2
1978	988.0	3.3	1994	1,630.9	2.2
1979	1,059.8	7.3	1995	1,668.1	2.3
1980	1,075.8	1.5	1996	1,715.0	2.8
1981	1,118.7	4.0	1997	1,745.7	1.8
1982	1,132.9	1.3	1998	1,775.8	1.7
1983	1,171.5	3.4	**Annual Compounded Percent Change**		
1984	1,262.8	7.8	1972–1998		3.1%
1985	1,331.3	5.4	1972–1980		3.6
1986	1,377.8	3.5	1980–1990		7.2
1987	1,464.2	6.3	1990–1998		0.9

Source: Bureau of Labor Statistics

1991 and 1992. Since 1992, hotel employment growth has stayed relatively consistent, between 1.2% and 2.8% per year.

Modes of Transportation

Other useful Category 2 data include statistics relating to the usage of different modes of transportation. When evaluating trends in lodging industry demand, data about air and car travel are most relevant. Table 3.8 sets forth the volume of American air and car travel between 1982 and 1997.

Between 1982 and 1997, air travel volume increased at an average annual compounded percentage rate of 3.8%. However, this growth rate decelerated to 2.0% annually between 1990 and 1997. Growth trends for air travel have been volatile, particularly in the 1990s. Air travel volume surged by roughly 28% in 1992, then plummeted in 1994. Car travel volume has increased more consistently. Between 1982 and 1997, car travel increased at an average annual compounded percentage rate of 2.5%, accelerating to a 3.1% growth rate between 1990 and 1997.

The data in Table 3.8 were gathered by the U.S. Travel Data Center and based on travel surveys. Additional information on airline passenger traffic is published by the Air Transport Association and based on actual airline usage. Table 3.9 shows

TABLE 3.8	National Travel Volume Segmented by Mode of Transportation			
Year	Air Travel (in millions)	Percent Change	Automobile Travel (in millions)	Percent Change
1982	91.2	–	366.5	–
1983	112.0	22.8%	349.2	(4.7)%
1984	114.5	2.2	335.8	(3.8)
1985	135.4	18.3	331.6	(1.3)
1986	138.2	2.1	357.6	7.8
1987	154.9	12.1	382.4	6.9
1988	149.0	(3.8)	416.7	9.0
1989	149.0	0.0	423.0	1.5
1990	139.7	(6.2)	426.7	0.9
1991	130.6	(6.5)	437.5	2.5
1992	166.7	27.6	455.6	4.1
1993	169.0	1.4	455.8	0.0
1994	135.8	(19.6)	502.7	10.3
1995	147.9	8.9	500.1	(0.5)
1996	145.4	(1.7)	511.9	2.4
1997	160.5	10.4	530.1	3.6
Annual Compounded Percent Change				
1982–1997		3.8%		2.5%
1990–1997		2.0		3.1

Source: U.S. Travel Data Center

TABLE 3.9	Airline Passenger Traffic			
Year	Revenue Passengers Enplaned (in thousands)	Percent Change	Revenue Passenger Miles (in thousands)	Percent Change
1980	296,903	—	255,192,114	—
1981	285,976	(3.7)%	248,887,801	(2.5)%
1982	294,102	2.8	259,643,870	4.3
1983	318,638	8.3	281,829,148	8.5
1984	344,683	8.2	305,115,855	8.3
1985	382,022	10.8	336,403,021	10.3
1986	418,946	9.7	366,545,855	9.0
1987	447,678	6.9	404,471,484	10.3
1988	454,614	1.5	423,301,559	4.7
1989	453,692	(0.2)	432,714,309	2.2
1990	465,560	2.6	457,926,286	5.8
1991	452,301	(2.8)	447,954,829	(2.2)
1992	475,108	5.0	478,553,708	6.8
1993	488,520	2.8	489,648,421	2.3
1994	528,848	8.3	519,381,688	6.1
1995	547,773	3.6	540,656,211	4.1
1996	581,234	6.1	578,663,005	7.0
1997	599,131	3.1	605,573,543	4.7
1998	614,168	2.5	619,455,758	2.3
Annual Compounded Percent Change				
1980–1998		4.1%		5.1%
1990–1998		3.5		3.8

Source: Air Transport Association

airline travel statistics, including revenue passengers enplaned (i.e., boarding an airplane) and the number of miles flown, between 1980 and 1998.

Between 1980 and 1998, the total number of passengers enplaned increased at an average annual compounded percentage rate of 4.1%. This rate of growth decelerated slightly to 3.5% between 1990 and 1998. Over the historical period, passenger volume decreased only in 1981, 1989, and 1991.

Between 1980 and 1998, passenger miles increased at an average annual compounded percentage rate of 5.1%, with the rate of growth decelerating to 3.8% between 1990 and 1998. The rates of growth for passenger miles have historically exceeded the rates of growth for passenger volume, indicating that the average distance traveled has also increased. This dynamic represents a positive trend for the hotel industry, as longer trips are more likely to require hotel stays.

An analysis of statistics on various modes of travel shows the relative importance of each. The automobile is by far the predominant means of transportation within the United States. It is also the primary means by which guests access lodging facilities. Air travel is second in importance, followed by bus and rail.

Table 3.10 summarizes the historical growth rates indicated in the preceding text, where such growth rates were indicated by the U.S. Travel Data Center findings. The growth rates generally indicate stronger expansion rates over the longer historical period, with decelerating growth indicated in the 1990s. These trends are chiefly a function of the early 1990s economic recession.

International Travel

Because travel is becoming more global, pertinent statistics pertain to visitors to the United States from foreign countries. Table 3.11 identifies historical trends in visitation from Mexico, Canada, and other countries between 1980 and 1997.

Between 1980 and 1997, travel to the United States from Mexico increased at an average annual compounded percentage rate of 5.8%, decelerating to 2.2% between 1990 and 1997. Travel to the United States from Canada increased at an average annual compounded percentage rate of 1.7% between 1980 and 1997, but receded at an average annual rate of 1.9% between 1990 and 1997. Significant declines were noted between 1993 and 1995, when the value of the Canadian dollar weakened relative to the American dollar. Among other countries growth has remained strong and consistent historically, with an average annual percentage growth rate of 7.1%. Overall, arrivals to the United States from foreign countries increased at an average annual compounded percentage rate of 4.6% between 1980 and 1997, with the rate of growth decelerating to 2.8% between 1990 and 1997.

The Department of Commerce provides an alternate measure of travel to the United States from foreign countries, which includes both the number of total visitors and total expenditures (i.e., total amount spent while visiting) between 1989 and 1998. The data are presented in Table 3.12.

TABLE 3.10   Rates of Growth Among Types of Travel

Category	Annual Compounded Percentage Change 1982–1997	Annual Compounded Percentage Change 1990–1997
Business	3.7%	1.8%
Pleasure	2.8	3.0
Vacation	—	.4
Weekend	—	4.3
Air	4.1	3.5
Automobile	5.1	3.8
Hotel	3.6	2.0

Source: U.S. Travel Data Center

TABLE 3.11	International Travel to the United States							
Year	Mexican (in millions)	Percent Change	Canadian (in millions)	Percent Change	Other (in millions)	Percent Change	Total (in millions)	Percent Change
1980	3.2	–	11.4	–	7.6	–	22.2	–
1981	3.8	18.8%	10.9	(4.4)%	8.8	15.8%	23.5	5.9%
1982	2.6	(31.6)	10.4	(4.6)	8.5	(3.4)	21.5	(8.5)
1983	1.8	(30.8)	12.0	15.4	7.7	(9.4)	21.5	0.0
1984	2.3	27.8	11.0	(8.3)	13.6	76.6	26.9	25.1
1985	2.5	8.7	10.9	(0.9)	12.0	(11.8)	25.4	(5.6)
1986	5.6	124.0	10.9	0.0	9.5	(20.8)	26.0	2.4
1987	6.7	19.6	12.4	13.8	10.3	8.4	29.4	13.1
1988	7.8	16.4	13.8	11.3	12.5	21.4	34.1	16.0
1989	7.2	(7.7)	15.3	10.9	14.1	12.8	36.6	7.3
1990	7.2	0.0	17.3	13.1	15.0	6.4	39.5	7.9
1991	7.7	6.9	19.1	10.4	16.1	7.3	42.9	8.6
1992	8.3	7.8	18.6	(2.6)	17.7	9.9	44.6	4.0
1993	9.8	18.1	17.3	(7.0)	18.7	5.6	45.8	2.7
1994	11.3	15.3	15.0	(13.3)	19.2	2.7	45.5	(0.7)
1995	9.6	(15.0)	13.7	(8.7)	20.2	5.2	43.5	(4.4)
1996	8.5	(11.5)	15.3	11.7	22.7	12.4	46.5	6.9
1997	8.4	(1.2)	15.1	(1.3)	24.3	7.0	47.8	2.8
Annual Compounded Percent Change								
1980–1997		5.8%		1.7%		7.1%		4.6%
1990–1997		2.2		(1.9)		7.1		2.8

Source: U.S. Travel & Tourism Administration

TABLE 3.12	International Travel to the United States			
Year	Visitors (in millions)	Percent Change	Expenditures (in millions)	Percent Change
1989	36.4	–	46.9	–
1990	39.4	8.2%	58.3	24.3%
1991	42.7	8.4	64.2	10.1
1992	47.3	10.8	71.4	11.2
1993	45.8	(3.2)	74.4	4.2
1994	44.8	(2.2)	75.4	1.3
1995	43.3	(3.3)	82.3	9.2
1996	46.5	7.4	90.2	9.6
1997	47.8	2.8	94.2	4.4
1998 (projected)	46.4	(2.9)	91.3	(3.1)
Annual Compounded Percent Change				
1989–1998		2.7%		7.7%

Source: Department of Commerce

Between 1989 and projected year-end 1998, international visitation to the United States increased at an average annual compounded percentage rate of 2.7%, while total expenditures increased at a rate of 7.7% per year over the same period.

Foreign travel to the United States represents an important source of national lodging demand because such travel usually requires the use of a hotel or motel. Historically, foreign travel to the United States has benefited key gateway and resort cities such as Boston, Washington, D.C., Orlando, Miami, Houston, Los Angeles, San Francisco, and Honolulu. Note that trends in foreign travel are commonly tied to trends in the strength of the American dollar. Periods in which the American dollar is weak tend to attract higher-than-usual levels of foreign travel, and often motivate domestic travelers to remain within the country rather than travel abroad. A strong American dollar has the opposite effect.

Statistics illustrating travel from the United States may also be pertinent in certain analyses. Table 3.13 sets forth historical trends in this variety of travel between 1985 and 1997.

American travel to Mexico increased at an average annual percentage rate of 4.4% between 1985 and 1997, decelerating to 1.1% between 1990 and 1997. A substantial decline was noted in 1996 as a result of political and financial instability in Mexico, although travel levels recovered in 1997, exceeding 1995 levels. Rates of growth in travel to Canada have remained relatively consistent histori-

TABLE 3.13	International Travel from the United States							
Year	To Mexico (in millions)	Percent Change	To Canada (in millions)	Percent Change	Overseas (in millions)	Percent Change	Total (in millions)	Percent Change
1985	10.5	—	12.1	—	12.7	—	35.3	—
1986	11.5	9.5%	14.1	16.5%	12.0	(5.5)%	37.6	6.5%
1987	13.0	13.0	13.3	(5.7)	13.6	13.3	39.9	6.1
1988	13.4	3.1	13.3	0.0	14.4	5.9	41.1	3.0
1989	14.2	6.0	12.2	(8.3)	14.8	2.8	41.2	0.2
1990	16.4	15.5	12.3	0.8	16.0	8.1	44.7	8.5
1991	15.0	(8.5)	12.0	(2.4)	14.5	(9.4)	41.5	(7.2)
1992	16.1	7.3	11.8	(1.7)	16.0	10.3	43.9	5.8
1993	15.3	(5.0)	12.0	1.7	17.2	7.5	44.5	1.4
1994	15.8	3.3	12.5	4.2	18.1	5.2	46.4	4.3
1995	15.8	0.0	12.9	3.2	18.7	3.3	47.4	2.2
1996	13.4	(15.2)	12.9	0.0	19.8	5.9	46.1	(2.7)
1997	17.7	32.1	13.4	3.9	21.6	9.1	52.7	14.3
Annual Compounded Percent Change								
1985–1997		4.4%		0.9%		4.5%		3.4%
1990–1997		1.1		1.2		4.4		2.4
Source: U.S. Travel & Tourism Administration								

cally, remaining in the range of 1.0% per year, while travel to other foreign countries has increased more sharply. Between 1985 and 1997, overseas travel increased at an average annual compounded percentage rate of 4.5%, slowing only slightly to 4.4% per year between 1990 and 1997. Overall, travel to foreign countries increased at an average annual compounded percentage rate of 3.4% between 1985 and 1997, slowing to 2.4% between 1990 and 1997.

Macro Demand by Market Segment

The preceding discussion of the macro demand for lodging facilities focused on the overall market without regard to specific types of travelers. Since most hotels are oriented toward one or more market segments, however, the major components of the travel market must be identified. Most macro data are divided into three primary market segments: business travelers, meeting and group travelers, and pleasure or leisure travelers. Each segment has its own historic growth trends and demographic characteristics.

Business Travel

Often identified as "commercial" demand, business travel is the lifeblood of most lodging markets in the United States. Not only does the business travel segment represent the largest volume of room night demand, but also on the whole it is the least price sensitive. A business-oriented hotel will generally achieve higher average room rates than will a comparable facility catering to meeting and group travelers.

The demographics of the business traveler are particularly interesting in evaluating the relative competitiveness of the various lodging facilities that attempt to attract this market segment. As illustrated in Table 3.2, statistics provided by the U.S. Travel Data Center indicate that the number of business trips increased at an average annual compounded percentage rate of 3.7% between 1982 and 1997, slowing to 1.8% between 1990 and 1997. Note that business trips, as defined by the U.S. Travel Data Center, include trips for conventions and other business meetings. Although specific travel characteristics associated with business travel in 1997 were also set forth earlier in this text, some pertinent statistics are summarized as follows:

- 60% of business trips consisted of "general business," while 9% of business trips consisted of a convention, seminar, or meeting.
- 71% of business trips involved only one household member.
- 64% of business trips required use of a hotel or motel.
- The average length of a business trip was 3.3 nights.
- 36% of business trips included an overnight weekend stay.
- Overall, 30% of business trips were combined with a pleasure-related purpose.

Certain types of businesses tend to generate more hotel room night demand than others. Whereas non-profit organizations tend to have a limited impact on lodging demand, firms involved in wholesale trade tend to generate the largest amount of hotel demand. The finance, insurance, and real estate (FIRE) sector also tends to generate a strong share of business travel.

Meeting and Group Travel

Meeting and group demand is an important market segment for full-service hotels with meeting and banquet space. This segment is usually subdivided into three categories of meetings: corporate, convention, and association. Each has somewhat different characteristics and hotel requirements. Corporate meetings are often organized by businesses and serve specific commercial needs. Conventions are large gatherings that can serve both business and social interests. Association meetings tend to be smaller than conventions and are commonly structured as business or educational functions.

The 1998 Meetings Market Report, conducted by the Cahners Travel Group's *Meetings & Conventions* magazine, is the primary source of meeting and group travel data. The magazine has conducted the biennial survey of the meetings, conventions, and incentive industries since 1974. Plog Research, a marketing research company based in Reseda, California, provided research for the 1998 report. Table 3.14 sets

TABLE 3.14	Meeting and Group Attendance							
Year	Avg. Annual Corporate (in millions)	Percent Change	Avg. Annual Convention (in millions)	Percent Change	Avg. Annual Associations (in millions)	Percent Change	Avg. Annual Total (in millions)	Percent Change
1974	24.3	–	11.6	–	4.1	–	40.0	–
1977	46.3	24.0%	9.0	(8.1)%	11.2	39.8%	66.5	18.5%
1979	39.2	(8.0)	8.0	(5.7)	14.0	11.8	61.2	(4.1)
1981	42.3	3.9	9.5	9.0	13.0	(3.6)	64.8	2.9
1983	36.8	(6.7)	12.1	12.9	14.4	5.2	63.3	(1.2)
1985	39.8	4.0	13.5	5.6	18.2	12.4	71.5	6.3
1987	47.3	9.0	10.7	(11.0)	16.3	(5.4)	74.3	1.9
1989	58.4	11.1	13.6	12.7	21.7	15.4	93.7	12.3
1991	49.6	(7.8)	8.6	(20.5)	22.6	2.1	80.8	(7.1)
1993	55.1	5.4	10.7	11.5	18.7	(9.0)	84.5	2.3
1995	49.3	(5.4)	13.0	10.2	15.1	(10.1)	77.4	(4.3)
1997	49.9	0.6	11.7	(5.1)	17.9	8.9	79.5	1.3
Annual Compounded Percent Change								
1974–1997		3.2%		0.0%		6.6%		3.0%
1991–1997		0.1		5.3		(3.8)		(0.3)

Source: 1998 Meetings Market Report conducted by Plog Research for *Meetings & Conventions* magazine
Updated reports available by calling (201) 902-7274.

forth the historical trends in meeting and group attendance, biennially, using data provided in the 1998 Meetings Market Report.

Between 1974 and 1997, total meeting and group attendance increased at an average annual compounded percentage rate of 3.0%, although attendance of this sort decreased at a rate of 0.3% between 1991 and 1997. Between 1974 and 1997, association attendance increased at the strongest rate, growing at an average annual compounded percentage rate of 6.6%, although this variety of visitation declined significantly between 1991 and 1997, pacing the overall decline through the 1990s. In contrast, convention visitation was essentially flat between 1974 and 1997 but increased at an average annual compounded percentage rate of 5.3% between 1991 and 1997.

Of the three sources of meeting and group attendance, the corporate segment accounts for the largest total share. This segment posted an average annual compounded percentage growth rate of 3.2% between 1974 and 1997 but remained flat between 1991 and 1997.

The 1998 Meetings Market Report also addresses the number of meetings held by each segment of meeting and group demand. Table 3.15 identifies these statistics, biennially, from 1987 to 1997.

Between 1987 and 1997, the total number of meetings and conventions decreased at an average annual compounded percentage rate of 0.3%, with a moderate gain in association meetings offset by a decline in the number of corporate meetings and conventions. The number of conventions and association meetings grew between 1995 and 1997, with growth rates equal to 1.8% and 3.9%, respectively. Corporate meetings, on the other hand, decreased by 0.8%. The number of corporate meetings has declined consistently since 1989, due to corporate downsizing and cuts in corporate travel budgets. Although the decline through 1991 was significant, decreases in corporate meetings since that time have been comparatively small.

TABLE 3.15   Number of Meetings

Year	Avg. Annual Corporate (in thousands)	Percent Change	Avg. Annual Convention (in thousands)	Percent Change	Avg. Annual Associations (in thousands)	Percent Change	Avg. Annual Total (in thousands)	Percent Change
1987	807.2	–	12.7	–	181.7	–	1,001.6	–
1989	866.8	3.6 %	12.6	(0.4)%	186.6	1.3%	1,066.0	3.2 %
1991	806.2	(3.6)	10.2	(10.0)	215.0	7.3	1,031.4	(1.6)
1993	801.3	(0.3)	11.8	7.6	206.5	(2.0)	1,019.6	(0.6)
1995	797.1	(0.3)	10.9	(3.9)	175.6	(7.8)	983.6	(1.8)
1997	783.9	(0.8)	11.3	1.8	189.5	3.9	984.7	0.1
Annual Compounded Percent Change								
1987–1997		(0.3)%		(1.2)%		0.4%		(0.2)%

Source: 1998 Meetings Market Report conducted by Plog Research for *Meetings & Conventions* magazine

Hotels and Motels–Valuations and Market Studies

TABLE 3.16   Total Expenditures—Meetings and Groups

Year	Avg. Annual Corporate (in billions)	Percent Change	Avg. Annual Convention (in billions)	Percent Change	Avg. Annual Associations (in billions)	Percent Change	Avg. Annual Total (in billions)	Percent Change
1987	$7.1	—	$11.8	—	$10.0	—	$28.9	—
1989	9.7	16.9%	15.0	12.7%	14.9	22.1%	39.6	17.1%
1991	8.7	(5.3)	11.0	(14.4)	15.3	1.3	35.0	(6.0)
1993	10.6	10.4	15.5	18.7	14.3	(3.3)	40.4	7.4
1995	8.6	(9.9)	16.8	4.1	12.0	(8.4)	37.4	(3.8)
1997	10.8	12.1	16.7	(0.3)	14.3	9.2	41.8	5.7
Annual Compounded Percent Change								
1987–1997	4.3%		3.5%		3.6%		3.8%	

Source: 1998 Meetings Market Report conducted by Plog Research for *Meetings & Conventions* magazine

Another important measure of meeting and group activity pertains to total meeting expenditures. Table 3.16 sets forth these statistics biennially between 1987 and 1997.

Between 1987 and 1997, total meeting and group expenditures rose at an average annual compounded percentage rate of 3.8%, with strong gains noted in each of the three segments. Corporate meeting expenditures rose at the strongest rate, with a 4.3% growth rate. Growth in convention and association spending equaled 3.5% and 3.6%, respectively. Whereas the preceding trends in attendance and the number of meetings indicate a mix of positive and negative trends, the comparatively steady increase in spending across the three segments is a positive indicator.

Table 3.17 specifies the frequency with which certain venues hosted corporate meetings, conventions, and association meetings. Downtown hotels hosted the majority of all three varieties of meeting and group demand. Sixty-one percent of those surveyed indicated that they had attended a corporate meeting at a down-

TABLE 3.17   Types of Facilities at which Meetings Were Held—1997

	Corporate Meetings	Conventions	Association Meetings
Downtown hotels	61%	56%	60%
Suburban hotels	44	21	36
Resort hotels	35	22	33
Convention centers	33	20	N/Av
Airport hotels	24	11	26
Golf resorts	20	10	14
Suite hotels	19	12	13
Residential conference centers	12	2	10

Source: 1998 Meetings Market Report conducted by Plog Research for *Meetings & Conventions* magazine

town hotel; 56% indicated that they had attended a convention at a downtown hotel; and 60% indicated that they had attended an association meeting at a downtown hotel. Suburban hotels, usually unpopular as convention sites, most commonly hosted corporate and association meetings. Resort hotels reflected a relatively balanced level of popularity among the three varieties of meeting and group demand.

Again, corporate meetings represent the largest of the three meeting and group segments. Table 3.18 describes this segment in greater detail. Plog Research's survey indicates that training seminars represent the most common variety of corporate meetings (aside from "other"), followed by sales meetings and management meetings. New product introductions generally feature the largest attendance, with an average of 129. Group incentive trips feature the second-largest average attendance at 102. Individual incentive trips reported the longest duration, with stays of 4.7 days, followed by group incentive trips at 4.4 days. The 1998 Meetings Market Report also indicates that, on average, it takes six months to plan corporate meetings.

Among the remaining meeting and group segments, association meetings tend to host about 100 people, comparable to the attendance of corporate meetings. Conventions, on the other hand, generally attract an average of 1,000 people. While lead planning time for associations is only slightly longer than that of corporate meetings, conventions often take years to plan.

The average meeting and convention size and the time required to plan them can be important considerations for a hotel appraiser. In valuing a hotel oriented toward the convention market, an appraiser should note the amount and size of the facility's meeting space. Doing so will help the appraiser determine whether or not the space suits an area's meeting demand. For example, if the market is composed mostly of corporate meetings, the meeting rooms should be relatively small and contain

TABLE 3.18 **Corporate Meeting Characteristics**

Type of Meeting	Average No. of Meetings/Year	Average Attendance	Average Duration (in days)
Sales meetings	6.2	63	2.8
Management meetings	5.0	39	2.6
Training seminars	7.4	58	2.6
Professional/technical meetings	4.5	63	2.7
New product introductions	4.1	129	2.5
Individual incentive trips	3.9	66	4.7
Group incentive trips	3.2	102	4.4
Stockholder meetings	1.8	35	2.1
Other meetings	12.4	95	2.6

Source: 1998 Meetings Market Report conducted by Plog Research for *Meetings & Conventions* magazine

appropriate audiovisual and computer equipment. A convention market, on the other hand, requires facilities that can accommodate large groups and exhibit space.

The lead time for different types of meetings is particularly important for hotels under development. If major conventions are planned and hotels and meeting accommodations are selected three years in advance, any new hotel scheduled to open within this period should be pre-marketed so that convention planners will consider it. As a hotel's meeting capacity increases, so must its marketing efforts prior to opening. A well-planned convention hotel will typically start its marketing program before construction begins.

Leisure Travel

Most of the sources for data on leisure travel were introduced earlier in this chapter. Visitation counts that the National Park Service compiles are also significant. Table 3.19 shows these data for the period from 1980 to 1998, for all parks as well as for several of the most popular destinations.

Between 1980 and 1998, national park visitation increased at an average annual compounded percentage rate of 1.5%, with a comparable growth rate of 1.4% noted between 1990 and 1998. With the exception of Sequoia National Park, each of the parks identified in the table posted stronger growth rates than that realized for all parks between 1980 and 1998. Between 1990 and 1998, visitation to Yellowstone National Park grew slightly below the national average, while visitation to Sequoia National Park receded.

Because each of the primary market segments displays specific characteristics that can affect the selection and use of a particular lodging facility, it helps to make a side-by-side comparison of typical traveler characteristics for the market's commercial, meeting and group, and leisure segments. Table 3.20 provides such a comparison.

Peak travel periods for commercial and leisure travelers are usually negatively correlated. Therefore, a hotel able to attract both of these segments is likely to have a smoother year-round occupancy pattern than a property largely dependent on one segment will. The same analogy applies to weekly travel peaks for these two market segments.

The average length of stay affects many operational aspects of a hotel property. A hotel with a shorter average stay requires more front desk personnel, luggage carriers, and accounting staff because more people will be checking in and out over the course of a week. More cleaning staff may also be needed because maids can generally clean the room of a stay-over guest in less time than it takes to prepare a room for a new occupant. Operating costs increase with the number of checkouts.

An extended-stay property that attracts guests who stay longer than seven days solves the problem of the weekend occupancy drop-off, which occurs when commercial travelers go home for the weekend. In this situation, longer stays actually increase the potential stabilized occupancy. From a layout point of view, however, a hotel with a

TABLE 3.19 U.S. National Park Visitation

Year	All Parks (in thousands)	Percent Change	Bryce Canyon (in thousands)	Percent Change	Yosemite (in thousands)	Percent Change	Mount Rushmore (in thousands)	Percent Change	Yellowstone (in thousands)	Percent Change	Grand Canyon (in thousands)	Percent Change	Sequoia (in thousands)	Percent Change
1980	220,463	—	571	—	2,490	—	1,285	—	2,000	—	2,305	—	862	—
1990	256,909	—	863	—	3,125	—	1,672	—	2,824	—	3,777	—	1,064	—
1991	264,438	2.9%	929	7.6%	3,423	9.5%	2,045	22.3%	2,921	3.4%	3,906	3.4%	1,120	5.3%
1992	271,638	2.7	1,018	9.6	3,820	11.6	1,917	(6.3)	3,144	7.6	4,547	16.4	961	(14.2)
1993	269,571	(0.8)	1,108	8.8	3,840	0.5	1,930	0.7	2,912	(7.4)	4,929	8.4	1,067	11.0
1994	266,427	(1.2)	1,028	(7.2)	3,962	3.2	2,044	5.9	3,046	4.6	4,704	(4.6)	1,034	(3.1)
1995	269,564	1.2	995	(3.2)	3,958	(0.1)	1,688	(17.4)	3,125	2.6	4,908	4.3	845	(18.3)
1996	265,796	(1.4)	1,270	27.6	4,046	2.2	1,905	12.9	3,012	(3.6)	4,877	(0.6)	838	(0.8)
1997	275,236	3.6	1,175	(7.5)	3,670	(9.3)	1,752	(8.0)	2,890	(4.1)	5,131	5.2	1,009	20.4
1998	286,715	4.2	1,166	(0.8)	3,657	(0.4)	2,014	15.0	3,121	8.0	4,558	(11.2)	861	(14.7)

Annual Compounded Percent Change

1980–1998	1.5%		4.0%		2.2%		2.5%		2.5%		3.9%		(0.0)%	
1990–1998	1.4		3.8		2.0		2.4		1.3		2.4		(2.6)	

Source: National Park Service

	TABLE 3.20 Typical Traveler Characteristics		
	Commercial Travelers	**Meeting and Group Travelers**	**Leisure Travelers**
Peak travel periods	Fall, winter,	Fall, winter, spring, and summer	North–summer and spring South–winter, spring
Weekly peaks	Mon.–Thurs.	Sun.–Thurs.	Variable
Average length of stay	Highway: 1–2 nts. Downtown: 2–3 nts.	3–5 nts.	Highway: 1 nt. Resort: 3–5 nts.
Double occupancy	1–1.3 ppl/room	High ADR conventions: 1.7–2.5 ppl./room Low ADR conventions: 1.3–1.7 ppl./room	1.2–1.4 ppl./room
Use of food facilities			
Breakfast	50–70%	60–80%*	75–80%**
Lunch	10–20	50–80*	10–50**
Dinner	30–50	40–80*	30–50**
Use of beverage facilities	20–60%	30–75%	30–75%
Degree of price sensitivity	Low	Medium	Medium–high
Special requirements	Entertainment Quiet rooms Desks with good lighting Convenient parking	Adequate function and exhibit space Active sales organization Large closets	Recreational facilities Large guest rooms Guest laundry

* Depends on the amount of banquet service
** Depends on the meal plan (American or European)
Source: HVS International

longer average length of stay, such as a resort, often requires larger closets and more clothing storage areas to accommodate a greater amount of luggage.

Double occupancy refers to the average number of guests per room. Leisure demand, which includes many traveling families, has a double occupancy rate ranging from 1.7 to 2.5 people per room. Commercial demand—typically composed of individual travelers—produces a double occupancy rate of 1.0 to 1.3 people per room. Many hotels are able to charge higher room rates for additional guests in a room, which tends to increase a property's overall average rate.

When it comes to room layout, a hotel with a high double occupancy rate requires more beds per room. A family-oriented resort should have at least two double beds in each room to accommodate its high double occupancy. On the other hand, a commercial-oriented property can offer a large number of rooms furnished with single, king-sized beds. Properties with high double occupancies usually require larger closets, two vanity sinks, and larger rooms.

The use of food and beverage facilities is higher for meeting and group travelers than other market segments since many groups incorporate banquets and other forms of food service into their function schedules.

Macro Travel Price Data

Macro travel data pertaining to the price of hotel accommodations are also important to hotel appraisers. Since a hotel's rooms revenue is calculated by multiplying the number of occupied rooms (demand) by the price of each occupied room, trends in macro hotel room rates can be a factor in forecasting future changes.

Each year the Travel Industry Association of America compiles data pertaining to the Travel Price Index (TPI) for various components of the travel industry, such as transportation costs, airfares, lodging costs, and food and beverage costs. These indices are similar to the Consumer Price Index (CPI) in that they show annual price increases caused by inflation and other factors. Table 3.21 shows the travel price indices for various travel components as well as the overall TPI.

Between 1988 and 1998, the total TPI increased at an average annual compounded percentage rate of 4.0%. A significant share of this growth was recorded between 1988 and 1991. In more recent years, the TPI has increased at levels below 4.0% per year. The most rapid rate of growth among the various TPI categories occurred in lodging, which grew at an average annual compounded percentage rate of 5.8% between 1988 and 1998. Unlike the overall TPI, lodging has experienced strong price increases in recent years. That is largely due to the fact that the general health of the national lodging industry allowed for strong gains in hotel pricing relative to the overall TPI, and, as noted in Table 3.22, the CPI. Airline fares are the only other TPI category where price increases exceeded those realized for the overall TPI. Table 3.22 illustrates historical trends in the lodging TPI and the

TABLE 3.21	Travel Price Index										
Year	Transport	Percent Change	Airline Fares	Percent Change	Lodging	Percent Change	Food and Beverages	Percent Change	Recreation Services	Percent Change	Total TPI	Percent Change
1988	99.8	–	124.2	–	132.9	–	122.2	–	131.1	–	119.7	–
1989	107.3	7.5%	131.6	6.0%	138.4	4.1%	127.8	4.6%	135.4	3.3%	125.7	5.0%
1990	121.4	13.1	148.4	12.8	152.5	10.2	133.8	4.7	143.2	5.8	136.0	8.2
1991	123.4	1.6	155.0	4.4	174.5	14.4	138.8	3.7	150.6	5.2	144.8	6.5
1992	123.3	(0.1)	155.2	0.1	184.2	5.6	141.7	2.1	155.8	3.5	148.9	2.8
1993	132.3	7.3	178.7	15.1	189.4	2.8	144.3	1.8	160.8	3.2	154.0	3.4
1994	135.5	2.4	185.0	3.5	195.5	3.2	146.8	1.7	166.8	3.7	157.7	2.4
1995	138.0	1.8	189.7	2.5	203.1	3.9	150.2	2.3	172.0	3.1	162.1	2.8
1996	142.8	3.5	192.5	1.5	213.7	5.2	154.0	2.5	178.1	3.5	168.1	3.7
1997	145.6	2.0	199.2	3.5	224.1	4.9	158.5	2.9	183.8	3.2	173.7	3.3
1998	140.2	(3.7)	205.3	3.1	234.5	4.6	162.6	2.6	189.0	2.8	177.1	2.0
Annual Compounded Percent Change											
1988–1998		3.5%		5.2%		5.8%		2.9%		3.7%		4.0%

Source: Travel Industry of America

overall TPI in relation to the CPI for all urban consumers (CPI-U), between 1979 and 1998.

Gains in the lodging TPI have historically outpaced gains in both the overall TPI and the CPI-U. A comparable premium in the rate of gain in lodging prices versus the overall TPI and the CPI-U is apparent for both periods of analysis, 1979 to 1998, and 1990 to 1998. Thus, whereas the average annual compounded percentage rate of lodging TPI gain decelerated to 5.5% between 1990 and 1998 (down from 6.9% between 1979 and 1998), the real gain relative to general inflation remained significant through the 1990s.

The preceding trends indicate that gains in hotel room rates are not totally tied to changes in the CPI; they can also be market-driven. For example, when hotel demand is strong and the market is undersupplied, occupancy levels will increase and room rates should show impressive gains. When hotel supply exceeds de-

TABLE 3.22 **Travel Price Index vs. Consumer Price Index**

Year	Lodging TPI	Percent Change	Total TPI	Percent Change	CPI-U*	Percent Change
1979	66.4	–	69.3	–	72.6%	–
1980	75.8	14.2%	81.2	17.2%	82.4	13.5%
1981	84.5	11.5	90.4	11.3	90.9	10.3
1982	94.2	11.5	95.5	5.6	96.5	6.2
1983	99.0	5.1	98.9	3.6	99.6	3.2
1984	106.8	7.9	103.6	4.8	103.9	4.3
1985	114.2	6.9	108.4	4.6	107.6	3.6
1986	118.4	3.7	109.0	0.6	109.6	1.9
1987	125.7	6.2	114.9	5.4	113.6	3.6
1988	132.9	5.7	119.7	4.2	118.3	4.1
1989	138.4	4.1	125.7	5.0	124.0	4.8
1990	152.5	10.2	136.0	8.2	130.7	5.4
1991	174.5	14.4	144.8	6.5	136.2	4.2
1992	184.2	5.6	148.9	2.8	140.3	3.0
1993	189.4	2.8	154.0	3.4	144.5	3.0
1994	195.5	3.2	157.7	2.4	148.2	2.6
1995	203.1	3.9	162.1	2.8	152.4	2.8
1996	213.7	5.2	168.1	3.7	156.9	3.0
1997	224.1	4.9	173.7	3.3	160.5	2.3
1998	234.5	4.6	177.1	2.0	163.0	1.6
Annual Compounded Percent Change						
1979–1998		6.9%		5.1%		4.3%
1990–1998		5.5		3.4		2.8

* Consumer Price Index for Urban Consumers, base period is 1982-1984
Source: Travel Industry Association of America

mand, occupancy levels will fall and hotel room rates will either level off or start to decline. The trends indicated in Table 3.22 support these observations. National lodging markets became substantially overbuilt by the early 1990s, and as hotel operators sacrificed average rates to retain viable occupancy levels, the rate of gain in the lodging TPI slowed. Between 1993 and 1995, the rate of gain ranged from 2.8% to 3.9%. As the lodging industry's recovery progressed in more recent years, the environment for average rate recovery also improved.

Future Changes in Hotel-Motel Macro Demand

If the past reflects the future, continuous changes in the transportation industry could significantly affect the characteristics of an average trip. Supersonic transport may prove to be as revolutionary as the jet plane, allowing travelers to make international trips in a single day. More expensive gasoline could reduce the mobility of the average vacation traveler, while greater use of mass transportation and the possible rebirth of rail service might prompt travelers to bypass highway facilities altogether. More sophisticated telecommunication systems may someday make in-person business meetings and conferences obsolete.

Future macro travel projections should also reflect potentially positive factors. In the past decade companies have given their employees more fringe benefits, including longer vacations. Some firms have even implemented a four-day workweek. Although these trends do not necessarily mean increased travel, they do add to the time that families can spend away from home.

A growing number of senior citizens with better retirement incomes and a desire to travel could also generate additional lodging demand. Increased foreign travel to the United States and a more travel-oriented society in general could mean more business for the lodging industry.

Micro Demand

In preparing a hotel market study and appraisal, accurate quantification of micro demand is essential. The room night is the unit of measurement commonly employed.

A *room night* is defined as one transient room occupied by one or more persons for one night. For example, a business traveler who stays at a motel for three nights accounts for three room nights. A family that uses one room for three nights also generates three room nights. If this family had occupied two guest rooms during their stay, the demand generated would have been six room nights.

The total number of room nights within a defined market area represents the total potential demand, which can be measured daily, weekly, monthly, or yearly, depending on local travel patterns.

The total demand for transient accommodations within a micro market is generally quantified by using the build-up approach based on an analysis of lodging activity; secondary support is provided by the build-up approach based on an analysis of demand generators.

To apply the build-up approach based on an analysis of lodging activity, an area's transient room night demand is estimated by totaling the rooms actually occupied in local hotels and motels. Through interviews with hostelry operators, owners, and other knowledgeable individuals, occupancy levels for individual lodging operations and area occupancy trends can be established. The percentage of occupancy for each property times the available number of rooms is multiplied by 365 days to produce the total number of room nights actually occupied each year. The area's total room night lodging demand can be quantified by combining the estimated number of occupied hotel rooms for each property and adding a factor for latent demand.

The build-up approach based on an analysis of demand generators involves interviews and statistical sampling market research. Lodging demand is estimated by totaling the room nights generated from sources of transient visitation. Drawing from a sample of major transient generators located within a defined market area, interviews and surveys are conducted to determine the amount of demand each source attracts during a specified period. When these data are combined with other survey information such as facility preferences, price sensitivity, the nature of the demand, and travel patterns, the analysis of demand generators provides both support and amplification for the findings derived from the analysis of lodging activity.

Appraisers use a combination of the two procedures to save time and effort researching. In practice, an overall area demand is first established by analyzing lodging activity. Then selective interviews are conducted at one or more major generators of visitation to verify the transient demand and establish traveler characteristics. By defining not only the quantity of transient demand but also its lodging characteristics, the analyst has enough data to develop a micro demand projection. Because each market area is unique, the analytic approach often must be adjusted to account for particular demand characteristics.

Build-Up Approach Based on an Analysis of Lodging Activity

The build-up approach based on an analysis of lodging activity is performed in seven steps.

1. Define the primary market area.
2. Define the area's primary market segments.
3. Identify all primary and secondary competitive lodging facilities in the market area and determine their individual room counts and competitive weighting factors.

4. Estimate the percentage of occupancy for each competitive hotel or motel annually and determine the percentage relationship between each market segment and the entire market.

5. Quantify the accommodated room night demand by multiplying each property's room count by its annual occupancy and then by the 365 days in a year. Each property's total accommodated room night demand is then allocated among the primary market segments (i.e., commercial, meeting and group, and leisure) within the market area.

6. Estimate fair share, market share, and penetration factors for each of the competitors.

7. Estimate latent demand, which includes both unaccommodated and induced demand.

8. Quantify the area's total room night demand.

After each of these steps is discussed, it will be demonstrated using a single case study example. The case study introduced in this chapter is developed and referenced throughout the book.

Define Primary Market Area

The first step in analyzing lodging activity is to define the subject's market area. The market area for a lodging facility is the geographical region where the sources of transient visitation (demand) and the competitive supply are located. To delineate the boundaries of a market area, four factors must be considered.

1. Travel time between the source of visitation and the subject property

2. Methods of travel commonly used

3. Sources of transient visitation

4. Location of competitive lodging facilities

Travel time is generally a better measure of distance than miles because highways, road conditions, and travel patterns differ. Most people are willing to travel up to 20 minutes to get from a source of visitation to their lodging accommodations. If most of visitors' travel time is spent on high-speed, interstate highways, the market area will be larger than if the route to the subject facility is along busy downtown streets.

The 20-minute market area radius is a rule of thumb that is usually appropriate for suburban areas. In rural regions the travel time radius can be significantly increased—sometimes to as much as four hours. Central business districts usually have a much shorter travel time radius of five to 10 minutes.

The transportation used also affects travel time. For example, a convenient rapid transit system can increase the market area by shortening the time needed to reach the subject property. Airport properties that depend on shuttle bus service should consider visitors' waiting time. These hostelries should be located no more than 10 minutes from the airport to allow for a 20-minute round trip.

The analyst should locate the subject property on a detailed road map and indicate points that could be reached within 20 minutes travel time. Connecting these points creates an irregular circle, which represents the boundaries of the initial market area. To determine the actual shape of the final market area, certain adjustments must be made to show the influence of competition and other demand characteristics.

Before any modifications are made, however, all potential sources of transient visitation within the initial market area should be identified and located on the map. Any attraction that draws out-of-town travelers who require commercial lodging facilities is a source of transient visitation. A representative list of visitation sources and the methods used to quantify their micro demand are presented later in this section.

After the initial market area has been determined, all competitive hostelries should be located on the map and their positions with respect to the subject property and sources of visitation should be noted. Travelers tend to stay at the lodging facility closest to their destination, assuming the property meets certain requirements. If a comparable hotel is located between a source of demand and the property being appraised, the competitive facility may attract patrons first, and the subject hostelry will receive the overflow. Care must be taken to evaluate the competition's drawing power because travelers will bypass one facility for another if it better suits their needs and budgets. The location of competitive properties between the property being appraised and the attraction generating business can decrease the size of the initial market area and may even eliminate some sources of visitation from consideration.

Local travel patterns and popular routes are important factors to consider when evaluating the competition. Travelers usually prefer to travel familiar routes and are not inclined to venture into unfamiliar areas. If the customary route to a source of demand happens to bypass the subject property, its potential for capturing that market is greatly reduced. The location of one or more comparable lodging facilities along the route also decreases the subject property's drawing power. Traffic counts and origination and destination studies prepared by state and local agencies can help pinpoint popular routes and identify area travel patterns. By plotting this information on the map showing the initial market area, appropriate adjustments can be made to the boundaries indicated. The resulting enclosure is the final market area and contains the sources of transient visitation available to the subject property.

This first step in the build-up approach for quantifying demand based on an analysis of lodging activity is demonstrated on the following pages.

The following case study is presented to illustrate the market analysis and valuation procedures described in this text. The example will be developed further in later chapters demonstrating the collection and development of data that lead to a final opinion of value. The case study explores two scenarios, one involving an existing 200-room Embassy Suites, and a second involving a proposed 250-room Sheraton Hotel. The proposed hotel is assumed to enter the same lodging market in which the existing Embassy Suites operates. The location is real, and although the data is realistic, it has been fabricated. In addition, the techniques employed to quantify demand and project income and expenses for this property apply to all types of lodging facilities.

Because every appraisal assignment is unique, the techniques used to collect and process data into an opinion of value must be tailored to meet the particular situation. Few assignments require the type of detailed analysis set forth in this case study. Many factors influence the applicability of the various approaches, including the availability of data, the nature of the market, the characteristics of the subject property, and time and economic considerations. An experienced hotel consultant can generally arrive at a credible opinion of value using a more abbreviated set of procedures.

Background

The subject lodging market consists of various hotels and motels located throughout suburban Long Island. The existing Embassy Suites and the site of the proposed Sheraton are both located in the same area, formed by the intersection of Interstate 495 and Route 110. The numerous benefits associated with this location have allowed the Embassy Suites to generate strong occupancy levels historically. Because the traffic volume is high in this location, the site receives a lot of exposure. Interstate 495 is a heavily traveled, east-west artery connecting various suburban communities with a nearby urban center; Route 110 is a four-lane, north-south feeder road that provides access to several large industrial and office parks.

The surrounding neighborhood has experienced strong growth over the past 10 years as the nearby urban center has extended its area of influence. What was once farmland now supports residential developments, regional shopping malls, office complexes, and industrial districts. Several large aerospace and communications manufacturers have established plants in the area; these manufacturers provide work for many smaller subcontracting production firms. These high technology businesses support an affluent population with large disposable incomes, attractive homes, and leisure-oriented lifestyles.

Although the aerospace industry tends to be highly cyclical, most of the larger plants have long-term government contracts. County planners expect moderate growth to continue. More than 40% of the land remains undeveloped and the area has been attracting many firms from the nearby urban center.

The Embassy Suites site measures approximately five acres and is located in the northwest quadrant of the intersection formed by Interstate 495 and Route 110. The hotel complies with the chain's construction standards and features 200 suites that surround a central high-rise atrium. Each guest suite has distinct living room and bedroom areas, separated by a wet bar and bathroom. The hotel also features a 100-seat restaurant and lounge, and approximately 5,000 square feet of meeting space. It is operated by Hotel Equity Investors under a franchise agreement.

As a result of the recent wave of economic growth, new first-class, full-service hotel development has the potential to be financially justified. A developer is considering developing a 250-room Sheraton Hotel on a seven-acre site located in the southeast quadrant of the intersection formed by Interstate 495 and Route 110. In addition to its 250 guest rooms, the hotel will have a 180-seat restaurant, a 50-seat lounge, a 40-seat lobby bar, and approximately 15,000 square feet of meeting space. The decor and construction specifications indicate a top-quality property capable of attracting first-class patrons. For purposes of this analysis, the Sheraton Hotel is assumed to open by the first day of the third year in the projection period.

Define Primary Market Area

The sites of the existing Embassy Suites and the proposed Sheraton Hotel are identified on a detailed highway map. Based on the sites' suburban locations, a 20-minute drive time is considered appropriate. A route is traced along each major highway starting at this intersection and ending at a point 20 driving minutes away based on average highway speeds and road conditions. The accompanying map illustrates the two, long radiating routes on Interstate 495 and Route 110. Secondary roads intersecting these two highways are also measured for travel time. The end points of all possible routes on the map are then joined by a continuous line; the resulting market area resembles a circle that has been pushed in on four sides. (The numbers on the map indicate demand generators, which will be discussed in greater detail later.)

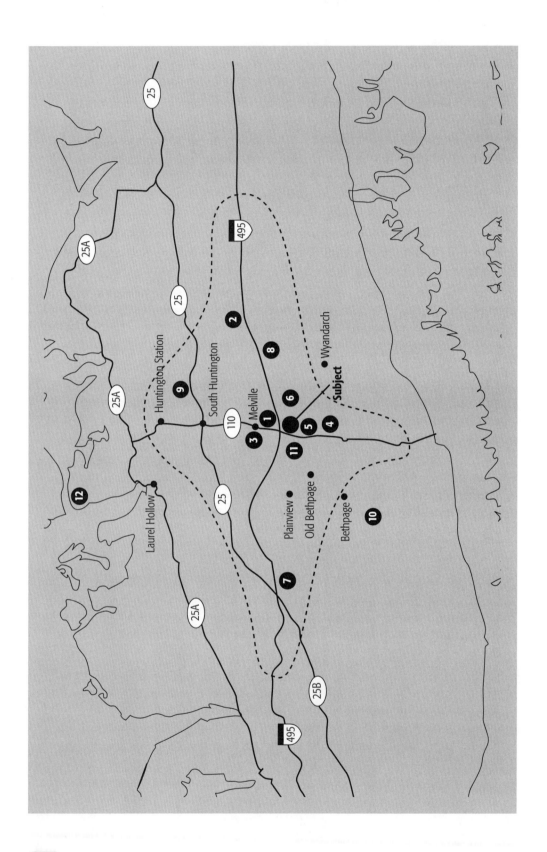

Most of the visitors to the market area arrive by car. Although limousine and taxi service from the nearby airport is available, rental cars are the preferred means of transportation.

Define Market Segments

Once the market area has been outlined, the appraiser should determine the primary segments of transient demand now using local hotels. The three market segments found in most areas are commercial, meeting and group, and leisure. Other market segments that are sometimes considered include extended-stay, government, airline crews, sports teams, military, truck drivers, and cruise ships.

Market segmentation is useful because individual market segments exhibit unique characteristics relating to future growth potential, seasonal aspects of demand, average length of stay, rates of double occupancy, facility requirements, price sensitivity, and other factors. Once the room night demand has been quantified by market segment and the individual characteristics of each segment have been defined, the future demand for transient accommodations can be more accurately forecast by making separate projections for each market segment. Some unique characteristics of the major market segments are described below.

Commercial Segment

The commercial market segment is composed of individual business people visiting the various firms within a market area. Commercial demand is strongest Monday through Thursday nights, declining significantly on Friday and Saturday and increasing somewhat on Sunday. A typical stay ranges from one to three days and the rate of double occupancy is low at 1.2 to 1.3 persons per room. Commercial demand is relatively constant throughout the year, with some drop-off in late December and during other holiday periods. Individual business travelers are not overly price-sensitive and usually use a hotel's food, beverage, and recreational facilities. Commercial travelers usually represent a desirable and lucrative market segment for hotels because such guests provide a consistent demand at room rates approaching the upper limit for the area.

Meeting and Group Segment

The meeting and group market includes individuals attending meetings, seminars, trade association shows, and similar gatherings for 10 or more people. Peak convention demand typically occurs in the spring and fall. Because many people take summer vacations, the summer months are the slowest period for this market segment; winter demand varies. The average stay for typical meeting and group travelers ranges from three to five days. Most commercial groups hold meetings Monday through Thursday, but associations and social groups sometimes meet on weekends. Commercial groups tend to have a low double occupancy of 1.3 to 1.5 persons per room, while social groups are likely to have somewhat higher double occupancy rates ranging from 1.5 to 1.9 persons per room. Hotels and motels often profit from meeting and group patronage. Although room rates are sometimes discounted for large groups, hotels benefit from the use of meeting space and the inclusion of in-house banquets and cocktail receptions.

Leisure Segment

The leisure segment consists of individuals and families spending time in the area or passing through en route to other destinations. Their purposes for travel may include sightseeing, recreation, relaxation, visiting friends and relatives, or other non-business activities. Leisure demand is strongest Friday through Saturday nights and all week during holiday periods and summer months. These peak periods of demand are negatively correlated with commercial visitation patterns, demonstrating the stabilizing effect on occupancy produced by capturing weekend and summer tourist travel. The typical length of stay for the leisure traveler ranges from one to four days, depending on the destination and the purpose of travel. The rate of double occupancy is often high—1.8 to 2.5 people per room. Leisure travelers constitute the most price-sensitive segment of the lodging market. Many prefer low-rise accommodations with adjacent parking; vacationers typically demand extensive recreational facilities and amenities. Highway accessibility and distance to vacation-related attractions are important considerations for vacationers choosing a location.

CASE STUDY

Define Market Segments

The primary market segments observed during fieldwork in the subject's market area were commercial, meeting and group, and leisure. In addition to these primary segments, a number of secondary segments, such as airline crews, bus tours, and military personnel, were noted. Because these secondary segments have little impact on total demand, they were categorized under the primary segments to which they were most similar.

Identify Primary and Secondary Competition, Room Counts, and Competitive Weighting Factors

The primary and secondary competitive lodging facilities located within a market area are part of the overall lodging supply, which can be defined as all transient accommodations catering to overnight visitors. Transient accommodations include hotels, motels, conference centers, bed and breakfasts, rooming houses, health spas, and other facilities. Although all transient lodging facilities operating in the same market area compete with one another to some extent, only those that are considered primary or secondary competition are included in the lodging analysis.

Hotels that are similar to the subject property—in terms of their class and facilities—and that appeal to the same type of transient visitor are considered primary competitive lodging facilities. Secondary competition consists of lodging facilities that would not normally attract the same type of transient visitor but become competitive because of special circumstances.

Determining which hotels represent primary or secondary competition and which provide no competition at all is largely subjective. Relative competitiveness can be evaluated by looking at area demand and identifying the different types of accommodations that transient visitors are selecting. Alternatively, competitive supply can be examined to identify accommodations that are similar to the subject in their market orientation (i.e., facilities, class, image, location, and other characteristics).

Demand generator interviews can provide information about the types of accommodations market area travelers are using. The responses to interview questions should allow the appraiser to pinpoint which lodging facilities are competitive with each other and why.

To evaluate the similarities of facilities and the market orientation of the hotels that make up the lodging supply, an appraiser may visit each property and judge its competitiveness using specific criteria. The following questions could be used to judge whether a lodging facility represents primary or secondary competition or does not compete with the subject property at all.

- Does the hotel occupy a similar location? Is it within 20 travel minutes of the demand generators? Is it identified with a specialized location such as an airport, convention center, downtown area, or resort?

- Is the hotel similar in terms of the types of facilities offered? Specialized types of hotels include convention, resort, suite, residence, conference center, casino, and health spa.

- Does the hotel offer similar amenities? Amenities may include restaurants, lounges, meeting rooms, pools (indoor or outdoor), health spas, tennis courts, and golf courses.

- Is the hotel similar in class—i.e., quality and price? Classes of lodging facilities include luxury, first-class, standard/mid-rate, economy/budget, and hard budget.

- Is the hotel similar in image? Image refers to the hotel's brand name, local reputation, management expertise, and unique characteristics.

Area hotels can be considered primary competition if they are similar to the subject property with respect to many of these criteria, particularly those related to types of facilities, class, and image. Secondary competition would include hotels that are similar in location-related characteristics but meet few of the other criteria, particularly class and image. Secondary properties are considered competitive because they occasionally attract the same market or travelers that the subject property and other primary competitors do.

When all primarily competitive hotels are sold out, travelers desiring these accommodations must settle for a secondarily competitive property. If, for example, a traveler wanted an upscale, first-class hotel, a budget property would be the secondary alternative. A budget traveler who found all the economy properties filled might have to patronize a first-class facility.

A secondary competitor is sometimes in demand because it has a particularly good location. A secondary property adjacent to a demand generator may do good business in inclement weather when people want to stay at the first hotel they see.

Generally a secondary hotel is not as competitive as a primary property is. To reflect this lesser degree of competitiveness, an appraiser will assign a weighting factor to a secondary property, which reduces the hotel's room count. For example, a 100-room, secondary hotel that is considered to be 25% competitive with the subject property is assumed to have an effective room count of only 25 rooms. This assumption not only reduces the existing supply of competitive hotel rooms, it also lowers the area's current room night demand. If the appraiser determines that more than one hotel can be considered secondarily competitive, then all of the secondary properties are typically combined into a single hotel using a weighted-average calculation in the market analysis. These combining calculations and the overall impact of secondary hotels will be illustrated in the case study example.

Usually a few hotels in the market area offer no competition to the subject property and are therefore not considered in the analysis of lodging activity. These properties are often so dissimilar to the subject property that any crossover of demand would be highly unlikely. Most travelers would probably defer their trip if they were unable to obtain accommodations in either the primary or secondary competitive properties.

To quantify hotel room night demand using the build-up approach based on lodging activity, it is necessary to determine the room counts of all competitive hotels. This information can be obtained directly from the properties or from various lodging directories. The room counts of any hotels that opened during the 12-month base year must be adjusted based on estimates of occupancy and market segmentation. For example, the 124-room Courtyard by Marriott identified subsequently in the case study opened in early July of the base year period, which extended from January 1 to December 31. Since the Courtyard only operated for six months of the base year period, its historic average room count (HARC) is 62 rooms (50 % × 124 = 62).

The *historic average room count* is the hotel's room count multiplied by the percentage of the base year that the property is actually open. In addition to weighting the impact of new hotels on the market, the HARC can also be used to adjust the room counts of seasonal properties that close for a portion of the year and existing hotels that add new rooms during the base year.

Identify Primary and Secondary Competition, Room Counts, and Competitive Weighting Factors

A survey of the subject market area revealed a total of 20 hotels containing 2,762 rooms. Of these 20 hotels, nine (including the Embassy Suites) were judged to represent primary competition (1,604 rooms) and six were considered secondarily competitive (743 rooms). Five hotels do not compete in the subject lodging market at all. The general criteria applied to identify primary and secondary competition are outlined below.

- Location. Competitive hotels are either within or near the previously defined market area.

- Facilities. All hotels must offer individual guestrooms on a transient basis.

- Amenities. To be considered primary competition, a hotel must offer a full range of amenities, including a restaurant, a lounge, meeting rooms, and a swimming pool. Secondarily competitive hotels must provide televisions, direct dial telephones, full baths, air-conditioning, 24-hour attended front desks, and daily maid service.

- Class, quality, and price. Primary competition includes first-class, full-service hotels. Secondary competition includes mid-rate, full-service hotels, a limited-service hotel, an extended-stay hotel, and a five-star luxury hotel. All competitive hotels must offer clean, comfortable, and safe accommodations.

- Image. A hotel needs a national affiliation or a strong local reputation to be considered primary competition. Hotels with poor reputations are not included in the primary or secondary competition.

Primary Competition

The hotels considered primarily competitive with the subject property are shown in Table 3.23. The room counts were obtained from lodging directories.

Secondary Competition

The hotels listed below are considered secondarily competitive within the subject competitive market. These hotels are identified as secondary competition rather than primary competition because of differences in their location, product quality, and/or market orientation.

- Red Roof Inn
- Super 8

- Microtel
- Residence Inn
- Delta Inn
- Four Seasons

These six secondarily competitive hotels were evaluated to determine their degree of competitiveness within the competitive market. Based on the competitive criteria outlined above, competitive weighting factors were assigned to each secondary hotel (see Table 3.24). When used in a supply and demand analysis, a competitive weighting factor effectively reduces a hotel's room count.

Five hotels in the market area are not considered either primary or secondary competition because they have poor local reputations, do not offer the required amenities, and have no national affiliation.

TABLE 3.23 Primary Competition

Hotel	Room Count
Embassy Suites	200
Hilton	275
Radisson Hotel	250
Holiday Inn	175
Courtyard	124*
Ramada Inn	150
Island Inn	135
Quality Inn	175
Days Inn	120
Total	1,604

* The Courtyard opened on July 1st of the base year, so its historic average room count (HARC) is 62 (.50 × 124 = 62)

TABLE 3.24 Secondary Competition

Hotel	Full Room Count	Competitive Weighting Factor	Weighted Room Count
Red Roof Inn	110	50%	55
Super 8	125	50	63
Microtel	100	25	25
Residence Inn	75	75	56
Delta Inn	83	40	33
Four Seasons	250	75	188
Total	743		420

Estimate Occupancy and Determine Market Segmentation

The key ingredient in the build-up approach based on an analysis of lodging activity is the occupancy estimate for each of the primary and secondary competitive hotels in the market area. The estimate of competitive occupancies should cover a full, 12-month period. Ideally this period, which is called the *base year*, will closely precede the first year projected in the supply and demand analysis.

When collecting occupancy and average room rate data, the appraiser should be aware of several factors that could skew the data and cause errors in the analysis. For example, occupancy is calculated as the number of rooms occupied over a period of time divided by the number of rooms available. The appraiser should first understand how the hotel defines "rooms." Generally, a room is synonymous with the term *hotel unit*, which is the smallest accommodation that can be rented to a guest. Each unit must have a full bath and its own entrance to a public hallway or to the exterior. Some hotel units are composed of two rooms, but since such a unit may have only one entrance or one bath, it would be impossible to rent it to two unrelated parties. If, on the other hand, each room has its own bath and entrance and the connection between the two rooms can be locked, then each room could be considered a separate unit.

The second factor to be examined in gathering occupancy data is how the hotel handles complimentary rooms. Most hotels have a small percentage of rooms that are provided on a complimentary basis to hotel guests. Since these rooms do not generate rooms revenue, they are sometimes omitted from the hotel's occupancy calculation. However, they do represent a form of hotel utilization and should be included in the calculations when the lodging activity approach is used to quantify hotel room night demand. The appraiser should therefore always ask for the percentage of occupancy that includes complimentary rooms. The inclusion of complimentary rooms also affects the calculation of average room rate, which will be discussed later.

The need to divide the market's overall room night demand into individual market segments has already been discussed. In applying the lodging activity approach, market segmentation is determined by interviewing competitive management about the percentage relationship of each market segment to the whole market. This information is usually not considered confidential and should be easily obtained from each of the hotels. The appraiser must define the market segments in detail before asking about percentage relationships so the interviewee will understand and employ the same basis in allocating the hotel's occupied rooms. The percentages should total 100% when all segments are considered.

Estimate Occupancy and Determine Market Segmentation

Occupancy, market segmentation, and historic average room counts have been calculated based on field interviews and in-house data. The current level of occupancy is estimated for each of the competitive hotels in the market. Because the fieldwork for the appraisal was performed in the first quarter of the year following the base year, the estimates of occupancy and market segmentation apply to the calendar base year. In addition to estimated occupancy levels, market segmentation percentages have been established for all the competitive hotels based on the relationship of each market segment to the whole. As described previously, this appraisal recognizes three market segments: commercial, meeting and group, and leisure. To account for hotels that open during the base year, the historic average room count (HARC) is used instead of the actual room count.

To reduce the number of calculations required, hotels considered secondary competition are combined into a single aggregate hotel by applying weighted averages. The aggregate hotel is called the *"secondary competition."* Table 3.25 sets forth the necessary calculations.

The weighted average is calculated by multiplying the effective room count of each hotel by the appropriate occupancy or market segmentation percentage. The sum of these products is then divided by the total effective room count (420). Table 3.26 shows the weighted-average calculation for occupancy.

Table. 3.27 shows the operating characteristics of each of the nine primary hotel competitors and the aggregate secondary competition. A similar weighted-average computation is made to determine the market-wide occupancy and market segmentation percentages.

TABLE 3.25 Weighted Average of Secondary Competition

| | | | Market Segmentation | | | |
Hotel	Weighted Room Count	Occupancy	Commercial	Meeting and Group	Leisure	Total
Red Roof Inn	55	82%	60%	5%	35%	100%
Super 8	63	78	60	5	35	100
Microtel	25	90	75	0	25	100
Residence Inn	56	77	80	5	15	100
Delta Inn	33	63	65	10	25	100
Four Seasons	188	72	60	25	15	100
Total	420	75%	64%	14%	22%	100%

TABLE 3.26 Occupancy–Secondary Competition

Hotel	Weighted Room Count	Occupancy	Effective Room Count Occupancy
Red Roof Inn	55	82%	45
Super 8	63	78	49
Microtel	25	90	23
Residence Inn	56	77	43
Delta Inn	33	63	21
Four Seasons	188	72	135
Total	420	75%	316
Weighted average	316 =	75%	420

TABLE 3.27 Room Count, HARC, Occupancy, and Market Segmentation

Hotel	Number of Rooms	HARC	Occupancy	Market Segmentation Commercial	Meeting and Group	Leisure	Total
Embassy Suites	200	200	78%	80%	5%	15%	100%
Hilton	275	275	72	40	50	10	100
Radisson Hotel	250	250	68	45	40	15	100
Holiday Inn	175	175	73	55	25	20	100
Courtyard	124	62	65	75	5	20	100
Ramada Inn	150	150	66	65	20	15	100
Island Inn	135	135	62	60	30	10	100
Quality Inn	175	175	78	50	10	40	100
Days Inn	120	120	74	70	5	25	100
Secondary competition	420	420	75	64	14	22	100
Total/weighted average	2,024	1,962	72%	58%	22%	19%	100%

Quantify Accommodated Room Night Demand

The current accommodated room night demand for each market segment is calculated separately for each competitive hotel using the following equation:

$$
\begin{aligned}
&\text{Historic average room count} \\
&\quad \times \text{occupancy} \\
&\quad \times \text{market segmentation} \times 365 = \text{Total accommodated} \\
&\qquad\qquad\qquad\qquad\qquad\qquad\quad \text{room night demand}
\end{aligned}
$$

The number of occupied rooms per market segment for all of the competitive hotels in the market area is then combined to yield the area's current accommodated room night demand. The accommodated room night demand represents the actual number of competitive rooms occupied during the base year. Table 3.28 shows the estimated accommodated room night demand divided by market segment.

TABLE 3.28	Accommodated Room Night Demand								
			— Market Segmentation —			— Market Segmentation —			
				Meeting			Meeting		
Hotel	HARC	Occupancy	Commercial	and Group	Leisure	Commercial	and Group	Leisure	
Embassy Suites	200	78%	80%	5%	15%	45,552	2,847	8,541	
Hilton	275	72	40	50	10	28,908	36,135	7,227	
Radisson Hotel	250	68	45	40	15	27,923	24,820	9,308	
Holiday Inn	175	73	55	25	20	25,646	11,657	9,326	
Courtyard	62	65	75	5	20	11,032	735	2,942	
Ramada Inn	150	66	65	20	15	23,488	7,227	5,420	
Island Inn	135	62	60	30	10	18,330	9,165	3,055	
Quality Inn	175	78	50	10	40	24,911	4,982	19,929	
Days Inn	120	74	70	5	25	22,688	1,621	8,103	
Secondary competition	420	75	64	14	22	73,820	16,148	25,376	
Accommodated room night demand						302,298	115,337	99,227	
Percent of total						58%	22%	19%	

Fair Share, Market Share, and Penetration Factors

Each competitive hotel's historical performance may be judged by comparing the respective occupancy rates. A statistical measure of each hotel's performance is called the *penetration factor*, which relates a specific hotel's performance (both overall and by segment) to that of the market at large. The penetration factor calculation is based on each hotel's fair share, which simply equates to a given property's room count divided by the market-wide room count. The fair share percentage functions as the denominator in all penetration factor calculations, whereas market share is the numerator. Market share represents that portion of demand actually accommodated by a particular property (either overall or by segment), divided by market-wide demand. Market share divided by fair share results in a penetration factor.

CASE STUDY

Fair Share, Market Share, and Penetration Factors

Table 3.29 shows the basis for the calculation of each competitive property's fair share factor. The fair share factor is calculated by dividing the HARC of each particular property by the market-wide HARC.

TABLE 3.29 Fair Share Factors

Hotel	HARC	% of Total
Embassy Suites	200	10.2%
Hilton	275	14.0
Radisson Hotel	250	12.7
Holiday Inn	175	8.9
Courtyard	62	3.2
Ramada Inn	150	7.6
Island Inn	135	6.9
Quality Inn	175	8.9
Days Inn	120	6.1
Secondary competition	420	21.4
Total	1,962	100.0%

Table 3.30 identifies the basis for the calculation of each competitive property's penetration factor. The penetration factors are calculated for each segment, as well as "overall."

Demonstrating the methodology, consider the 148.0% penetration factor achieved by the Embassy Suites in the commercial segment. In the base year, the Embassy Suites accommodated 45,552 room nights of commercial segment demand. Dividing this figure by the market-wide commercial demand of 302,298

TABLE 3.30 Penetration Factors

Hotel	Room Nights Sold by Market Segment — Commercial	Mtg. & Group	Leisure	Total	Fair Share	Penetration by Segment — Commercial	Mtg. & Group	Leisure	Overall
Embassy Suites	45,552	2,847	8,541	56,940	10.2%	148.0%	24.0%	84.0%	108.1%
Hilton	28,908	36,135	7,227	72,270	14.0	68.0	224.0	52.0	99.8
Radisson Hotel	27,923	24,820	9,308	62,050	12.7	72.0	169.0	74.0	94.2
Holiday Inn	25,646	11,657	9,326	46,629	8.9	95.0	113.0	105.0	101.1
Courtyard	11,032	735	2,942	14,710	3.2	115.0	20.0	94.0	90.1
Ramada Inn	23,488	7,227	5,420	36,135	7.6	102.0	82.0	71.0	91.4
Island Inn	18,330	9,165	3,055	30,551	6.9	88.0	115.0	45.0	85.9
Quality Inn	24,911	4,982	19,929	49,823	8.9	92.0	48.0	225.0	108.1
Days Inn	22,688	1,621	8,103	32,412	6.1	123.0	23.0	134.0	102.5
Secondary competition	73,820	16,148	25,376	115,344	21.4	114.0	65.0	119.0	104.2
Total	302,298	115,338	99,226	516,862	100.0%	100.0%	100.0%	100.0%	100.0%

generates a market share factor of 15.1%. Dividing this market share factor of 15.1% by the Embassy Suites' fair share of 10.2% (calculated by dividing 200 by 1,962) results in the penetration factor of 148.0%. In other words, the Embassy Suites accommodated 148% of its fair share of commercial demand in the base year, demonstrating its great success and appeal in this particular market segment. Overall, the Embassy Suites accommodated 108.1% of its fair share of market demand, matching the level of market penetration recorded in the base year by the Quality Inn. These two hotels led the competitive market. The Days Inn, the Holiday Inn, and the aggregate of secondary competitors also accommodated more than their fair share of market demand in the base year. The remaining competitors attracted less than their fair share of market demand. Also of note, the Embassy Suites led the market in commercial segment penetration, while the Hilton was particularly strong in the meeting and group segment. The Quality Inn led the market in the leisure segment.

Estimate Latent Demand

The area's current accommodated room night demand is based on actual occupancies and accounts for only those hotel rooms that guests have used. It does not consider other types of demand that may have been present in the market but, for one reason or another, have not been accommodated by the current supply of lodging facilities. This additional demand is called *latent demand* and is composed of both unaccommodated demand and induced demand.

Unaccommodated Demand

Unaccommodated demand represents transient travelers who seek accommodations within a market area but, because all local lodging facilities are full, must defer their trips, settle for less desirable accommodations, or stay outside the market area.

Since this type of demand is not actually accommodated by the area's lodging facilities, it is not included in the room nights quantified in the previous steps of the lodging activity approach.

Unaccommodated demand is actually a form of excess demand that develops as a result of the hotel business's cyclical nature. For example, in markets dominated by commercial demand, area occupancy levels Monday through Thursday often approach 100%, indicating that many travelers are not being accommodated locally. Many resort market areas also sell out during peak vacation periods, thereby generating unaccommodated room night demand. Because hotels cannot expand or contract in response to cyclical lodging demand, unaccommodated transient visitation is normal in many market areas.

In quantifying the current hotel room night demand, unaccommodated demand only becomes a factor when the number of competitive rooms in the market increases. As the supply of hotel rooms increases, more of the previously unaccommodated demand will be accommodated during periods of peak visitation. Since these uncounted room nights will help offset the impact of new rooms entering the market, it is important to quantify the number of unaccommodated travelers trying to use lodging facilities in the area.

Quantifying the room nights that are not being accommodated in a market is difficult and requires experience and good judgment. The following list outlines factors that should be considered when deriving this type of estimate:

- *The nature of the demand.* Is the area demand cyclical and concentrated at certain times (e.g., Monday through Thursday, vacation periods, special events)?

- *Area occupancy.* Considering the nature of the area's transient demand, are most of the local lodging facilities operating at stabilized levels of occupancy? For example, in a typical, commercially oriented market where lodging demand is high Monday through Thursday and drops considerably over the weekend, one might expect that a strong stabilized level of occupancy would be approximately 70%. Under these circumstances an area-wide occupancy of 78% could produce a significant amount of unaccommodated demand. If most of the area's hotels were operating at 60% occupancy, however, the amount of the unaccommodated demand would probably be negligible.

- *Fill nights.* How many fill nights are area hotels experiencing? In conducting competitive interviews the appraiser should try to determine the number of nights area hotels are actually filled to capacity. Once this number has been established, the number of turn-away room nights can be quantified. Sometimes hotels with centralized reservation systems keep monthly denial reports, which show the number of people who called to make reservations at a specific hotel but were denied because the property was booked. Occasionally individual hotels also track the number of walk-ins turned away on days when the hotel is booked.

- *Alternative accommodations.* If it appears that a sizable amount of unaccommodated demand exists in an area, the appraiser might want to conduct interviews at alternative accommodations to identify the sources of their demand and to determine if any of the customers would choose other facilities if they were available. Alternative accommodations might include lodging facilities outside the market area or hotels within the area that are considered less desirable.

In most instances data on fill nights and turn-away frequency are not available. Appraisers should try to obtain as much information as possible, but they must be prepared to estimate unaccommodated room night demand without a strong factual basis. The appraiser's experience plays an important role in quantifying unaccommodated demand. By observing numerous market areas that have experienced cycles of building, declining occupancies, and recovery, appraisers can develop an appropriate estimate of unaccommodated demand.

Unaccommodated demand is estimated as a percentage of the accommodated demand for each market segment. The range for unaccommodated demand typically extends from 0% to 30% of accommodated demand. The high end of this range would be appropriate for exceptionally strong markets where nearly every hotel is experiencing high levels of occupancy, many fill nights, and a large amount of turn-away demand. In strong hotel markets 5% to 10% is a reasonable level of unaccommodated demand. Since unaccommodated demand is difficult to quantify, a conservative estimate is usually warranted.

Unaccommodated demand is brought into the market analysis as accommodated demand when there are sufficient new rooms available to absorb this form of latent demand. Care must be taken to ensure that the amount of unaccommodated demand converted into accommodated demand is justified by the number of new rooms opening in the market. The capacity (new rooms) available to convert unaccommodated demand into accommodated demand is called the *accommodatable latent demand*. It will be covered later.

Induced Demand

Induced demand is the second type of latent demand. It represents the additional room nights that will be attracted to the market area. Induced demand may be created by specific circumstances such as

- *The opening of new hotels that offer new amenities, including extensive meeting and group space and specialized recreational amenities such as golf courses, ski slopes, or health spas.* These hotels are expected to attract a new market segment that does not currently seek accommodations in the subject's market area. For example, if a new hotel with a 60,000-square-foot exhibit hall opens in a market that does not have a similar facility, this hotel will probably attract into the area groups that had previously selected hotels elsewhere.

- *The aggressive marketing efforts of individual properties.* Some major hotel chains have been able to bring new room nights into the market by aggressively marketing the properties they operate. Convention-oriented lodging chains frequently are able to move convention groups around to various hotels within their systems, thereby creating induced demand for any new hotels they operate.

- *The opening of a new major demand generator such as a convention center, commercial enterprise, retail complex, transportation facility, or recreational attraction.* The development of Disney World is an example of an induced demand generator. Airport expansions commonly induce new demand, particularly if the facility develops as a major hub for many airlines.

Because induced demand can be traced to one or more specific factors, quantifying these additional room nights is somewhat easier than estimating unaccommodated demand. The procedure used is similar to the build-up approach based on an analysis of demand generators. The appraiser evaluates each generator of induced demand to determine the number of room nights that will be attracted to the market area. Induced demand may either enter the market all at once or gradually.

Induced demand is occasionally factored into the market on a temporary basis. Examples of this scenario involve one-time or cyclical events hosted by a given lodging market, such as the Olympics and the Super Bowl. Movie crews in town for extended shoots are another common example of temporary induced demand. In such cases, appraisers must factor the associated demand levels in and out of the projections at the appropriate times.

Unaccommodated demand and induced demand combined equal the total latent demand for the market area. The following case study demonstrates the procedures for estimating the unaccommodated and induced demand for the subject's market area.

CASE STUDY

Estimate Latent Demand

Analysis of the subject's market area indicates the presence of latent hotel demand composed of both unaccommodated and induced room night demand. To show the market's true depth, latent demand must be quantified.

The composition of demand in the market, area-wide occupancy, the number of fill nights, and the amount of turned-away demand all indicate that the local market has a certain amount of unaccommodated room night demand.

The composition of local hotel demand shows a definite commercial orientation (58% of total demand), suggesting an influx of room nights on Monday, Tuesday, Wednesday, and Thursday with a significant drop off on Friday, Saturday, and Sunday. Moreover, the groups currently using the area's lodging facilities are business-related and tend to meet Mondays through Thursdays rather than on weekends. Given these findings, more than 80% of the local room night demand is likely to need accommodations during the week. This demand pattern could produce an overflow condition and create unaccommodated demand.

The area-wide occupancy calculated from accommodated demand was 72% in the base year. Considering the commercial market's depth and the Monday through Thursday orientation of the demand, 72% occupancy reflects a healthy hotel market. This observation further supports the presence of unaccommodated demand.

To quantify the amount of unaccommodated demand, the number of commercial and meeting and group fill nights must be estimated. Assuming that 90% of the base year's commercial demand and 80% of the meeting and group demand are concentrated Monday through Thursday, a total of 364,338 room nights are demanded during this period.

Commercial demand	302,298 × 90%	=	272,068
Meeting demand	115,337 × 80%	=	92,270
Total			364,338

Dividing this demand by 208—the number of times per year that this period occurs—results in a demand of 1,752 rooms per average day (364,338/208=1,752). Since the market had a HARC of 1,962 during the base year, it is reasonable to assume that fill nights occur often. If the fill nights occur Tuesday and Wednesday nights and Monday and Thursday capture the remaining demand, the following table shows the occupancy calculation for Monday and Thursday nights:

Total Monday through Thursday demand	364,338 RN
(Assume sellout Tuesday and Wednesday.) 2 days × 52 weeks × 1,962 rooms	204,048 RN
Demand remaining Monday and Thursday	160,290 RN
Average occupancy Monday and Thursday	160,290
	204,048
	78.6%

Based on these calculations, it is reasonable to assume that the local market experiences at least 104 fill nights (Tuesday and Wednesday) per year as a result of the concentration of commercial and meeting and group demand. If this should occur as demonstrated above, Monday and Thursday nights would still achieve occupancies averaging nearly 80%. This estimate of fill nights was confirmed by manager interviews conducted during fieldwork.

Most of the estimated unaccommodated demand comes from the commercial and meeting and group segments. Because the market has a relatively strong leisure orientation as well, a certain amount of unaccommodated leisure demand is also anticipated.

Based on the preceding analysis, the unaccommodated demand estimates shown in Table 3.31 were made for the subject market area.

Unaccommodated demand for the commercial and meeting and group segments amounts to an average of 288 room nights per night for the 104 Tuesday and Wednesday nights per year. This number seems reasonable

TABLE 3.31 **Unaccommodated Demand**

	Commercial	Meeting and Group	Leisure
Accommodated demand	302,298	115,338	99,226
Unaccommodated percentage	× 8.0%	× 5.0%	× 3.0%
Unaccommdated demand	24,184	5,767	2,977

considering the size of the market and was supported by data accumulated during fieldwork.

Unaccommodated demand for the leisure segment is concentrated during the summer months, when vacationers travel through the area en route to Manhattan attractions and nearby beach resorts.

The opening of the proposed Sheraton Hotel is expected to create induced demand in the meeting and group segment. Because the Sheraton has ample meeting facilities and a positive image in the meetings market, the area will attract additional room nights of demand solely as a result of the new hotel's opening. In addition, the county's convention center has recently been renovated and expanded to accommodate larger groups. A new rooms tax dedicated to the local convention bureau should enable this agency to market its facility to a broader group of meeting and group users. Based on discussions with the Sheraton developer and representatives of the convention bureau, it is anticipated that approximately 15,000 room nights of additional meeting and group demand will be attracted to this market each year.

The induced demand that will be attracted to the local market over the next several years is reflected in the phase-in schedule shown in Table 3.32. Note that the induced demand is not expected to enter the market until the third projection year, the projected date of the Sheraton Hotel's opening.

TABLE 3.32 **Induced Demand Phase-In—Meeting & Convention Segment**

Projection Year	Induced Demand Potential Induced Demand	Percentage Phase-in	Induced Meeting & Group Demand
3	15,000	20%	3,000
4	15,000	60	9,000
5	15,000	100	15,000

Quantify Total Room Night Demand

Totaling the area's existing and potential room night demand is the last step in the build-up approach based on an analysis of lodging activity. This demand includes both accommodated and latent demand, which were identified in the preceding steps. The following case study will show how this demand is quantified.

CASE STUDY

Quantify Total Room Night Demand

Based on the data developed during the previous steps, the total potential room night demand for the subject market area in the base year can be calculated. This procedure is identified in Table 3.33

TABLE 3.33 Total Potential Room Night Demand

Accommodated demand	
Commercial	302,298
Meeting & group	115,338
Leisure	99,226
Total	516,862
Unaccommodated demand	
Commercial	24,184
Meeting & group	5,767
Leisure	2,977
Total	32,928
Induced demand	None*
Total potential demand	549,790

* Induced demand is phased in over three years starting in Year 3.

Build-up Approach Based on an Analysis of Demand Generators

In markets with few demand generators, it is sometimes appropriate to quantify the existing hotel room night demand by interviewing demand generators. As markets become more complex and the number of generators increases, it becomes more difficult to identify all of the demand generators and conduct an accurate survey. Most markets are too complex to rely solely on this approach, so the analysis of lodging activity is usually emphasized and selective demand generator interviews are used to determine the characteristics of the transient demand.

The build-up approach based on an analysis of demand generators is typically performed in three steps:

1. Identify generators of transient visitation.

2. Interview or survey selected demand generators and identify the characteristics of the demand.

3. Quantify room night demand.

Each step in the analysis of demand generators will be discussed. Then all three steps will be illustrated as the process is applied to the case study property.

Identify Generators of Transient Visitation

The generators of transient visitation are identified when the final market area is defined. There may be many sources of transient visitation, and efforts should be made to compile a complete list. The following methods can be used to identify generators of hotel demand:

1. *Interview local hotel and motel managers to determine the sources of their occupancy.* Ask for a percentage breakdown on the types of customers (i.e., commercial, convention, leisure) and try to learn the names of firms or groups that use the facility regularly.

2. *Obtain a directory of local businesses and identify those with regional or national operations that are likely to attract out-of-town customers, suppliers, vendors, or company representatives.*

3. *Obtain statistics pertaining to area visitation from the local convention and visitors bureau.* Request a list of recent conventions and meetings that used local hostelries. Determine if the primary market area has any popular tourist or vacation attractions. Visitor counts and projections can be helpful if their reliability can be verified.

4. *Visit car rental agencies, especially those at local airports, to determine which firms regularly rent cars.* This information will indicate which area businesses attract out-of-town visitors. These agencies also can supply information about which motels are popular among their clients.

5. *Drive around the area looking for concentrations of out-of-state cars in industrial parks, office complexes, government centers, regional hospitals, and other facilities.* Parking lots at local hostelries also contain many market indicators. Do most of the cars belong to out-of-state or in-state residents? Do they belong to businessmen traveling alone (clean and neat) or families on vacation (with luggage, games, and roadmaps)? A late-night parking lot count can indicate a highway motel's occupancy, assuming one vehicle per room. Even more important, a parking lot count can indicate the relative competitiveness of area hostelries if all are surveyed on the same night. One night's count is not necessarily indicative of annual occupancy, so additional factors should also be considered.

6. *Interview chamber of commerce officials, visitor information center employees, taxi drivers, gas station operators, and restaurant managers;* they can help identify

potential sources of transient visitation. The local building department can also provide information on proposed projects and changes in highway patterns.

Identifying the prime demand generators within a market area is relatively simple. When the survey is completed, the list will probably contain one or more of the following:

- Businesses–office buildings, industrial parks, research facilities, and manufacturing plants
- Government centers
- Airports
- Convention centers and conference facilities
- Colleges and universities
- Tourist attractions
- Vacation and recreation areas
- Parks and scenic areas
- Hospitals
- Sports attractions
- Casinos
- Military bases
- Trade and professional associations
- Convenient highway stopping points
- Regional shopping centers
- Special events, state fairs and parades

For market areas with many demand generators, the list should rank the sources in order of their estimated potential to generate demand. Prime sources with the greatest ability to attract out-of-town visitors should be researched first so that the appraiser can conduct a thorough analysis.

Interview or Survey Selected Demand Generators

Quantifying the total demand into measurable units—i.e., room nights—is the most important step in the survey process. By estimating the number of room nights attributable to each generator of visitation in the subject market area, the total micro demand can be determined.

In addition to quantifying total demand, the appraiser's survey should outline the general characteristics of the travelers who make up the potential market. The following list indicates factors that can help define the demand and may be useful in designing a proposed hostelry.

Demand Factors

- Number of nights per stay
- Number of people per room
- Periods of use during the year
- Definition of seasonality

  Fluctuations in use during the year

  Fluctuations in use during the month

  Fluctuations in use during the week

- Price willing to pay
- Food, beverage, entertainment, and telephone usage

Design Factors

- Number of people per guest room

  Space requirements

  Bed requirements

  Bathroom requirements

  Closet and storage requirements

- Use of guest rooms for purposes other than sleeping (i.e., meetings, entertainment, interviewing, or displays)

  Space requirements

  Furniture and layout

  Lighting and decor

- Restaurant and lounge facilities

  Space requirements

  Decor, menu, and price

  Kitchen equipment

  Staffing

- Meeting and banquet facilities

  Space requirements

  Types of configuration

  Special equipment

- Methods of travel

  Parking requirements

  Entrance, loading, and baggage requirements

- Recreational facilities

The list of demand generators must be analyzed in order to select market-surveying techniques that will be most effective in quantifying potential demand and defining specific traveler characteristics. Research techniques may include personal and telephone interviews, questionnaires, and use of available data and surveys.

Regardless of the techniques chosen, it is most important to locate and question the individuals most knowledgeable on the subject. For a hotel demand study, these people are typically those who make hotel reservations—e.g., secretaries, executive transfer departments, travel departments, personnel and recruitment departments, convention and visitors bureau placement departments, tour operators and travel agents, airline flight service and customer relations departments, and college alumni and athletic offices. The people who actually book reservations for out-of-town visitors are called *bookers*. Purchasing agents and buyers, executives, receptionists, college admissions officers, and park rangers who greet out-of-town visitors might also be questioned. Security departments, convention and visitors bureau registration and research departments, and hospital admissions departments that control visitation data are other good sources. People who see and come into contact with out-of-town visitors are called *seers*.

Personal interviews produce the most reliable data, but they are usually time-consuming. In areas with many sources of visitation, personal interviews can be limited to those with the greatest potential for generating room nights. A checklist of essential items to cover should be devised and interview time should be limited to five or 10 minutes. Use appointments only if an initial drop-in visit produces no results.

Key questions typically asked during an interview include

- How many out-of-town visitors do you average each week, month, or year?
- What is the purpose of the visitation?
- How long do the visitors stay?
- Are the visitors visiting any other demand sources in the area?
- Where are the visitors staying now?
- What rates are they willing to pay?

Once these questions are answered, more detailed questions should be asked to identify some of the market's characteristics. The demand and design factors listed previously can be used as a guide. The interviewer should always ask if any other people in the organization have contact with visitors. The interviewer should also specify the interview's purpose, because the more information the interviewer is willing to provide, the more information he or she will receive.

Telephone interviews are less time-consuming but rarely produce the same quality of data. Less important demand sources can be interviewed over the phone and later seen personally if greater potential is discovered.

Questionnaires, on the other hand, are useful for mass surveys when hundreds of identifiable demand generators are involved. A short, simple form that can be completed in less than five minutes usually yields the best results. It is important to contact the person best suited to answer the questions when using this type of survey. A brief letter explaining the survey's purpose should accompany each questionnaire. A greater response will be obtained if someone who is well known in the community signs the letter. A self-addressed, stamped envelope for returning replies must be enclosed.

Occasionally, various groups and municipal agencies compile data pertaining to local transient demand. These data are usually part of larger studies conducted in connection with urban renewal or redevelopment projects, proposed convention centers, and master development plans. Organizations that may perform such market surveys include chambers of commerce, convention bureaus, municipal planning departments, redevelopment agencies, financial institutions, and utility companies. Data obtained from these sources should be verified. If the information is usable it can serve as a starting point for defining the local transient market.

All major generators of transient visitation should be surveyed with a personal or telephone interview or a mailed questionnaire. In market areas with many secondary generators of visitation, however, these techniques may not be practical. Time restraints and the inability to identify smaller generators often require some form of sampling.

Quantify Room Night Demand

Sampling is a market research procedure in which conclusions about a large population are drawn from a thorough analysis of a representative portion of the population. Properly applied, sampling can yield more accurate results than complete surveys can because more time can be devoted to correct interviewing and data collection techniques.

Selecting the unit of comparison that best reflects the total market is key to proper sampling. Counting room nights per square foot of office space is one frequently used measure for determining potential commercial traveler demand. Interviewing a representative sample of office space users and estimating how many out-of-town visitors are received over a given period can be used to develop a unit of comparison. The number of visitor room nights is divided by the total square footage of office space within the sample. Multiplying this factor by the amount of office space within the market area produces an indication of the potential commercial demand. If necessary, adjustments can be made to avoid double counting of travelers visiting more than one firm.

Other units of comparison that may reflect transient visitation include population, employment, university enrollment, hospital beds, traffic counts, retail sales, and convention attendance. Many books have been written about correct sampling and market research procedures. Although every market area requires a somewhat specialized approach, three basic rules should be followed.

1. The sample must be representative of the total market.

2. Data and information from the sample must be factual and unbiased.

3. The units of comparison applied should reflect market behavior.

Analyzing demand generators provides an estimate of the total number of room nights available in the market area as well as specific information about the demand's characteristics. The total potential demand must be divided among all the competitive lodging facilities before the market capture rate for the subject property can be estimated.

The build-up approach based on an analysis of demand generators is demonstrated in the following case study.

CASE STUDY

Identify Generators of Transient Visitation

Local chamber of commerce officials, county planners, and various hotel and real estate professionals were interviewed to identify the generators of transient visitation in the market area. Most of the major businesses and attractions in the area that draw overnight visitors are described in the following list. The generators can be located by number on the area map.

1. *Office park.* A 2,000,000-square-foot office park is located directly across Interstate 495 from the site of the proposed Sheraton Hotel. This fully developed and leased office park houses many regional sales and service departments as well as national firms.

2. *Aerospace firm.* This major aircraft component manufacturer has 3,500,000 square feet of building space and employs more than 15,000 people. It is situated one exit east of the subject, along Interstate 495.

3. *Communications firm.* The research division of a national communications firm is housed in a major office complex two miles north of the subject, off Route 110. It employs 10,000 people in a facility of more than three million square feet.

4. *Aircraft engineer producer.* This jet engine manufacturer currently employs 5,000 people and occupies more than two million square feet of building space. The firm is located approximately three miles south of the Sheraton site, off Route 110.

5. *High-technology research park.* An office park of 25 communication-oriented research facilities owned by major manufacturers is located adjacent to the Sheraton site, directly to the south. The park is fully developed and contains approximately one million square feet of laboratory and office space.

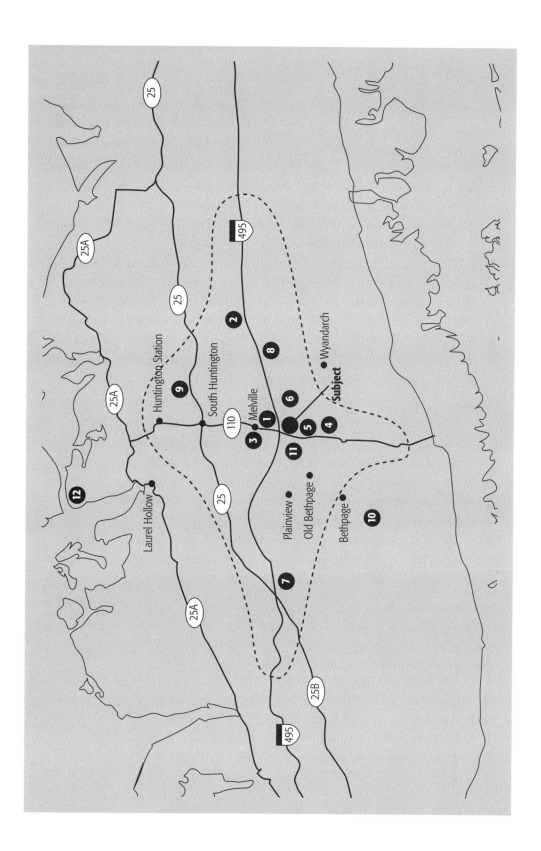

6. *Industrial park.* This established industrial park houses 100 small and medium-sized manufacturing firms that perform subcontracting work for the aircraft engine producer (4). Located one mile east of the proposed Sheraton on a service road next to Interstate 495, the industrial park has excess land for future expansion. The current total building area of the firms located in the park is approximately two million square feet.

7. *Office district.* A downtown-type office district with an inventory of 2,520,000 square feet of high-rent office space is located nine miles west of the subject property, next to an Interstate 495 interchange. Financial, legal, and insurance firms primarily occupy the space in this office district.

8. *New industrial park.* This new, 700-acre industrial park includes approximately 200 acres that are currently developed. It lies five miles east of the subject site, at an Interstate 495 exit. The park has 1,350,000 square feet of space still under lease, and favorable future growth trends are indicated.

9. *Regional mall.* Located on a secondary highway approximately five miles northeast of the proposed Sheraton site, this 75-acre regional shopping mall has 135 stores and 1,500,000 square feet of space.

10. *State hospital.* A 1,000-bed state mental hospital located eight miles southwest of the subject on a secondary highway generates commercial visitation.

11. *Convention center.* The 10-year-old convention center recently expanded its exhibit space from 75,000 to 100,000 square feet of floor area. It is located on Route 110, near the subject site, just south of a nearby Hilton Hotel. The convention center, used primarily for trade shows and local events, can accommodate up to 10,000 people.

12. *Resort area.* A beach resort area, which attracts vacationers during the summer and weekend travelers throughout the rest of the year, is a 30-minute drive from the Sheraton site.

Survey Selected Generators

These 12 potential demand generators indicate that the transient market is composed of commercial, meeting and group, and leisure travelers.

The commercial demand in the area uses lodging facilities five nights per week. Some commercial visitors arrive Sunday night to start work Monday morning. Commercial demand is low Sunday night, then increases and remains fairly level Monday, Tuesday, Wednesday, and Thursday nights; demand drops off significantly on Friday and Saturday.

The meeting and group demand is generated primarily by the convention center and by several research-oriented firms holding conferences and training sessions in the area. The bulk of this demand is felt during the fall, winter, and spring; Sunday through Thursday are the peak convention days. Although commercial travelers rarely use lodging facilities on Friday or Saturday nights, certain types of conventions take place on weekends and during holiday periods, when rates are typically lower.

The area immediately surrounding the proposed Sheraton has no tourist attractions, however, a summer beach resort approximately 30 minutes to the south draws numerous leisure travelers on weekends during the spring and fall and all week during the summer. Because this resort area is seasonal, there are only a few, small, family-owned motels near the beach. Consequently, many overnight visitors must find accommodations farther away. Since the beach resort is accessed primarily via Interstate 495 and Route 110, many vacationers stay in hotels surrounding the subject site. The leisure demand this resort area generates tends to be negatively correlated to the commercial and meeting and group patronage attracted to the area's business and convention center. Local lodging facilities benefit from this situation, which tends to create level occupancy throughout the year.

The subject market area has a number of primary generators of transient demand, many of which comprise secondary generators such as office parks that house multiple tenants. Therefore, it has been determined that the build-up approach based on an analysis of demand generators is not an appropriate method for quantifying the existing transient demand. The demand generators identified have been analyzed, however, to assess the nature of the transient demand and the characteristics and desires of local visitors. Personal interviews, telephone surveys, and letter questionnaires were used to gather information from several demand generators. A summary of the appraiser's findings follows.

Commercial Demand

- *Aerospace firm* (2). This large manufacturer's security department provided the best information on transient visitation. Based on an analysis of the visitor registration log over a two-year period, the appraiser estimates that the aerospace firm attracts approximately 110 outside visitors every week; these visitors stay at local hotels for an average of two nights per visit. Over the past several years, this type of visitation has remained fairly stable.

- *Aircraft engine producer* (4). This firm recently moved into the area and maintains few records on outside visitation. Before constructing the plant, however, the company had to submit to the county an economic impact study outlining the firm's potential benefits to the area. One of the benefits cited was that the plant's visitors would stay at local hotels and therefore bring business to the area. A footnote to the study stated that the company's visitation estimate was based on visitation histories from the firm's other plants throughout the United States. According to this study, roughly 12,850 room nights would be generated during the first year—an average of 247 room nights per week. This figure is estimated to increase by 5% annually.

- *Office district* (7). A list of office district tenants was compared to a list of the tenants occupying the office park (1). The office district has more local firms (i.e., accounting and legal firms), which would probably not generate as much visitation as the regional and national firms with offices in the park would.

- *New industrial park* (8). The tenants occupying the new industrial park were more national in scope than those at the established industrial park (6).

- *Regional mall* (9). Many tenants of the regional mall are national retailers. Home office personnel, who take inventories and prepare audits, visit each store regularly.

- *State hospital* (10). State officials visit this property weekly to perform various administrative functions.

Meeting and Group Demand

- *Convention and visitors bureau.* The local convention and visitors bureau, which is responsible for booking and tracking this type of visitation, was the primary source of information on the meeting and group segment. Discussions with the director of the local bureau revealed that the area has three main generators of meeting and group demand: the convention center (11); the communications firm (3), which sponsors training sessions; and the research park (5), which holds seminars.

- *Convention center* (11). The 10-year-old convention center has operated at a stable level for several years. In the past, efforts to attract larger conventions failed because exhibit space was limited. The renovation and expansion of this facility was recently completed, though, and now the facility is expected to contribute to future meeting and group demand growth.

- *Communications firm* (3). Most of the outside visitation to this firm consists of meeting and group demand. Transient commercial visitors consist mostly of out-of-town suppliers, salespeople, and manufacturers' representatives. Many of these visitors pass through the firm's purchasing department.

- *Research park* (5). While assessing the commercial demand generated by the research park, the appraiser discovered that strong meeting and seminar demand was created by this concentration of research-oriented businesses.

Leisure Demand

- *Resort area* (12). Discussions with the local visitors bureau in the resort community revealed that interest in the area is growing in response to the recent development of several resort amenities, such as an 18-hole public golf course, several miniature golf courses, a bowling alley, an amusement park, and an aquarium. These amenities not only attract visitors to this destination, they also provide incentive for visitors to extend their stays, creating more room night demand.

Forecasting Room Night Demand

By analyzing lodging activity and/or demand generators, the appraiser has quanti-fied the total room night demand in the current market. This existing demand consists of either accommodated demand or latent demand, or both. Latent demand consists of unaccommodated demand and induced demand.

Because a market study and valuation requires the appraiser to look into the future, the existing room night demand must be forecast over the projection period. Future hotel demand will increase, decrease, or remain level. The direction and rate of change is estimated by analyzing various economic and demographic indicators.

An excellent context for future demand growth projections may be provided by historical demand growth trends for the lodging market in question. Smith Travel Research (STR) is the leading independent data consulting firm serving the lodging industry. Located in Hendersonville, Tennessee, STR offers composite demand, supply, occupancy, and average rate trends for a specified group of hotels. The trends are generally available over five- and 10-year periods, but may be custom-ized. As for hotel populations, nearly all nationally recognized hotel chains report their data directly to STR. Before placing a request, STR provides a list of hotels in a specific area (county, city, zip code, etc.) that have reported their data histori-cally. Users may then select the hotels they want to include in the survey. STR maintains some base reporting rules in order to prevent a user from isolating the data of any single hotel or chain of hotels. STR may be reached at (615) 824-8664, or online at www.str-online.com. Demand trends are particularly useful in develop-ing market demand projections.

Apart from STR data, demand projections are based on the analysis of economic and demographic data gathered during fieldwork. Forecasts depend on how well economic and demographic data reflect changes in hotel room night demand. Data that mirror future trends in transient visitation are given greater weight in the appraiser's analysis than those that do not. Since changes in hotel demand are often tied to specific types of visitation, individual market segments—such as commercial, meeting and group, and leisure—are analyzed. Table 3.34 shows the three primary market segments and the types of data that feasibly could change hotel room night demand. Other market segments, such as extended stay demand, have profiles or characters that align with one of the three primary segments.

Commercial hotel demand is greatly influenced by trends that relate to business activity, such as office space absorption, employment, new businesses moving into the area, and airport enplanements. Population growth is not a strong indicator of changes in commercial demand, but it usually sets the lower limit for potential growth in commercial visitation. For example, if an area's population is expected to

TABLE 3.34	Data Reflecting Changes in Demand	
Commercial	**Meeting & Group**	**Leisure**
Total employment by category	Convention center patronage	Tourist visitation
Office space	Total employment by category	Highway traffic counts
absorption	Airport enplanements	Visitor counts at attractions
inventory	Air cargo data	Employment by category
under development	Tourist visitation	Restaurant Activity Index (RAI)
vacancy rate	Retail sales	Restaurant Growth Index (RGI)
Retail space	Visitor counts at attractions	
absorption	Office space	
inventory	absorption	
under development	inventory	
vacancy rate	under development	
Industrial space	vacancy rate	
absorption	Retail space	
inventory	absorption	
under development	inventory	
vacancy rate	under development	
New businesses entering area	vacancy rate	
Highway traffic counts	Industrial space	
Airport enplanements	absorption	
Air cargo data	inventory	
Commercial building permits	under development	
Housing starts	vacancy rate	
Assessed values	New businesses entering area	
Population		
Retail sales		
Effective buying income		
Personal income		

grow at an annual compounded rate of 1.5%, it is likely that commercial hotel demand will grow by at least the same rate. Other indicators may justify using a higher rate.

There are fewer indicators of meeting and group demand, and many of them provide only an indirect basis for projecting trends in hotel demand. Convention center activity, particularly that which generates visitation from outside the area, is probably the best indicator of meeting and group demand. The commercial activity reflected in employment trends and office and industrial space absorption indirectly indicates meeting and group demand, because many meetings result from business activity. Meeting and group demand is also created through the sales efforts of individual hotels. This type of induced demand was discussed in a previous section of the text.

Few indicators of leisure demand are available. However, visitor statistics, especially in resort areas, do indicate leisure demand trends. Attendance data for area tourist attractions are also useful.

Changes in hotel demand are projected by market segment for periods ranging from three to 10 years. In forecasting lodging demand, it is wise to keep the projection period as short as possible. The annual compounded percent of change should reflect the most probable trend in hotel room night demand. Many hotel market studies and valuations seem to project continuous growth in lodging demand, but demand trends do not have to be positive, nor does growth have to increase by the same percentage each year.

The forecast direction and rate of change in hotel room night demand are applied to both accommodated and unaccommodated demand components, which tend to move in tandem with one another.

Changes in induced demand are not usually related to projected changes in the accommodated and unaccommodated components of demand. Rather, induced demand depends on the latent demand characteristics exhibited by the specific demand generator. For example, if a large convention hotel is expected to open in a market enabling the area to attract major groups that previously could not be accommodated, the growth and ultimate size of this induced demand will reflect the hotel operator's marketing ability as well as the hotel's capacity to handle these groups. Depending on the convention hotel's size, the additional demand will usually be expected to increase over a period of time and then stabilize as the hotel approaches its capacity. Although growth in induced demand does not usually depend on growth in an area's convention demand, the surrounding meeting and group market should be considered when quantifying induced demand.

Forecasting Room Night Demand

Table 3.35 identifies the market-wide demand and supply trends provided to the appraisers by Smith Travel Research for the subject lodging market. The "Trend Report" pertains to all suburban Long Island hotels. Due to this survey's breadth, the supply and demand figures do not align with the market-wide data otherwise identified in this case study. Nevertheless, the general trends contribute to the context of this analysis. Between 1990 and 1999, demand among suburban Long Island hotels increased at an average annual compounded percentage rate of 3.2%. The rate of growth ranged from 4.0% to 6.9% per year between 1994 and 1999.

Otherwise, the basis for the room night demand projection is based on the local economic and demographic trends. Table 3.36 summarizes the types of data accumulated in the field and analyzed in-house. It indicates if the data are actual (historic) or projected, and the average annual compounded percent of change observed over that period.

Based on these data, the following analysis was undertaken to estimate the demand growth rates to be used in projecting future hotel room night demand for the subject market area.

Commercial Demand

Historic economic and demographic trends in the subject market area show strong growth. The local population has grown at an annual compounded rate of 2.2% over the past 10 years; commercial indicators for the FIRE, trade, and services employment sectors have increased 2.5%, 1.6%, and 4.0%, respec-

TABLE 3.35 Trend Report for Suburban Long Island

Year	Room Night Demand	Percent Change	Market Supply	Percent Change	Market-wide Occupancy
1990	691,075	—	990,083	—	69.8%
1991	685,125	(0.9)%	1,018,286	2.8%	67.3
1992	663,639	(3.1)	1,028,256	1.0	64.5
1993	671,023	1.1	1,036,876	0.8	64.7
1994	707,644	5.5	1,058,952	2.1	66.8
1995	740,023	4.6	1,109,618	4.8	66.7
1996	783,857	5.9	1,165,655	5.1	67.2
1997	837,987	6.9	1,205,831	3.4	69.5
1998	880,664	5.1	1,238,459	2.7	71.1
1999	916,270	4.0	1,283,078	3.6	71.4
Avg. annual % change, 1990–1999:		3.2%		2.9%	

TABLE 3.36 Room Night Demand Growth Indicators		
Type of Data	**Historic (Actual) or Projected Date of Data**	**Annual Compounded Percentage Change**
Population	Historic	2.2%
Population	Projected	1.7
Retail sales	Historic	2.5
Retail sales	Projected	2.1
Effective buying income	Historic	3.2
Effective buying income	Projected	1.2
Personal income	Historic	3.1
Personal income	Projected	1.3
Employment by category		
Manufacturing	Historic	1.0
Construction	Historic	2.0
TCPU*	Historic	2.0
FIRE**	Historic	2.5
Trade	Historic	1.6
Services	Historic	4.0
Government	Historic	0.5
Assessed values	Historic	1.8
Housing starts	Historic	2.5
Commercial building permits	Historic	4.0
Airport enplanements	Historic	3.8
Airport enplanements	Projected	1.5
Air cargo data	Historic	3.0
Highway traffic counts	Historic	2.0
Inventory of office space	Projected	2.9
Office space absorption	Projected	3.1
Office space construction	Projected	2.0
Inventory of industrial space	Projected	2.7
Industrial space absorption	Projected	2.9
Industrial space construction	Projected	2.0
Inventory of retail space	Projected	2.4
Retail space absorption	Projected	3.3
Retail space construction	Projected	2.2
New businesses to area	Historic	2.3
Convention center usage	Historic	1.0
Tourist visitation	Projected	1.0
Visitor counts at attractions	Historic	1.0
Restaurant Activity Index	Historic	2.3
Restaurant Growth Index	Historic	2.7

* Transportation, communications, and public utilities

**Finance, insurance, and real estate

tively. Airport enplanements were strong at 3.8% and new business showed an annual gain of 2.3%. Future projections suggest continued growth, but probably not at the levels previously experienced. Office space, industrial space, and retail space absorption is expected to grow at 3.1%, 2.9%, and 3.3%, respectively. Population growth is projected to slow to 1.7%, while airport enplanement growth will likely decelerate to 1.5% in the near term.

Based on this analysis, the appraisers have projected commercial demand growth of 5.0% in the first projection year, slowing to 4.0% in the second projection year, and 3.0% in the third projection year. Commercial segment demand growth is expected to stabilize at 3.0% every year thereafter.

Meeting and Group Demand

Whereas the historical rate of meeting and group demand growth in the subject lodging market has been measured at rates of 1% to 2% per year, the recent completion of the convention center's renovation and expansion justifies the use of a stronger growth rate throughout our projection period. The convention center now features greater potential for attracting large groups. Based on these considerations, the appraisers have projected annual meeting and group demand growth of 2.00% in the first projection year, 2.50% in the second projection year, and 2.75% in the third projection year. Meeting and group demand growth is projected to stabilize at 2.75% every year thereafter.

Leisure Demand

Visitor counts in the resort area south of the subject site have grown at an annual rate of 1.0% for the past five years. According to the local visitors bureau, the resort's upgraded amenities are helping to improve overnight tourist visitation. As such, an annual leisure segment demand growth factor of 1.50% has been applied for the purposes of this analysis.

Table 3.37 shows the projected growth in hotel room night demand for each of the three market segments.

These compounded annual growth rates are applied to both accommodated and unaccommodated room night demand. Induced demand is projected to grow to 15,000 room nights in the fifth projection year and then remain level for the remainder of the projection period. Table 3.38 shows the projected room night demand for each of the three market segments for the next five years.

Now the micro demand analysis for the subject market area is complete. The next component of the market study is an analysis of the competitive lodging supply, which will form the basis for allocating the total area-wide room night demand among the competitive hotels in the market.

TABLE 3.37 Projected Demand Growth Rates

Segment	Year 1	Year 2	Year 3	Year 4	Year 5
			Projection Year		
Commercial	5.00%	4.00%	3.00%	3.00%	3.00%
Meeting and group	2.00	2.50	2.75	2.75	2.75
Leisure	1.50	1.50	1.50	1.50	1.50
Weighted average	3.71%	3.23%	2.68%	2.68%	2.69%

TABLE 3.38 Projection of Market Demand (Unadjusted for Unaccommodatable Demand)

	Base Year	Year 1	Year 2	Year 3	Year 4	Year 5
			Projection Year			
Commercial Segment						
Growth rate	—	5.00%	4.00%	3.00%	3.00%	3.00%
Accommodated demand	302,298	317,413	330,110	340,013	350,213	360,719
Unaccommodated demand	24,184	25,393	26,409	27,201	28,017	28,858
Induced demand	0	0	0	0	0	0
Total demand	326,482	342,806	356,519	367,214	378,230	389,577
Meeting and Group Segment						
Growth rate	—	2.00%	2.50%	2.75%	2.75%	2.75%
Accommodated demand	115,338	117,645	120,586	123,902	127,309	130,810
Unaccommodated demand	5,767	5,882	6,029	6,195	6,365	6,540
Induced demand	0	0	0	3,000	9,000	15,000
Total demand	121,105	123,527	126,615	133,097	142,674	152,350
Leisure Segment						
Growth rate	—	1.50%	1.50%	1.50%	1.50%	1.50%
Accommodated demand	99,226	100,714	102,225	103,758	105,314	106,894
Unaccommodated demand	2,977	3,022	3,067	3,113	3,160	3,207
Induced demand	0	0	0	0	0	0
Total demand	102,203	103,736	105,292	106,871	108,474	110,101
Total Demand–all segments	549,790	570,069	588,426	607,182	629,378	652,028

Supply of Transient Accommodations

A hotel appraiser should be familiar with both macro and micro hotel supply factors. Long-term macro supply trends often affect local hotels significantly, particularly with respect to hotel size, layout, design, chain affiliation, financial structure, and type of management. An understanding of the micro supply is needed to predict the relative competitiveness of area properties and to estimate the subject property's probable market share.

Macro Supply

It has traditionally been difficult to determine the macro supply for transient lodging accommodations within the United States because there was no uniform, long-term census that annually quantified the number of hotel units. One of the problems relates to definition. What constitutes a lodging facility? Should properties such as rooming houses, residential hotels, dormitories, camps, seasonal resorts, and motels with fewer than 10 units be included? The U.S. Bureau of the Census has information dating back to 1939, but the definition of a lodging facility used at that time included many properties that would not be considered competitive lodgings today.

Today the hotel data-consulting firm Smith Travel Research (STR) addresses the problem of quantifying the supply of hotel and motel rooms in the United States. STR tracks the number of lodging units currently operating in the United States and compiles occupancy, average room rate, and other operational statistics about thousands of hotels and motels throughout the nation. This information is then published in composite form and made available to subscribers of *Lodging Outlook* magazine. STR can also be commissioned to generate specific data such as information about market share and penetration, or to produce a trend report detailing supply, demand, occupancy, average rate, and RevPAR trends for a specific collection of hotels. (RevPAR is defined later.) As noted previously in this text, STR may be contacted at (615) 824-8664, or on-line at www.str-online.com.

Occupancy, Average Rate, and RevPAR Data

Table 4.1 identifies historical and projected trends in supply, demand, and occupancy for the United States, based on data provided by STR, as well as HVS International. Between 1970 and 1998, the number of hotel rooms in the United States increased at an average annual compounded percentage rate of 2.4%. Between 1990 and 1998, the rate of growth equated to 1.8% per year. Recession in the early 1990s, and oversupply throughout the industry, slowed growth to a low of 0.3% in 1993. As the industry stabilized, the environment for additional gains in supply improved. Gains of 3.5% and 3.9% were noted in 1997 and 1998, respectively. Demand growth was outpaced by supply growth between 1970 and 1998, driving the national occupancy rate down from 71.4% in 1970 to 64.0% in 1998. The national occupancy rate has generally remained in the 60% to 65% range since 1983. The strongest national occupancy rate noted on the chart, 72.3%, was recorded in 1979. The lowest national occupancy rate, 61.9%, was recorded in 1991.

STR also records average rate and RevPAR trends for the nation. Table 4.2 identifies historical and projected trends in national average rate, occupancy rate, and RevPAR. RevPAR equates to revenue per available room and is calculated as the product of occupancy and average rate. Because it accounts for both occupancy and average rate together, this figure provides the best overall measure of revenue-generating results for a single property or group of hotels. For example, a hotel operating at a 55% occupancy rate with a room rate of $65 has a RevPAR of $35.75 (55% x $65). This hotel is generating more rooms revenue than a hotel with a 70% occupancy rate and a room rate of $50, which has a RevPAR of $35 (70% × $50). Table 4.2 also sets forth the CPI-U (Consumer Price Index for Urban Consumers). A comparison of national average rate growth trends with the CPI-U is meaningful.

Between 1973 and 1998, the national average rate increased at an average annual compounded percentage rate of 6.2%, slowing to 3.7% between 1990 and 1998. In both cases, hotel average rate growth has exceeded the rate of gain in the CPI-U. In 1998, the national average rate increased by 4.4%, compared to the 1.6% gain in the CPI-U. RevPAR growth has also outpaced the rate of change in the CPI-U. The rate of change in hotel expenses conforms with that of the CPI-U, and the fact that average rate gains (and therefore hotel revenues) have increased at a superior pace is positive from the standpoint of overall profit margins.

Table 4.3 sets forth supply levels for each of the 50 states and Washington, D.C., as of year-end 1989 and 1994, and as of September 30, 1999. As of 1999, the states with the largest quantity of hotel rooms (in descending order) were California, Florida, and Texas. Between 1994 and 1999, the highest rates of supply growth were noted in Mississippi, Minnesota, and Nevada.

Year	Net Rooms Added (in thousands)	Rooms Available Supply (in thousands)	Percent Change	Demand (in thousands)	Percent Change	Occupancy	Percent Change
1970	–	1,911	–	1,364	–	71.4%	–
1971	59	1,970	3.1%	1,375	0.8%	69.8	(2.2)%
1972	83	2,053	4.2	1,448	5.3	70.5	1.1
1973	109	2,162	5.3	1,526	5.4	70.6	0.1
1974	138	2,300	6.4	1,482	(2.9)	64.4	(8.7)
1975	60	2,360	2.6	1,512	2.0	64.1	(0.6)
1976	21	2,381	0.9	1,577	4.3	66.2	3.4
1977	24	2,405	1.0	1,627	3.2	67.7	2.1
1978	27	2,432	1.1	1,694	4.1	69.7	3.0
1979	34	2,466	1.4	1,783	5.3	72.3	3.8
1980	19	2,485	0.8	1,766	(1.0)	71.1	(1.7)
1981	38	2,523	1.5	1,723	(2.4)	68.3	(3.9)
1982	17	2,540	0.7	1,703	(1.2)	67.0	(1.8)
1983	31	2,571	1.2	1,667	(2.1)	64.8	(3.3)
1984	38	2,609	1.5	1,682	0.9	64.5	(0.6)
1985	73	2,682	2.8	1,704	1.3	63.5	(1.4)
1986	89	2,771	3.3	1,743	2.3	62.9	(1.0)
1987	94	2,865	3.4	1,814	4.1	63.3	0.7
1988	112	2,977	3.9	1,891	4.2	63.5	0.3
1989	101	3,078	3.4	1,983	4.9	64.4	1.4
1990	99	3,177	3.2	2,022	2.0	63.6	(1.2)
1991	45	3,222	1.4	1,993	(1.4)	61.9	(2.8)
1992	24	3,246	0.7	2,035	2.1	62.7	1.4
1993	11	3,257	0.3	2,071	1.8	63.6	1.4
1994	34	3,291	1.0	2,133	3.0	64.8	1.9
1995	43	3,334	1.3	2,172	1.8	65.1	0.5
1996	77	3,411	2.3	2,220	2.2	65.1	(0.1)
1997	118	3,529	3.5	2,275	2.5	64.5	(0.9)
1998	139	3,668	3.9	2,346	3.1	64.0	(0.8)
1999*	128	3,796	3.5	2,409	2.7	63.5	(0.8)
2000*	114	3,910	3.0	2,472	2.6	63.2	(0.4)
2001*	102	4,012	2.6	2,533	2.5	63.1	(0.1)
2002*	92	4,104	2.3	2,592	2.3	63.2	0.0

Annual Compounded Percent Change

1970–1998			2.4%		2.0%		(0.4)%
1990–1998			1.8		1.9		0.1
1998–2002			2.8		2.5		(0.3)

* Projected

Source: Smith Travel Research and HVS International

TABLE 4.2 Average Rate, Occupancy Rate, and RevPAR—U.S. Lodging Industry

Year	Average Room Rate	Percent Change	Consumer Price Index*	Percent Change	Hotel Occupancy	Revenue Per Room (RevPAR)	Percent Change
1973	$17.36	—	44.4	—	70.6%	$12.25	—
1974	18.68	7.6%	49.3	11.0%	64.4	12.04	(1.8)%
1975	20.04	7.3	53.8	9.1	64.1	12.84	6.7
1976	21.68	8.2	56.9	5.8	66.2	14.36	11.8
1977	23.44	8.1	60.6	6.5	67.7	15.86	10.4
1978	26.72	14.0	65.2	7.6	69.7	18.61	17.4
1979	31.27	17.0	72.6	11.3	72.3	22.61	21.5
1980	36.03	15.2	82.4	13.5	71.1	25.61	13.3
1981	39.64	10.0	90.9	10.3	68.3	27.07	5.7
1982	42.04	6.1	96.5	6.2	67.0	28.19	4.1
1983	44.21	5.2	99.6	3.2	64.8	28.67	1.7
1984	47.27	6.9	103.9	4.3	64.5	30.47	6.3
1985	49.45	4.6	107.6	3.6	63.5	31.42	3.1
1986	51.04	3.2	109.6	1.9	62.9	32.10	2.2
1987	53.12	4.1	113.6	3.6	63.3	33.63	4.8
1988	54.98	3.5	118.3	4.1	63.5	34.92	3.8
1989	56.84	3.4	124.0	4.8	64.4	36.62	4.9
1990	58.68	3.2	130.7	5.4	63.6	37.35	2.0
1991	58.78	0.2	136.2	4.2	61.9	36.36	(2.6)
1992	59.61	1.4	140.3	3.0	62.7	37.37	2.8
1993	61.27	2.8	144.5	3.0	63.6	38.96	4.2
1994	63.54	3.7	148.2	2.6	64.8	41.18	5.7
1995	66.65	4.9	152.4	2.8	65.1	43.42	5.4
1996	70.93	6.4	156.9	3.0	65.1	46.16	6.3
1997	75.31	6.2	160.5	2.3	64.5	48.55	5.2
1998	78.62	4.4	163.0	1.6	64.0	50.28	3.6
1999**	81.76	4.0	166.3	2.0	63.5	51.89	2.0
2000**	84.70	3.6	170.4	2.5	63.2	53.55	2.5
2001**	87.41	3.2	175.2	2.8	63.1	55.19	2.8
Annual Compounded Percent Change							
1973–1998		6.2%		5.3%			5.8%
1990–1998		3.7		2.8			3.8
1998–2001		3.6		2.4			3.1

* Consumer Price Index for Urban Consumers, base period is 1982–1984

**Projected

Source: Smith Travel Research, Bureau of Labor Statistics, and HVS International

Hotels and Motels—Valuations and Market Studies

TABLE 4.3 — Lodging Industry Census by State

State	No. of Properties 1989	1994	1999*	Percent Change 1989–1994	1994–1999	No. of Rooms 1989	1994	1999*	Percent Change 1989–1994	1994–1999
Alabama	412	464	610	12.6%	31.5%	41,694	44,449	54,569	6.6%	22.8%
Alaska	148	153	168	3.4	9.8	11,636	12,235	14,326	5.1	17.1
Arizona	621	660	857	6.3	29.8	68,599	71,530	91,701	4.3	28.2
Arkansas	357	397	466	11.2	17.4	28,557	31,304	35,883	9.6	14.6
California	3,608	3,796	3,991	5.2	5.1	360,213	381,403	402,726	5.9	5.6
Colorado	743	764	934	2.8	22.3	68,640	70,551	87,436	2.8	23.9
Connecticut	238	246	260	3.4	5.7	24,522	25,164	28,174	2.6	12.0
Delaware	116	119	131	2.6	10.1	8,498	9,116	10,253	7.3	12.5
Florida	2,353	2,451	2,768	4.2	12.9	292,788	316,052	358,136	7.9	13.3
Georgia	878	976	1,356	11.2	38.9	103,705	110,958	142,276	7.0	28.2
Hawaii	309	315	313	1.9	(0.6)	66,455	69,270	69,240	4.2	(0.0)
Idaho	166	189	220	13.9	16.4	13,194	14,737	17,579	11.7	19.3
Illinois	812	900	1,096	10.8	21.8	103,837	111,387	130,388	7.3	17.1
Indiana	435	484	663	11.3	37.0	47,608	51,170	64,889	7.5	26.8
Iowa	371	425	516	14.6	21.4	28,167	31,183	37,463	10.7	20.1
Kansas	319	334	398	4.7	19.2	24,731	25,463	30,753	3.0	20.8
Kentucky	345	391	507	13.3	29.7	34,559	37,344	45,653	8.1	22.2
Louisiana	326	331	438	1.5	32.3	49,201	47,976	58,615	(2.5)	22.2
Maine	314	320	326	1.9	1.9	19,956	20,753	21,396	4.0	3.1
Maryland	426	423	469	(0.7)	10.9	46,931	48,332	53,191	3.0	10.1
Massachusetts	563	567	599	0.7	5.6	57,607	58,817	64,373	2.1	9.4
Michigan	802	830	974	3.5	17.3	76,726	78,558	90,556	2.4	15.3
Minnesota	504	561	697	11.3	24.2	44,608	42,802	58,119	(4.0)	35.8
Mississippi	256	297	417	16.0	40.4	26,165	29,636	43,083	13.3	45.4
Missouri	563	653	821	16.0	25.7	63,123	71,242	85,435	12.9	19.9
Montana	259	280	316	8.1	12.9	17,052	18,454	21,228	8.2	15.0
Nebraska	288	307	368	6.6	19.9	18,798	20,221	24,156	7.6	19.5
Nevada	469	487	551	3.8	13.1	105,881	132,371	171,300	25.0	29.4
New Hampshire	221	221	231	0.0	4.5	15,482	15,564	16,697	0.5	7.3
New Jersey	484	496	537	2.5	8.3	62,174	65,055	71,168	4.6	9.4
New Mexico	351	402	493	14.5	22.6	27,446	31,183	38,484	13.6	23.4
New York	1,127	1,151	1,219	2.1	5.9	138,256	142,608	150,284	3.1	5.4
North Carolina	1,125	1,168	1,457	3.8	24.7	95,354	98,570	125,129	3.4	26.9
North Dakota	121	139	155	14.9	11.5	9,748	10,817	12,039	11.0	11.3
Ohio	790	854	1,092	8.1	27.9	87,679	91,825	112,422	4.7	22.4
Oklahoma	356	375	448	5.3	19.5	35,044	36,127	40,658	3.1	12.5
Oregon	525	574	665	9.3	15.9	38,926	42,373	51,563	8.9	21.7
Pennsylvania	774	833	970	7.6	16.4	83,545	89,081	103,404	6.6	16.1
Rhode Island	61	65	69	6.6	6.2	5,721	6,313	6,736	10.3	6.7
South Carolina	636	682	845	7.2	23.9	66,293	69,662	82,964	5.1	19.1
South Dakota	219	260	292	18.7	12.3	12,777	15,077	17,326	18.0	14.9
Tennessee	780	878	1,104	12.6	25.7	79,784	86,467	104,860	8.4	21.3
Texas	1,671	1,742	2,395	4.2	37.5	205,823	210,252	269,443	2.2	28.2
Utah	364	372	454	2.2	22.0	28,243	29,174	36,850	3.3	26.3
Vermont	198	200	203	1.0	1.5	13,632	14,093	14,491	3.4	2.8
Virginia	842	878	1,023	4.3	16.5	96,221	101,628	114,110	5.6	12.3
Washington	583	642	745	10.1	16.0	49,214	54,816	66,113	11.4	20.6
Washington, D.C.	103	98	103	(4.9)	5.1	24,446	23,820	24,799	(2.6)	4.1
West Virginia	170	180	217	5.9	20.6	17,118	18,036	21,222	5.4	17.7
Wisconsin	667	720	834	7.9	15.8	50,138	54,255	63,481	8.2	17.0
Wyoming	250	258	272	3.2	5.4	17,951	18,466	19,539	2.9	5.8
Total U.S.	29,419	31,308	37,053	6.4%	18.3%	3,114,466	3,307,740	3,876,679	6.2%	17.2%

* 1999 data are as of the 12 months ending in September; all other data are year-end.
Source: Smith Travel Research

STR also sorts lodging industry census data by hotel location, i.e., urban, suburban, airport, highway, and resort. Table 4.4 shows these census data. In terms of the number of rooms, suburban supply increased most dramatically between 1994 and 1999, while the resort sector recorded the smallest increase in inventory. Table 4.5 shows the share of total supply contributed by each of the various location types. The suburbs account for the largest single share, at 34%.

TABLE 4.4	**Lodging Industry Census by Location**									
	— No. of Properties —			Percent Change		— No. of Rooms —			Percent Change	
Type	1989	1994	1999*	1989–1994	1994–1999	1989	1994	1999*	1989–1994	1994–1999
Urban	2,843	2,887	3,472	1.5%	20.3%	520,875	531,019	609,160	1.9%	14.7%
Suburban	9,749	10,690	13,506	9.7	26.3	968,361	1,053,187	1,304,085	8.8	23.8
Airport	1,738	1,937	2,392	11.4	23.5	277,679	296,959	341,916	6.9	15.1
Highway	12,989	13,638	15,404	5.0	12.9	948,977	1,001,744	1,142,255	5.6	14.0
Resort	2,100	2,156	2,279	2.7	5.7	398,574	430,231	479,263	7.9	11.4
Total U.S.	29,419	31,308	37,053	6.4%	18.3%	3,114,466	3,313,140	3,876,679	6.4%	17.0%

* 1999 data are as of the 12 months ending in September; all other data are year-end.

Source: Smith Travel Research

TABLE 4.5	**Hotel Locations (1999 Room Count)**	
	Location	**Percent of Total**
	Urban	16%
	Suburban	34
	Airport	9
	Highway	29
	Resort	12

Source: Smith Travel Research

STR also sorts lodging industry census data by property type, i.e., gaming, convention, conference center, all-suites, and standard hotels. Table 4.6 shows these data. In terms of the number of rooms, the number of all-suites hotels increased by 68.8%, while gaming hotels increased by 38.0%. Only minor increases in convention and conference center hotels were noted. Table 4.7 shows the share of total supply contributed by each property type.

Table 4.8 sets forth occupancy levels for each of the 50 states and Washington, D.C., for 1989, 1994, and the 12 months ending September 30, 1999. In 1999, the highest occupancy rates were recorded by Nevada, Rhode Island, and New York. The lowest occupancy rates were recorded by Wyoming, South Dakota, and Arkansas. Between 1994 and 1999, the strongest rates of occupancy gain were realized by Maine, Connecticut, and Vermont.

TABLE 4.6 **Lodging Industry Census by Property Type**

Type	— No. of Properties —			Percent Change		—— No. of Rooms ——			Percent Change	
	1989	1994	1999*	1989–1994	1994–1999	1989	1994	1999*	1989–1994	1994–1999
Gaming	153	173	206	13.1%	19.1%	85,837	104,203	143,843	21.4%	38.0%
Convention	140	147	156	5.0	6.1	117,699	122,824	126,270	4.4	2.8
Conference center	107	115	122	7.5	6.1	25,002	27,231	28,375	8.9	4.2
All suites	1,343	1,601	2,810	19.2	75.5	169,750	207,979	351,097	22.5	68.8
Hotel	27,675	29,272	33,781	5.8	15.4	2,716,558	2,851,390	3,228,505	5.0	13.2
Total U.S.	29,418	31,308	37,075	6.4%	18.4%	3,114,846	3,313,627	3,878,090	6.4%	17.0%

* 1999 data are as of the 12 months ending in September; all other data are year-end.

Source: Smith Travel Research

TABLE 4.7 **Share of Total Supply Contributed by Hotel Types (1999 Room Count)**

Type	Percent of Total
Gaming	4%
Convention	3
Conference center	1
All suites	9
Hotel	83

Source: Smith Travel Research

Table 4.9 sets forth occupancy rate levels by location type. Urban hotels posted the strongest occupancy rate in 1999; the urban location was the only one to realize a gain in occupancy between 1994 and 1999.

Table 4.10 sets forth occupancy rate levels by property type. Gaming hotels posted the highest occupancy level in 1999, although this sector's occupancy levels actually declined between 1994 and 1999. Between 1994 and 1999, occupancy rates increased for both the convention and conference center sectors.

Table 4.11 sets forth average rate levels for each of the 50 states in the nation, as well as for the District of Columbia, for 1989, 1994, and the 12 months ending September 30, 1999. In 1999, the highest average rate levels were recorded by New York, Hawaii, Massachusetts, and Washington, D.C. The lowest average rate levels were recorded in North Dakota, Oklahoma, and Arkansas. Between 1994 and 1999, the strongest rates of average rate gain were realized by New York, Connecticut, and Delaware.

Table 4.12 sets forth average rate levels by location type. Resorts and urban hotels posted the strongest average rate levels in 1999. Urban hotels experienced the strongest rate of average rate growth between 1994 and 1999.

Table 4.13 sets forth average rate levels by property type. Convention and conference center hotels posted the highest average rate levels in 1999. These sectors also recorded the strongest rate of average rate growth between 1994 and 1999.

	Hotel Occupancy Levels by State				
TABLE 4.8	——— Occupancy Rate ———			——— Percent Change ———	
State	**1989**	**1994**	**1999***	**1989–1994**	**1994–1999**
Alabama	61.2%	63.4%	57.4%	3.6%	(9.5)%
Alaska	70.5	65.1	63.1	(7.7)	(3.1)
Arizona	65.2	67.6	60.9	3.7	(9.9)
Arkansas	55.8	59.8	55.6	7.2	(7.0)
California	68.7	63.2	68.4	(8.0)	8.2
Colorado	55.6	63.6	60.4	14.4	(5.0)
Connecticut	60.4	60.8	66.5	0.7	9.4
Delaware	59.7	61.9	66.2	3.7	6.9
Florida	68.3	64.4	66.5	(5.7)	3.3
Georgia	60.5	66.6	61.6	10.1	(7.5)
Hawaii	78.5	75.5	71.7	(3.8)	(5.0)
Idaho	63.7	64.1	60.5	0.6	(5.6)
Illinois	64.1	65.4	64.8	2.0	(0.9)
Indiana	61.5	62.9	57.0	2.3	(9.4)
Iowa	59.6	60.1	58.7	0.8	(2.3)
Kansas	61.1	65.2	59.9	6.7	(8.1)
Kentucky	61.7	63.0	57.8	2.1	(8.3)
Louisiana	61.0	70.0	65.7	14.8	(6.1)
Maine	63.4	56.3	62.6	(11.2)	11.2
Maryland	62.1	63.2	67.0	1.8	6.0
Massachusetts	61.9	62.8	67.9	1.5	8.1
Michigan	58.8	61.9	61.5	5.3	(0.6)
Minnesota	61.5	64.5	62.1	4.9	(3.7)
Mississippi	59.4	67.4	58.9	13.5	(12.6)
Missouri	60.4	62.0	58.6	2.6	(5.5)
Montana	60.7	60.6	57.8	(0.2)	(4.6)
Nebraska	60.4	65.1	59.7	7.8	(8.3)
Nevada	76.1	79.6	75.7	4.6	(4.9)
New Hampshire	56.1	56.0	60.1	(0.2)	7.3
New Jersey	63.6	65.7	67.9	3.3	3.3
New Mexico	59.1	68.9	59.4	16.6	(13.8)
New York	68.8	66.7	71.1	(3.1)	6.6
North Carolina	60.2	63.5	59.4	5.5	(6.5)
North Dakota	65.2	57.6	57.4	(11.7)	(0.3)
Ohio	62.9	62.3	59.1	(1.0)	(5.1)
Oklahoma	54.4	56.2	56.2	3.3	0.0
Oregon	68.8	63.4	57.3	(7.8)	(9.6)
Pennsylvania	64.9	63.5	63.0	(2.2)	(0.8)
Rhode Island	65.7	63.4	72.2	(3.5)	13.9
South Carolina	65.1	64.3	60.5	(1.2)	(5.9)
South Dakota	54.3	55.4	55.4	2.0	0.0
Tennessee	60.4	64.2	58.3	6.3	(9.2)
Texas	59.9	64.9	61.3	8.3	(5.5)
Utah	62.8	68.3	57.6	8.8	(15.7)
Vermont	64.4	56.3	61.3	(12.6)	8.9
Virginia	63.7	63.6	62.9	(0.2)	(1.1)
Washington	68.9	65.2	63.2	(5.4)	(3.1)
Washington, D.C.	71.0	67.1	70.7	(5.5)	5.4
West Virginia	63.3	67.9	58.6	7.3	(13.7)
Wisconsin	60.5	60.5	57.6	0.0	(4.8)
Wyoming	54.6	55.2	53.9	1.1	(2.4)
Total U.S.	64.4%	64.8%	N/Av	0.6%	N/Av

* 1999 data are for the 12 months ending in September.
Source: Smith Travel Research

Hotels and Motels—Valuations and Market Studies

TABLE 4.9 — Hotel Occupancy Levels by Location Type

Location	Occupancy Rate			Percent Change	
	1989	1994	1999*	1989–1994	1994–1999
Urban	65.3%	67.7%	68.0%	3.7%	0.4%
Suburban	63.1	65.9	64.1	4.4	(2.7)
Airport	67.4	69.2	67.1	2.7	(3.0)
Highway	63.1	62.8	60.2	(0.5)	(4.1)
Resort	68.9	67.6	67.4	(1.9)	(0.3)

* 1999 data are for the 12 months ending in September.

Source: Smith Travel Research

TABLE 4.10 — Hotel Occupancy Levels by Property Type

Type	Occupancy Rate			Percent Change	
	1989	1994	1999*	1989–1994	1994–1999
Gaming	85.7%	86.0%	81.8%	0.4%	(4.9)%
Convention	70.8	71.3	72.8	0.7	2.1
Conference center	62.9	67.7	68.0	7.6	0.4
All suites	69.3	73.7	70.5	6.3	(4.3)
Hotel	63.8	64.9	63.3	1.7	(2.5)

* 1999 data are for the 12 months ending in September.

Source: Smith Travel Research

Table 4.14 sets forth RevPAR levels for each of the 50 states and Washington, D.C., for 1989, 1994, and the 12 months ending September 30, 1999. In 1999, the highest RevPAR levels were recorded by New York, Hawaii, and Massachusetts, as well as Washington, D.C. The lowest RevPAR levels were recorded by North Dakota, Oklahoma, and Arkansas. Between 1994 and 1999, the strongest rates of RevPAR gain were realized by Connecticut, New York, and Rhode Island.

Table 4.15 sets forth RevPAR levels by location type. Resorts and urban hotels posted the strongest RevPAR levels in 1999 and the strongest rates of RevPAR growth between 1994 and 1999.

Table 4.16 sets forth RevPAR levels by property type. Convention and conference center hotels posted the highest RevPAR levels in 1999 as well as the strongest rates of RevPAR growth between 1994 and 1999.

Classification of Lodging Facilities

Hotels and motels are designed and located to attract specific markets. Because hotel designs, facilities, amenities, and locations differ and directly impact financial operating results, it is important to define and accurately classify the different characteristics of lodging facilities.

| TABLE 4.11 | Hotel Average Room Rate by State |

	Average Room Rate			Percent Change	
State	1989	1994	1999*	1989–1994	1994–1999
Alabama	$40.19	$45.12	$54.17	12.3%	20.1%
Alaska	69.94	89.91	96.94	28.6	7.8
Arizona	56.69	69.44	84.81	22.5	22.1
Arkansas	36.65	42.06	52.33	14.8	24.4
California	62.29	69.44	92.17	11.5	32.7
Colorado	55.31	71.15	87.12	28.6	22.4
Connecticut	61.17	62.03	86.79	1.4	39.9
Delaware	53.25	52.15	71.87	(2.1)	37.8
Florida	59.58	66.86	85.76	12.2	28.3
Georgia	47.71	55.51	69.68	16.3	25.5
Hawaii	98.30	104.05	129.38	5.8	24.3
Idaho	40.09	51.33	61.10	28.0	19.0
Illinois	61.71	69.06	91.07	11.9	31.9
Indiana	44.75	51.24	63.42	14.5	23.8
Iowa	40.30	45.15	54.70	12.0	21.2
Kansas	39.13	45.16	56.31	15.4	24.7
Kentucky	41.65	46.70	57.44	12.1	23.0
Louisiana	55.93	68.19	85.38	21.9	25.2
Maine	56.07	59.74	71.12	6.5	19.0
Maryland	58.22	62.24	80.58	6.9	29.5
Massachusetts	78.97	83.11	111.23	5.2	33.8
Michigan	51.64	55.40	69.53	7.3	25.5
Minnesota	47.54	58.47	70.69	23.0	20.9
Mississippi	37.05	46.37	54.39	25.2	17.3
Missouri	47.57	54.33	64.86	14.2	19.4
Montana	36.93	46.69	53.88	26.4	15.4
Nebraska	37.43	43.59	54.18	16.5	24.3
Nevada	48.32	56.90	78.30	17.8	37.6
New Hampshire	61.28	60.74	74.14	(0.9)	22.1
New Jersey	79.08	70.90	93.39	(10.3)	31.7
New Mexico	41.37	53.53	58.96	29.4	10.1
New York	87.77	95.23	134.41	8.5	41.1
North Carolina	42.58	47.65	61.29	11.9	28.6
North Dakota	36.53	39.94	44.69	9.3	11.9
Ohio	46.79	53.16	66.19	13.6	24.5
Oklahoma	38.10	43.58	51.74	14.4	18.7
Oregon	45.65	56.54	68.57	23.9	21.3
Pennsylvania	56.74	63.14	80.71	11.3	27.8
Rhode Island	77.23	76.09	100.01	(1.5)	31.4
South Carolina	47.89	55.27	65.99	15.4	19.4
South Dakota	37.21	45.04	54.67	21.0	21.4
Tennessee	45.60	52.37	62.97	14.8	20.2
Texas	46.59	56.64	69.98	21.6	23.6
Utah	45.22	57.54	69.14	27.2	20.2
Vermont	65.38	73.18	82.86	11.9	13.2
Virginia	53.88	59.34	75.01	10.1	26.4
Washington	49.83	62.05	77.83	24.5	25.4
Washington, D.C.	101.12	113.01	138.73	11.8	22.8
West Virginia	41.65	46.50	56.41	11.6	21.3
Wisconsin	46.21	54.48	63.20	17.9	16.0
Wyoming	39.57	50.96	62.10	28.8	21.9
Total U.S.	$51.23	$57.78	N/Av	11.8%	N/Av

* 1999 data are for the 12 months ending in September.
Source: Smith Travel Research

TABLE 4.12	**Hotel Average Room Rate by Location Type**				
	——— **Average Room Rate** ———			——— **Percent Change** ———	
Location	**1989**	**1994**	**1999***	**1989–1994**	**1994–1999**
Urban	$79.91	$91.73	$121.08	14.8%	32.0%
Suburban	54.50	61.04	76.16	12.0	24.8
Airport	56.73	60.96	78.33	7.5	28.5
Highway	42.29	47.19	59.23	11.6	25.5
Resort	87.24	97.96	125.89	12.3	28.5

* 1999 data are for the 12 months ending in September.
Source: Smith Travel Research

TABLE 4.13	**Hotel Average Room Rate by Property Type**				
	——— **Average Room Rate** ———			——— **Percent Change** ———	
Type	**1989**	**1994**	**1999***	**1989–1994**	**1994–1999**
Gaming	$64.71	$60.36	$74.65	(6.7)%	23.7%
Convention	103.93	110.75	148.87	6.6	34.4
Conference center	84.07	106.49	148.41	26.7	39.4
All suites	79.41	86.83	94.98	9.3	9.4
Hotel	55.82	63.47	81.29	13.7	28.1

* 1999 data are for the 12 months ending in September.
Source: Smith Travel Research

Hotels and motels can be classified by

- Type of facilities offered
- Class or quality of facilities and services
- Location

Using this classification procedure, a hotel could be described as a mid-rate, convention hotel with an airport location. Its class or quality level is mid-rate, the facilities are specifically designed to accommodate conventions, and the property is located near an airport. Each of the three categories will be discussed and illustrated by examples.

Type of Facilities Offered
The type of facilities refers to the physical hotel property as well as to the amenities and services available to guests. The types of lodging facilities commonly found in the United States include

- Commercial
- Convention
- Resort

	TABLE 4.14	**Hotel RevPAR by State**			
		RevPAR		**Percent Change**	
State	**1989**	**1994**	**1999***	**1989–1994**	**1994–1999**
Alabama	$24.60	$28.61	$31.09	16.3%	8.7%
Alaska	49.31	58.53	61.17	18.7	4.5
Arizona	36.96	46.94	51.65	27.0	10.0
Arkansas	20.45	25.15	29.10	23.0	15.7
California	42.79	43.89	63.04	2.6	43.7
Colorado	30.75	45.25	52.62	47.1	16.3
Connecticut	36.95	37.71	57.72	2.1	53.0
Delaware	31.79	32.28	47.58	1.5	47.4
Florida	40.69	43.06	57.03	5.8	32.5
Georgia	28.86	36.97	42.92	28.1	16.1
Hawaii	77.17	78.56	92.77	1.8	18.1
Idaho	25.54	32.90	36.97	28.8	12.3
Illinois	39.56	45.17	59.01	14.2	30.7
Indiana	27.52	32.23	36.15	17.1	12.2
Iowa	24.02	27.14	32.11	13.0	18.3
Kansas	23.91	29.44	33.73	23.2	14.6
Kentucky	25.70	29.42	33.20	14.5	12.8
Louisiana	34.12	47.73	56.09	39.9	17.5
Maine	35.55	33.63	44.52	(5.4)	32.4
Maryland	36.15	39.34	53.99	8.8	37.3
Massachusetts	48.88	52.19	75.53	6.8	44.7
Michigan	30.36	34.29	42.76	12.9	24.7
Minnesota	29.24	37.71	43.90	29.0	16.4
Mississippi	22.01	31.25	32.04	42.0	2.5
Missouri	28.73	33.68	38.01	17.2	12.8
Montana	22.42	28.29	31.14	26.2	10.1
Nebraska	22.61	28.38	32.35	25.5	14.0
Nevada	36.77	45.29	59.27	23.2	30.9
New Hampshire	34.38	34.01	44.56	(1.1)	31.0
New Jersey	50.29	46.58	63.41	(7.4)	36.1
New Mexico	24.45	36.88	35.02	50.8	(5.0)
New York	60.39	63.52	95.57	5.2	50.5
North Carolina	25.63	30.26	36.41	18.0	20.3
North Dakota	23.82	23.01	25.65	(3.4)	11.5
Ohio	29.43	33.12	39.12	12.5	18.1
Oklahoma	20.73	24.49	29.08	18.2	18.7
Oregon	31.41	35.85	39.29	14.1	9.6
Pennsylvania	36.82	40.09	50.85	8.9	26.8
Rhode Island	50.74	48.24	72.21	(4.9)	49.7
South Carolina	31.18	35.54	39.92	14.0	12.3
South Dakota	20.21	24.95	30.29	23.5	21.4
Tennessee	27.54	33.62	36.71	22.1	9.2
Texas	27.91	36.76	42.90	31.7	16.7
Utah	28.40	39.30	39.82	38.4	1.3
Vermont	42.10	41.20	50.79	(2.1)	23.3
Virginia	34.32	37.74	47.18	10.0	25.0
Washington	34.33	40.46	49.19	17.8	21.6
Washington, D.C.	71.80	75.83	98.08	5.6	29.3
West Virginia	26.36	31.57	33.06	19.8	4.7
Wisconsin	27.96	32.96	36.40	17.9	10.4
Wyoming	21.61	28.13	33.47	30.2	19.0
Total U.S.	$36.62	$41.18	N/Av	12.5%	N/Av

* 1999 data are for the 12 months ending in September.
Source: Smith Travel Research

TABLE 4.15 **Hotel RevPAR by Location Type**

	RevPAR			Percent Change	
Location	**1989**	**1994**	**1999***	**1989–1994**	**1994–1999**
Urban	$52.18	$62.10	$82.33	19.0%	32.6%
Suburban	34.39	40.23	48.82	17.0	21.4
Airport	38.24	42.18	52.56	10.3	24.6
Highway	26.68	29.64	35.66	11.1	20.3
Resort	60.11	66.22	84.85	10.2	28.1

* 1999 data are for the 12 months ending in September.
Source: Smith Travel Research

TABLE 4.16 **Hotel RevPAR by Property Type**

	RevPAR			Percent Change	
Type	**1989**	**1994**	**1999***	**1989–1994**	**1994–1999**
Gaming	$55.46	$51.91	$61.06	(6.4)%	17.6%
Convention	73.58	78.96	108.38	7.3	37.2
Conference center	52.88	72.09	100.92	36.3	40.0
All suites	55.03	63.99	66.96	16.3	4.6
Hotel	35.61	41.19	51.46	15.7	24.9

* 1999 data are for the 12 months ending in September.
Source: Smith Travel Research

- All-suites
- Extended-stay
- Microtel
- Conference center
- Casino
- Bed and breakfast
- Health spa

Commercial

Commercial facilities cater primarily to individual commercial travelers, who travel to conduct business within the market area surrounding the hotel. Consequently, these properties are usually located near concentrations of office and industrial buildings, restaurants, entertainment outlets, and transportation services. Facilities and amenities usually include a restaurant and lounge (on site or nearby), meeting and conference rooms, recreational facilities (e.g., swimming pool, fitness center) and shops. These target commercial travelers and often include room service, secretarial support, computer terminals, photocopy and fax services, concierge and valet services, airport pickup, local transportation, and auto rentals. Commercial hotels typically experience high occupancy rates Monday through Thursday nights with a significant drop-off on Friday, Saturday, and Sunday nights. This weekly occupancy pattern can sometimes be balanced by supplementing the low weekend commercial demand with meeting and group patronage.

Convention

Convention hotels are designed to accommodate large groups and functions. They provide facilities such as large ballrooms with break-out areas for meetings and conferences, exhibit space for trade shows, sample and display rooms for sales meetings, extensive restaurant and lounge capacity, and the same recreational amenities found in commercial hotels. Meeting space, which should amount to at least 30 square feet per guest room, is the key component of a convention hotel. Convention hotels are often located near commercial hotels and sometimes adjacent to convention centers. Because convention hotels are intended for group use, they often include meeting planning and meeting support services, efficient check-in, check-out and billing procedures, audiovisual, computer, and communications equipment rentals, entertainment, and the services previously described for commercial hotels. Occupancy trends at convention hotels usually remain strong Monday through Thursday nights then drop off on weekends. Since some groups prefer to meet on weekends, a convention hotel may post higher weekend occupancies than most commercial hotels. Convention hotels are also affected by monthly occupancy trends because many groups do not meet during the summer or over the holidays.

Resort

Because resort hotels target leisure travelers, they either provide or are located near recreation facilities such as swimming pools, tennis courts, golf courses, ski slopes, ice rinks, or horseback riding and hiking trails. Usually located in scenic areas such as the mountains or the coast, resort hotels often offer limited amounts of meeting and banquet space, restaurants, lounges, entertainment outlets, fitness centers, concierge and valet services, and transportation and tour services. At some resorts meals are included in the room rate. An American Plan provides breakfast, lunch, and dinner; The Modified American Plan includes breakfast and dinner only; and a European Plan does not include meals in room rates at all.

All-inclusive resorts are becoming increasingly popular, predominantly at Caribbean and Mexican resorts. In this pricing plan, any activity that might generate extra charges, such as meals, beverages, recreation activities, etc., is included in the tariff. Resort hotels are often impacted by seasonality. Depending on the nature of the resort area, resorts might have noticeably high or low levels of occupancy at different times of the year. For example, a ski resort booms during the winter months and sometimes during the summer. The shoulder months in the spring and fall, however, are usually slow. These fluctuations in occupancy create operational inefficiencies that hurt a property's financial performance.

All-Suites

All-suites hotels have guest rooms that include both a sleeping area and a separate living area in a single unit. In some hotels the suites are two-room modules that are side-by-side; others have elongated suites where the living area is located in the front and the sleeping area in the rear. The living area typically contains armchairs, a coffee table, a dining table, a television, and a couch that converts into a bed. Most offer a kitchen with a microwave oven and a small refrigerator. Some are more elaborate and contain full kitchens. The bedrooms have less area than standard hotel rooms but their furnishings are typical. The economics of the all-suites concept are based on eliminating or reducing the hotel's public space (i.e., restaurant, lounge, meeting space, and lobby area) and transferring this square footage to the guest rooms. All-suites hotels cater primarily to individual commercial and leisure travelers who do not need a large amount of public space. Transferring public space to the guest rooms maintains the same total building area, so an all-suites hotel can charge the same room rate that a comparable, full-facility property can. For the traveler who does not require public space, the all-suites product is usually an excellent value.

All-suites hotels offer most of the amenities normally found in commercial hotels, but in some instances they are downsized. Amenities may include a swimming pool, a fitness center, and a restaurant that serves in the evenings as a lounge. The services are comparable to those at a commercial hotel. In many chain hotels, all-suites service includes a full breakfast and a complimentary cocktail hour. All-suites can be located in any area suitable for commercial hotels.

In the past two decades, a number of all-suites have been occupancy leaders in their individual markets, demonstrating that the concept has been well received by the U.S. travel market.

Extended-Stay

The extended-stay hotel is a cross between an apartment complex and an all-suites hotel. Its guestroom units are larger than those found in a standard, all-suites hotel and contain more living space, larger closets, and a full kitchen. Because the guest units are designed to accommodate travelers who stay more than 10 days, they are equipped with full-size refrigerators, stoves with ovens, microwaves, sinks, and dishwashers. They also include cooking equipment, dishes, and eating utensils. The property's exterior generally resembles a garden apartment complex and has a residential atmosphere. The amenities and services offered by an extended-stay hotel are similar to those provided by all-suites facilities. Some chains include a free continental breakfast along with a complimentary cocktail reception. At least one extended-stay chain offers grocery shopping service. Hotel staff will purchase the items requested on a guest's shopping list and deliver the order by the end of the day. Residential or commercial areas where guests have access to daily conveniences such as grocery stores, dry cleaners, pharmacies, restaurants, movie theaters, and other entertainment are the best locations for extended-stay hotels.

The extended-stay concept works best when the market has a sufficient number of travelers who are staying for five or more consecutive days and can account for at least 70% of the property's overall occupancy. This customer mix enables the hotel to achieve high weekend occupancy, which greatly enhances the property's operational efficiencies. Well-operated extended-stay hotels routinely operate at more than 80% occupancy when there is a sufficient amount of long-term patronage.

Microtel

The microtel was one of the new hotel products introduced into the market in the second half of the 1980s. This low-end budget product is based on the idea that much of the floor area in a typical hotel guest room is unnecessary and can be eliminated, thereby lowering the property's development cost, reducing operating expenses, and allowing the microtel to charge lower room rates than other budget hotels do. While the standard budget or economy hotel room has more than 250 square feet of space, the microtel provides a queen-sized bed, a dresser, nightstands, a desk, a sitting alcove, and a full bath with a combination shower and tub in an area of less than 195 square feet. The concept can go further by eliminating many of the expensive amenities that have recently been creeping into budget properties, including swimming pools, continental breakfasts, and morning newspapers. The French have taken the microtel concept one step further by providing only a sink in each guest room and communal commodes and showers accessed from the corridors. This allows the hotel to shrink the size of guest rooms and reduce the number of bathroom fixtures. It remains to be seen whether the American traveling public will accept a guest room without a lavatory and bath.

Conference Center

Dedicated conference centers are unique hotel products designed specifically to accommodate small groups and meetings. Unlike commercial hotels with attached conference space that derive demand from all market segments, conference centers usually concentrate on the meeting market. Some even exclude other segments that might distract the in-house groups. Ideally, a conference center provides an environment conducive to productive, successful meetings. To this end, the following facilities and services are usually offered: high technology meeting space with the latest audiovisual and computer equipment; conference planning services; group meals and coffee breaks, packaged in an all-inclusive price; recreational facilities such as swimming pools, tennis courts, golf courses, and fitness equipment; and guest rooms suitable for studying. Conference centers are often situated in remote locations to eliminate any distractions that could disrupt the meeting. Therefore, efficient transportation is essential and driving time to and from a major airport is usually less than an hour.

Conference centers typically cater to small groups that are meeting for training or educational purposes. Social activities are usually minimized so as not to distract the attendees. During weekends and holiday periods, when meeting demand is low, conference centers will either try to attract leisure travelers or close down altogether.

The marketing of a conference center is highly specialized because the facilities are directed almost totally toward the high-end meeting planner. Conference center operators must have established contacts in this market niche to capture this segment of the market. Once stable revenue can be established, the profitability of a dedicated conference center is generally good because facility usage is regulated and controlled.

In addition to commercially oriented conference centers, a number of educational institutions and large companies have their own dedicated meeting and lodging facilities.

Casino

Casino hotels combine a transient hotel with a full casino facility. In most instances the guest rooms, restaurants, lounges, and other hotel amenities are designed to attract guests to the casino and keep them on the property. The rooms are actually amenities to the casino. Casino hotels seek to attract groups and individual leisure travelers who enjoy gambling. Operating a casino hotel requires specialized expertise, not only in marketing the product to the gambler-user but also in controlling the actual gaming activities.

Bed and Breakfast

During the past two decades, the bed and breakfast inn experienced a tremendous increase in popularity. This product, which is not much more than a spruced-up rooming house, offers relatively low-cost accommodations in a comfortable, residential-like atmosphere. Many establishments are historic-type houses with period furnishings. Breakfast is usually included in the price. Bed and breakfast establishments are typically owner-operated. They are basically large homes where roomers are taken in to help supplement the property's operating expenses. Because the economics or income-generating capability of such small lodging facilities can seldom support absentee ownership, sales comparison is usually the most appropriate appraisal approach for bed and breakfast properties.

A bed and breakfast facility traditionally has a residential-like external appearance and a historical feel. Certain older, independent, small motels feature the same type of ownership and economics as bed and breakfasts; however, these are generally referred to as *mom and pop motels*.

Health Spa

Dedicated health spa resorts are similar in concept to dedicated conference centers in that they cater almost exclusively to one market segment. Health spas cater to the health-conscious leisure traveler. A number of hotels offer health and fitness facilities but usually do not provide the total environment of a dedicated health spa. Health spas offer all-inclusive programs that include accommodations, meals, a medical check-up, individually designed health-related activities (usually exercise programs), and counseling. Guests normally stay for three days to two weeks and are not encouraged to partake in meals or activities off the premises unless they are under the supervision of the spa's staff. This type of regulation is designed to help the guest achieve a desired, health-related goal. These properties are usually located in resort areas. Their facilities typically include those normally found in resort hotels with heavy emphasis on fitness equipment, exercise rooms, and similar amenities. Health spas require highly specialized marketing and operating expertise, particularly when it comes to exercise, fitness, and health management. The ratio of staff to guests is high, so a constant, year-round occupancy is important for operating efficiency.

Class or Quality of Facilities and Services

The class of a lodging facility is a way of describing the property's quality and the level of service the staff provides. Generally, class is reflected in a hotel's ability to achieve a particular room rate. A hotel's class relates to its particular market area. The facilities and level of service that might be considered first-class in Amarillo, Texas, may not get such a rating in San Francisco. Usually the best hotel in a market is classified as the area's first-class property; other facilities in the same area that offer lower levels of quality or service are assigned lower rankings.

America's lodging industry does not recognize a uniform system of hotel classes. Terms such as first-class, luxury, and super-luxury mean different things to different people. Table 4.17 shows some of the class categories frequently used in the United States and their typical ranges of 1999 room rates.

Hotel chains try to market their properties to particular classes of travelers. For example, Motel 6 caters to the rate-sensitive budget traveler, while Four Seasons hotels attract an upper-end, luxury-oriented clientele. Table 4.18 sets forth an informal ranking of various major American lodging chains based on pricing. This was based on a study performed by HVS International that surveyed hundreds of hotels in the central United States and developed an average published room rate for each chain. This table shows the room rate positioning of each chain as of 1990, 1992, and 1996. The table also divides the group into five classes. Because hotels that operate under the same name brands have varying levels of product quality, it is difficult to rank chains definitively. Nevertheless, this table provides a general indication of the identified brands' respective class levels, in ascending order.

TABLE 4.17	Hotel Class and Room Rates	
Normal Class	**Range of Room Rates**	
Microbudget	$30 to $40	
Economy	$40 to $50	
Luxury-budget	$50 to $65	
Mid-rate	$65 to $100	
First-class	$100 to $135	
Luxury	$135 and above	

Over the years there has been little movement between classes by hotel chains. Most chains try to create and maintain a specific image through the quality of amenities and services they provide. Days Inn and Rodeway Inn are two exceptions to this rule. Over the past two decades, Days Inn officials have raised the quality of its affiliates so much that the brand has been promoted from the economy class to the luxury-budget category. Rodeway Inn, originally known as a mid-rate chain, is now part of the economy class.

In the United States the *Mobil Travel Guide* and the American Automobile Association (AAA) regularly inspect and rate hotels and motels based on factors such as cleanliness, quality of service and facilities, staff professionalism, and provided amenities. Their findings are published annually and include a quality rating. Mobil ranks lodging facilities using one to five stars and AAA uses one to five diamonds. Many travelers choose lodging facilities based on the information in these guides.

Location

Lodging facilities can also be classified by location. A property's location affects many factors, including the market segments served, the types of facilities and services required, and occupancy cycles. Hotel locations may be classified as airport, highway, center city, suburban, convention center, and resort.

Airport

An airport hotel is situated near a commercial airport and serves out-of-town visitors. This type of location attracts mostly flight crews and airline passengers whose flights have been canceled or delayed. Airport hotels are also natural sites for small and medium-sized meetings when some or all of the attendees are coming from out of town. Most airport hotels are designed to accommodate commercial travelers as well as meeting and group patronage. Leisure demand does not normally constitute a significant portion of an airport hotel's market area. Lodging facilities that rely on a significant amount of airline-generated business such as airline crews and delayed passengers tend to trade room rates for occupancy. This type of demand is extremely price-sensitive, so the property's average room rate must be low. The offsetting benefit of higher occupancy sometimes makes this strategy effective.

TABLE 4.18	**Lodging Brands Arranged by Published Room Rates**		
Microbudget/Economy	**1990 Average**	**1992 Average**	**1996 Average**
Red Roof Inns	$34	$27	$33
Microtel	n/a	35	44
Super 8	38	32	44
Best Inns	40	35	45
Knights Inn	n/a	36	45
Econo Lodge	33	33	46
Thriftlodge	n/a	36	47
Luxury Budget			
Budgetel	n/a	n/a	51
Fairfield Inn by Marriott	37	n/a	52
Travelodge	47	37	52
HoJo Inns	n/a	n/a	52
Days Inn	46	45	54
Sleep Inns	n/a	38	58
Signature Inns	n/a	49	60
La Quinta	52	52	60
Howard Johnson	61	47	60
Rodeway Inns	41	34	61
Ramada Limited	n/a	n/a	61
Best Western	57	48	63
Comfort Inns	61	47	64
Mid Rate			
Quality Inns	62	54	65
Hampton Inns	52	50	67
Holiday Inn Express	n/a	n/a	67
Country Lodging	n/a	n/a	67
Ramada Inns	66	58	71
Holiday Inns	76	75	76
Comfort Suites	65	62	78
Clarion	65	75	81
Courtyard by Marriott	62	62	88
Wyndham Garden	n/a	n/a	92
Four Points	n/a	n/a	96
AmeriSuites	n/a	n/a	96
First Class			
Radisson	100	92	106
Homewood Suites	n/a	n/a	108
Sheraton Hotels	90	88	113
Residence Inns	103	93	117
Crowne Plaza	n/a	n/a	121
Hilton Hotel Hotels	110	99	122
Marriott Hotels	121	114	126
Doubletree Hotels	n/a	n/a	128
Embassy Suites	119	117	130
Luxury			
Renaissance Hotels	137	123	140
Wyndham Hotels	n/a	n/a	147
Summerfield Suites	n/a	n/a	157
Omni Hotels	142	129	163
Hyatt Hotels	148	159	166
Westin Hotels	163	150	172
Doubletree Guest Suites	115	115	179
Ritz-Carlton	164	139	195
Four Seasons	200	189	294

Source: HVS International

Hotels and Motels–Valuations and Market Studies

Most airport hotels provide passenger pick-up and delivery using hotel cars and vans. Depending on the flight schedule, airport shuttle service can be intermittent or continuous. In either case, operating an airport van is expensive and this expense should be considered when projecting operating expenses.

Airport hotels generally experience stable year-round occupancy patterns and usually have higher weekend occupancies than commercial hotels do.

Highway

A highway-oriented lodging facility is located near a major travel route. Visibility and accessibility are important. Highway hotels usually attract individual commercial and leisure travelers. These properties are not often used by the meeting and group segment, so several, small meeting rooms usually suffice. A highway hotel should have either its own restaurant or be near a food service facility that serves three meals a day. The long-term success of a highway hotel depends on auto travel, which has at times been scarce in response to fuel shortages. Changes in highway traffic patterns caused by the construction of new roads, highways, and interchanges can also impact a particular location's desirability. These are some of the risks inherent in a lodging facility that depends on a single mode of travel access. The occupancy patterns of highway hotels typically reflect the type of travelers using the adjacent highway. Their average length of stay is usually short, ranging from one to three days.

Center City

A center city hotel is located in an urban, downtown area. Thus, it attracts individual commercial travelers as well as members of the meeting and group market. Some center city hotels in popular destinations such as Boston, New York City, Washington, D.C., New Orleans, and San Francisco also attract leisure demand. To be successful, a center city hotel should provide adequate parking (usually on-site or valet), security, quiet rooms away from street noise, and room service. In areas with a broad selection of nearby restaurants a center city hotel needs only minimal food and beverage facilities, unless the property depends on a significant amount of meeting and banquet business. Center city hotels are usually high-rises and are more expensive to operate than their suburban counterparts. These properties are almost always subject to higher property taxes, energy costs and labor rates. Moreover, due to site constraints, a center city hotel's layout is not always efficient.

Suburban

Suburban hotels are located just outside the center city near commercial areas with concentrations of office, retail, and industrial businesses. These properties cater to individual commercial travelers, meeting and group demand, and some leisure business—particularly on weekends and holidays. Many suburban hotels are constructed as mid-rise buildings and provide a full range of amenities, including restaurants, lounges, meeting and banquet rooms, swimming pools (indoor and outdoor), health and fitness clubs, tennis courts, and jogging tracks. Parking is generally free and readily available. Developing a suburban hotel usually costs less than developing a comparable center city property.

Convention Center

As the number of convention centers throughout the United States has grown, so has the number of hotels affiliated with them. Some of these hotels are physically attached to convention centers, while others are located nearby. These hotels may capture a substantial portion of the room nights generated by the convention center, but even the best convention centers are used only for about half the year. This statistic can be easily verified. Assuming that a typical, four-day convention takes two days to set up and two days to dismantle, the facilities are really only in use 50% of the time, or 180 days per year. If this is the maximum potential use, and summer and holiday periods are slow, it is easy to see why convention facilities do not generate lodging demand consistently.

Resort

Leisure travelers go to resorts to relax and have fun. Resort locations often offer special recreational and aesthetic attractions, such as water sports, winter activities, entertainment, and breathtaking scenery. Many resort locations also attract leisure-oriented meeting and group demand, but most are not frequented by commercial travelers. Immediate site access and visibility are often unimportant to leisure travelers and can even ruin the privacy and serenity many of them seek at a resort. Area access can be critical, however, particularly for remote locations. Other factors that can affect the desirability of resort locations include: climate (especially adverse periods such as hurricane season in the Caribbean), perceived safety and guest comfort, political stability (in foreign countries), and distance and travel time from the starting point to the resort.

Hotel Chains

Every year the American Hotel and Lodging Association compiles a directory of hotel-motel chains. A chain is defined as any group of three or more hotels, motels, or resorts operated under a common name or by a single owner or operator. Generally a hotel chain is equated with a recognizable name such as Marriott, Holiday Inn, or Super 8 rather than an independent hotel with no brand-name affiliation. Over the past 20 years, chain affiliation has become increasingly prevalent in the hotel industry. Whereas 35% of all hotels were chain-affiliated in 1970, the current ratio is estimated to be 80%. The rapid growth of hotel chains over the last three decades can be attributed to three factors: franchising, management contracts, and internal expansion.

Table 4.19 identifies the top 50 hotel chains as of 1998 based on the total number rooms they have. The identified hotel chains operate under recognized trade names. Trade names are used by individual lodging facilities in one of three ways.

	Table 4.19	Hotel Chains Ranked by Number of Rooms—1998	
Rank	**Brand**	**No. of Rooms**	**No. of Properties**
1	Best Western	313,247	4,037
2	Holiday Inn	284,911	1,516
3	Days Inn	162,472	1,888
4	Marriott	141,125	369
5	Comfort Inns & Suites	140,087	1,815
6	Ramada Hotels, Inns & Limiteds	131,603	1,047
7	Sheraton	121,312	372
8	Super 8	115,318	1,893
9	Hampton Inn	102,483	982
10	Radisson	93,295	399
11	Hilton Hotel	88,824	281
12	Motel 6	86,000	800
13	Holiday Inn Express	81,479	1,021
14	Quality Inns, Hotels & Suites	78,304	731
15	Hyatt Regency	71,305	163
16	Courtyard by Marriott	67,009	471
17	Mercure Hotel	60,236	562
18	Howard Johnson	50,489	497
19	Novotel	49,219	318
20	Golden Tulip	48,500	400
21	Travelodge	48,111	575
22	Westin	46,547	103
23	Econo Lodge	45,193	722
24	Doubletree	43,912	162
25	Crowne Plaza	43,393	144
26	Inter-Continental	43,392	122
27	La Quinta	39,155	302
28	Fairfield Inn by Marriott	38,973	414
29	Residence Inn by Marriott	38,753	324
30	Red Roof Inn	38,000	330
31	Renaissance	36,994	95
32	Embassy Suites	36,375	151
33	Sterling	32,550	176
34	Summit	31,500	169
35	Wyndham*	30,200	114
36	Extended Stay America	26,048	202
37	Sofitel	24,186	135
38	Clarion	22,519	142
39	Four Points	21,760	116
40	Knights Inn	18,609	233
41	Nikko	18,375	54
42	Homestead Village	18,176	136
43	Sleep Inn	17,523	228
44	Baymont Inn (Budgetel)	17,064	170
45	Country Inns & Suites by Carlson	15,664	203
46	St. Regis	14,720	59
47	Suburban Lodge	14,428	107
48	Microtel	13,325	180
49	AmeriSuites	12,467	97
50	Best Value Inn	12,005	152

* 1999 numbers were not available; 1998 figures are presented.
Source: *Hotel Business Magazine*

First, a hotel may actually be owned by the hotel chain. For example, most Red Roof Inns and Motel 6 hotels are owned by the chain; they rarely franchise or operate under management contracts. Second, a hotel may be independently owned by a person who uses the trade name under a franchise arrangement with the hotel chain. Third, a hotel may be owned by an independent owner and managed by the hotel chain, which provides management service and the trade name identification. Most hotels in the United States are operated under a franchise arrangement. Some hotels use the chain's management services but few are actually owned by the lodging chain. Since chain affiliation can directly impact a hotel's value, appraisers should be familiar with hotel franchising and management contracts.

Franchising

A *franchise* is an agreement between a hotel-motel company (usually a national or regional chain) and an independent hotel owner in which the owner pays a fee to use the name, trademarks, and various services offered by the chain. A franchise agreement creates certain benefits and costs for both the owner and the chain. The benefits and costs to a chain are discussed later in this chapter.

Benefits to Owner (Franchisee)

1. *Instant identity, recognition, and image.* Every chain has its own image, which indicates its price level (economy, standard, or luxury) and market (leisure, commercial, or convention). To have a positive effect, the franchise image must conform to the facilities offered and to the available market.

2. *Reservation or referral service.* Most franchises have some type of centralized reservation system that enables guests to reserve a room by calling a toll-free number. Most of the chains offer computerized services; others have teletype and phone connections with individual properties. A good reservation system generates approximately 15% to 30% of a property's occupancy.

3. *Chain advertising and sales.* All major franchises publish a directory that briefly describes each property and provides location and rate information. The extent of media advertising and actual sales solicitation varies from chain to chain. In most cases the business generated through the reservation system and national or regional promotions cannot support an individual hotel; sales efforts on a local level are also necessary.

4. *Procedures manual.* Chains urge all of their properties to follow standardized systems and procedures. Operating manuals are provided, and each affiliated facility is inspected periodically to ensure that policies and standards are being observed. Some chains have training schools to instruct management on basic operational techniques.

5. *Management assistance.* Most chains can provide franchises with specialized assistance in the various aspects of hotel-motel development and management

such as planning, operations, and marketing. These services generally are not covered by the normal franchise fee and are contracted for separately.

6. *Group purchasing.* Chains require that affiliated properties use certain identity items such as ashtrays, monogrammed towels, silverware, china, and uniforms. They offer group purchasing programs that reduce the cost of these items to owners.

Costs to Owner

Hotel franchise fees are the compensation paid to the franchiser for the use of the chain's name, logo, identity, image, goodwill, procedures and controls, marketing, and referral and reservation systems. Franchise fees normally include an initial fee with the franchise application, plus continuing fees paid periodically throughout the term of the agreement.

The initial fee typically takes the form of a minimum dollar amount based on a hotel's room count. For example, the initial fee may be a minimum of $45,000 plus $300 per room for each room over 150. Thus, a hotel with 125 rooms would pay $45,000 and a hotel with 200 rooms would pay $60,000. The initial fee is paid upon submission of the franchise application. This amount covers the franchiser's cost of processing the application, reviewing the site, assessing market potential, evaluating the plans or existing layout, inspecting the property during construction, and providing services during the pre-opening or conversion phases.

If the hotel is existing and the franchise represents a conversion, the initial fee structure is occasionally reduced. Some franchisers will return the initial fee if the franchise is not approved, while others will keep a portion (5% to 10%) to cover the cost of reviewing the application.

Converting the affiliation of an existing hotel may require the purchase of towels, brochures, operating supplies, and paper items imprinted with the franchiser's logos. The potential affiliate may have to undertake a property refurbishment or renovation (ranging from installing a higher grade of carpeting to enclosing a property's exterior corridors.) New franchises and converting franchises will also have to pay for signage. Although these potential costs are not quantified in our analysis, they must be considered when measuring the costs and benefits of affiliation. Requirements of this kind will vary from hotel to hotel and among various franchise organizations.

Continuing Fees

Payment of continuing franchise fees begins when the hotel assumes the new franchise affiliation; the fees are paid monthly over the term of the agreement. Continuing fees generally include a royalty fee, an advertising or marketing contribution fee, and a reservation fee. In addition, continuing fees may include a frequent traveler program and other miscellaneous fees. The continuing fees we analyzed are broken down as follows.

1. *Royalty fee.* Almost all franchisers collect a royalty fee, which represents compensation for the use of the chain's trade name, service marks and associated logos, goodwill, and other franchise services. A significant profit is generally factored into this fee.

2. *Advertising or marketing contribution fee.* Chainwide advertising and marketing consists of national or regional advertising in various types of media, the development and distribution of a chain directory, and marketing geared toward specific groups and segments. In many instances, the advertising or marketing fee goes into a fund that is administered by the franchiser on behalf of all members of the chain. These dollars must be used to promote the chain and normally do not represent a source of profit to the franchiser.

3. *Reservation fee.* If the franchise chain has a reservation system, the reservation fee supports the cost of operating and paying for the central office, telephones, computers, and reservation personnel. The reservation fee is designed to cover the cost of the reservation system and (like advertising and marketing fees) generally provides little profit to the franchiser.

4. *Frequent traveler program.* Some franchisers maintain incentive programs that reward guests for frequent stays; these programs are designed to encourage loyalty to the chain. The cost of administrating the program is financed by a frequent traveler assessment.

5. *Other miscellaneous fees.* Some of these fees, which include fees payable to the franchiser for additional systems or procedures such as required training programs, travel agent commissions and global distribution system (GDS) fees, are often minimal and unprofitable. Other miscellaneous fees are associated with the costs of any computer hardware and software that a franchise requires. Technology is becoming more prevalent and franchisers are requiring more in the way of computer systems; hence, we thought it was important to reflect these potential costs.

Sometimes the franchiser offers additional services for a fee. These services may include any of the following: consulting, purchasing assistance, computer equipment or satellite communication equipment rental, optional training programs, on-site opening assistance, or additional advertising services. The fees for these services are typically not qualified in the disclosure documents. Our analysis considers only those costs that are mandatory and quantified by the franchiser.

Calculation of Continuing Franchise Fees

Assessing continuing franchise fees is based on several formulas. In general, royalty fees are calculated on a percentage of rooms revenue. Typically, the royalties range from 2.0% to 6.5%. Advertising, marketing, and training fees are usually calculated as a percentage of rooms revenue, and typically range from 1.0%

to 3.75%; however, the formula for calculating these fees may use a dollar amount per available room, per month.

Reservation fees may also be based on a percentage of rooms revenue (0.8% to 2.5%) or dollar amount per available room, per month ($3.00 to $8.65). In some cases, the reservation fee is based on an amount for each reservation that is sent to the property through the central reservation system ($1.00 to $11.00). Some franchisers use a combination of two or all three of these methods to calculate reservation fees.

Frequent traveler program assessments are typically based on a percentage of total or rooms-only revenues (0.3% to 5%) generated by a program member staying at a hotel, or a fixed dollar amount ($1.25 to $15.00) for each room occupied by a program member. Many programs also require hotels to contribute a one-time participation fee of approximately $10.00 per guestroom, while others use a combination of all three methods. In determining the frequent traveler program fees we have not considered any costs associated with the granting of frequent flyer miles.

For the most part, these various fee formulas are applied individually, but in some cases, franchisers combine a number of formulas (e.g., a marketing fee that might be the greater of $0.50 per available room per day or 2.0% of rooms revenue.) Many also have first-month contingency fees in lieu of recorded revenues (e.g., a royalty fee of $24.00 per room for the first month and then 5% of gross revenues in the following months.)

Each fee structure offers advantages and disadvantages for the individual property. A fee based entirely on a percentage of rooms revenue is favorable for hotels that bring in significant income from food and beverage sales. Fees based on an amount per available room are fixed and tend to benefit high-volume hotels and penalize properties with lower operating results. Paying a reservation fee based on the number of reservations received is equitable, as long as the reservations equate to occupied room nights and not to no-shows.

Analysis of Franchise Fees

To provide a comparison of hotel franchise fees, HVS International periodically researches hotel franchise fees from information presented in the Uniform Franchising Offering Circular (UFOC) documents prepared by the respective franchisers. Tables 4.21, 4.22, and 4.23 deal with different classes of lodging facilities (i.e., level of quality), so comparisons can be made specifically among chains within the same class. The economy chains include chains that are classified as economy chains by Smith Travel Research; the mid-rate chains include chains that are classified as mid-scale chains with and without food and beverage by Smith Travel Research; and the first-class chains include chains that are classified as upscale or upper upscale chains by Smith Travel Research. Table 4.20 summarizes the assumptions incorporated in Tables 4.21, 4.22, and 4.23.

TABLE 4.20   Assumptions Incorporated into Each Data Table

1998 Assumptions	Economy Hotel	Mid-Rate Hotel	First-Class Hotel
Room count	100 rooms	200 rooms	300 rooms
Average room rate (Year 1)	$50.00	$80.00	$110.00
Room rate growth	3% per year	3% per year	3% per year
Occupancy:			
Year 1	60%	60%	60%
Year 2	70%	70%	70%
Years 3–10	75%	75%	75%
Projection period	10 years	10 years	10 years
Total room nights	266,450	532,900	799,350
Total rooms revenue			
during 10-year period	$15,323,447	$49,035,031	$101,134,752
Total food and beverage revenue			
during 10-year period	N/A	N/A	$60,680,851
Number of reservations			
From franchiser:	15% of occupied rooms	15% of occupied rooms	15% of occupied rooms
Percent of rooms occupied			
By frequent travelers:	8% of occupied rooms	8% of occupied rooms	8% of occupied rooms
Percent of rooms occupied			
By third-party reservation travelers:	5% of occupied rooms	5% of occupied rooms	5% of occupied rooms
Percent of rooms occupied			
By Internet reservation travelers:	2% of occupied rooms	2% of occupied rooms	2% of occupied rooms
Average length of stay	2 nights	2 nights	2 nights
Days in year	365	365	365

The HVS International model assumes that each affiliation is capable of generating the same portion of occupancy from its reservation system. In actuality, some affiliations generate more demand and some contribute less.

Tables 4.21, 4.22, and 4.23 summarize the franchise fee information relating to each franchise affiliation. The first column lists the franchiser name; the second column shows the initial fee based on the room count assumed for each class of facility; columns three through seven outline the continuing fees, which are divided into royalty, reservation, marketing, frequent traveler program, and miscellaneous costs. They were calculated on an annual basis and represent the total amount the franchisee would pay over the 10-year projection period. The eighth column illustrates the sum of the initial and continuing fees, while the final column shows the percentage relationship between the total projected franchise fees and the total projected rooms revenue.

A total of 73 franchise groups, including 27 economy, 24 mid-rate, and 22 first-class franchisers, participated in the analysis. The trend toward continued fran-

TABLE 4.21 **Summary Table of Chain Franchise Fees–Economy Hotels**

	Chain	1998 Initial Cost	Royalty Cost	Frequent Reservation Cost	Marketing Cost	Traveler Cost	1998 Total Misc. Cost	10-Year Cost	Total Cost as a % of Total Rooms Revenue
1	AmericInn	$30,000	$766,172	$0	$306,469	$74,606	$0	$1,177,247	7.7%
2	Budget Host	5,000	73,750	39,500	5,000	0	4,800	128,050	0.8
3	Baymont	35,000	766,172	153,234	306,469	2,500	139,242	1,402,618	9.2
4	Best Inns/Suites of America	35,000	731,114	191,543	191,543	0	36,600	1,185,800	7.7
5	Days Inn	36,000	996,024	352,439	0	0	127,368	1,511,831	9.9
6	EconoLodge	25,000	612,938	268,160	268,160	0	115,566	1,289,825	8.4
7	Guesthouse Inns	16,000	456,250	193,689	36,500	0	106,938	809,378	5.3
8	Homegate Suites	30,000	689,555	229,813	306,469	0	316,508	1,572,345	10.3
9	Howard Johnson Inns	36,000	612,938	383,086	306,469	31,974	134,939	1,505,406	9.8
10	Key West Inn	25,000	459,703	193,202	153,234	0	0	831,140	5.4
11	Knights Inn	16,000	689,555	229,852	229,852	0	108,600	1,273,858	8.3
12	Mainstay Suites	30,000	689,555	191,543	191,543	0	329,416	1,432,058	9.3
13	Microtel	35,000	884,349	161,999	161,999	0	36,100	1,279,447	8.3
14	Motel 6	25,000	612,938	229,852	229,852	0	133,790	1,231,431	8.0
15	Passport Inn	10,000	536,321	36,000	153,234	0	0	735,555	4.8
16	Ramada Ltd.	36,000	612,938	344,778	344,778	0	132,399	1,470,892	9.6
17	Red Carpet Inn	15,000	612,938	36,000	153,234	0	0	817,172	5.3
18	Red Roof Inn	40,000	677,501	306,469	383,086	0	32,625	1,439,681	9.4
19	Rodeway Inn	25,000	536,321	191,543	191,543	0	115,566	1,059,973	6.9
20	Scottish Inns	10,000	536,321	36,000	153,234	0	0	735,555	4.8
21	Shoney's Inns	25,000	536,321	153,234	153,234	0	107,293	975,083	6.4
22	Shoney's Suites	25,000	766,172	153,234	153,234	0	107,293	1,204,935	7.9
23	Super 8	21,000	766,172	229,852	229,852	0	26,511	1,273,387	8.3
24	Thriftlodge	36,000	689,555	324,719	324,719	0	133,364	1,508,357	9.8
25	TownePlace Suites	40,000	766,172	305,244	229,852	12,259	146,707	1,500,234	9.8
26	Travelodge	36,000	689,555	324,719	324,719	0	133,364	1,508,357	9.8
27	Villager Lodge	15,000	766,172	153,234	153,234	0	19,970	1,107,611	7.2

chise expansion and segmentation was exhibited by a 14.1% increase in the number of study participants from 1996 to 1998. The Budget Host organization led the latest analysis, with only 0.8% of its projected 10-year revenue going toward expenses related to franchise fees. Other organizations achieving low percentages included Best Western at 1.8%, Scottish Inns at 4.8%, and Candlewood at 5.1%. Study results showed that the percent of rooms revenue figures ranged from 0.8%

TABLE 4.22   Summary Table of Chain Franchise Fees—Mid-Rate Hotels

	Chain	1998 Initial Cost	Royalty Cost	Frequent Reservation Cost	Marketing Cost	Traveler Cost	1998 Total Misc. Cost	10-Year Cost	Total Cost as a % of Total Rooms Revenue
1	Best Western	$44,000	$51,290	$269,342	$500,050	$0	$0	$864,682	1.8%
2	Candlewood	80,000	2,374,605	0	0	0	58,221	2,512,826	5.1
3	Clarion	60,000	1,838,814	612,938	490,350	196,140	398,673	3,596,915	7.3
4	Club Hotel by Doubletree	90,000	1,961,401	858,113	858,113	0	300,990	4,068,617	8.3
5	Comfort Inn	60,000	2,574,339	858,113	1,029,736	196,140	397,673	5,116,001	10.4
6	Comfort Suites	60,000	2,451,752	858,113	1,029,736	196,140	397,673	4,993,414	10.2
7	Country Inn & Suites	35,000	1,905,308	219,821	1,436,011	0	154,553	3,750,693	7.6
8	Fairfield Inn	80,000	2,206,576	853,430	1,225,876	68,649	100,453	4,534,984	9.2
9	Four Points	80,000	2,451,752	679,815	490,350	198,140	471,372	4,371,429	8.9
10	Hampton Inn/ Suites	90,000	1,961,401	980,701	980,701	0	415,890	4,428,692	9.0
11	Holiday Inn	100,000	2,574,339	767,258	612,938	198,140	395,764	4,648,439	9.5
12	Holiday Inn Select	100,000	2,574,339	767,258	612,938	198,140	395,764	4,648,439	9.5
13	Holiday Inn Sunspree	100,000	2,574,339	889,845	735,525	198,140	395,764	4,893,614	10.0
14	Holiday Inn Express	100,000	2,451,752	889,845	735,525	55,290	395,764	4,628,177	9.4
15	Howard Johnson Hotel	71,000	1,961,401	1,225,876	980,701	63,948	346,115	4,649,040	9.5
16	Master Host Inns	30,000	2,206,576	72,000	490,350	0	0	2,798,927	5.7
17	Park Inn	51,000	2,451,752	735,525	490,350	0	339,819	4,068,447	8.3
18	Quality Inn	60,000	1,961,401	858,113	1,029,736	196,140	397,673	4,503,063	9.2
19	Quality Suites	60,000	1,961,401	612,938	1,029,736	196,140	397,673	4,257,888	8.7
20	Ramada	71,000	1,961,401	1,103,288	1,103,288	0	333,264	4,572,242	9.3
21	Sierra Suites	30,000	2,451,752	419,659	1,225,876	0	308,550	4,435,836	9.0
22	Sleep Inn	60,000	1,961,401	858,113	1,029,736	196,140	397,673	4,503,063	9.2
23	Wellesley Inn	50,000	2,206,576	735,525	980,701	0	395,314	4,368,116	8.9
24	Wingate Inns	71,000	2,206,576	980,701	980,701	309,082	371,900	4,919,959	10.0

to 10.3% in the economy category, 1.8% to 10.4% in the mid-rate category, and 7.1% to 11.4% in the first-class category. Low percentage leaders in each category were Budget Host, Best Western, and Omni, respectively. The overall range was a low of 0.8% to a high of 11.4%, with a median of 8.8%.

Some of the lower franchise fee percentages belong to chains such as Budget Host and Best Western; technically, these represent associations or referral organi-

TABLE 4.23   **Summary Table of Chain Franchise Fees–First-Class Hotels**

	Chain	1998 Initial Cost	Royalty Cost	Frequent Reservation Cost	Marketing Cost	Traveler Cost	1998 Total Misc. Cost	10-Year Cost	Total Cost as a % of Total Rooms Revenue
1	AmeriSuites	$90,000	$5,056,738	$1,517,021	$2,022,695	$0	$549,728	$9,236,182	9.1%
2	Courtyard	120,000	5,562,411	1,531,100	2,022,695	225,764	223,681	9,685,651	9.6
3	Crowne Plaza	150,000	5,056,738	1,748,501	1,625,021	407,539	689,497	9,677,296	9.6
4	Doubletree	150,000	4,045,390	1,769,858	1,769,858	0	580,821	8,315,927	8.2
5	Doubletree Guest Suites	150,000	4,045,390	1,769,858	1,769,858	0	580,821	8,315,927	8.2
6	Embassy Suites	150,000	4,045,390	1,769,858	1,769,858	0	793,821	8,528,927	8.4
7	Hawthorn Suites	120,000	5,056,738	1,264,184	1,264,184	0	50,500	7,755,606	7.7
8	Hilton Hotel	55,000	5,056,738	2,021,691	1,011,348	415,662	1,070,417	9,630,855	9.5
9	Hilton Garden Inn	55,000	5,056,738	2,021,691	1,011,348	415,662	858,492	9,418,930	9.3
10	Hilton Suites	55,000	5,056,738	2,021,691	1,011,348	415,662	1,070,417	9,630,855	9.5
11	Homewood Suites	135,000	4,045,390	2,022,695	2,022,695	0	684,821	8,910,601	8.8
12	Marriott	90,000	7,888,511	670,662	1,011,348	517,810	1,333,680	11,512,011	11.4
13	Omni	50,000	3,034,043	1,769,858	1,769,858	303,404	245,000	7,172,163	7.1
14	Radisson	50,000	4,045,390	0	4,192,228	0	639,547	8,927,166	8.8
15	Renaissance	60,000	4,897,623	574,886	1,517,021	517,810	1,398,720	8,966,060	8.9
16	Residence Inn	120,000	6,068,085	0	2,528,369	97,089	343,618	9,157,161	9.1
17	Sheraton	120,000	5,056,738	1,240,381	1,011,348	650,262	635,033	8,713,761	8.6
18	Staybridge Suites	150,000	5,056,738	1,264,184	1,264,184	404,539	699,392	8,839,038	8.7
19	Summerfield Suites	40,000	5,056,738	629,488	2,528,369	0	458,550	8,713,145	8.6
20	Westin	85,000	3,814,006	1,011,348	2,022,695	323,631	386,896	7,643,576	7.6
21	Wyndham	40,000	5,056,738	569,537	1,517,021	0	508,550	7,691,846	7.6
22	Wyndham Garden	50,000	5,056,738	569,537	1,517,021	0	508,550	7,701,846	7.6

zations rather than franchises. These groups are structured for the benefit of their member hotels, so fees are oriented more toward covering operating costs than producing large profits. Consequently, their percentages represent the actual cost of operating a franchise organization and indicate the margin of profit realized by other chains.

As shown in the tables, a Marriott affiliation is still the most expensive, and in 1998, this was the only franchiser whose royalty fees were based on a percentage of the combined rooms and food and beverage revenues. Marriott's frequent traveler award program also contributes to the above-average cost of this affiliation. However, few would dispute the success of Marriott's operating abilities or their favorable customer image and goodwill. Often, there is a direct relationship between a hotel's goodwill and potential for asset value enhancement. Thus, although affiliating with this type of franchiser may prove feasible and prudent, it will be comparatively costly.

In 1998, 30 franchisers offered frequent traveler programs that involved costs to the franchisee, up from 16 in 1996, 13 in 1994, and 7 in 1991. This represents an increase of 329% from 1991 to 1998. The increase can be attributed, in part, to franchisers dividing their franchise offerings into different property types, including suite and extended-stay hotels.

Long-Term Strategies

Tables 4.24, 4.25, and 4.26 compare the results of the past five HVS International franchise fee studies.

As mentioned earlier, the trend toward continued franchise expansion and segmentation was exhibited by a 14.1% increase in the number of 1998 study participants. In 1996, 64 franchises were included in the study, compared to 57 in 1994, 51 in 1991, and 37 in the original 1989 study. There has been a 97% net increase in study participation since 1989.

Nine economy, 13 mid-rate, and seven first-class franchises participated in all five studies. Throughout all five studies, Scottish Inns in the economy segment, Best Western in the mid-rate segment, and Omni in the first-class segment maintained the lowest overall average percent of rooms revenue at 4.0%, 1.6%, and 6.8%, respectively. Days Inn logged the five-study average high, 9.0%.

The overall franchise class average showed steady growth over the course of the five studies; however, some of the cost increase in the 1998 study can be attributed to the inclusion of costs associated with required computer equipment and systems, because these costs were not included in the previous studies. The

TABLE 4.24 Summary of 1989, 1991, 1994, 1996, and 1998 Economy Results

Chain	Total 10-Year Cost					Total Cost as a Percentage of Rooms Revenue					Five-Year Average
	1989	1991	1994	1996	1998	1989	1991	1994	1996	1998	
Best Inns/Suites of America	$245,885	$481,770	$485,644	$485,645	$1,185,800	2.1%	4.1%	4.1%	4.1%	7.7%	4.4%
Days Inn*	3,539,366	3,947,255	3,939,005	3,951,355	1,511,831	8.1	9.0	9.0	9.0	9.9	9.0
Econo Lodge	786,626	786,626	925,981	910,078	1,289,825	6.7	6.7	7.9	7.8	8.4	7.5
Microtel	437,799	319,856	319,856	966,680	1,279,447	3.7	2.7	2.7	8.2	8.3	5.1
Red Carpet Inn	444,799	451,799	628,712	640,712	817,172	3.8	3.8	5.3	5.4	5.3	4.7
Rodeway Inn	786,626	693,862	809,076	639,379	1,059,973	6.7	5.9	6.9	5.4	6.9	6.4
Scottish Inn	323,856	328,856	564,741	576,741	735,555	2.7	2.8	4.8	4.9	4.8	4.0
Super 8	727,655	845,597	845,597	969,739	1,508,357	6.2	7.2	7.2	8.2	8.3	7.4
Travelodge	781,626	882,347	1,010,040	1,047,042	1,508,357	6.6	7.5	8.6	8.9	9.8	8.3
Averages						5.2%	5.5%	6.3%	6.9%	7.7%	6.3%

* Historically, was included as a mid-rate chain

TABLE 4.25 — Summary of 1989, 1991, 1994, 1996, and 1998 Mid-Rate Results

Chain	Total 10-Year Cost					Total Cost as a Percentage of Rooms Revenue					Five-Year Average
	1989	1991	1994	1996	1998	1989	1991	1994	1996	1998	
Best Western	$414,142	$660,953	$849,618	$735,154	864,682	0.9%	1.5%	1.9%	1.7%	1.8%	1.6%
Clarion*	5,200,259	5,584,740	5,603,073	4,898,850	3,596,915	5.4	5.8	5.8	5.1	7.3	5.9
Comfort Inn**	772,622	827,827	1,058,883	1,100,895	5,116,001	6.6	7.0	9.0	9.3	10.4	8.5
Country Inn & Suites	2,775,661	3,963,511	3,871,696	3,507,750	3,750,693	6.3	9.0	8.8	8.0	7.6	7.9
Hampton Inn/ Suites	861,626	926,597	1,015,240	991,022	4,428,692	7.3	7.9	8.6	8.4	9.0	8.2
Holiday Inn	2,793,501	3,259,777	3,752,918	3,717,115	4,648,439	6.4	7.4	8.6	8.5	9.5	8.1
Howard Johnson	3,173,885	3,431,637	3,799,510	3,801,835	4,649,040	7.2	7.8	8.7	8.7	9.5	8.4
Master Host Inn**	446,799	451,799	687,683	699,683	2,798,927	3.8	3.8	5.8	5.9	5.7	5.0
Park Inn	2,219,918	1,771,934	2,645,944	2,665,876	4,068,447	5.1	4.0	6.0	6.1	8.3	5.9
Quality Inn	2,329,853	2,909,053	3,123,974	3,355,258	4,503,063	5.3	6.6	7.1	7.7	9.2	7.2
Quality Suites	2,329,853	2,909,053	3,123,974	3,355,258	4,257,888	5.3	6.6	7.1	7.7	8.7	7.1
Ramada	3,329,877	3,785,860	3,799,510	3,806,273	4,572,242	7.6	8.6	8.7	8.7	9.3	8.6
Sleep Inn**	875,622	932,305	957,481	998,591	4,503,063	7.4	7.9	8.1	8.5	9.2	8.2
Averages						5.7%	6.5%	7.2%	7.3%	8.1%	7.0%

* Historically, was included as a first-class chain
**Historically, was Included as an economy chain

TABLE 4.26 — Summary of 1989, 1991, 1994, 1996, and 1998 First-Class Results

Chain	Total 10-Year Cost					Total Cost as a Percentage of Rooms Revenue					Five-Year Average
	1989	1991	1994	1996	1998	1989	1991	1994	1996	1998	
Crowne Plaza	$6,490,163	$7,511,036	$8,542,530	$8,178,372	$9,677,296	6.8%	7.8%	8.9%	8.5%	9.6%	8.3%
Embassy Suites	7,030,298	7,309,966	7,472,068	7,357,281	8,528,927	7.3	7.6	7.8	7.7	8.4	7.8
Hawthorn Suites	6,361,763	6,362,263	6,361,763	7,322,534	7,755,606	6.6	6.6	6.6	7.6	7.7	7.0
Hilton Hotel	5,702,366	6,363,760	7,361,188	8,223,698	9,630,855	5.9	6.6	7.7	8.6	9.5	7.7
Omni	6,290,263	6,291,763	6,291,763	6,610,844	7,172,163	6.6	6.6	6.6	6.9	7.1	6.8
Radisson	7,260,334	7,829,060	8,595,937	7,806,699	8,927,166	7.6	8.2	9.0	8.1	8.8	8.3
Sheraton	5,550,356	6,811,972	7,691,514	7,703,520	8,713,761	5.8	7.1	8.0	8.0	8.6	7.5
Averages						6.7%	7.2%	7.8%	7.9%	8.5%	7.6%

economy class maintained a five-study average of 6.3%, the mid-rate class carried a 7.0% average, and the first-class group had a five-study average of 7.6%. The economy group exhibited the lowest averages in all five studies, while the first-rate group logged the highest.

Liability of Owner

In granting a franchise, a chain offers no guarantee of or financial commitment to the property's success. Should the property fail, the chain can immediately withdraw its franchise and demand that all forms of identity be removed. The owner assumes all financial liabilities.

Benefits to Chain (Franchiser)

1. *Inexpensive, low-risk expansion.* Franchising allows hotel chains to expand their operations with minimal capital and personnel investment. Increased representation improves the chain's recognition, which tends to increase occupancies. The cash flow from franchise fees and royalties appeals to publicly held companies.

2. *Allied expansion.* Several chains have developed allied businesses to support their franchises and company-owned operations. These businesses include interior designers, building contractors, furniture equipment and supply dealers, travel agencies, and tour packagers.

Costs to Chain

1. *Franchise services.* Chains must provide the services described in the franchise agreement. Maintaining the reservation system and advertising the chain are the bulk of their responsibility.

2. *Quality control.* Inspection, supervision, and enforcement of franchise procedures and standards are essential. One neglected property can ruin the reputation of an entire chain. The need for strict quality control has led some chains to abandon their franchise programs because they found it impossible to enforce operational standards.

From a valuation standpoint, a franchise is neither a requirement nor a guarantee of success. A franchise well-suited to the local market demand can provide a competitive advantage over independent properties and those with less desirable affiliations. Naturally, any competitive advantage enhances the business value of a property.

It is important to remember that franchises are not permanent and are commonly terminated when the property is sold. New owners must apply for and be granted a new franchise, which could require that an outdated hotel be brought up to current chain standards. It may cost hundreds of thousands of dollars to maintain a franchise affiliation; the appraiser must keep this in mind when determining a property's present value.

Management Contracts

A *management contract* is an agreement between a management company (operator) and a property owner (investor) whereby the operator assumes complete responsibility for managing the hotel. For this service the operator is paid a fee based on a prescribed formula. The owner has little say in operational policies, procedures, and day-to-day management, but he or she is financially responsible for the property and must replenish operating capital if necessary. A management contract differs from a lease in that under a management contract the residual income (or loss) after payment of all expenses, including the management fee, goes to the owner; in a lease arrangement the residual income (or loss) after payment of rent goes to the tenant, or operator.

A hotel management company can be classified as either a *first-tier management company* or a *second-tier management company* depending on the types of services they offer.

A first-tier management company operates lodging facilities for third parties under a management contract and provides two types of services: 1) day-to-day operational supervision and property management, and 2) national or regional customer recognition through affiliation with a chain. Marriott, Hilton Hotel, and Hyatt are examples of first-tier management companies.

A second-tier management company, which also operates lodging facilities for third parties under a management contract, provides day-to-day operational supervision and property management but offers no trade name customer recognition. Second-tier management companies often use hotel franchises for identification. Examples of second-tier management companies include MeriStar Hotels & Resorts, Lodgian, Richfield Hospitality Services, and Ocean Hospitalities.

Hotel management contracts offer both benefits and costs to the property owner (investor) and the management company.

Benefits to Investor

1. *Professional management.* Management contracts allow an inexperienced investor to participate in the benefits of hotel ownership without becoming involved in day-to-day management. Management companies offer professional talent, proven methods of operation, and relief from most of the operational burden. An owner who contracts with a first-tier management company benefits from the chain's image, reservation system, and advertising programs.

2. *Profitable affiliation.* Some chains do not franchise, so the only way an owner can benefit from a potentially profitable affiliation with such a chain is through a management contract with a first-tier management company.

3. *Borrowing power and possible operator investment.* Many lenders are more willing to make loans on hotels that are managed by reputable management companies rather than by individual operators. Occasionally a management company will pay to obtain an especially desirable contract. It may invest initial working capital, inventories, or furniture, fixtures, and equipment.

Costs to Investor

1. *Management fees.* Unlike a franchise fee, the individual investor and operator typically negotiate management fees. These fees may be influenced by projected operating results, the expected ratio of food and beverage volume to rooms

revenue, the services offered by the operator, the operator's financial investment, and the property's desirability. The fee for management contracts is structured in one of three ways: 1) a percentage of a defined gross revenue (usually 2% to 6%); 2) a percentage of a defined gross as a basic fee, plus a percentage of a defined operating income as an incentive fee (usually 1% to 4% of the gross and 5% to 10% of the net); 3) a percentage of a defined operating income (usually 10% to 25%).

From an investor's point of view, a fee structure based on a percentage of the hotel's operating profit is more desirable than one based on a percentage of gross revenue. Because the investor receives only the residual income after all expenses have been paid, a fee structure that provides an incentive to maximize revenue and minimize costs is a logical choice.

2. *Required facilities and standards.* Management companies require that the properties they operate meet certain physical specifications pertaining to size, layout, design, and decor. Operators actively participate in the planning of new hotels and the renovation of existing ones. The investor must provide sufficient funds to maintain the property properly and to replace short-lived items periodically.

Benefits to Operator

1. *Inexpensive expansion with quality control.* Like franchises, hotel chains can expand with a low capital investment and still keep quality under control with in-house management.

2. *Good profit potential.* Management contracts offer good potential for profit, especially with high-volume operations. Because the owner is responsible for all expenses, the financial risk to the operator is minimal.

Costs to Operator

Management services. In addition to providing the standard franchise services of a reservation system and chain advertising, the operator employs a staff of regional managers, supervisors, and specialists in food and beverage service, accounting, marketing, and engineering.

The quality of the management provided by a professional hotel company varies depending on the chain and the individual property. The appraiser should thoroughly evaluate management's effectiveness to determine if current operating results indicate competent supervision. The assumption of competent management is discussed later.

Choice of Management

Using either a first-tier or second-tier hotel management company has advantages and disadvantages.

Advantages of a First-Tier Management Company

• Often it costs less than using a second-tier management company and a franchise affiliation.

- Some chain affiliations are only available by management contracts (e.g., Four Seasons and Ritz-Carlton.)
- It combines the operating company and the entity that carries the name recognition, which tends to produce more unified management.
- Usually it provides a larger, more effective convention and group sales infrastructure.

Disadvantages of a First-Tier Management Company
- Sometimes it is not available for smaller properties.
- It is less likely to manage distressed properties.
- The term of contract is usually longer.
- Termination provisions often are more difficult to obtain.
- It is more difficult to negotiate an owner-oriented management contract.

Advantages of a Second-Tier Management Company
- It is easier to negotiate an owner-oriented management contract.
- A smaller management company is likely to give a property more individual attention.
- It is more likely to manage unique hotels that are small, distressed, or operating in specialized markets, secondary locations, or secondary cities.

Disadvantages of a Second-Tier Management Company
- Lenders are less likely to approve financing.
- The perceived risk of the company is higher.
- It can be more expensive when a management fee is added to a national franchise fee. (Some second-tier management companies attempt to negotiate a first-tier fee structure.)

Management Contract Provisions

Management Fees

As has historically been the case, the management fee paid to hotel companies typically consists of a two-tiered structure: a *base fee* and an *incentive fee*. The base fee is commonly defined as a percentage of gross revenues, while the incentive fee is tied to profit criteria.

Historically (in the 1970s and 1980s), the base fee ranged from 3% to 5% of gross revenues and constituted the greater part of the compensation achieved by the operator. Incentive fees were typically defined as a percentage of defined net operating income. This amount was sometimes subordinated to debt service, but often it was also subject to accruals. In virtually all cases, the revenue derived from the base fee was significantly greater than the revenue derived from the incentive fee.

Common examples from this period include typical Marriott contracts that generally provided for a base fee of 3% of gross revenues plus an incentive fee of 20% of defined net income that, if deferred, was often subject to accruals. Typical Hyatt contracts dating from this period provided for a management fee equal to the greater of 5% of gross revenues or 20% of net income. As this structure required the management company to achieve a net income level of 25% of gross revenues in order to have the incentive fee surpass the base fee, the incentive factor was somewhat limited.

Today, the emphasis has shifted from the base fee to the incentive fee. Base fees now range from 1.5% to 4% of gross revenues, and 2% to 3% is the most common range. With the higher base fees (3% and above), it is not uncommon for a portion of the base fee to be subordinated to debt service and/or some owner's priority whereby the operator receives a reduced management fee if certain objectives are not achieved.

Incentive fees are now deal-specific—not based on a standardized formula. Common structures include a percentage of gross operating profit over a defined amount (hurdle), usually related to the historic or budgeted performance of the property. Depending on the threshold, these fees range from 10% to 25% of the defined amount. Moreover, incentive fees are virtually always subordinate to debt service and, in many cases, also to an owner's priority return. These amounts may be influential in determining the hurdle for the incentive fee to be earned. The strategy behind these structures is to align the operator with the owner's position by exposing the operator to a similar level of risk as related to both the operation and the capital structure of the deal.

Termination Provisions

Termination provisions set forth the circumstances in which a management contract may be canceled by either the owner or the operator. Termination provisions may be divided into two categories: those related to hotel ownership, and those that are "for cause." While many specific terms may influence termination "for cause," the most common are related to the performance of the two parties in fulfilling their obligations under the contract.

Historically, the termination provisions in hotel management contracts were extremely limited and related to the financial health of the parties to the contract. The most common reason for termination was the bankruptcy or other financial breach by one of the parties. With respect to termination upon the sale of the property, such provisions, when included, usually addressed the operator's right to terminate the contract upon the sale of the hotel; typically, the owner had no such right. Some contracts also provided the owner with the right to terminate in the event that the operator did not perform to some standard. In some instances, the standard was defined on the basis of performance as compared to operating history or budget, or in terms of market share. However, these clauses were often poorly defined and difficult to enforce. One common cause was "failure to operate and maintain the hotel in a first-class manner," or some similar vague language, which could result in years of dispute.

In management contracts that are currently being negotiated, the termination provision is often the most crucial clause. In some cases, the owner has the right to terminate the contract upon sale of the property, with minimal notice (30 to 60 days.) This clause is particularly important to the owner in terms of enhancing the hotel's marketability. Unencumbered by an existing management contract, a hotel will be attractive to a broader universe of buyers, including hotel companies that only own properties they can also manage. In the early 1990s, many contracts (particularly those of the second-tier companies) also provided the owner the right to terminate with minimal notice, for no specific cause (i.e., without the sale of the property.) Today, these latter provisions are tempered by buy-out clauses, whereby the owner may terminate the contract on short notice but must make a payment to the management company—generally 0.5 to 3.0 times the management fee paid during the past 12 months.

Term of the Contract

The term of the contract refers to the time for which the contract will be in force. Included in this category are renewals of the initial term, which may be invoked at the request of the owner or the operator.

Given the prevalence of termination provisions, the significance of the contract's term has been somewhat undermined. Recently, some contracts were written with relatively short terms, ranging from one to five years, with no renewal provision. The majority of these were shorter (one to two years); some were actually month-to-month. This contrasts dramatically with the 10- to 30-year terms—with as many as 50 years of renewal options—that historically prevailed.

The current standard has shifted away from the extreme short term, and now ranges from three to 10 years for second-tier operators and 10 to 20 years for first-tier companies. Renewals are most commonly subject to negotiation within the year prior to the original term's expiration. These more extended terms recognize the benefit of long-term, consistent management and are often seen as a way to "reward" management companies for their performance.

Other Contract Issues

The following issues are also subject to negotiation in hotel management contracts. The ranges and standards set forth represent the terms currently employed in today's hotel management contracts.

- *Financial reporting requirements.* Monthly statements should be provided within 10 to 15 days of the end of the month. Annual budgets should be prepared for owner review and approval 60 days in advance.

- *Operator independence/owner control.* Owner should have right of approval of budget and any expenditures exceeding a defined amount ($10,000 to $20,000 depending on the size of the hotel.)

- *Owner versus operator as employer of personnel.* This issue is generally dictated by the specific circumstances of the owner, as well as the management company's structure. Institutional owners typically require all employees to be employed by the operator.

- *Allocation of home office expense.* Current standards indicate a wide range of fees charged under this heading. These charges typically include reservation fees, central marketing expenses, charges for frequent guest programs, and possibly some accounting or computer use fees. Reservation fees are most often charged on a dollar-per-reservation transaction, which can include both the making of and the canceling of a reservation. These charges range from $4.00 to $6.00 per reservation. Central marketing fees typically range from 2% to 3% of revenue, and may be supplemented by the cost of participation in select (voluntary) marketing programs. The cost of frequent guest programs varies dramatically depending on the program's nature and cannot be standardized. Similarly, the accounting and computer use fees vary from chain to chain; the latter are often minimal and depend on the sophistication of the management company's MIS systems.

- *Reserve for replacement.* This is one area where owners and operators are increasingly in agreement as they recognize the need for and importance of keeping the asset in marketable condition. Although most contracts now provide a reserve for replacement equal to a minimum of 3% of gross revenues, appraisers have also seen 4% and 5% reserves with increasing frequency.

- *Capital contributions by the operator.* In today's highly competitive market for management contracts, a number of operators now assume an actual ownership position in a hotel. Thus, capital contributions may be seen as crucial to the successful attainment of a management contract.

- *Restrictive covenants concerning other hotels and contracts.* This issue is most important in the case of first-tier management companies, and generally depends on the likelihood that multiple hotels with the same brand will be located in a given market area. Restrictive covenants are still used, but the specific scope of the restriction is subject to negotiation based on market circumstances and the brand's strength.

Internal Expansion

Some of the growth hotel chains experienced between 1970 and 2000 can be attributed to internal expansion. The availability of capital allowed many chains to construct new facilities and purchase existing properties. It is not uncommon for a hotel chain to purchase hotels that are already operating under its franchise.

Future of Chains

Hotel-motel chains should continue to dominate the supply of transient accommodations; in fact, their market share is expected to increase. After economic recession in the early 1990s, a new wave of construction began to take shape in 1995 and has continued through 1999. Nearly all new hotel construction involves chain-affiliated projects, and a number of new brands have been introduced, most notably in the increasingly segmented extended-stay sector.

Independent Hotels and Motels

The number of nonaffiliated hotels and motels has been declining rapidly. Most of these properties are small "mom-and-pop" motels constructed during the 1950s and 1960s that are now on the brink of functional and external obsolescence due to the proliferation of larger, more modern chain operations. New budget chains have hurt independent lodging facilities deeply. With the exception of a few isolated market areas where independent hotels continue to dominate (e.g., Cape Cod, New Orleans' French Quarter), the national lodging market is dominated by chain-affiliated hotels.

Most independent hostelries lack a solid identity, and as a result, travelers pass them by, opting instead for a known product that offers services, accommodations, and rates within an expected range. An independent can, however, create its own identity with a massive advertising campaign, a highly visible and convenient location, a large clientele, or superior facilities and services.

When valuing an independent hotel or motel, the appraiser should know the risk factors involved. Unless circumstances clearly indicate that the independent can overcome the competitive disadvantages, the market will usually reflect either a lower stabilized net income or a higher capitalization rate for an independent hotel property.

Micro Supply

Another term for the micro supply of hotels and motels is *competition*. The previous section described how to classify lodging accommodations by the type of facilities offered (e.g., commercial, convention, resort, suite, extended-stay), the class (e.g., luxury, first-class, mid-rate, economy) and the location (e.g., highway, downtown, airport, resort.) Compiling this information on all the hotels within the local market area allows an appraiser to identify the primary and secondary competition and evaluate the relative competitiveness of each property. These tasks are fundamental to the build-up approach based on the analysis of lodging activity.

The appraiser's next step is to determine the future guest room supply considering both the addition of new properties into the market and the removal of existing rooms. From this information the total room nights available can be projected. The accommodatable latent demand and the total usable latent demand are then calculated to project annual area-wide occupancy.

The last step in the market analysis phase of the appraisal is to evaluate the relative competitiveness of all hotels within the market area. This evaluation will form a basis for projecting the future market share of the subject property. Once the market share has been determined, the number of room nights captured and the resulting projected occupancy can be calculated.

Total Guestroom Supply

The total guestroom supply consists of the existing area hotels (primary and secondary competition), which were previously identified in the build-up approach based on an analysis of lodging activity, plus any facilities under construction and proposed projects likely to be completed. Information on the room counts of existing hotels and those under construction is fairly simple to obtain.

Most proposed hotels are never developed, so it is sometimes difficult to pinpoint projects that could feasibly be completed. Local building departments, development agencies, chambers of commerce, hotel associations, newspapers, American Hotel and Lodging Association development reports, developers, hotel managers, real estate brokers, lenders, and other appraisers all provide useful information about proposed hotels. In addition, construction industry consultant F.W. Dodge can be commissioned to produce standard and customized reports detailing hotel developments in a particular area. The company may be reached at 1-800-FWDODGE, or online at www.fwdodge.com.

Determining whether or not the project will ultimately be developed is key to evaluating a proposed hotel. The following list of criteria can help answer this question:

- Does the developer have all necessary zoning approvals, building permits and licenses? These approvals must be obtained before construction can begin. A project planned for a jurisdiction with restrictive development policies has less of a chance of reaching the development stage.

- Is the project financing in place? The entire financing package, including both debt and equity capital, must be fully committed and implemented before a proposed hotel is considered definite. Hotel financing has always been difficult to secure and most of the projects that are discontinued during the development process fail because they lack some form of financing.

- Does the project have a franchise and/or management company commitment (contractually obligated)? Sophisticated lenders generally require a franchise affiliation and an experienced operator before agreeing to finance a project. In markets where appropriate identification is unavailable, the development probability is reduced.

- Does the developer have a history of successful hotel projects? Most first-time developers fail to complete their contemplated hotel projects, and lenders are often reluctant to finance inexperienced hotel developers.

- What is the current supply and demand situation in the local hotel market? If the lodging market is overbuilt or suffering from decreased demand, proposed hotel projects are generally reconsidered and either postponed or terminated. An appraiser should investigate the competitive environment several years into the future to determine the probable impact of definite additions to supply over the projection period. Should the anticipated area-wide occupancy drop below an acceptable level, it becomes more likely that some of the proposed hotel projects will be withdrawn.

- What is the hotel financing market's current condition? Over the past 40 years, the availability of hotel financing has followed a cyclical trend. Since few hotel projects are developed without some form of financing, a downward trend in the availability of debt and/or equity money will usually curtail many proposed projects.

Using these criteria the appraiser evaluates each proposed hotel within the market area and determines whether the project should be considered a definite addition to the future lodging supply or disregarded as unlikely to be built. A third alternative would be to assign a probability factor to the project based on its chance of being developed. Using the criteria set forth above, the project can be considered a future addition to the competitive supply, but its room count would be weighted to reflect its development probability. For example, assume that a 200-room hotel is planned for a site within a given market area. Based on the preceding development criteria and discussions with the building department and developer, the appraiser estimates that there is a 50% chance that this project will be built. When projecting the competitive supply, the appraiser would include this project but apply a 50% probability factor and consider it a 100-room hotel rather than a 200-room hotel.

The total guestroom supply is estimated for each projection year by totaling the existing supply of hotel rooms. Actual room counts are used for those hotels that are considered primary competition, and appropriately weighted room counts are used for properties considered secondarily competitive. To this existing supply are added any new rooms currently under construction and rooms in proposed hotels that are likely to be completed. If a hotel that is under construction or proposed is expected to open at some point during one of the projection years, its room count is weighted for that year based on the ratio of 12 minus the month opened divided by 12. If a hotel will be removed from the market during the projection period, its room count is deducted after it is appropriately weighted for the number of rooms available.

The total room nights available is quantified by multiplying the total guestroom supply for each projection year by 365.

Total Accommodatable Latent Demand

If the appraiser projects any type of latent demand, a calculation should be made to determine what portion of the latent demand can be accommodated by the new additions to the guestroom supply. Accommodatable latent demand is calculated for each projection year by multiplying the number of new hotel rooms that have opened since the base year by 365. This calculation indicates the number of new rooms available per year, which is then multiplied by the estimated area-wide occupancy for that year. The portion of the latent demand that cannot be accommodated by the new rooms entering the market is known as the *unaccommodatable latent demand* and is calculated as follows:

Latent demand − accommodatable latent demand = unaccommodatable latent demand

Since the supply of hotel rooms is insufficient to accommodate the unaccommodatable latent demand, the unaccommodatable latent demand must be deducted from the previously calculated total demand to produce an accurate estimate of occupancy and total usable demand. The unaccommodatable latent demand is allocated to each market segment based on the percentage relationship between each segment's latent demand and the market's total latent demand.

Total Usable Latent Demand

The total usable latent demand for any given projection year is either the total latent demand or the total accommodatable latent demand, whichever is less.

The following case study illustrates quantification of the area's total guestroom supply, the total room nights available, the area occupancy, the accommodatable latent demand, and the total usable latent demand.

CASE STUDY

Total Guestroom Supply

In addition to the 250-room subject Sheraton Hotel, which is expected to open on January 1st of the third projection year, a 140-room Best Western Hotel is scheduled to open on October 1st of the first projection year, and a 200-room Marriott Suites is scheduled to open on January 1st of the second projection year. Financing for both of these projects has been secured, and the likelihood of their completion appears to be high. In addition, each of these hotels is expected to enter the market at 100% competitiveness.

Rumors have spread that Hyatt is interested in developing a 300-room convention hotel within the subject market. A site has not been selected and suitable zoning would be difficult to obtain as a result of a local water moratorium. At this preliminary stage, the development is highly speculative; even if a site and approvals could be obtained, this property would probably not enter the market for six to eight years. For these reasons, a new Hyatt is not included in this supply analysis. Table 4.27 shows the projected guestroom supply for the market area.

TABLE 4.27 Projection of Market Supply									
					Projection Year				
Hotel	**Base Year**	**Year 1**	**Year 2**	**Year 3**	**Year 4**	**Year 5**	**Year 6**	**Year 7**	**Year 8**
Existing supply (HARC)	1,962	1,962	1,962	1,962	1,962	1,962	1,962	1,962	1,962
Proposed Sheraton	–	–	–	250	250	250	250	250	250
Marriott Suites	–	–	200	200	200	200	200	200	200
Best Western	–	35	140	140	140	140	140	140	140
Change in HARC	–	62	62	62	62	62	62	62	62
Total	1,962	2,059	2,364	2,614	2,614	2,614	2,614	2,614	2,614
Total room nights available	716,130	751,535	862,860	954,110	954,110	954,110	954,110	954,110	954,110

Total Rooms Available

During the base year, the total existing supply (HARC) equated to 1,962 rooms. Along with accounting for the new hotels, our analysis reflects the impact of the Courtyard by Marriott's partial year of operation in the base year. This 124-room hotel opened on July 1st of the base year, thus, its room count for the base year was pro-rated to 62. The remaining 62 rooms must be factored into the analysis by the first projection year. In addition, only 35 of the Best Western's 140 rooms are allocated to the first projection year, reflecting that hotel's projected opening on October 1st. Pro-rating the 140 rooms to account for three months of operation (140 × 25%) render the Year 1 allocation of 35 rooms. In the second projection year, the Best Western is open for the full year, which effectively adds another 105 rooms to the market.

Once the total number of rooms has been quantified, this figure may be multiplied by 365 in order to generate the market's total room nights available per year.

Unadjusted and Adjusted Market-wide Occupancy

Before the market-wide occupancy can be properly calculated, the accommodatable latent demand and the total usable latent demand must be determined. Table 4.28 begins by presenting an unadjusted forecast of market-wide occupancy, using the room night demand levels developed in the previous chapter, and the room night supply levels identified above. As

| TABLE 4.28 | Unadjusted and Adjusted Market-wide Occupancy Forecast |

Hotel	Base Year	Year 1	Year 2	Year 3	Year 4	Year 5	Year 6	Year 7	Year 8
				Projection Year					
Total room night demand	549,790	570,069	588,426	607,182	629,378	652,028	669,144	686,739	704,828
Total room nights available	716,130	751,535	862,860	954,110	954,110	954,110	954,110	954,110	954,110
Unadjusted market-wide occupancy rate	76.8%	75.9%	68.2%	63.6%	66.0%	68.3%	70.1%	72.0%	73.9%
New rooms	0	97	402	652	652	652	652	652	652
New room nights available	0	35,405	146,730	237,980	237,980	237,980	237,980	237,980	237,980
Accommodatable room nights	0	26,856	100,062	151,447	156,983	162,633	166,902	171,291	175,803
Total latent demand	32,928	34,297	35,505	39,509	46,542	53,605	54,699	55,825	56,983
Unaccommodatable demand	(32,928)	(7,441)	0	0	0	0	0	0	0
Usable latent demand	0	26,856	35,505	39,509	46,542	53,605	54,699	55,825	56,983
Allocation Ratio									
Commercial	73.4%	74.0%	74.4%	68.8%	60.2%	53.8%	54.3%	54.8%	55.3%
Meeting & group	17.5%	17.2%	17.0%	23.3%	33.0%	40.2%	39.7%	39.2%	38.8%
Leisure	9.0%	8.8%	8.6%	7.9%	6.8%	6.0%	6.0%	5.9%	5.9%
Unaccommodated Demand by Segment									
Commercial	(24,184)	(5,509)	0	0	0	0	0	0	0
Meeting & group	(5,767)	(1,276)	0	0	0	0	0	0	0
Leisure	(2,977)	(656)	0	0	0	0	0	0	0
Total	(32,928)	(7,441)	0	0	0	0	0	0	0
Adjusted Market Demand by Segment									
Commercial	302,298	337,297	356,519	367,214	378,230	389,577	401,265	413,303	425,702
Meeting & group	115,338	122,251	126,615	133,097	142,674	152,350	156,127	160,008	163,996
Leisure	99,226	103,080	105,292	106,871	108,474	110,101	111,752	113,428	115,130
Total	516,862	562,628	588,426	607,182	629,378	652,028	669,144	686,739	704,828
Adjusted market-wide occupancy rate	72.2%	74.9%	68.2%	63.6%	66.0%	68.3%	70.1%	72.0%	73.9%

indicated, an unadjusted market-wide occupancy rate of 76.8% is calculated for the base year, followed by 75.9% in the first projection year.

Since the market-wide occupancy projection for each year contains latent demand, this occupancy figure may be overstated because latent demand cannot be accommodated until new rooms are added to the market. Further calculations are needed to determine the actual market-wide occupancy based on total usable latent demand.

During the base year, the accommodatable latent demand is always zero. As a result, all of the latent demand is considered unaccommodatable latent demand, and the total usable latent demand is zero. Only after new inventory enters the market can latent demand begin to be realized as accommodatable demand. Table 4.28 identifies the quantity of new rooms that is scheduled to enter the subject lodging market. In the first projection year, a total of 97 new rooms will enter the market, offering a total of 35,405 room nights per year (97 rooms × 365 nights/year). This new supply component is then multiplied by the unadjusted market-wide occupancy rate (75.9%) in order to calculate the share of rooms that could logically be expected to accommodate latent demand. The result, in the first projection year, is 26,856 (35,405 × 75.9%) accommodatable room nights. In the successive years, the new inventory component is calculated on a rolling basis, as opposed to incrementally.

In order to test how usable the latent demand is, it is compared to the accommodatable room nights allocated to the new supply. In the first projection year, latent demand amounts to 34,297 room nights, exceeding the accommodatable room nights of 26,856 by 7,441 room nights. The 7,441 room nights represent unaccommodatable demand. From the second projection year forward, the new inventory features far more capacity than the available latent demand does. As such, unaccommodatable demand drops to zero for the remainder of the projection period.

Once the overall unaccommodatable demand figures have been quantified for the base year and each projection year, this total must be allocated to each specific demand segment. The bottom half of Table 4.28 is devoted to this methodology. The allocation ratio is figured by calculating the share of latent demand generated by each segment for each year. Table 4.29 identifies this process. Based on the calculated allocation ratios, the amount of base year unaccommodatable demand is estimated as follows: 24,184 room nights in the commercial segment; 5,767 room nights in the meeting and group segment; and 2,977 room nights in the leisure segment. Table 4.30 identifies these calculations, while Table 4.31 illustrates the calculation of the adjusted room night demand levels, by segment, for the base year. After adjustment, the base year market-wide occupancy rate equates to 72.2%, as illustrated in Table 4.28. Tables 4.32 and 4.33 set forth the calculations associated with the adjustment of the Year 1 projections. Table 4.28 shows that, after adjustment, the Year 1 market-wide occupancy rate equates to 74.9%.

TABLE 4.29   Calculation of Allocation Ratios for Unaccommodatable Demand

Hotel	Base Year	Projection Year							
		Year 1	Year 2	Year 3	Year 4	Year 5	Year 6	Year 7	Year 8
Unaccommodated Demand									
Commercial	24,184	25,393	26,409	27,201	28,017	28,858	29,724	30,616	31,534
Meeting & group	5,767	5,882	6,029	6,195	6,365	6,540	6,720	6,905	7,095
Leisure	2,977	3,022	3,067	3,113	3,160	3,207	3,255	3,304	3,354
Total	32,928	34,297	35,505	36,509	37,542	38,605	39,699	40,825	41,983
Induced Demand									
Commercial	0	0	0	0	0	0	0	0	0
Meeting & group	0	0	0	3,000	9,000	15,000	15,000	15,000	15,000
Leisure	0	0	0	0	0	0	0	0	0
Total	0	0	0	3,000	9,000	15,000	15,000	15,000	15,000
Total Latent Demand									
Commercial	24,184	25,393	26,409	27,201	28,017	28,858	29,724	30,616	31,534
Meeting & group	5,767	5,882	6,029	9,195	15,365	21,540	21,720	21,905	22,095
Leisure	2,977	3,022	3,067	3,113	3,160	3,207	3,255	3,304	3,354
Total	32,928	34,297	35,505	39,509	46,542	53,605	54,699	55,825	56,983
Percentage of Total									
Commercial	73.4%	74.0%	74.4%	68.8%	60.2%	53.8%	54.3%	54.8%	55.3%
Meeting & group	17.5%	17.2%	17.0%	23.3%	33.0%	40.2%	39.7%	39.2%	38.8%
Leisure	9.0%	8.8%	8.6%	7.9%	6.8%	6.0%	6.0%	5.9%	5.9%
Total	99.9%	100.0%	100.0%	100.0%	100.0%	100.0%	100.0%	99.9%	100.0%

TABLE 4.30   Base Year Unaccommodatable Demand, by Segment

Market Segment	Unaccommodatable Latent Demand		Percent of Total		Allocation to Each Segment
Commercial	32,928	×	73.4%	=	24,184
Meeting & group	32,928	×	17.5%	=	5,767
Leisure	32,928	×	9.0%	=	2,977
Total			99.9%		32,928

TABLE 4.31   Base Year Adjusted Room Night Demand, by Segment

Market Segment	Unadjusted Room Night Demand		Unaccommodatable Latent Demand		Adjusted Room Night Demand
Commercial	326,482	−	24,184	=	302,298
Meeting & group	121,105	−	5,767	=	115,338
Leisure	102,203	−	2,977	=	99,226
Total	549,790		32,928		516,862

TABLE 4.32 Year 1 Unaccommodatable Demand, by Segment

Market Segment	Unaccommodatable Latent Demand		Percent of Total		Allocation to Each Segment
Commercial	7,441	×	74.0%	=	5,509
Meeting & group	7,441	×	17.2%	=	1,276
Leisure	7,441	×	8.8%	=	656
Total			100.0%		7,441

TABLE 4.33 Year 1 Adjusted Room Night Demand, by Segment

Market Segment	Unadjusted Room Night Demand		Unaccommodatable Latent Demand		Adjusted Room Night Demand
Commercial	342,806	−	5,509	=	337,297
Meeting & group	123,527	−	1,276	=	122,251
Leisure	103,736	−	656	=	103,080
Total	570,069		7,441		562,628

The projected market-wide occupancy provides an indication of the future health of the local lodging market and a rough estimate of occupancy for any proposed lodging facility.

When projected area-wide occupancies are anticipated to fall below 55% to 60%, the normal breakeven point for hotels, the health of the local lodging market could be jeopardized. In these situations the average hotel within a market is unable to generate sufficient cash flow to meet debt service, so competition often intensifies and hotels reduce their rates to hold onto their market share. If the market does not recover within a short time, owners run out of loss reserves and hotels are taken back by lending institutions. These situations can sometimes be avoided by carefully considering the economic impact on both existing lodging facilities and any proposed hotels before recommending that a new hotel be developed in a seriously overbuilt market.

A rough estimate of occupancy can be developed for a proposed hotel using the following rules of thumb:

- A new hotel entering the market should achieve an occupancy rate in Year 1 that is 5% to 15% below the market-wide occupancy level.

- In its second year of operation a new hotel should achieve an occupancy rate that is approximately equal to the market-wide level.

- In Year 3 a new hotel should achieve an occupancy rate approximately 5% to 15% higher than the market-wide level.

As with all general rules, there are many exceptions, but this procedure provides a basis for a quick-go or no-go decision before proceeding to the next step in the analysis.

Market-wide Occupancy

The market-wide occupancy for the base year and each of the projection years is set forth in Table 4.34.

TABLE 4.34 **Market-wide Occupancy**

Year	Market-wide Occupancy Rate
Base	72.2%
1	74.9
2	68.2
3	63.6
4	66.0
5	68.3
6	70.1
7	72.0
8	73.9

Market-wide occupancy levels are expected to decline significantly beginning in the second projection year as the new wave of inventory enters the market and absorbs all of the latent demand. Market-wide occupancy is expected to reach a low of 63.6% in Year 3, when the proposed Sheraton is slated to open. Thereafter, as supply levels stabilize and demand continues to grow, market-wide occupancy levels are expected to improve and return to levels higher than 70% by the sixth projection year.

Allocate Area Demand to All Competitive Hotels

Once the relationship between supply and demand has been quantified with the estimate of market-wide occupancy, all of the competitive hotels are evaluated to quantify their relative competitiveness. Evaluating each hotel's competitive characteristics helps the appraiser fit any new properties into the market and calculate how much of the room night demand each hotel is likely to attract.

The percentage of the market captured by an individual lodging facility is called its *market share;* the market shares of all competing properties, including the subject, should total 100% for each market segment.

The allocation of the area's total room night demand among the lodging facilities in the area can be accomplished through analyzing customer preference items or penetration factors. Just as the two build-up approaches for quantifying an area's demand analyze the actual generators of transient visitation and the demand indicated by all lodging activity, the two approaches for allocating the total demand to individual properties concentrate on the nature of the visitation and the characteristics of the lodging activity. Due to the similarities in these methodologies, demand allocation based on an analysis of customer preference items is generally used in conjunction with the build-up approach based on an analysis of demand generators, while demand allocation based on an analysis of penetration factors is usually applied in conjunction with the build-up approach based on an analysis of lodging activity.

Demand Allocation Based on an Analysis of Customer Preference Items

Demand allocation based on an analysis of customer preference items generally begins after the build-up approach based on an analysis of demand generators has been completed. Once the final market area is defined and the sources of transient visitation are identified, surveyed, and quantified, the procedure can be applied. First, the area's competing lodging facilities must be identified by type and class. As described previously, hotels and motels can be categorized by type (commercial, convention, resort, etc.) and each type can be further divided into classes (luxury, standard, economy). Interviews with area hotel managers and a review of published room rate information can facilitate categorization.

Second is to allocate the demand that each source of visitation has generated among the subject property and the other area hotels. The allocation should be based on the demand's characteristics and on the supply's relative competitiveness. This allocation is based on customer preference items.

Choosing a hotel or motel is actually a complex procedure. Several customer preference items influence the selection of a particular lodging facility. Hotel and motel patrons can be grouped into three categories based on the primary purpose of their trips.

1. Commercial—business travel, either alone or in groups of fewer than five.

2. Convention—gathering for groups, meetings, lectures, seminars, or trade shows.

3. Leisure—recreation, sightseeing, or visiting friends and relatives.

A further breakdown of each group reveals customers' reactions to room rates; economy accommodations will appeal to highly rate-conscious travelers; standard rates draw moderately rate-conscious customers; and individuals indifferent to cost will probably choose luxury lodgings.

Combining the three customer categories with the three rate reactions produces nine types of guests (e.g., commercial-economy rate, convention-standard rate, leisure-luxury rate.) Each customer preference item represents a specific characteristic guests consider in choosing one hotel over another. Six of the most prominent customer preference items are shown in Table 4.35.

Ranking the six customer preference items in order of importance establishes a basis for predicting how guests will choose among several lodging facilities in a particular market area. Table 4.36 ranks the preference items listed above.

TABLE 4.35 **Customer Preferences and Considerations**

Item	Consideration
Price	Economic
Travel distance	Time, convenience
Quality of facilities	Comfort, status, atmosphere
Amenities	Comfort, status, recreation, convenience, atmosphere
Management	Comfort, atmosphere
Image	Status

TABLE 4.36 **Customer Preference Items by Market Segment**

		Economy	Standard	Luxury
Commercial				
Most important	1	Price	Travel time	Image
	2	Travel time	Quality	Quality
	3	Quality	Price	Management
	4	Management	Image	Travel time
	5	Amenities	Management	Amenities
Least important	6	Image	Amenities	Price
Meeting & Group				
Most important	1	Price	Amenities	Image
	2	Amenities	Quality	Amenities
	3	Quality	Price	Quality
	4	Management	Image	Management
	5	Travel time	Management	Travel time
Least important	6	Image	Travel time	Price
Leisure				
Most important	1	Price	Amenities	Image
	2	Amenities	Quality	Amenities
	3	Quality	Price	Quality
	4	Management	Image	Management
	5	Travel time	Management	Travel time
Least important	6	Image	Travel time	Price

Source: HVS International

Hotels and Motels—Valuations and Market Studies

For example, an economy-minded commercial traveler will drive farther (more travel time) to stay at a hotel that offers favorable prices. This same traveler will probably select a property with good-quality facilities over a lower-quality hotel with more amenities. A standard-rate leisure traveler on the other hand places primary emphasis on a hotel's amenities and price, regarding travel time as less important.

A market share distribution can be constructed by carefully analyzing the preferences and characteristics of the typical transient traveler visiting the market area and matching these selection criteria with the competitive hotel-motel supply. Each competitive property should receive a portion of the overall market share; the size of the portion will depend on the property's relative competitiveness and its ability to attract a particular type of traveler. The sum of all the allocated market shares for each generator of demand should equal 100%.

The number of room nights captured by an individual property can be calculated by multiplying each generator's percentage market share allocated to the hotel by the total number of room nights quantified in the build-up approach based on an analysis of demand generators. The total of all allocated room nights from all generators of demand is divided by the property's room count (multiplied by 365) to produce the estimate of occupancy. The following example illustrates how customer preference information can be used to allocate the room nights generated by a source of visitation among the subject property and all competing lodging facilities. Table 4.36 illustrates the importance of various hotel characteristics to different market segments.

EXAMPLE

The subject property is a proposed nationally franchised, commercial motor hotel offering typical amenities at standard rates. Three competing lodging facilities lie within the market area. Competition A is a luxury-rate, nationally franchised, commercial hotel with high-quality facilities and a reputable image. Competition B is a standard-rate, nationally franchised, commercial motel with good-quality facilities. Competition C is an economy-rate, independent commercial motel with fair facilities.

A prominent national manufacturing company's home office generates transient visitation within the market area. Based on a survey of various department heads, an estimate of the firm's out-of-town visitation is developed, as shown in Table 4.37.

The property being appraised will be built approximately eight travel minutes away from this source of visitation. The other properties are also

TABLE 4.37	Estimate of Out-of-Town Visitation		
Type of Visitor	Typical Rate Preference	Estimated Total Yearly Room Nights	Facilities Currently Used
Corporate executives	Luxury	3,700	Competition A
Middle management	Standard	5,000	Competition B
Visiting sales representatives	Standard and economy	7,500	Competition B and C

nearby. Competition A is 15 minutes from the source of visitation, Competition B is 12 minutes away, and Competition C is 10 minutes away.

In allocating the room nights generated by this source of visitation, the appraiser assumes that most corporate executives will continue to travel the extra seven minutes to stay at Competition A because it offers the best image and quality. Some may use the new facility if Competition A is full or inclement weather or some other factor makes a closer location more desirable. The allocation of room nights based on customer preference items for this market segment is shown in Table 4.38.

Middle-management visitors will choose either the new property or Competition B. Because the property being appraised will be newer and four minutes closer, it may capture a sizable portion of this market. Competition B may respond by upgrading its facilities and/or lowering its rates. If differences in travel time are minimal, the quality of the facilities, price, image, and management could be deciding factors. The allocation of room nights for this market segment is shown in Table 4.39.

TABLE 4.38	Allocation of Room Nights For Corporate Executives	
Lodging Facility	Estimated Market Share	Room Nights
New property	5%	185
Competition A	94	3,478
Competition B	1	37
Competition C	0	0

TABLE 4.39	Allocation of Room Nights for Middle Management	
Lodging Facility	Estimated Market Share	Room Nights
New property	65%	3,250
Competition A	1	50
Competition B	29	1,450
Competition C	5	250

Economy-minded visiting salespeople will probably drive the extra two minutes to take advantage of the low rate offered by Competition C. Standard-rate salespeople, like the middle-management visitors, must choose between the new property and Competition B. The allocation of room nights for this market segment is shown in Table 4.40.

Table 4.41 indicates that the total demand from this particular source of visitation allocated to the appraised property is 5,685 room nights: 185 room nights for corporate executives, 3,250 for middle management, and 2,250 for visiting salespeople. If the subject has 150 guest units, the 5,685 room nights would equate to approximately 10% of occupancy.

TABLE 4.40 Allocation of Room Nights for Visiting Sales Representatives

Lodging Facility	Estimated Market Share	Room Nights
New property	30%	2,250
Competition A	1	75
Competition B	24	1,800
Competition C	45	3,375

TABLE 4.41 Total Demand to Subject from Manufacturing Company

Company Staff	Room Nights to Subject Property
Corporate executives	185
Middle management	3,250
Visiting sales representatives	2,250
Total	5,685

Quantifying the total demand generated by all sources of visitation and allocating the room nights between the subject and competing properties is accomplished using the procedure described below. The result is an estimate of occupancy, calculated as the total number of room nights allocated to the appraised property divided by the property's total available rooms per year.

$$\frac{\text{Total number of room nights}}{\text{Number of rooms} \times 365} = \text{Estimated occupancy}$$

Demand Allocation Based on an Analysis of Penetration Factors

Demand allocation based on an analysis of penetration factors is usually employed in conjunction with the build-up approach based on an analysis of lodging activity. The approach assumes that the accommodated room night demand for each competitive hotel has been determined and allocated among the appropriate market segments. To calculate new market shares for area hostelries when another lodging facility is added to the market, a rating factor known as the *penetration factor* is used.

Penetration factors show how well each property in the market area competes for a particular market segment. The penetration factor is calculated by dividing a given hotel's market share by its fair share. *Market share* represents that portion of total demand accommodated by a given property. *Fair share* represents that portion of total supply accounted for by the same property. A 100-room hotel in a 1,000-room market has a fair share of 10%. If that same hotel accommodates 12% of the market's total demand, then its penetration factor is 120% (12%/10%). In other words, this hotel attracts 120% of its fair share of the market's demand. When a new hotel enters the market, the projection of future penetration factors is somewhat complicated and requires the use of a market share adjuster.

EXAMPLE

Assume that the local market consists of three competitive lodging facilities with a total of 675 rooms. Hotel A has 300 rooms, therefore its fair share equates to 44.44% (300/675). Market research indicates that, over the past 12 months, Hotel A has operated at 80% occupancy; 50% of its total accommodated demand comes from the commercial segment of the market. The number of accommodated room nights per year in the commercial segment for Hotel A is calculated as follows:

$$300 \text{ rooms} \times 365 \text{ days} \times 0.80 \times 0.50 = 43,800 \text{ commercial room nights}$$

After doing similar calculations for the other hotels in the market, Hotels B and C, the total level of commercial demand is estimated at 83,836 room nights. As such, Hotel A's commercial segment market share equates to 52.24% (43,800/83,836). With known fair share and market share ratios, Hotel A's commercial segment penetration factor can be calculated as follows:

$$\frac{52.24\%}{44.44\%} = 118\%$$

Commercial segment penetration factors for each of the hotels in the competitive market are presented in Table 4.42.

| | | Percent | | | | | |
Hotel	Number of Rooms	Yearly Occupancy	Commercial Demand	Room Nights Per Year	Market Share	Fair Share	Penetration Factor
A	300	80%	50%	43,800	52.24%	44.44%	118%
B	250	75	30	20,531	24.49	37.04	66
C	125	95	45	19,505	23.27	18.52	126
Total	675			83,836	100.00%	100.00%	

TABLE 4.42 Penetration Factors

The penetration factors show that Hotel C is somewhat more competitive than Hotel A in the commercial segment, and that both Hotel A and Hotel C are significantly more competitive than Hotel B. As noted, Hotel A's fair share equates to 44.44%. If it were to capture its fair share of the commercial market it would receive 44.44% of the demand and have a penetration factor of 100%. Hotel C is the most competitive property for commercial demand, with a penetration factor of 126%. However, it has only 125 rooms, so it captures 23.27% of the commercial market, which is the smallest share noted among the three competitors.

Now assume that Hotel D enters the market, adding 200 rooms to the total supply. Market research and analysis of its location, amenities, management, and other competitive characteristics indicate that Hotel D will be more competitive than Hotel B for commercial demand but somewhat less competitive than Hotel A. The penetration factor for Hotel D should fall somewhere between 66% and 118%, but probably closer to 118%. It is also anticipated that Hotel D will become increasingly competitive during its first two years of operation. Therefore, based on market research and the appraiser's judgment, the penetration factor for Hotel D is estimated to be 97% in Year 1 and 105% in Year 2.

Because this new property has entered the market, the commercial demand must be reallocated among four hotels and the market shares and commercial room nights captured must be recalculated. In this process, note that penetration factors of the existing hotels are expected to remain stable, and our projections also assume that the level of demand in the market remains fixed. Table 4.43 illustrates this procedure.

The fair share of each property is multiplied by its projected penetration factor to yield the market share adjuster. Each property's market share adjuster is then divided by the total of all the market share adjusters, rendering a revised market share. The market share adjuster re-establishes the market share factors for each property, which is necessary due to the pro-

Hotel	Number of Rooms	Commercial Penetration Factor	Commercial Fair Share	Market Share Adjuster	Market Share	Room Nights Captured

TABLE 4.43   Demand, Market Share, and Capture

Hotel	Number of Rooms	Commercial Penetration Factor	Commercial Fair Share	Market Share Adjuster	Market Share	Room Nights Captured
Year 1						
A	300	118%	34.29%	40.3%	40.6%	34,022
B	250	66	28.57	18.9	19.0	15,948
C	125	126	14.29	17.9	18.1	15,150
D	200	97	22.86	22.2	22.3	18,716
Total	875		100.00%	99.3%	100.0%	83,836
Year 2						
A	300	118%	34.29%	40.3%	39.8%	33,407
B	250	66	28.57	18.9	18.7	15,659
C	125	126	14.29	17.9	17.7	14,876
D	200	105	22.86	24.0	23.7	19,893
Total	875		100.00%	101.1%	100.0%	83,836

jected opening of the new hotel. Note that Hotel A's market share declines from the historical level of 52.24% shown in Table 4.42 to 40.6% in Table 4.43. The decline is chiefly a function of the hotel's decreased fair share. When the market expanded by 200 rooms, Hotel A's fair share declined from 44.44% to 34.29%. Because the new hotel is expected to increase its penetration in the second projection year, Hotel A's market share declines further that year, falling to 39.8%.

The opening of Hotel D is not expected to increase the actual number of commercial room nights accommodated within the market area, so the current demand of 83,836 must be reallocated among the four hotels.

Key to this example is the use of a market share adjuster in the calculation of a property's market share. This unique factor allows an analyst to compare many competitive aspects of a lodging establishment regardless of the property's room count or changes in the overall supply of accommodations. The example assumes that the relative competitiveness of the original three hotels remains constant, while the new hotel becomes more competitive. This is generally experienced by established lodging facilities operating at stabilized penetration levels. If market research indicates that any of these properties is becoming more or less competitive, however, its penetration factor can be modified upward or downward, as demonstrated in the case study.

The example illustrates demand allocation based on an analysis of penetration factors for the commercial market segment. The same procedure could be used to allocate meeting and group demand, leisure demand, or any other quantifiable source of visitation within the market area. The ultimate result is a total room night estimate for the subject property, which can be converted into a projection of occupancy by dividing the total projected room nights by the number of available room nights. The results are shown in Table 4.44.

In practice, analysts generally use a combination of customer preference items and penetration factors to allocate room night demand among competitive lodging facilities. Both approaches call for judgments on a wide variety of competitive factors. Experience in hotel operations and analysis can prove invaluable in determining the most probable sequence of events.

TABLE 4.44 **Hotel D—Projected Room Nights**

	Year 1	Year 2
Commercial	18,716	19,893
Meeting & group	26,270	27,560
Leisure	9,420	10,185
Total	54,406	57,638
Available room nights:		
200 × 365	73,000	73,000
Projected occupancy	74.5	79.0

CASE STUDY

Penetration Factors

The relative competitiveness of the existing area hotels will be compared using penetration factors. The penetration factors for each hotel in the market are calculated by dividing the properties' market shares by their fair shares in each market segment. Table 4.45 summarizes the base year penetration factors for the hotels included in the market analysis.

Penetration factors must now be assigned to each new lodging facility as it enters the market. Moreover, if the relative competitiveness of any area hotel is expected to change, its penetration factors need to be adjusted. Assigning penetration factors to new properties or adjusting the factors of existing properties is largely subjective; the factors of similar hotels operating within the market can be used as a basis for these judgments.

The following things should be considered when assigning penetration factors:

TABLE 4.45	Historical Penetration Factors, by Segment			
	Penetration Factors—Base Year			
Hotel	Commercial	Meeting and Group	Leisure	Total
Embassy Suites	148.0%	24.0%	84.0%	108.1%
Hilton Hotel	68.0	224.0	52.0	99.8
Radisson Hotel	72.0	169.0	74.0	94.2
Holiday Inn	95.0	113.0	105.0	101.1
Courtyard	115.0	20.0	94.0	90.1
Ramada Inn	102.0	82.0	71.0	91.4
Island Inn	88.0	115.0	45.0	85.9
Quality Inn	92.0	48.0	225.0	108.1
Days Inn	123.0	23.0	134.0	102.5
Secondary competition	114.0	65.0	119.0	104.2

- A new hotel generally becomes increasingly competitive in its initial years of operation, as it builds toward a stabilized occupancy rate.

- Factors that could alter the penetration factors of an existing hotel include: a major renovation or addition; a change in management or franchise; a change in market orientation; and growing levels of physical or functional obsolescence.

- Hotels with particularly high penetration factors in one market segment usually have a relatively low penetration factor in another.

After reviewing the various factors that affect the relative competitiveness of all of the hotels within the market area, the following rationale was developed and used in projecting each hotel's future penetration factors.

The Embassy Suites opened four years ago and is therefore considered a relatively new product. It is commercially oriented and its competitive position in the market is strong and stable. The property is well located relative to the competition and demand generators. Its facilities are up-to-date and well maintained. Management operates the property competently, and frequent travelers are familiar with the Embassy Suites name. The market penetrations presently achieved by the Embassy Suites are expected to continue at similar levels into the future.

The Hilton Hotel was constructed 10 years ago as a convention-oriented hotel. Currently, it is the largest hotel in the market. Its extensive meeting and banquet space, along with aggressive group marketing and skilled management, makes this property the most competitive product in the meeting and group market. But with so much emphasis on meeting and group demand, the Hilton Hotel is the area's least competitive hotel in the commercial market. Essentially, most of the Hilton Hotel's commercial demand has been purposely displaced by meeting and group patronage. A recent renovation has brought this property up to first-class condition, and it should continue to be the meeting and group leader for a while more. The market penetration factors presently achieved by the Hilton Hotel are also expected to continue into the future.

The Radisson Hotel is a convention hotel that competes with the Hilton Hotel for group patronage. Constructed 14 years ago, this property completed an extensive renovation approximately 18 months ago. The upgrade enabled the Radisson to maintain its competitive position. The square footage of its meeting space is somewhat less than that of the Hilton Hotel, making the property less appealing to large groups and banquets. Like the Hilton Hotel, the Radisson focuses on group patronage, which displaces much of the commercial business that would normally use the hotel Monday through Thursday. The market penetration levels presently achieved by the Radisson are expected to continue at similar levels into the future.

The Holiday Inn is one of the area's newest hotels, having opened five years ago. Its facilities include extensive recreational amenities. Like most Holiday Inns, this property benefits from a strong reservation system that draws a mix of commercial, meeting and group, and leisure demand. The sports facilities are particularly appealing to weekend visitors who come to the property for various organized escape packages. The Holiday Inn also has quality meeting and banquet space, which attracts small groups and conferences. Like the group-oriented Radisson and Hilton Hotel, the meeting and group demand displaces some of the commercial patronage that would normally use the hotel during the week. The hotel is well maintained and operated by a competent management company. The market penetration levels presently achieved by the Holiday Inn are also expected to continue at similar levels.

The Courtyard by Marriott opened mid-way through the base year and realized strong penetration factors immediately upon opening. The hotel demonstrated particular strength in the commercial and leisure markets. Its excellent location, strong management, and connection with the Marriott brand should make the Courtyard one of the occupancy leaders in the area.

With only six months of operating history, the Courtyard has not yet achieved a stabilized level of competitiveness. Gains are expected in all three market segments. The market mix of the Courtyard is expected to be similar to that of the Embassy Suites (i.e., strong commercial, minimal meeting and convention, and good leisure.) It should undercut the Embassy Suites in room rate, capturing price-sensitive travelers, particularly in the leisure market. On the other hand, the suite concept seems to be uniformly more competitive in the commercial segment. These factors should enable the Courtyard to be more competitive in the leisure segment, somewhat more competitive in the meeting and group segment and nearly as competitive as the Embassy Suites in the commercial segment. Based on this analysis, the market penetration levels for the Courtyard by Marriott are set forth in Table 4.46.

TABLE 4.46	Penetration Factors—Courtyard by Marriott						
Segment	Base Year	Year 1	Year 2	Year 3	Year 4	Year 5	Year 6
Commercial	115.0%	125.0%	135.0%	135.0%	135.0%	135.0%	135.0%
Meeting & group	20.0	23.0	25.0	25.0	25.0	25.0	25.0
Leisure	94.0	98.0	100.0	100.0	100.0	100.0	100.0

The Ramada Inn is a 17-year-old property that suffers from some deferred maintenance and a second-rate location in an older industrial park. It has a similar market orientation as the Holiday Inn but does not capture as much meeting and group or leisure business. The neighborhood surrounding the Ramada consists of warehouses and industrial buildings, which is not conducive to either meeting or leisure demand. Ownership has renovated the property on a regular basis so its competitive position is not expected to deteriorate. The market penetration levels presently achieved by the Ramada Inn are expected to continue at similar levels into the future.

The Island Inn is the oldest hotel in the market, having been constructed 25 years ago. Frequent changes in ownership, along with indifferent management, has hindered this property's operating results over the past five years. The Island Inn was originally a Sheraton Hotel but lost its franchise four years ago. Without a national identification, reservation system, or sufficient revenue to maintain this property at an attractive level, it is likely that the Island Inn's competitive position will decline over the coming years. The market penetration levels presently achieved by the Island Inn are expected to decline in the future as well. Declines in competitiveness are anticipated in all three market segments. Based on this analysis, the market penetration levels for the Island Inn are set forth in Table 4.47.

The Quality Inn opened four years ago with immediate success. Its location next to a growing office complex and an established recreational theme park has enabled this property to capture an attractive mix of commercial and

TABLE 4.47	Penetration Factors–Island Inn						
Segment	Base Year	Year 1	Year 2	Year 3	Year 4	Year 5	Year 6
Commercial	88.0%	84.0%	82.0%	80.0%	80.0%	80.0%	80.0%
Meeting & group	115.0	102.0	93.0	85.0	85.0	85.0	85.0
Leisure	45.0	40.0	40.0	40.0	40.0	40.0	40.0

leisure patronage. Weekends and holiday periods are particularly strong for the Quality Inn, enabling it to achieve the area's highest market penetration in the leisure segment. Ownership is presently considering adding more meeting space, which currently is limited. Initial indications show, however, that the property has a good market mix and any increase in meeting and group usage would just displace commercial demand and ultimately lower the average room rate. The property is well maintained and in acceptable physical condition. Its management is competent, especially in marketing to the leisure segment. The market penetration levels presently achieved by the Quality Inn are expected to continue at similar levels into the future.

The Days Inn is a commercially oriented property that opened 12 years ago. Its convenient highway location enables this hotel to attract a sizable amount of weekend leisure demand along with a high level of commercial patronage. On the other hand, limited meeting space hinders the Days Inn's performance in the meeting and group segments, but it does attract some rate-sensitive groups. The property has been well maintained and effectively managed. It benefits from a strong reservation system and moderate prices. The market penetration levels presently achieved by the Days Inn are expected to continue at similar levels.

The composition and competitiveness of the secondary competition is not expected to change over the projection period, so the consolidated market penetration factors presently achieved by these properties should continue at the current levels.

In addition to these existing hotels, three new hotels are expected to enter the competitive set over the near term.

The proposed Sheraton Hotel is expected to open at the beginning of the third projection year. It will reportedly be designed as a convention-oriented hotel with approximately the same amount of meeting space as the Radisson Hotel. To maximize rooms revenue, the Sheraton hopes to attract both the meeting and group and commercial segments in such a way that the higher-rated commercial demand will not be displaced by lower-priced meeting and group patronage. The new facilities the Sheraton offers and its excellent location should make it competitive in the local market. Its market penetration levels in all three segments are expected to stabilize at a level somewhat above those experienced by the Radisson. Based on this analysis, the market penetration factors projected for the proposed Sheraton Hotel are set forth in Table 4.48.

TABLE 4.48 Penetration Factors–Proposed Sheraton Hotel							
Segment	Base Year	Year 1	Year 2	Year 3	Year 4	Year 5	Year 6
Commercial	–	–	–	75.0%	78.0%	80.0%	80.0%
Meeting & group	–	–	–	160.0	175.0	180.0	180.0
Leisure	–	–	–	60.0	70.0	75.0	75.0

The Marriott Suites hotel will be the second Marriott product in the marketplace. It is expected to open at the beginning of the second projection year and will cater to a more upscale traveler than the Courtyard does. Thus, it will achieve a higher average room rate. Plans call for limited meeting space similar to the Embassy Suites, but the property will have a more upscale décor. With a projected room rate somewhat higher than the Embassy Suites, the Marriott Suites should be slightly less competitive in the commercial and leisure segments as far as occupancy is concerned. Marriott's strength in marketing to meeting planners is anticipated to make this property more competitive than the Embassy Suites in the meeting and convention segment. Based on this analysis, the market penetration factors projected for the Marriott Suites hotel are set forth in Table 4.49.

TABLE 4.49 Penetration Factors–Proposed Marriott Suites							
Segment	Base Year	Year 1	Year 2	Year 3	Year 4	Year 5	Year 6
Commercial	–	–	120.0%	134.0%	140.0%	140.0%	140.0%
Meeting & group	–	–	17.0	25.0	34.0	34.0	34.0
Leisure	–	–	60.0	71.0	71.0	71.0	71.0

The Best Western Hotel is expected to open in October of the first projection year. Its facilities will be oriented toward the rate-sensitive commercial traveler and weekend leisure patronage. Meeting space will be limited, so its competitiveness in this segment is anticipated to be minimal. The Best Western has building plans that look attractive, but the property will have an inferior location near the interstate. Based on this competitive analysis, the Best Western should be slightly less competitive than the nearby Days Inn for highway-oriented leisure patrons. Its competitiveness in the commercial segment is expected to be just below that of the Quality Inn, which is also a new property with limited meeting space. The market penetration factors projected for the Best Western Hotel are set forth in Table 4.50.

Tables 4.51 through 4.53 show the penetration factors forecasted for each existing and new hotel, by market segment, over the projection period.

The penetration factors form the basis for calculating the market share of each hotel within the market. Once the market share is known, the number of room nights captured by each hotel can be projected, which then leads to an estimate of occupancy.

The process of converting the penetration factor projections into an occupancy forecast includes the following steps:

- Fair share calculations are performed to determine the fair share for each hotel in the market, over the projection period. Because the market-wide

TABLE 4.50 Penetration Factors–Proposed Best Western Hotel

Segment	Base Year	Year 1	Year 2	Year 3	Year 4	Year 5	Year 6
Commercial	–	74.0%	80.0%	87.0%	87.0%	87.0%	87.0%
Meeting & group	–	9.0	17.0	17.0	17.0	17.0	17.0
Leisure	–	111.0	121.0	131.0	131.0	131.0	131.0

TABLE 4.51 Historical and Projected Penetration Factors–Commercial Segment

Hotel	Base Year	Year 1	Year 2	Year 3	Year 4	Year 5	Year 6
Embassy Suites	148.0%	148.0%	148.0%	148.0%	148.0%	148.0%	148.0%
Hilton Hotel	68.0	68.0	68.0	68.0	68.0	68.0	68.0
Radisson Hotel	72.0	72.0	72.0	72.0	72.0	72.0	72.0
Holiday Inn	95.0	95.0	95.0	95.0	95.0	95.0	95.0
Courtyard	115.0	125.0	135.0	135.0	135.0	135.0	135.0
Ramada Inn	102.0	102.0	102.0	102.0	102.0	102.0	102.0
Island Inn	88.0	84.0	82.0	80.0	80.0	80.0	80.0
Quality Inn	92.0	92.0	92.0	92.0	92.0	92.0	92.0
Days Inn	123.0	123.0	123.0	123.0	123.0	123.0	123.0
Secondary competition	114.0	114.0	114.0	114.0	114.0	114.0	114.0
New Hotels							
Proposed Sheraton	–	–	–	75	78	80	80
Marriott Suites	–	–	120	134	140	140	140
Best Western	–	74	80	87	87	87	87

TABLE 4.52	Historical and Projected Penetration Factors—Meeting & Group Segment						
Hotel	**Base Year**	**Year 1**	**Year 2**	**Year 3**	**Year 4**	**Year 5**	**Year 6**
Embassy Suites	24.0%	24.0%	24.0%	24.0%	24.0%	24.0%	24.0%
Hilton Hotel	224.0	224.0	224.0	224.0	224.0	224.0	224.0
Radisson Hotel	169.0	169.0	169.0	169.0	169.0	169.0	169.0
Holiday Inn	113.0	113.0	113.0	113.0	113.0	113.0	113.0
Courtyard	20.0	23.0	25.0	25.0	25.0	25.0	25.0
Ramada Inn	82.0	82.0	82.0	82.0	82.0	82.0	82.0
Island Inn	115.0	102.0	93.0	85.0	85.0	85.0	85.0
Quality Inn	48.0	48.0	48.0	48.0	48.0	48.0	48.0
Days Inn	23.0	23.0	23.0	23.0	23.0	23.0	23.0
Secondary competition	65.0	65.0	65.0	65.0	65.0	65.0	65.0
New Hotels							
Proposed Sheraton	–	–	–	160	175	180	180
Marriott Suites	–	–	17	25	34	34	34
Best Western	–	9	17	17	17	17	17

TABLE 4.53	Historical and Projected Penetration Factors—Leisure Segment						
Hotel	**Base Year**	**Year 1**	**Year 2**	**Year 3**	**Year 4**	**Year 5**	**Year 6**
Embassy Suites	84.0%	84.0%	84.0%	84.0%	84.0%	84.0%	84.0%
Hilton Hotel	52.0	52.0	52.0	52.0	52.0	52.0	52.0
Radisson Hotel	74.0	74.0	74.0	74.0	74.0	74.0	74.0
Holiday Inn	105.0	105.0	105.0	105.0	105.0	105.0	105.0
Courtyard	94.0	98.0	100.0	100.0	100.0	100.0	100.0
Ramada Inn	71.0	71.0	71.0	71.0	71.0	71.0	71.0
Island Inn	45.0	40.0	40.0	40.0	40.0	40.0	40.0
Quality Inn	225.0	225.0	225.0	225.0	225.0	225.0	225.0
Days Inn	134.0	134.0	134.0	134.0	134.0	134.0	134.0
Secondary competition	119.0	119.0	119.0	119.0	119.0	119.0	119.0
New Hotels							
Proposed Sheraton	–	–	–	60	70	75	75
Marriott Suites	–	–	60	71	71	71	71
Best Western	–	111	121	131	131	131	131

inventory commonly changes yearly due to the opening of new hotels, fair share levels generally shift over the projection period.

• For each hotel, the market penetration factor is multiplied by its appropriate fair share, resulting in a factor referred to as the market share adjuster.

The market share adjuster is then divided by the total of all the market share adjusters for the area's competitive hotels. This calculation results in each property's market share percentage. These calculations are performed separately for each segment, by year.

- The segmented market share percentages are then multiplied by the total market demand for each segment. This step produces the actual room nights captured by each hotel, in each market segment.
- The room nights captured by segment are added to figure the total room night capture for each hotel.
- Each property's occupancy rate is then determined by dividing the total room nights captured by the hotel's number of available rooms per year (room count $\times$ 365).

Table 4.54 sets forth the fair share factors calculated for each of the hotels in the competitive market. Note that the sum of all the fair share factors always equates to 100.0%.

Table 4.55 demonstrates the calculation of the market share adjuster associated with the Embassy Suites, by segment, for each projection year. The penetration factor is multiplied by the fair share factor to produce the market share adjuster.

TABLE 4.54 **Historical and Projected Fair Share Factors**

Hotel	Base Year	Year 1	Year 2	Year 3	Year 4	Year 5	Year 6
Embassy Suites	10.2%	9.7%	8.5%	7.7%	7.7%	7.7%	7.7%
Hilton Hotel	14.0	13.4	11.6	10.5	10.5	10.5	10.5
Radisson Hotel	12.7	12.1	10.6	9.6	9.6	9.6	9.6
Holiday Inn	8.9	8.5	7.4	6.7	6.7	6.7	6.7
Courtyard	3.2	6.0	5.2	4.7	4.7	4.7	4.7
Ramada Inn	7.6	7.3	6.3	5.7	5.7	5.7	5.7
Island Inn	6.9	6.6	5.7	5.2	5.2	5.2	5.2
Quality Inn	8.9	8.5	7.4	6.7	6.7	6.7	6.7
Days Inn	6.1	5.8	5.1	4.6	4.6	4.6	4.6
Secondary competition	21.4	20.4	17.8	16.1	16.1	16.1	16.1
New Hotels							
Proposed Sheraton	–	–	–	9.6	9.6	9.6	9.6
Marriott Suites	–	–	8.5	7.7	7.7	7.7	7.7
Best Western	–	1.7	5.9	5.4	5.4	5.4	5.4
Total	99.9%	100.0%	100.0%	100.0%	100.0%	100.0%	100.0%

TABLE 4.55 **Market Share Adjusters–Embassy Suites**

Hotel	Year 1	Year 2	Year 3	Year 4	Year 5	Year 6
Penetration factor						
Commercial	148.0%	148.0%	148.0%	148.0%	148.0%	148.0%
Meeting & group	24.0	24.0	24.0	24.0	24.0	24.0
Leisure	84.0	84.0	84.0	84.0	84.0	84.0
Fair share factor						
Commercial	9.7%	8.5%	7.7%	7.7%	7.7%	7.7%
Meeting & group	9.7	8.5	7.7	7.7	7.7	7.7
Leisure	9.7	8.5	7.7	7.7	7.7	7.7
Market share adjuster						
Commercial	14.38%	12.52%	11.32%	11.32%	11.32%	11.32%
Meeting & group	2.33	2.03	1.84	1.84	1.84	1.84
Leisure	8.16	7.11	6.43	6.43	6.43	6.43

In Tables 4.56 through 4.58, the market share adjusters for each segment, for each competitive hotel are set forth. Note that the sum of the market share adjusters is roughly 100.

TABLE 4.56 **Market Share Adjusters–Commercial Segment**

Hotel	Year 1	Year 2	Year 3	Year 4	Year 5	Year 6
Embassy Suites	14.4%	12.5%	11.3%	11.3%	11.3%	11.3%
Hilton Hotel	9.1	7.9	7.2	7.2	7.2	7.2
Radisson Hotel	8.7	7.6	6.9	6.9	6.9	6.9
Holiday Inn	8.1	7.0	6.4	6.4	6.4	6.4
Courtyard	7.5	7.1	6.4	6.4	6.4	6.4
Ramada Inn	7.4	6.5	5.9	5.9	5.9	5.9
Island Inn	5.5	4.7	4.1	4.1	4.1	4.1
Quality Inn	7.8	6.8	6.2	6.2	6.2	6.2
Days Inn	7.2	6.2	5.6	5.6	5.6	5.6
Secondary competition	23.3	20.3	18.3	18.3	18.3	18.3
New Hotels						
Proposed Sheraton	–	–	7.2	7.5	7.7	7.7
Marriott Suites	–	10.2	10.3	10.7	10.7	10.7
Best Western	1.3	4.7	4.7	4.7	4.7	4.7
Total	100.3%	101.5%	100.5%	101.2%	101.4%	101.4%

TABLE 4.57 **Market Share Adjusters—Meeting & Group Segment**

Hotel	Year 1	Year 2	Year 3	Year 4	Year 5	Year 6
Embassy Suites	2.3%	2.0%	1.8%	1.8%	1.8%	1.8%
Hilton Hotel	29.9	26.1	23.6	23.6	23.6	23.6
Radisson Hotel	20.5	17.9	16.2	16.2	16.2	16.2
Holiday Inn	9.6	8.4	7.6	7.6	7.6	7.6
Courtyard	1.4	1.3	1.2	1.2	1.2	1.2
Ramada Inn	6.0	5.2	4.7	4.7	4.7	4.7
Island Inn	6.7	5.3	4.4	4.4	4.4	4.4
Quality Inn	4.1	3.6	3.2	3.2	3.2	3.2
Days Inn	1.3	1.2	1.1	1.1	1.1	1.1
Secondary competition	13.3	11.5	10.4	10.4	10.4	10.4
New Hotels						
Proposed Sheraton	–	–	15.3	16.7	17.2	17.2
Marriott Suites	–	1.4	1.9	2.6	2.6	2.6
Best Western	0.2	1.0	0.9	0.9	0.9	0.9
Total	95.3%	84.9%	92.3%	94.4%	94.9%	94.9%

TABLE 4.58 **Market Share Adjusters—Leisure Segment**

Hotel	Year 1	Year 2	Year 3	Year 4	Year 5	Year 6
Embassy Suites	8.2%	7.1%	6.4%	6.4%	6.4%	6.4%
Hilton Hotel	6.9	6.0	5.5	5.5	5.5	5.5
Radisson Hotel	9.0	7.8	7.1	7.1	7.1	7.1
Holiday Inn	8.9	7.8	7.0	7.0	7.0	7.0
Courtyard	5.9	5.2	4.7	4.7	4.7	4.7
Ramada Inn	5.2	4.5	4.1	4.1	4.1	4.1
Island Inn	2.6	2.3	2.1	2.1	2.1	2.1
Quality Inn	19.1	16.7	15.1	15.1	15.1	15.1
Days Inn	7.8	6.8	6.2	6.2	6.2	6.2
Secondary competition	24.3	21.1	19.1	19.1	19.1	19.1
New Hotels						
Proposed Sheraton	–	–	5.7	6.7	7.2	7.2
Marriott Suites	–	5.1	5.4	5.4	5.4	5.4
Best Western	1.9	7.2	7.0	7.0	7.0	7.0
Total	99.8%	97.6%	95.4%	96.4%	96.9%	96.9%

Table 4.59 demonstrates how the Embassy Suites' market share adjusters are converted into market share percentages. In each segment, in each year, the Embassy Suites' market share adjuster is divided by the sum of all market share adjusters.

In Tables 4.60 through 4.62, the market share percentages for each segment, for each competitive hotel are set forth. In this portion of the analysis, the sum of the market share percentages is always 100.0%.

TABLE 4.59 **Market Share Percentages—Embassy Suites**

	Year 1	Year 2	Year 3	Year 4	Year 5	Year 6
Commercial market share adjuster	14.38%	12.52%	11.32%	11.32%	11.32%	11.32%
÷ Total of all market share adjusters	100.2	101.5	100.3	101.1	101.3	101.3
= Market share	14.35	12.33	11.29	11.20	11.17	11.17
Meeting & group market share adjuster	2.33%	2.03%	1.84%	1.84%	1.84%	1.84%
÷ Total of all market share adjusters	95.3	84.9	92.2	94.4	94.9	94.9
= Market share	2.44	2.39	2.00	1.95	1.94	1.94
Leisure market share adjuster	8.16%	7.11%	6.43%	6.43%	6.43%	6.43%
÷ Total of all market share adjusters	99.8	97.6	95.4	96.4	96.8	96.8
= Market share	8.18	7.28	6.74	6.67	6.64	6.64

TABLE 4.60 **Market Share Percentages—Commercial Segment**

Hotel	Year 1	Year 2	Year 3	Year 4	Year 5	Year 6
Embassy Suites	14.34%	12.33%	11.29%	11.20%	11.18%	11.18%
Hilton Hotel	9.06	7.79	7.13	7.08	7.07	7.07
Radisson Hotel	8.72	7.50	6.86	6.81	6.80	6.80
Holiday Inn	8.05	6.93	6.34	6.29	6.28	6.28
Courtyard	7.51	6.98	6.38	6.34	6.32	6.32
Ramada Inn	7.41	6.38	5.83	5.79	5.78	5.78
Island Inn	5.49	4.61	4.12	4.09	4.08	4.08
Quality Inn	7.80	6.71	6.14	6.09	6.08	6.08
Days Inn	7.15	6.15	5.63	5.59	5.58	5.58
Secondary competition	23.2	20.0	18.3	18.1	18.1	18.1
New Hotels						
Proposed Sheraton	–	–	7.2	7.4	7.6	7.6
Marriott Suites	–	10.0	10.2	10.6	10.6	10.6
Best Western	1.3	4.7	4.6	4.6	4.6	4.6
Total	100.0%	100.0%	100.0%	100.0%	100.0%	100.0%

TABLE 4.61   Market Share Percentages–Meeting & Group Segment

Hotel	Year 1	Year 2	Year 3	Year 4	Year 5	Year 6
Embassy Suites	2.45%	2.39%	1.99%	1.95%	1.94%	1.94%
Hilton Hotel	31.41	30.70	25.55	24.97	24.84	24.84
Radisson Hotel	21.54	21.06	17.52	17.13	17.04	17.04
Holiday Inn	10.08	9.86	8.20	8.02	7.98	7.98
Courtyard	1.45	1.55	1.29	1.26	1.25	1.25
Ramada Inn	6.27	6.13	5.10	4.99	4.96	4.96
Island Inn	7.02	6.26	4.76	4.65	4.63	4.63
Quality Inn	4.28	4.19	3.48	3.41	3.39	3.39
Days Inn	1.41	1.38	1.14	1.12	1.11	1.11
Secondary competition	13.9	13.6	11.3	11.1	11.0	11.0
New Hotels						
Proposed Sheraton	–	–	16.6	17.7	18.1	18.1
Marriott Suites	–	1.7	2.1	2.8	2.7	2.7
Best Western	0.2	1.2	1.0	1.0	1.0	1.0
Total	100.0%	100.0%	100.0%	100.0%	99.9%	99.9%

TABLE 4.62   Market Share Percentages–Leisure Segment

Hotel	Year 1	Year 2	Year 3	Year 4	Year 5	Year 6
Embassy Suites	8.18%	7.28%	6.74%	6.67%	6.64%	6.64%
Hilton Hotel	6.96	6.20	5.73	5.68	5.65	5.65
Radisson Hotel	9.00	8.02	7.42	7.34	7.31	7.31
Holiday Inn	8.94	7.96	7.37	7.29	7.26	7.26
Courtyard	5.91	5.37	4.97	4.92	4.90	4.90
Ramada Inn	5.18	4.61	4.27	4.23	4.21	4.21
Island Inn	2.63	2.34	2.17	2.14	2.13	2.13
Quality Inn	19.16	17.06	15.79	15.63	15.55	15.55
Days Inn	7.82	6.97	6.45	6.38	6.35	6.35
Secondary competition	24.3	21.7	20.0	19.8	19.7	19.7
New Hotels						
Proposed Sheraton	–	–	6.0	6.9	7.4	7.4
Marriott Suites	–	5.2	5.7	5.6	5.6	5.6
Best Western	1.9	7.3	7.4	7.3	7.2	7.2
Total	100.0%	100.0%	100.0%	100.0%	100.0%	100.0%

Room Nights Captured

The projected room nights captured by any hotel can be calculated by multiplying the hotel's market share percentage by the total room night demand for the corresponding segment. This process is repeated for each market segment and the results are totaled to yield the number of room nights captured.

CASE STUDY

Room Nights Captured

Table 4.63 demonstrates how the market share percentages calculated for the Embassy Suites are converted into an estimate of room nights captured, by segment. In each year, the Embassy Suites' market share ratio is applied to segmented market-wide demand levels.

In Tables 4.64 through 4.66, the segmented room night capture levels for each of the competitive hotels are set forth. In Table 4.67, the segmented demand levels are added and presented as a total room night capture.

In the Embassy Suites case, the occupancy rate is calculated in Table 4.68. The total capture is divided by the number of room nights available per year. This table also identifies the demand segmentation and the overall penetration factor projected for the hotel. Demand segmentation calculations are based on the segmented demand forecast for the property. The overall penetration factor is calculated by dividing the overall market share by the hotel's fair share.

Table 4.69 sets forth the same set of data and conclusions as Table 4.68, although this table pertains to the projections for the proposed Sheraton Hotel. As indicated, the Sheraton is expected to realize an overall penetration factor of approximately 94% in its initial year of operation, improving to approximately 105% in its third year of operation. These penetration factors reflect a normal occupancy build-up for new properties such as the proposed Sheraton.

Demand capture levels for each competitive hotel have been divided by their respective supply levels, rendering a forecast of occupancy over the projection period. The results are set forth in Table 4.70.

TABLE 4.63   Room Nights Captured–Embassy Suites

	Year 1	Year 2	Year 3	Year 4	Year 5	Year 6
Commercial						
Market-wide demand	337,297	356,519	367,214	378,230	389,577	401,265
Market share	14.34%	12.33%	11.29%	11.20%	11.18%	11.18%
Room nights captured	48,373	43,975	41,450	42,378	43,567	44,874
Meeting & Group						
Market-wide demand	122,251	126,615	133,097	142,674	152,350	156,127
Market share	2.45%	2.39%	1.99%	1.95%	1.94%	1.94%
Room nights captured	2,992	3,029	2,649	2,776	2,949	3,023
Leisure						
Market-wide demand	103,080	105,292	106,871	108,474	110,101	111,752
Market share	8.18%	7.28%	6.74%	6.67%	6.64%	6.64%
Room nights captured	8,427	7,664	7,199	7,234	7,307	7,416
Total capture	59,792	54,669	51,298	52,388	53,823	55,313

TABLE 4.64   Room Nights Captured–Commercial Segment

Hotel	Year 1	Year 2	Year 3	Year 4	Year 5	Year 6
Embassy Suites	48,373	43,975	41,450	42,378	43,567	44,874
Hilton Hotel	30,560	27,782	26,186	26,773	27,524	28,349
Radisson Hotel	29,416	26,742	25,206	25,770	26,493	27,288
Holiday Inn	27,169	24,699	23,280	23,802	24,470	25,204
Courtyard	25,331	24,870	23,441	23,966	24,639	25,378
Ramada Inn	25,004	22,730	21,425	21,905	22,519	23,195
Island Inn	18,532	16,446	15,124	15,462	15,896	16,373
Quality Inn	26,311	23,919	22,545	23,050	23,697	24,408
Days Inn	24,121	21,928	20,669	21,132	21,725	22,376
Secondary competition	78,247	71,133	67,048	68,549	70,472	72,587
New Hotels						
Proposed Sheraton	–	–	26,256	27,918	29,437	30,320
Marriott Suites	–	35,656	37,529	40,087	41,212	42,448
Best Western	4,233	16,639	17,056	17,438	17,927	18,465
Total	337,297	356,519	367,215	378,230	389,578	401,265

TABLE 4.65 Room Nights Captured—Meeting & Group Segment

Hotel	Year 1	Year 2	Year 3	Year 4	Year 5	Year 6
Embassy Suites	2,992	3,029	2,649	2,776	2,949	3,023
Hilton Hotel	38,398	38,877	34,000	35,627	37,851	38,789
Radisson Hotel	26,336	26,665	23,320	24,435	25,961	26,605
Holiday Inn	12,327	12,480	10,915	11,437	12,151	12,452
Courtyard	1,778	1,956	1,711	1,793	1,905	1,952
Ramada Inn	7,667	7,763	6,789	7,114	7,558	7,745
Island Inn	8,583	7,924	6,334	6,637	7,051	7,226
Quality Inn	5,236	5,301	4,636	4,858	5,161	5,289
Days Inn	1,720	1,742	1,523	1,596	1,696	1,738
Secondary competition	17,017	17,230	15,068	15,789	16,775	17,191
New Hotels						
Proposed Sheraton	–	–	22,078	25,303	27,651	28,336
Marriott Suites	–	2,146	2,760	3,933	4,178	4,282
Best Western	196	1,502	1,314	1,376	1,462	1,499
Total	122,250	126,615	133,097	142,674	152,349	156,127

TABLE 4.66 Room Nights Captured—Leisure Segment

Hotel	Year 1	Year 2	Year 3	Year 4	Year 5	Year 6
Embassy Suites	8,427	7,664	7,199	7,234	7,307	7,416
Hilton Hotel	7,173	6,524	6,128	6,158	6,219	6,313
Radisson Hotel	9,280	8,440	7,927	7,967	8,046	8,167
Holiday Inn	9,217	8,383	7,874	7,913	7,992	8,112
Courtyard	6,096	5,657	5,314	5,340	5,393	5,474
Ramada Inn	5,342	4,859	4,564	4,586	4,632	4,701
Island Inn	2,709	2,464	2,314	2,325	2,349	2,384
Quality Inn	19,751	17,963	16,873	16,956	17,125	17,382
Days Inn	8,066	7,336	6,890	6,924	6,994	7,098
Secondary competition	25,071	22,801	21,417	21,523	21,737	22,063
New Hotels						
Proposed Sheraton	–	–	6,428	7,536	8,155	8,277
Marriott Suites	–	5,474	6,085	6,115	6,176	6,269
Best Western	1,949	7,728	7,859	7,898	7,977	8,096
Total	103,081	105,293	106,872	108,475	110,102	111,752

TABLE 4.67 Total Room Nights Captured

Hotel	Year 1	Year 2	Year 3	Year 4	Year 5	Year 6
Embassy Suites	59,792	54,669	51,298	52,388	53,823	55,313
Hilton Hotel	76,131	73,182	66,314	68,557	71,594	73,451
Radisson Hotel	65,032	61,846	56,453	58,172	60,500	62,060
Holiday Inn	48,713	45,562	42,069	43,151	44,612	45,767
Courtyard	33,204	32,483	30,466	31,099	31,937	32,804
Ramada Inn	38,013	35,352	32,778	33,605	34,709	35,642
Island Inn	29,824	26,833	23,771	24,424	25,296	25,982
Quality Inn	51,298	47,183	44,054	44,864	45,983	47,079
Days Inn	33,908	31,006	29,083	29,652	30,414	31,213
Secondary competition	120,335	111,164	103,533	105,861	108,985	111,841
New Hotels						
Proposed Sheraton	–	–	54,762	60,757	65,243	66,934
Marriott Suites	–	43,276	46,373	50,135	51,566	52,999
Best Western	6,378	25,869	26,229	26,712	27,366	28,060
Total	562,628	588,425	607,183	629,377	652,028	669,145

TABLE 4.68 Projected Occupancy, Segmentation, Overall Penetration–Embassy Suites

	Year 1	Year 2	Year 3	Year 4	Year 5	Year 6
Commercial	48,373	43,975	41,450	42,378	43,567	44,874
Meeting & group	2,992	3,029	2,649	2,776	2,949	3,023
Leisure	8,427	7,664	7,199	7,234	7,307	7,416
Total capture	59,792	54,669	51,298	52,388	53,823	55,313
Available room nights	73,000	73,000	73,000	73,000	73,000	73,000
Occupancy rate	81.91%	74.89%	70.27%	71.77%	73.73%	75.77%
Rounded	82%	75%	70%	72%	74%	76%
Demand Segmentation						
Commercial	81%	80%	81%	81%	81%	81%
Meeting & group	5%	6%	5%	5%	5%	5%
Leisure	14%	14%	14%	14%	14%	13%
Total	100%	100%	100%	100%	100%	100%
Subject capture	59,792	54,669	51,298	52,388	53,823	55,313
÷ Marketwide demand	562,628	588,426	607,182	629,378	652,028	669,144
Subject market share	10.63%	9.29%	8.45%	8.32%	8.25%	8.27%
Subject room count	200	200	200	200	200	200
÷ Marketwide supply	2,059	2,364	2,614	2,614	2,614	2,614
Subject fair share	9.71%	8.46%	7.65%	7.65%	7.65%	7.65%
Overall penetration	109.41%	109.82%	110.42%	108.79%	107.89%	108.04%

TABLE 4.69 — Projected Occupancy, Segmentation, Overall Penetration—Proposed Sheraton

	Year 1	Year 2	Year 3	Year 4	Year 5	Year 6
Commercial	–	–	26,256	27,918	29,437	30,320
Meeting & group	–	–	22,078	25,303	27,651	28,336
Leisure	–	–	6,428	7,536	8,155	8,277
Total capture	–	–	54,762	60,757	65,243	66,933
Available room nights	–	–	91,250	91,250	91,250	91,250
Occupancy rate	–	–	60.01%	66.58%	71.50%	73.35%
Rounded	–	–	60%	67%	71%	73%
Demand Segmentation						
Commercial	–	–	48%	46%	45%	45%
Meeting & group	–	–	40%	42%	42%	42%
Leisure	–	–	12%	12%	12%	12%
Total	–	–	100%	100%	99%	99%
Subject capture	–	–	54,762	60,757	65,243	66,934
÷ Marketwide demand	–	–	607,182	629,378	652,028	669,144
Subject market share	–	–	9.02%	9.65%	10.01%	10.00%
Subject room count	–	–	250	250	250	250
÷ Marketwide supply	–	–	2,614	2,614	2,614	2,614
Subject fair share	–	–	9.56%	9.56%	9.56%	9.56%
Overall penetration	–	–	94.30%	100.94%	104.62%	104.59%

TABLE 4.70 — Occupancy Projections—All Hotels

Hotel	Year 1	Year 2	Year 3	Year 4	Year 5	Year 6
Embassy Suites	81.9%	74.9%	70.3%	71.8%	73.7%	75.8%
Hilton Hotel	75.8	72.9	66.1	68.3	71.3	73.2
Radisson Hotel	71.3	67.8	61.9	63.8	66.3	68.0
Holiday Inn	76.3	71.3	65.9	67.6	69.8	71.7
Courtyard	73.4	71.8	67.3	68.7	70.6	72.5
Ramada Inn	69.4	64.6	59.9	61.4	63.4	65.1
Island Inn	60.5	54.5	48.2	49.6	51.3	52.7
Quality Inn	80.3	73.9	69.0	70.2	72.0	73.7
Days Inn	77.4	70.8	66.4	67.7	69.4	71.3
Secondary competition	78.5	72.5	67.5	69.1	71.1	73.0
New Hotels						
Proposed Sheraton	–	–	60.0	66.6	71.5	73.4
Marriott Suites	–	59.3	63.5	68.7	70.6	72.6
Best Western	49.9	50.6	51.3	52.3	53.6	54.9

Stabilized Occupancy

When projecting a property's room nights captured and occupancy rates into the future, the assumptions of continued growth and no new additions to the competitive supply will ultimately produce unreasonably high capture and occupancy levels. As a result, appraisers use the concept of a stabilized occupancy.

A property's stabilized occupancy level reflects the anticipated level of occupancy over its remaining economic life of the property, given any or all periods of build-up, plateau, and decline in its life cycle. The concept of stabilized occupancy excludes from consideration any abnormal relationship between supply and demand as well as any transitory or nonrecurring conditions, whether favorable or unfavorable, that may result in unusually high or low levels of occupancy. Although it is common for a hotel to operate at occupancies above its stabilized level, it is equally possible that new competition and temporary downturns in the economy could force actual occupancy below stabilized occupancy.

Projections become more uncertain the farther into the future they are made. The use of a single stabilized occupancy rate produces the same results as a forecast that attempts to reflect the inevitable upward and downward occupancy cycles that a typical lodging facility experiences. Furthermore, discounting future economic benefits tends to smooth out the cycle, providing additional support for using a stabilized level of occupancy.

For new hotels like the proposed Sheraton described in the case study, a two- to five-year build-up in occupancy is generally factored into the projection. Few hotels stabilize in their initial year of operation. Since the initial years tend to generate operating losses, the build-up period must be included in the projection to illustrate the actual start-up cash requirements.

Several factors influence the selection of a stabilized level of occupancy. The following list identifies some key considerations.

Market-Specific Considerations
- Market area demand trends
- Composition of local demand
- Supply and competitive trends
- Historic occupancy cycles

Property-Specific Considerations
- Location-specific factors
- Competitiveness
- Age
- Management and image
- Obsolescence

The best indicator to analyze when establishing a stabilized level of occupancy is probably the nature of the local hotel demand. Different types of travelers have different travel patterns (i.e., days of travel, length of stay, and seasonality), so the mix of visitors within a given market will influence the area's overall occupancy level.

For example, assume a market has a strong business base, which generates a significant room night demand Monday through Thursday nights. However, the local area has no leisure attractions, so few people use local hotels and motels on Friday and Saturday nights. Some commercial demand is experienced Sunday night as business travelers try to get a head start on Monday's activities. Because of this occupancy pattern, the maximum market-wide occupancy would be approximately 67%, assuming near sellouts every Monday through Thursday. Table 4.71 illustrates how this maximum occupancy level was established.

TABLE 4.71   Maximum Occupancy

Day	Percentage of Occupancy
Monday	80%
Tuesday	85
Wednesday	90
Thursday	80
Friday	30
Saturday	45
Sunday	60
Weekly average	67%

Considering market conditions and the nature of the existing lodging demand, a stabilized occupancy rate higher than 67% could not be justified unless the property has competitive or physical attributes that enable it to capture more than its fair share of weekday demand as well as the existing weekend demand.

The historic occupancy cycles experienced in the market area also indicate where the stabilized occupancy rate should fall. Table 4.72 shows the 20-year occupancy cycle of three different hypothetical cities.

Statistical data relating to the 20-year occupancy cycles are shown in Table 4.73.

The stabilized occupancy for each of these cities should approximate the average occupancy, which is generally the midpoint between the highest and lowest occupancy levels recorded during the 20-year period.

The following case study illustrates the estimation of stabilized occupancy.

TABLE 4.72   **20-Year Occupancy History**

Year	City A	City B	City C
1	71.0%	72.0%	57.0%
2	66.0	74.0	68.0
3	63.0	76.0	62.0
4	69.0	75.0	56.0
5	60.0	69.0	50.0
6	61.0	68.0	47.0
7	63.0	69.0	49.0
8	66.0	70.0	51.0
9	64.0	69.0	46.0
10	66.0	64.0	57.0
11	68.0	71.0	59.0
12	69.0	71.0	61.0
13	72.0	77.0	63.0
14	72.0	78.0	60.0
15	69.0	76.0	63.0
16	66.0	72.0	62.0
17	59.0	68.0	61.0
18	65.0	68.0	60.0
19	69.0	70.0	57.0
20	70.0	69.0	60.0
Average	66.4%	71.3%	57.5%
Standard deviation	3.8	3.6	5.8

TABLE 4.73   **20-Year Occupancy Cycles**

Year	City A	City B	City C
Average occupancy	65.5%	71.3%	57.0%
Highest occupancy	72.0	78.0	68.0
Lowest occupancy	59.0	64.0	46.0
Difference	13.0 pts.	14.0 pts.	22.0 pts.
Standard deviation	3.8	3.6	5.8

Estimating Stabilized Occupancy

The supply and demand analysis ultimately results in a yearly estimate of occupancy over a given period of time. The appraiser must now evaluate each yearly occupancy estimate and determine whether or not it is appropriate to use when projecting income and expenses. This evaluation also includes determination of the subject's stabilized occupancy level. Table 4.74 shows the yearly occupancy projections for the market at large, the existing Embassy Suites, and the proposed Sheraton Hotel.

The occupancy for the market area peaks at 75% in the first projection year and declines to a low of about 64% in the third projection year. Thereafter, market-wide occupancy levels are expected to improve.

Projected occupancy levels for the Embassy Suites rise to 82% in the first projection year then decline substantially to 70% in Year 3. Based on the Embassy Suites' popular design and stable market presence, a stabilized occupancy rate of 72%, as realized in the fourth projection year, is considered to be appropriate. Table 4.75 sets forth the projection of occupancy through the stabilized year for the Embassy Suites. For the proposed Sheraton, the new hotel may be expected to achieve a stabilized occupancy of 71%, which is projected to occur in its third year of operation (the fifth projection year). Table 4.76 sets forth the projection of occupancy through the stabilized year for the proposed Sheraton Hotel.

TABLE 4.74 Yearly Occupancy Projections

Year	Market Area	Embassy Suites	Proposed Sheraton
Base	72%	78%	–
1	75	82	–
2	68	75	–
3	64	70	60%
4	66	72	67
5	68	74	71
6	70	76	73
7	72	78	75
8	74	80	77

TABLE 4.75 Projected Stabilized Occupancy–Embassy Suites	Occupancy Rate
Year	
1	82%
2	75
3	70
Stabilized	72

TABLE 4.76 Projected Stabilized Occupancy–Proposed Sheraton	Occupancy Rate
Year	
3	60%
4	67
Stabilized	71

Average Rate Per Occupied Room

After occupancy has been estimated, the average rate per occupied room is needed to forecast a hotel's rooms revenue. Like occupancy, the projected average rate is derived through market analysis. A hotel's ability to achieve a satisfactory average room rate can impact its financial feasibility as well as its market value. Appraisers must understand the definition of average rate per occupied room, how it is estimated, and what factors can affect its future movement.

The *average rate per occupied room* is defined as the net rooms revenue derived from the sale of guest rooms divided by the number of paid rooms occupied. The *Uniform System of Accounts for Hotels* defines the components of this formula as follows:

- Net rooms revenue—Total rooms revenue less allowances.
- Allowances—Rebates and overcharges or revenue not known at the time of sale but adjusted at a subsequent date. Allowances may also include revenue foregone as a result of hotel promotions or complimentary services.
- Paid rooms occupied—Rooms occupied by hotel guests on a paid basis. It should be noted that the overall average rate per occupied room does not include any occupancy derived from complimentary rooms.

Since most hotels have many rate categories, depending on the size of the accommodations, view and location, age and condition, and types of travelers served, the average room rate represents the weighted average of all of these rate categories. Several of the rate categories used by hotels are described on the following page.

- Rack rate—An undiscounted room rate generally given to anyone who does not qualify or ask for a special discounted rate. The term is derived from the room rack, a front desk feature that is less common in the computer age. The room rack traditionally contains information about each room's rate, including the highest rate that can be charged for that particular accommodation. When a hotel is expected to be full during a certain period or a guest arrives without a reservation, the rack rate is often the only rate available. The average room rate is always less than the rack rate.

- Published rate—The rate listed in directories and other publications. This rate is usually quoted as a range (i.e., single: $70-$100) and represents the various rack rates for specific types of accommodations. Published room rates usually set the upper limits of average rates. Average room rates tend to be closer to published rates for single rooms than for double rooms.

- Commercial rate—A discounted room rate available to certain commercial travelers. Some hotels will charge any commercial traveler a commercial rate upon request, while others offer it only to established accounts based on their projected usage of the hotel. Commercial rates often differ because they are individually negotiated between the commercial business and the hotel. Commercial rates are always below the rack and published rates and, depending on the market mix, will often approximate the property's average room rate.

- Contract rate—A discounted room rate available to specific high-volume users such as airlines, convention groups, and bus tours. Contract rates are negotiated by the user and the hotel and often apply to a block of rooms that are reserved on an ongoing basis and paid for whether they are used or not. For example, an airline may contract for 35 rooms per night for a full year. Two crews may utilize these rooms in a day, if scheduling permits. The rooms may not be used at all, however, if a flight is delayed or canceled. Depending on the amount and timing of the usage, a contract rate may be heavily discounted and fall significantly below both the average rate and the commercial rate.

The mix of business it attracts in various rate categories affects a hotel's average room rate. A hotel that caters to numerous airline crews or convention groups will likely have a lower average room rate than will a property used primarily by commercial travelers.

Hotel operators continually try to maximize their room rates. With computer software that can perform yield management, hotels can coordinate projected future usage by market segment and employ a continuously sliding scale of room charges to achieve the best room rates. The ability to adjust room rates constantly in order to maximize the yields produced by changes in room night demand is one advantage of hotel investment.

Estimating the Average Rate per Occupied Room

Various procedures are used to forecast the average rate per occupied room for existing and proposed hotels. An existing hotel has an operating history that establishes an actual average room rate, which serves as a starting point for forecasting future rates. Proposed hotels have no operating history, so the initial average room rate must be derived by analyzing the competitive rates actually achieved by local hotels with comparable facilities. The various procedures for forecasting average room rates for existing and proposed hotels are outlined in the following sections.

Forecasting Average Room Rates for an Existing Hotel

In forecasting average room rates for an existing hotel, the property's operating history is used as a starting point and future rate changes are forecasted based on market conditions and the property's relative competitiveness. Seven steps are involved in this process.

1. Compile the subject's overall average room rates by month for the past three to five years.

2. Analyze historical trends in the subject's average room rates.

3. Consider the historical relationship between the average room rate and occupancy.

4. Research the average room rates for the subject property's primary and secondary competition.

5. Compare the average room rates of the subject and the competition.

6. Project future changes in average room rates.

7. Project the subject property's average room rate.

First, the subject's overall average rates are compiled monthly for the last three to five years. A monthly analysis is used to highlight seasonality in a property's ability to charge desirable rates.

Next, historical trends in the subject's average room rates are studied and the compounded annual growth rate is calculated. If sufficient data are available, growth trends should be evaluated on a monthly basis and by individual market segments.

Since average room rate and occupancy are often related, the historic relationship between these two components should be analyzed. Average room rate can be affected by changes in occupancy. In markets where occupancies are declining, for example, average room rates will usually soften and sometimes even fall. In markets where hotel patronage is rising, average room rates will often show real growth in excess of inflation. These fluctuations can be attributed to competitiveness and price sensitivities. When a market experiences a decrease in lodging demand or an increase in the supply of hotel rooms, occupancy levels tend to decline. Individual properties react to this depletion of patronage by becoming more competitive and rate-conscious or by holding a hard rate policy when negotiating for new business or contracts. As market-wide occupancy levels fall further, hotels are pressured to slash rates even more in order to hold onto their market shares. By understanding the historic occupancy pattern experienced by the subject property, the appraiser is better able to explain past movements in average room rates based on this room rate-occupancy relationship.

In addition to the external market factors that influence average room rates, a hotel will generally experience an increase in its average rate as a result of increased occupancy. This increase can be attributed to the fact that as a hotel approaches 100% occupancy, management is able to sell more of the property's expensive rooms and is less willing to offer discounts and other incentives to promote occupancy. A potential customer making a reservation at a hotel with one room remaining will probably pay the full or rack rate. By selling out its higher-priced rooms, a hotel can increase its average room rate faster than either inflation or local market conditions would allow.

Next, the appraiser should research the average room rates of the subject property's primary and secondary competitors. This information is usually gathered during competitive interviews. The appraiser should ensure that the data represent recent average room rates rather than published or rack rates.

The subject's average room rate is compared with the rates of its competition. Differences can be attributed to factors such as location, scope of the physical facilities, management, image, quality, and the market segments served. If the average room rate comparison reveals differences that cannot be adequately explained, further investigation is needed.

To project future changes in average room rates, many factors must be considered. A hotel's ability to increase room rates over time is influenced by supply and demand, inflation, competitive standards, and specific property improvements.

As discussed previously, the relationship between the local supply of transient accommodations and the demand for lodgings is a determining factor contributing to future trends in hotel occupancy and average room rates. A market that is overbuilt or losing demand will probably not experience any significant increases in average room rates. In fact, as this situation becomes more severe, room rates may even decline.

Price increases caused by inflation also affect room rates, albeit indirectly. When a hotel operator sees profits dwindling in response to increased operating costs, there is a natural tendency to raise room rates as a means of offsetting higher expenses. If other hotels in the market are in the same situation, the competitive environment will probably allow them all to raise their rates.

Room rates can also increase due to an improvement in the competitive standard. In established hotel markets where the stock of existing lodging facilities shows physical and functional obsolescence, room rates may lag behind inflation. This trend often reverses when a new, upscale property is introduced into the market. The new hotel must quickly achieve a higher-than-usual room rate to be economically justified. Most existing hotels in the same market benefit from the introduction of the higher-priced competition because it exerts upward pressure on room rates and enables all operators to raise their rates.

Changes in the subject property that make the property more or less appealing to transient visitors can affect future trends in average room rates. The expansion, renovation, upgrading, or addition of facilities and amenities, new management, or a different franchise affiliation can allow a hotel to increase room rates more rapidly than usual. Similarly, lack of periodic maintenance and replacement can make a property less competitive and cause room rates to decline.

After evaluating all of the room rate data available and forming appropriate conclusions, the appraiser is ready to forecast the subject's average room rate over the projection period. Until the subject property reaches stabilized occupancy, movement in the average room rate is generally attributed to the property-specific and market-specific factors described above. After the hotel achieves stable occupancy, most forecasters assume that room rates will continue to increase at the anticipated rate of inflation over the remainder of the projection period. Since each market situation is unique, this inflation assumption should be validated before it is utilized.

Forecasting Average Room Rates for a Proposed Hotel

Forecasting the average room rate for a proposed hotel is similar to the procedure applied to an existing property except the appraiser does not have an operating history and a benchmark rate from which to project room rates into the future. The appraiser should begin by compiling a complete database of information relative to the room rates actually achieved by competitive properties in the area. In addition to collecting room rate data (by market segment if possible), the appraiser should examine the relative competitiveness of each property to identify the reasons for any room rate differentials. This information is then used to project average room rates for the proposed subject property.

Three methods can be used to forecast average room rates:

1. Competitive positioning
2. Market segmentation
3. Rule-of-thumb

Competitive positioning method. The competitive positioning method starts with an analysis of the average room rates currently achieved by local competitive hotels. These rates establish a range within which the room rate for a proposed hotel is likely to fall. The projected average rate for the subject property is then set close to the average rate of the hotel in the sample that is most similar to the subject in quality, size, facilities, amenities, market orientation, location, management image, and affiliation. Upward and/or downward adjustments are then made to the average rate to reflect any differences between the comparable and the subject property.

The competitive positioning method works well if the local market contains a hotel that is relatively comparable to the proposed subject property. It can also be used to verify that the average room rates achieved by an existing hotel represent an optimum level for the market.

Market segmentation method. In applying the market segmentation method, the appraiser develops an average room rate by individual market segments. This method starts with the previously developed demand forecast for the subject property, which includes a projection of the number of room nights captured for each market segment (commercial, meeting and group, leisure, etc.) Using the rates charged by competitive properties as a base, a room rate estimate is developed for each market segment. The estimated room rate for each market segment is multiplied by the projected number of room nights captured and the results are totaled to yield the total rooms revenue. An average rate is then calculated by dividing total rooms revenue by the number of rooms occupied.

The advantage of the market segmentation method is its ability to adjust the projected average room rate for changes in market mix. For example, a new, convention-oriented hotel is likely to experience a build-up of convention capture during its initial years as sales efforts become more effective and groups are drawn to the property. If convention rates are lower than the property's commercial rates, the change in the market mix away from commercial business and toward more convention patronage will probably slow the growth of the average rate. This room rate sensitivity can only be examined by assigning an individual rate to each market segment and using the market segmentation method.

Rule-of-thumb method. In the hotel industry there is a rule of thumb that states that for every $1,000 of total project cost (on a per-room basis), a hotel must achieve an average room rate of at least $1.00 to be financially feasible. Therefore, if it costs $90,000 per room to construct a new hotel, the property must attempt to achieve an average rate of $90.

The rule-of-thumb method provides a target indicating where the average room rate should be set; it is not a market-based approach and does not consider the various local competitive factors investigated in the other methods. However, in markets where several new properties have recently been added, the upward pressure on room rates generated by the economics inherent in this thumb rule often causes the entire market to raise rates.

Because the rule-of-thumb method is simple, it must rely on numerous assumptions. Some of the many assumptions built into this method pertain to the subject's occupancy rate, the ratio of food and beverage revenue to rooms revenue, operating costs, fixed expenses and capital costs. Properties that do not fit the national norms for these characteristics are apt to require more or less than $1.00 of average rate to justify $1,000 per room of development cost. For example, assume that this rule of thumb works for hotels with an occupancy rate of 72%. If the subject property is projected to achieve only 68% stabilized occupancy, then it will take more than $1.00 of average room rate to cover $1,000 per room in development costs. In this case an adjusted rule of thumb of $1.25 to $1.50 of average room rate might be needed to justify each $1,000 of cost per room.

Room Rate Discounts

It is not unusual for new hotels to discount their room rates during the initial years of operation in an attempt to increase the hotel's market share and generate occupancy. If this strategy is likely to be utilized, the appraiser should adjust the average room rates established by the previously described methods downward to reflect appropriate room rate discounts.

In the following case study, average room rates are projected for an existing hotel as well as for a proposed lodging facility.

CASE STUDY

Projecting Average Room Rates

The average room rates for the existing Embassy Suites and the proposed Sheraton Hotel will be estimated for each projection year until the hotel achieves stabilized occupancy.

Since hotel room rates depend largely on the local competitive market, it is necessary to survey the average rates achieved by the competition. Table 4.77 shows the average room rates for the primary competition (including the Embassy Suites) in the base year. The weighted average of the average room rates is also presented; it accounts for the size and base year occupancy level of the properties.

In the base year, the Embassy Suites posted the strongest average rate, at $151. This hotel led the market by virtue of its all-suites guestroom facilities, the quality of its location, and the popularity and strong loyalty engendered by the Embassy Suites brand. The market's Hilton Hotel, Courtyard, and Radisson affiliates also achieved relatively high average rate levels, each exceeding the market average of $130.57. Overall, the Embassy Suites' actual results for the base year adequately reflect its competitive position, requiring no material adjustment.

In order to project future increases in the Embassy Suites' average rate levels, additional context for rate growth trends may be derived from market data provided by Smith Travel Research (STR). Table 4.78 sets forth average rate trends for all hotels located in suburban Long Island, as compiled and

TABLE 4.77 Average Room Rates—Base Year

Hotel	Average Rate Per Occupied Room
Embassy Suites	$151.00
Hilton Hotel	136.00
Radisson Hotel	131.00
Holiday Inn	127.00
Courtyard	133.00
Ramada Inn	124.00
Island Inn	110.00
Quality Inn	125.00
Days Inn	121.00
Weighted Average	$130.57

published by STR. Note that this survey pertains to a broader market area than that defined for the subject property. Nevertheless, the data are worthy indicators of general pricing trends.

Between 1990 and 1999, the average rate in the suburban Long Island market area increased at an average annual compounded percentage rate of 5.5%. This growth rate encompasses the early 1990s, during years of economic recession, as well as the economic expansion of the late 1990s. Whereas the market's average rate actually declined in 1991, dramatic growth of 11.5% was noted in 1998. In 1999, average rate growth slowed slightly, but remained strong at 9.0%.

In future years, as new hotels begin to enter the competitive market, average rate growth may be expected to slow significantly. Occupancy levels are expected to soften in the near term, and therefore limit prospects for the type of aggressive pricing increases noted in the past four years. These considerations are reflected in the projection of average rate for the Embassy Suites, as detailed in Table 4.79.

In projecting the average rate of the proposed Sheraton, the appraisers have used the market segmentation method. Because the appraisers have access to the historical segmented average rate results realized by the Embassy Suites, the data may be used as a basis for estimating the subject property's segmented average rates. Table 4.80 identifies the Embassy Suites' data, as well as the projections for the Sheraton. As noted, the Sheraton's average rate is expected to be lower than that of the Embassy Suites in each demand segment, owing to the popularity of the Embassy Suites operating concept and the fact that each of its guest units are two-room suites. After accounting for the proposed Sheraton's higher share of discounted meeting

TABLE 4.78 Suburban Long Island Average Rate Trends

Year	Market-wide Average Rate	Percent Change
1990	$81.21	–
1991	80.81	(0.5)%
1992	82.43	2.0
1993	85.31	3.5
1994	88.98	4.3
1995	92.98	4.5
1996	100.42	8.0
1997	107.95	7.5
1998	120.37	11.5
1999	131.20	9.0
Avg. annual % change, 1990–1999		5.5%

TABLE 4.79 Projected Average Rates—Embassy Suites

Year	Projected Increase in Market-wide ADR	Projected Increase in Embassy Suites ADR	Embassy Suites Average Rate
Base	–		$151.00
1	5% to 7%	6.0%	160.06
2	4% to 6%	5.0	168.06
3	3% to 5%	4.0	174.79
4	3% to 4%	3.0	180.03
5	3% to 4%	3.0	185.43
6	3% to 4%	3.0	190.99
7	3% to 4%	3.0	196.72

and group demand relative to the Embassy Suites, the resulting average rate will also account for the impact that market segmentation has on a given hotel's overall average rate.

In order to project future changes in the segmented rates selected for the Sheraton, Table 4.81 sets forth the appraiser's estimate of future changes in market-wide average rates. Variations in the overall pricing trends may be reflected in a given market segment; however, in the case of the subject market area, the appraisers have projected uniform increases of 6.0% in Year 1, 5.0% in Year 2, 4.0% in Year 3, and 3.0% in Year 4 and thereafter. Table 4.82 sets forth the basis for the segmented average rate forecast. In Table 4.83, the projected segmented average rates are multiplied by the segmented demand forecast for the proposed Sheraton, beginning as of Year 3, the hotel's first year of

TABLE 4.80 Segmented ADR–Embassy Suites

	Embassy Suites			Proposed Sheraton
Market Segment	No. of Room Nights	% of Total	Average Rate	Positioned Average Rate
Commercial	45,552	80.0%	$154.00	$148.00
Meeting & group	2,847	5.0	142.00	135.00
Leisure	8,541	15.0	138.00	130.00
Total	56,940	100.0%	$151.00	

TABLE 4.81 Projected Average Rate Growth–Market

Year	Projected Increase in Market–wide ADR
Base	–
1	5% to 7%
2	4% to 6%
3	3% to 5%
4	3% to 4%
5	3% to 4%
6	3% to 4%
7	3% to 4%

operation. Each year's revenue is totaled and divided by the total demand, resulting in a forecast of weighted average rate.

Since the projected average room rates for the proposed Sheraton were estimated through comparison with the average rates achieved by similar, but more established hotels in the market, the initial years' rates must be adjusted downward to account for factors such as discounting, occupancy build-up, and customer acceptance. Most new hotels will discount their room rates during the first year or two to offer a competitive advantage and build occupancy. This strategy tends to set a new property's actual average rate below that of a comparable hotel operating at its stabilized level of occupancy. As occupancy builds up, room rates tend to increase because the hotel is selling more of its higher-priced rooms and suites. Management can usually begin to be less flexible in offering discounts and acquires more experience in maximizing yield. Finally, as a hotel matures, customer acceptance becomes more established, and this loyalty often allows the operator to raise room rates.

To account for all of the factors that depress room rates during the initial years of operation, an appropriate discount must be applied to the projected

TABLE 4.82 **Segmented Rate and Rate Growth Factors**

Year	Commercial	Percent Change	Meeting & Group	Percent Change	Leisure	Percent Change
Base	$148.00	–	$135.00	–	$130.00	
1	156.88	6.0%	143.10	6.0%	137.80	6.0%
2	164.72	5.0	150.26	5.0	144.69	5.0
3	171.31	4.0	156.27	4.0	150.48	4.0
4	176.45	3.0	160.95	3.0	154.99	3.0
5	181.75	3.0	165.78	3.0	159.64	3.0
6	187.20	3.0	170.76	3.0	164.43	3.0

TABLE 4.83 **Segmented Rate and Rate Growth Factors**

	Commercial	Meeting & Group	Leisure	Total	Wtd. Avg. Rate
Year 3					
Demand	26,256	22,078	6,428	54,762	
Segment rate	$171.31	$156.27	$150.48		
Total revenue	$4,498,006	$3,450,017	$967,223	$8,915,247	$162.80
Year 4					
Demand	27,918	25,303	7,536	60,757	
Segment rate	$176.45	$160.95	$154.99		
Total revenue	$4,926,175	$4,072,591	$1,168,005	$10,166,772	$167.34
Year 5					
Demand	29,437	27,651	8,155	65,243	
Segment rate	$181.75	$165.78	$159.64		
Total revenue	$5,350,060	$4,584,005	$1,301,850	$11,235,915	$172.22
Year 6					
Demand	30,320	28,336	8,277	66,934	
Segment rate	$187.20	$170.76	$164.43		
Total revenue	$5,675,888	$4,838,579	$1,361,013	$11,875,480	$177.42

average rates derived from comparable hotels. Generally the size of this discount is inversely proportional to the hotel's overall competitiveness. The discount may also be related to the general health of the local hotel market, which might suggest deeper discounts when occupancy levels are depressed.

Based on the appraiser's analysis, the discounts shown in Table 4.84 were applied to the proposed Sheraton's average rate during its first two years of operation.

TABLE 4.84	Discount Factors			
Projection Year	Operational Year	ADR Projection Before Discount	Discount Factor	Discounted Average Rate
3	First	$162.80	10.0%	146.52
4	Second	167.34	5.0	158.97
5	Stabilized	172.22	0.0	172.22

CHAPTER 5

Forecasting Revenues and Expenses

To develop a supportable estimate of value using the income capitalization approach, the appraiser must make forecasts of income and expenses that reflect the outlook of typical hotel investors. Hotels and motels are unique forms of real estate with many unusual characteristics, including intensive use of labor, cost-of-goods-sold expense categories, and a retail product identity. Special knowledge and data are required to estimate a hotel's future income. This chapter describes step-by-step procedures for projecting income and expenses using data sources available to all appraisers.

Existing Facility vs. Proposed Facility

Valuing an existing hotel generally requires less fieldwork than valuing a proposed facility does. In the case of an existing hotel, the appraiser first reviews the local supply and demand situation and projects the subject's future revenue. Then, using the property's operating ratios obtained from previous years' financial statements, various expense categories are estimated. These estimates should be compared to the operating results of similar properties, if available, or to national averages; any differences should be resolved. Discrepancies may occur for several reasons, including

- *Unusual property characteristics.* Some hotels are more expensive to operate than others. For example, beachfront hotels have higher maintenance costs, properties in the Northeast United States pay more for energy, commercial hotels have more credit card commissions, and airport hotels incur shuttle bus expenses.

- *Assumed competent management.* Projected expenses reflect competent management, while the actual management may be better than, equal to, or less capable than normal.

- *Different levels of occupancy and average rate.* When comparing expense ratios for two properties, the appraiser must ascertain that they operate at similar occupancy levels and have similar average rates. Lodging facilities generally experience more efficient operations as their rates and occupancies increase.

The final income and expense estimate for an existing hostelry should be a blend of past operating results and future expectations.

Assembling sufficient market information and comparable data for a proposed facility requires more research. Market analysis should help appraisers accumulate enough information to formulate estimates of occupancy and average rate. Once these two factors have been established, rooms revenue and other income sources may be computed.

Because a proposed hotel has no operating history on which to base an expense projection, the appraiser must either obtain data from existing comparable properties or use national averages. Statistics from either of these sources can be processed to project income and expenses for the proposed subject property. Because national averages are available to all appraisers, they are used here to demonstrate the projection procedure. However, actual operating performance data from a comparable property are generally preferred.

National Averages

Each year, several firms compile operating statistics and ratios for hundreds of hotels and motels throughout the United States. This information is generally categorized according to property size, room rate, geographical location, and other characteristics. The data represent average operating results and typical management ability and may be used to evaluate an existing operation or to project income and expenses for a proposed facility. Currently, Smith Travel Research is the best source of national hotel operating data.

Uniform System of Accounts for Hotels

The data found in most hotel financial statements are arranged in accordance with the Uniform System of Accounts for the Lodging Industry (USALI). This system was established by the Hotel Association of New York City in 1926 and was later adopted by the American Hotel and Lodging Association. The ninth revised edition of the format, designed to conform to evolving accounting practices, was issued in 1998.

The USALI provides a simple formula for classifying the accounts used by hotels of all types and sizes. The system's universality allows appraisers to compare individual properties or groups of properties that have similar characteristics.

A complete set of financial statements for a hotel or motel should include a balance sheet, a statement of income and expenses, a statement of changes in financial position, and any disclosures needed to comply with accepted accounting principles. The appraiser is primarily interested in the data contained in the statement of income and expenses.

The following list is extracted from the *Uniform System of Accounts for the Lodging Industry* (1998), published by the Educational Institute of the American Hotel and Motel Association, Orlando, Florida. It shows how various hotel activities are classified in income and expense statements.

Operated departments

- Rooms
- Food
- Beverage
- Telephone
- Garage, parking lot
- Guest laundry
- Golf course
- Golf pro shop
- Tennis, racquet club
- Tennis pro shop
- Health club
- Swimming pool, cabanas, baths
- Other operated departments
- Rentals and other income

Undistributed operating expenses

- Administrative and general expenses
- Human resources
- Information systems
- Security
- Transportation
- Marketing
- Guest entertainment
- Franchise fee
- Property operation and maintenance
- Energy costs

House profit

- Management fee

Total income before fixed charges

- Rent, property taxes, and insurance
- Interest expense
- Depreciation and amortization

Income before income taxes

- Income taxes

Net income

The total income after expenses for each major revenue-producing department is listed separately. If there are other departments with revenues and expenditures, they too are enumerated. The expenses incurred by undistributed overhead departments and capital expenses are then listed. The entries are totaled to determine the property's income before taxes. Then state and federal income taxes are deducted to arrive at the property's net income.

Because this format does not address the specific needs of the appraiser, who must capitalize income after property taxes and insurance but before interest, depreciation, and amortization, a slightly modified system is required to indicate:

Total income before fixed charges

- Property taxes
- Insurance
- Reserve for replacement

Income before debt service

Under the USALI, salaries and wages are allocated to individual departments and expense categories as follows:

Rooms

- Assistant managers
- Front office
- Housekeeping
- Service (doorman, front)
- House officers and watchmen

Food

- Food preparation
- Food service

Beverage

- Beverage service

Administrative and general

- Manager's office
- Accounting office
- Data processing
- Front office bookkeeping
- Night auditors
- Credit office
- Timekeepers
- Receiving clerks
- Employment office
- Employees' locker attendants

Marketing

- Sales department
- Advertising
- Merchandising
- Public relations and publicity
- Research

Guest entertainment

- Manager
- Entertainment director
- Stagehands

Property operation, maintenance, and energy costs

- Chief engineer and assistant
- Engineers
- Painters and paperhangers
- Radio and television repair
- Grounds and landscape
- Office and storeroom

Forecast of Revenue and Expense

The forecast of revenue and expense begins by converting the occupancy and average rate projections into an estimate of rooms revenue. Using data collected in the market and industry statistics, the appraiser then develops a forecast of other revenue items such as food, beverage, telephone, and other income as well as normal hotel operating expenses. Combining all this information produces a highly documented forecast of revenue and expenses, which becomes a key component in estimating market value and evaluating the economics of the investment. This chapter will demonstrate how all types of hotel revenues and expenses are forecasted.

Rooms Revenue Defined

The primary components of rooms revenue—occupancy and average room rate— were discussed and projected in Chapter 3. A projection of rooms revenue is derived using the following formula:

$$\text{Occupancy} \times \text{average room rate} \times \text{room count} \times 365 = \text{Rooms revenue}$$

The following case study demonstrates the projection of rooms revenue.

CASE STUDY

Rooms Revenue

The rooms revenue projection for the proposed Sheraton Hotel is calculated in Table 5.1, while the rooms revenue projection for the existing Embassy Suites is calculated in Table 5.2. In each case, the occupancy rate is multiplied by the number of rooms in the hotel per year (room count × 365) in order to generate an estimate of the number of occupied rooms. Rooms revenue is then calculated as the product of occupied rooms multiplied by average rate.

TABLE 5.1 Rooms Revenue Projection–Proposed Sheraton

	Year 3	Year 4	Year 5 (Stab.)
No. of rooms	250	250	250
× Days/year	365	365	365
No. of rooms/year	91,250	91,250	91,250
× Occupancy rate	60.0%	67.0%	71.0%
No. of occupied rooms	54,750	61,138	64,788
× Average rate	$146.52	$158.97	$172.22
Rooms revenue (in thousands)	$8,022	$9,719	$11,158

TABLE 5.2 Rooms Revenue Projection–Embassy Suites

	Year 1	Year 2	Year 3	Year 4 (Stab.)
No. of rooms	200	200	200	200
× Days/year	365	365	365	365
No. of rooms/year	73,000	73,000	73,000	73,000
× Occupancy rate	82.0%	75.0%	70.0%	72.0%
No. of occupied rooms	59,860	54,750	51,100	52,560
× Average rate	$160.06	$168.06	$174.79	$180.03
Rooms revenue (in thousands)	$9,581	$9,201	$8,932	$9,462

Hotels and Motels–Valuations and Market Studies

Fixed and Variable Component Approach to Forecasting

Before projecting individual items of hotel revenue and expense, appraisers must understand the fixed and variable component approach to forecasting. This approach produces one of the most accurate models of a hotel's financial performance; it forms the basis for many computerized hotel forecasting programs utilized by hotel appraisal firms, hotel companies, investors, lenders, and developers.

Theoretical Basis

The fixed and variable component approach is based on the premise that hotel revenue and expenses have one component that is fixed and another that varies directly with occupancy and the use of the facility. A projection can therefore be made by examining a known level of revenue or expense and calculating the portion that is fixed and the portion that is variable. Then the fixed component is held at a constant level, while the variable component is adjusted to reflect the percentage change between the projected occupancy and facility utilization and the actual occupancy and facility utilization that produced the known revenue or expense. This process is demonstrated in the following example.

EXAMPLE

A 200-room commercial hotel operated last year with an occupancy of 70%, an average room rate of $104.33, and a rooms department expense of $1,226,000, or 23% of rooms revenue. A projection for this year indicates that the subject's occupancy is expected to fall to 61% because several new hotels will open in the area during the year. This year's rooms department expense can be calculated with the procedure described below.

First, last year's rooms department expense is expressed in this year's dollars by applying a 3% inflation rate.

$$\$1,226,000 \times 1.03 = \$1,263,000 \text{ (rounded)}$$

The appraiser has determined that 60% of the rooms expense is typically fixed and the remaining 40% varies with occupancy. Thus, fixed and variable components of this year's rooms expense are estimated as follows:

$$\text{Fixed: } 0.60 \times \$1,263,000 = \$758,000 \text{ (rounded)}$$
$$\text{Variable: } 0.40 \times \$1,263,000 = \$505,000 \text{ (rounded)}$$

Next, the variable component is adjusted for the decline in occupancy from 70% to 61%. The percentage decline in occupancy (occupancy adjustment) is calculated by dividing the projected occupancy by the known occupancy.

$$0.61 \div 0.70 = 0.8714$$

Multiplying the occupancy adjustment by the variable component yields the adjusted variable component.

$$0.8714 \times \$505,000 = \$440,000 \text{ (rounded)}$$

Finally, the fixed component and the adjusted variable component are combined to produce the estimated rooms department expense at 61% occupancy.

Fixed component	$758,000
Adjusted variable component	440,000
Projected rooms department expense	$1,198,000

Assuming the hotel's average rate remains at $104.33 in the first projection year, the hotel's rooms departmental expense ratio will increase from 23.0% to 25.8%.

The fixed component of rooms expense represents items such as front desk salaries and the cost of cleaning public areas that must be maintained regardless if the hotel is operating at zero or full occupancy. The variable component is made up of items such as maids' salaries and guest supplies, which vary directly with the level of occupancy.

Application of the Approach

The process of forecasting hotel revenue and expenses by the fixed and variable component approach is accomplished in the nine steps outlined below.

Step 1. All revenue and expense items are projected based on information found in the financial statements of the subject and/or comparable hotels. If the subject property is an existing hotel, then its past operating performance is generally used to establish future projections. For proposed hotels the appraiser must rely on the operating results of hotels considered comparable to the subject property.

Step 2. Comparable financial statements usually must be adjusted or modified to reflect the subject property's unique characteristics. These adjustments may include changing the average room rate, modifying the income and expense ratios, and altering the fixed charges. These changes are made to create a one-year financial statement that uses the subject property's first-year average room rate—expressed in current dollars prior to any initial year discounts—and the income and expense ratios that represent the occupancy level that the comparable experiences. This profit and loss statement is called the *base* (or *comparable base*) and will form a foundation for calculating fixed and variable component relationships.

Step 3. The revenue and expense figures that make up the base are revised (inflated or deflated) to reflect current dollars for each forecast year. The rate of change applied should reflect the anticipated price change for the individual line item in the income and expense statement. The average room rate used in the base is derived from the average rate projection. Any discounting of average room rates is disregarded in developing the base for each projection year. Step 3 aims to put the comparable financial data constituting the base into the inflated dollars anticipated for that year.

Step 4. Fixed and variable percentages are estimated for each revenue and expense category. Table 5.3 shows typical ranges of fixed and variable percentages and the index used to measure the amount of variable change.

TABLE 5.3 Fixed And Variable Percentages			
Revenue and Expense Category	**Percent Fixed**	**Percent Variable**	**Index of Variability**
Revenues			
Rooms	N/A	N/A	N/A
Food	10–50%	50–90%	Occupancy
Beverage	0–30	70–100	Food revenue
Telephone	10–40	60–90	Occupancy
Other income	30–60	40–70	Occupancy
Departmental Expenses			
Rooms	50–70%	30–50%	Occupancy
Food	35–60	40–65	Food revenue
Beverage	35–60	40–65	Beverage revenue
Telephone	55–75	25–45	Telephone revenue
Other income	40–60	40–60	Other income
Undistributed Operating Expenses			
Administrative and general	65–85%	15–35%	Total revenue
Transportation	65–90	10–35	Occupancy
Human resources	80–95	5–20	Total revenue
Information systems	80–100	0–20	Total revenue
Security	65–90	10–35	Occupancy
Marketing	65–85	15–35	Total revenue
Franchise fee	0	100	Rooms revenue
Property operation & maintenance	55–75	25–45	Total revenue
Energy (utilities)	80–95	5–20	Total revenue
Fixed Expenses			
Management fee	0%	100%	Total revenue
Property taxes	100	0	Total revenue
Insurance	100	0	Total revenue
Reserve for replacement	0	100	Total revenue

These fixed and variable percentages were developed from a regression analysis that evaluated hundreds of financial statements to determine which portion of each revenue and expense category was fixed and which was variable.

The index of variability refers to the factor that controls the movement of the variable component. For example, the variable component of food revenue moves in response to occupancy changes. Beverage revenue seems to be tied directly to food revenue. Food and beverage expense levels depend largely on changes in food and beverage revenue. The variable components of undistributed operating expenses and all fixed expenses seem to move in relation to total revenue.

Step 5. Each individual line item in a hotel's financial statement is projected separately using the fixed and variable calculations. The fixed component is estimated by multiplying the appropriate fixed percentage by the base revenue or expense line item for the corresponding projection year. The variable component is estimated in steps 6 through 8.

Step 6. Variable components are assumed to vary directly with the index of variability established in Step 4. The amount of variable change is quantified by dividing the appropriate projected index of variability by the index of variability for the base. For example, assume that the projected occupancy percentage for the subject property in Year 1 was 62%. The occupancy of the base was 73%. Dividing the projected occupancy by the base occupancy results in the following variable percentage change:

$$\frac{\text{Projected occupancy}}{\text{Base occupancy}} = \frac{0.620}{0.730} = 0.849, \text{ or } 84.9\%$$

Basically, this calculation shows that, as of that projected year, the subject's occupancy is estimated to be 84.9% of the occupancy percentage found in the comparable base data.

Step 7. The unadjusted variable component is calculated by multiplying the appropriate base revenue or expense item for the projected year by the variable percentage estimated in Step 4. Note that the total of the fixed and variable percentages for each line item must equal 100%.

Step 8. The unadjusted variable component must now be adjusted for variability in the index by multiplying the results of Step 7 by the variable percentage change calculated in Step 6. The product is known as the *adjusted variable component.*

Step 9. The forecast for the revenue or expense category is the total of the fixed component calculated in Step 5 and the adjusted variable component calculated in Step 8.

Step 1: Obtain Comparable Financial Statements

Obtaining operating information on hotels and motels is relatively simple for firms that regularly appraise existing lodging facilities, but for those who only perform this type of assignment occasionally, comparable financial data can be more difficult to obtain.

The key to selecting financial data for use in projecting hotel income and expenses is to rely on only recent financial statements from properties that are truly comparable to the subject. Employing the financial comparable selection procedure facilitates this process. Lodging facilities vary in many respects, including differences attributable to location, size, facilities, class, management, occupancy, and average room rate. Each of these factors can impact a hotel's financial operating results. When a number of financial statements are available, the financial comparable selection procedure shown below indicates the order in which factors should be considered to screen out the statements of hotels that are less similar to the subject.

1. Average room rate (class)

2. Facilities

3. Room count

4. Management (image & service)

5. Occupancy

6. Geographic location

In evaluating several financial statements, the appraiser should first look for income and expense data from hotels that are similar to the subject property in terms of average room rate. A hotel's class or rate structure directly impacts both income and expense ratios, particularly fixed expenses that are measured on a per-available-room basis. Generally, hotel operating data should not be compared unless the properties are either in the same class or no more than one class away from each other. Most hotels can be categorized in one of the following room rate classifications: luxury, first-class, mid-rate, economy (budget), or sub-budget.

After the appraiser has accumulated financial statements from other properties with similar room rates, attention is focused on hotels with facilities that are most comparable to those of the subject property. The term "facilities" is first used broadly. Hotels can be classified by the types of facilities they offer—e.g., commercial, convention, resort, conference, health spa, suite, or extended stay. Within these broad classifications financial comparability can be further refined by matching properties with similar physical components. For example, the term convention hotel can include a wide range of properties, from a 250-room suburban hotel to a 2,000-room convention center. Some resort hotels may just offer rooms on a beach, while others may provide a full resort complex with all types of recreational amenities. The facility's age and condition should also be considered. Financial comparability can be enhanced by using the financial statements of properties with similar facilities, particularly if these facilities generate large amounts of revenue (food and beverage) or operating expenses (golf courses).

Room count is the next consideration in the financial comparable selection order. The financial data used in projecting income and expense are generally more reliable when they come from comparable properties that are similar in size to the subject property. In assessing comparability, size can be defined broadly. A small hotel might be defined as one with 0 to 150 rooms. A mid-sized property would have between 150 and 300 rooms, and properties of 300 to 1,000 rooms would be considered large. A mega-property would have 1,000 rooms or more. These categories can overlap, so size must be evaluated on a case-by-case basis.

When a hotel's future management is known, it is often appropriate to use the financial operating ratios exhibited by other properties managed by this particular operator as a basis for forecasting income and expense. Although more weight should be given to the previous considerations in the financial comparable selection order (i.e., average room rate, facilities, and rooms count), the obvious strengths and weaknesses of the contemplated management should be factored into the analysis, particularly if the property is subject to a long-term management contract.

Occupancy is one of the least important considerations in the evaluation of comparability. When the fixed and variable income and expense forecasting model is used, differences in occupancy levels between the comparable and the subject property are automatically adjusted. Nevertheless, appraisers should avoid using financial data from hotels that exhibit widely divergent occupancies.

Geographic considerations are generally given minimal weight in selecting comparable financial data. Most hotel operating expenses are not dependent on the property's geographic location. However, two specific expense categories— energy cost and property taxes—are strongly affected by local factors. In addition, data from markets such as New York City, Washington, D.C., and San Francisco, which are burdened by unusually high labor costs, should not be compared to properties that are not similarly affected.

Appraisers should recognize that the financial comparable selection order provides a quick method for identifying financial data that may be comparable to the subject property. In certain situations it may be appropriate to use data that do not fall within the process described as long as the desired effect—i.e., a proper base for projecting income and expense—is ultimately obtained.

CASE STUDY

Financial Comparable Selection Order

The following statement of income and expense (Table 5.4) was obtained from a hotel that is considered to be closely comparable to the proposed Sheraton.

Table 5.5 shows the areas of similarity between the comparable and the proposed Sheraton Hotel.

Several adjustments will be made to these financial data to make them comparable to the physical, operational, and location-specific characteristics contemplated for the proposed Sheraton.

TABLE 5.4   Comparable Statement of Income and Expense

Number of rooms:	290			
Occupancy rate:	68%			
Occupied rooms:	71,978			
Average rate:	$144.50			
	Total $ (in thousands)	**Percent of Gross**	**Per Available Room (PAR)**	**Per Occupied Room (POR)**
Revenue				
Rooms	$10,401	57.7%	$35,865	$144.50
Food	4,734	26.3	16,325	65.77
Beverage	1,544	8.6	5,324	21.45
Telephone	474	2.6	1,636	6.59
Other income	870	4.8	3,000	12.09
Total revenue	$18,023	100.0%	$62,150	$250.40
Departmental Expenses*				
Rooms	$2,444	23.5%	$8,428	$33.96
Food & beverage	4,709	75.0	16,237	65.42
Telephone	199	42.0	687	2.77
Other income	413	47.5	1,425	5.74
Total departmental expenses	$7,765	43.1%	$26,777	$107.89
Departmental Income	$10,258	56.9%	$35,373	$142.51
Undistributed Operating Expenses (UDOE)				
Administrative & general	$1,361	7.5%	$4,692	$18.90
Marketing	608	3.4	2,095	8.44
Franchise fee	551	3.1	1,900	7.66
Property operation & maintenance	790	4.4	2,724	10.98
Energy	720	4.0	2,483	10.00
Total UDOE	$4,030	22.4%	$13,894	$55.98
Income Before Fixed Charges	$6,228	34.5%	$21,479	$86.53
Fixed Charges				
Management fee	$586	3.3%	$2,021	$8.14
Property taxes	560	3.1	1,931	7.78
Insurance	189	1.0	650	2.62
Reserve for replacement	503	2.8	1,734	6.99
Total fixed charges	1,838	10.2	6,336	25.53
Net Income	$4,390	24.3%	$15,143	$61.00
Ratios				
Food revenue to rooms revenue	45.5%			
Food and beverage revenue to rooms revenue	60.4			
Telephone revenue to rooms revenue	4.6			
Other income to rooms revenue	8.4			
Beverage revenue to food revenue	32.6			

* Departmental expenses expressed as a ratio to departmental revenues

TABLE 5.5   **Hotel Comparison**

	Comparable Hotel	**Proposed Sheraton**
Average room rate	$144.50 (base year)	$148.56 (stabilized, deflated to base year dollars)
Facilities	Convention-commercial orientation with 50 square feet of meeting and banquet space per room. Fairly extensive restaurant and lounge facilities which, combined with banquet and meeting space, produce food and beverage revenue that equates to approximately 68% of rooms revenue. Normal amount of recreational amenities. This hotel is four years old.	Convention-commercial orientation with 42 square feet of meeting and banquet space per room. Somewhat lower concentration of restaurant and lounge space than the comparable. Similar recreational amenities are anticipated.
Room count	290 rooms	250 rooms
Management	National hotel management with experience in operating first-class convention hotels	Similar to comparable
Occupancy	68% (base year)	71% (stabilized)
Geographic location	Midwest	Northeast

Step 2. *Adjust comparable financial statements*

Comparability among hotels is never precise, so adjustments must be made to individual categories (line items) of income and expense to bring the comparable's actual operating results closer to the expectations for the subject.

Comparable financial data are adjusted in two stages. In Stage 1, the comparable operating data for a particular income or expense category are projected for the subject property using an appropriate unit of comparison. This produces a general estimate of each income and expense category. In Stage 2, each of the subject's projected revenue and expense categories is fine-tuned by factoring the property's unique physical, operational and location-specific attributes into the final projection. Both of these stages are described.

When projecting income and expense using comparable financial data, it is first necessary to break down the comparable income and expense statement into specific units of comparison. For hotels, these units of comparison include

- Percent of total revenue
- Percent of rooms revenue
- Percent of food and beverage revenue

- Dollars per available room
- Dollars per occupied room

Applying units of comparison puts the financial data on a common basis so that the comparable's operating results can be analyzed and projected for the subject. A given unit of comparison may be better suited to some revenue and expense categories than others. Certain units are more applicable because of specific volume relationships, which cause individual revenue and expense categories to react differently to changes in a hotel's occupancy, average room rate, and food and beverage volume. If, for example, a revenue or expense category varies in relation to changing occupancy levels or average room rates, the appropriate unit of comparison would be the percentage of rooms revenue or total revenue. If the category is primarily fixed, then greater emphasis should be placed on the dollars per available room unit of comparison. A category that is food and beverage-sensitive would be expressed as a percentage of food and beverage revenue.

Table 5.6 shows the primary units of comparison applied in projecting each category of hotel income and expense from a comparable financial statement.

TABLE 5.6   Units of Comparison Applied

Unit of Comparison	Sensitivity Factors	Used to Project the Following Income and Expense Categories
Percent of total revenue	Occupancy Average room rate Food & beverage revenue	Administrative and general Management fee Marketing Property operation and maintenance
Percent of rooms revenue	Occupancy Average room rate	Food revenue Telephone revenue Other income Rooms expense
Percent of food and beverage revenue	Food & beverage revenue	Food and beverage expense
Dollars per available room	Fixed categories	Administrative and general Marketing Property operation and maintenance Energy Insurance Property taxes
Dollars per occupied room	Occupancy	Food revenue Beverage revenue Telephone revenue Other income Rooms expense Energy

Each of the five units of comparison in the first column is sensitive to the various factors shown in the second column. For example, the percentage of total revenue is sensitive to a hotel's occupancy, average room rate, and food and beverage revenue. The last column shows which income and expense categories are best projected by a specific unit of comparison. Since most items of income and expense have both a fixed component and a variable component, it is sometimes appropriate to use more than one unit of comparison.

Once a projection for a category of income and expense is made using the units of comparison described, it is often necessary to fine-tune the projection to account for the physical, operational, and location-specific differences between the comparable and subject property. Primary differences that should be adjusted for include

- Differences in average room rate, particularly if the subject property is in a higher or lower class (e.g., economy, mid-rate, first, luxury) than the comparable
- Substantial differences in size (room count)
- Differences in food and beverage volume, particularly if one property has significantly more or less beverage or banquet revenue
- Location-specific differences, which generally affect energy costs and property tax expense

Since fixed and variable analysis adjusts for differences in occupancy between the comparable and the subject property, no specific adjustment is needed to account for a variance in occupancy at this point in the projection process.

When fine-tuned adjustments are required to account for differences between properties, the unit of comparison used in the projection is adjusted either upward or downward in the manner described below.

Percent of total revenue. Adjusting the percentage of total revenue unit of comparison upward for an expense item causes the dollar amount of that expense to increase. When the comparable has an average room rate that is higher than the rate of the subject property, its operating expense ratios based on a percentage of total revenue tend to be lower. If such an unadjusted percentage were to be applied to the subject property, it would be understated; therefore, the unit of comparison should be fine-tuned upward.

It is difficult to determine how to adjust the percentage of total revenue based on the property's size. In general, if the comparable is slightly larger than the subject property, its operating expense ratios, which utilize a percentage of total revenue, tend to be lower because some of the fixed expenses (such as payroll) can be spread out over a greater amount of revenue. This advantage ends at the point when added costs must be incurred to handle the additional rooms. For example, a single general manager might operate a 100-room hotel efficiently. That same individual could probably handle an additional 75 rooms, which would decrease the management payroll expressed as a percentage of total revenue. Once the room count exceeds 175, however, it may be necessary to hire an assistant manager to take over some of the operational responsibilities. This extra expense quickly increases the expense ratio.

When the comparable has more food and beverage revenue than the subject property does, its operating expense ratios, based on a percentage of total revenue, tend to be lower and should be fine-tuned upward when projecting expenses for the subject property.

Percent of rooms revenue. The fine-tuned adjustments for this unit of comparison are the same as those just described for the percentage of total revenue.

Percent of food and beverage revenue. This unit of comparison is used primarily to project food and beverage department expenses. As the volume of food and beverage increases, the food and beverage expense ratio usually decreases. If the comparable has more food and beverage revenue than the subject property does, its food and beverage expense ratio would be lower and should be adjusted upward to project the subject's food and beverage department expenses. An even greater upward adjustment is needed if the comparable has a considerable amount of beverage or banquet business, which tends to operate at a greater profit margin.

Ample banquet space adds to a hotel's food and beverage revenue. Often this amenity is necessary for the sale of guest rooms.

Dollars per available room. Adjusting the dollars per available room unit of comparison upward for an expense item causes the dollar amount of that expense to increase.

When the comparable has an average room rate that is higher than the subject property's rate, it is likely to be providing a superior level of service. This would likely increase the cost of operations on a per-available-room basis. In this instance the unit of comparison used to project expenses for the subject property should be adjusted downward.

The preceding discussion of an efficient room count also applies to the dollars per available room unit of comparison. If the comparable has a room count that is less efficient than the subject's, its operating expenses expressed on a per-available-room basis could be overstated and may have to be adjusted downward when making a projection for the subject property.

If the comparable has a greater amount of food and beverage revenue than the subject property does, its operating expenses will probably be higher when expressed on a per-available-room basis. In this case the unit of comparison used to project expenses for the subject property should be adjusted downward.

Dollars per occupied room. Since the occupancy level used for the subject property's base profit and loss statement will be the same as the occupancy of the comparable, the adjustments made to this unit of comparison should be identical to those used for the dollars per available room.

CASE STUDY

Adjusting Comparable Financial Data

The process of adjusting comparable financial data will be illustrated for the proposed Sheraton Hotel. First, each income and expense category is projected using an appropriate unit of comparison (Stage 1) and then the results are fine-tuned (Stage 2). Each category of income and expense is analyzed and adjusted separately using the comparable statement of income and expense (Table 5.4), which was selected for the proposed Sheraton through application of the financial comparable selection order. This process will result in a one-year financial statement that incorporates the subject's base year average room rate expressed in current dollars (before initial year discounting), and income and expense ratios that reflect the level of occupancy actually experienced by the comparable. This profit and loss statement, which is called the *base* or *comparable base,* will form a foundation for calculating the fixed and variable component relationships.

Rooms Revenue

The base rooms revenue is calculated by multiplying the occupancy rate by the average room rate, the room count, and 365. Since the fixed and variable component approach will automatically adjust for differences in occupancy, the comparable property's occupancy level will be used for the subject property. The Sheraton's average room rate was projected at $172.22 in the fifth year. Deflating this figure back to base year dollars at the assumed underlying inflation rate of 3.0% renders a result of $148.56. The base rooms revenue is therefore calculated as follows:

$$0.68 \times \$148.56 \times 250 \times 365 = \$9,218,000 \text{ (rounded)}$$

Food and Beverage Revenue

Food and beverage revenue is generated by a hotel's restaurants, lounges, coffee shops, snack bars, banquet rooms, and room service. These outlets are both revenue sources and necessary amenities for the sale of guest rooms. Although some hotels have active lounges and banquet facilities that attract local residents, in most hotels guests represent a substantial portion of the food and beverage patrons.

In the *Uniform System of Accounts for the Lodging Industry,* food revenue is defined as "revenue derived from the sale of food, including coffee, milk, tea and soft drinks. Food sales do not include meals charged on employees' (staff) checks." Beverage revenues are "derived from the sale of beverages." In addition to the revenue generated through the sale of food and beverages, hotels normally produce other related income derived from meeting room rental, cover charges, service charges, and miscellaneous banquet revenue. The combination of food income, beverage income, and other food and beverage income equals total food and beverage revenue.

Table 5.7 shows the various revenue categories that compose the food and beverage department within a hotel.

TABLE 5.7 Food and Beverage Revenue

Category	Percent of Category	Fixed Revenue	Variable Revenue		
			Occupancy Sensitive	Rate Sensitive	Food and Beverage Sensitive
Food	60–85%	–	Moderately	–	Highly
Beverage	15–40	–	Moderately	–	Highly
Other income					
Public room rentals	0–2	–	Moderately	–	Slightly
Cover and minimum charges	0–3	–	Moderately	–	Highly
Sundry banquet income	0–4	–	Slightly	–	Highly

The comparable statement of income and expense (Table 5.4) provides the following data, which will be used to project the base food revenue for the proposed Sheraton.

Total food revenue	$4,734,000
Food revenue per available room	$16,325
Food revenue per occupied room	$65.77
Ratio of food revenue to rooms revenue	46% (rounded)
Ratio of food revenue to total revenue	26% (rounded)

The description of the comparable hotel provided in Table 5.5 indicates that this hotel has larger, more elaborate food and beverage facilities than are planned for the proposed Sheraton. Specifically, the comparable has 50 square feet of meeting and banquet space per room compared to the subject's 42 square feet—a difference of about 16%. In addition, the Sheraton will have a lower concentration of restaurant and lounge space.

These differences between the food facilities of the comparable and those planned for the subject indicate that the food revenue per available room unit of comparison should be adjusted downward. Offsetting this downward adjustment would be a slight upward adjustment to reflect the Sheraton's new facilities and higher average room rate, which could lead to lower menu prices. Based on this analysis, the comparable property's food revenue per available room will be adjusted downward by 15%. When this adjustment is applied, the following base food revenue is produced:

$$\$16,325 \times 0.85 \times 250 \text{ rooms} = \$3,469,000 \text{ (rounded)}$$

The ratio of food revenue to rooms revenue would also be an appropriate unit of comparison. This unit of comparison would be adjusted downward to compute the subject's food base. However, the ratio of food revenue to total revenue is generally a less reliable unit of comparison.

Beverage revenue is derived from the sale of alcoholic beverages in a hotel's restaurants and banquet rooms and from the sale of both alcoholic and nonalcoholic beverages in the hotel's bars and lounges. Beverage revenue can be projected in a manner similar to food revenue using the fixed and variable component method. Appraisers should recognize that much of the beverage revenue a hotel generates usually comes from its lounge outlet. Lounge customers tend to be fickle, however, frequenting a popular spot one year and another the next. Since management plays an important role in the ultimate success of a hotel's beverage operation, it is often wise to use comparable beverage revenue data that reflect the same level of beverage management expertise that the subject property will experience.

Beverage revenue tends to be highly variable, changing directly with food revenue. The most appropriate unit of comparison, therefore, is a percentage of food revenue. The ratio of beverage revenue to food revenue for the comparable is approximately 33%. While the proposed Sheraton will have a similar ratio of beverage facilities to food facilities as the comparable, a downward adjustment to the unit of comparison is appropriate to account for the comparable property's highly successful lounge. Using a ratio of beverage revenue to food revenue of 27%, the following calculation shows the base beverage revenue for the subject property.

$$\$3,469,000 \times 0.27 = \$937,000 \text{ (rounded)}$$

Telephone Revenue

Telephone revenue is generated from hotel guests charging local and long-distance calls to their rooms and from out-of-town patrons using the hotel's public telephones. Before deregulation of the telephone industry in the early 1980s, hotels were limited to a 15% commission on long-distance calls. This mark-up was generally too low to generate a profit for most hotels' telephone departments, which typically ran at a loss. Today, however, the mark-up at which hotels can resell telephone services to guests is not regulated. As a result of this freedom and the development of sophisticated call accounting equipment, the telephone department is generally able to profit. State-of-the-art telephone equipment can provide functions as sophisticated as least cost routing, automatic price billing, and post telephone charging to guest folios. Moreover, hotels can select among various providers of long-distance services and can work with any one of a number of Alternative Operator Services (AOS), which route and price calls and may also provide additional telephone-related guest services.

In recent years the hotel industry has seen diverging trends in telephone revenue. The number of long-distance calls billed per occupied room has decreased due to the use of long-distance carrier services accessed via calling cards, as well as increased reliance upon cell phones. When hotel guests charge long-distance calls to their personal or business telephone accounts, the hotel loses the revenue from the long-distance tariff and mark-up and can generally charge only an access fee.

Table 5.8 shows the various accounts that compose telephone revenue according to the *Uniform System of Accounts for the Lodging Industry*.

Telephone revenue varies directly with changes in occupancy. The small portion of this revenue category that is fixed represents pay station revenue generated by unregistered patrons using the hotel's food and beverage outlets and meeting rooms. The appropriate units of comparison would be revenue per occupied room and revenue per available room.

TABLE 5.8   **Telephone Revenue**

				Variable Revenue	
Category	Percent of Category	Fixed Revenue	Occupancy Sensitive	Rate Sensitive	Food and Beverage Sensitive
Local	25–60%	–	Highly	–	–
Long distance	35–60	–	Highly	–	–
Service charges	0–10	–	Highly	–	–
Commissions–local	0–10	–	Highly	–	–
Commissions–long-distance	0–10	–	Highly	–	–

The comparable statement of income and expense shows the following data, which provide a basis for projecting the base telephone revenue for the proposed Sheraton.

Total telephone revenue	$474,000
Telephone revenue per available room	$1,636
Telephone revenue per occupied room	$6.59
Ratio of telephone revenue to rooms revenue	4.6%
Ratio of telephone revenue to total revenue	2.6%

Because the comparable property has about 15% more meeting, banquet, restaurant, and lounge facilities than the proposed Sheraton does, it probably attracts 15% more unregistered food and beverage patrons who would use the pay telephones. If outside usage represents 10% of the total telephone revenue (the fixed component), then the comparable data should be adjusted downward by approximately 1.5% (15% × 10% = 1.5%). Based on this analysis, the comparable property's telephone revenue per occupied room is adjusted downward by 1.5%. With this adjustment, the base telephone revenue is calculated as follows:

$$\$6.59 \times 0.985 \times 250 \text{ rooms} \times 0.68 \times 365 = \$403,000 \text{ (rounded)}$$

The same base telephone revenue could have been calculated using the telephone revenue per available room. The ratio of telephone revenue to rooms revenue or to total revenue are considered secondary units of comparison because small changes in a hotel's average room rate often have little impact on telephone service charges. If the comparable were a different class of hotel, then the potential difference in telephone rates charged would have been considered.

Other Income

Other income represents revenue derived from sources other than the sale of guest rooms, food and beverages, and telephone service. Depending on the type of hotel and the facilities and amenities offered, other income may include the following revenue items:

- Rents charged for stores, office space, concession space, clubs, and storage
- Commissions from auto rental, photography, telegrams, and vending services
- Concession revenue paid by others for the privilege of operating departments that might otherwise be operated by the hotel itself; gift shops, barbers, and beauty shops are typically concessions.
- Revenue derived from in-room movie charges
- Cash discounts earned from creditors' accounts for payment within the discount period; trade discounts, which are deducted from the cost of goods sold, are not considered other income.
- Electronic games and pinball machines
- Forfeited advance deposits and guaranteed no-shows
- Service charges added to customers' accounts for service that does not have to be paid to service personnel
- Interest income from house accounts
- Salvage revenue from the sale of old and obsolete items

Other income is highly sensitive to occupancy and slightly sensitive to food and beverage usage, so the appropriate units of comparison would be either a percentage of rooms revenue adjusted for any unusual food and beverage volume or revenue per occupied room. When a hotel has extensive retail or office rental space, recreational amenities, or other significant sources of other income, a separate revenue category may be used to show the extent of this income.

The following data from the comparable statement provides a basis for projecting the base other income for the proposed Sheraton.

Total other income	$870,000
Other income per available room	$3,000
Other income per occupied room	$12.09
Ratio of other income to rooms revenue	8.4%
Ratio of other income to total revenue	4.8%

Using the ratio of other income to rooms revenue as the unit of comparison, several fine-tuned adjustments would be appropriate. A downward adjustment is needed to reflect the comparable property's more extensive restaurant and banquet space, which should generate more other income than the subject. A slight upward adjustment should also be applied to reflect the subject's higher average rate, newer facilities, and greater ability to use these advantages to generate proportionately more other income than the comparable does.

Based on this analysis, the comparable property's 8.4% ratio of other income to rooms revenue will be adjusted downward to 8.0%. When this adjustment is applied, the following base other income is produced:

$$0.08 \times \$9,218,000 = \$737,000 \text{ (rounded)}$$

Total Revenue

The base total revenue is calculated by adding the five revenue components.

Rooms	$9,218,000
Food	3,469,000
Beverage	937,000
Telephone	403,000
Other income	737,000
Total	$14,764,000

Rooms Expense

Rooms expense consists of items relating to the sale and upkeep of guestrooms and public space. Table 5.9 outlines the components of the rooms department expense category according to the *Uniform System of Accounts for the Lodging Industry.*

Most of the categories that compose rooms expenses appear to be moderately occupancy-sensitive and highly rate-sensitive, indicating that a portion of the category is fixed and the remainder is occupancy-variable.

Salaries, wages, and employee benefits account for a substantial portion of the rooms expense. Although a portion of the payroll expense is occupancy-variable in that management can schedule maids, bell personnel, and house cleaners to work only when occupancy requires, much of the rooms payroll is fixed. Front desk personnel, public area cleaners, housekeepers, and other supervisory staff are needed regardless of the occupancy level. As a result, salaries, wages, and employee benefits are only moderately occupancy-sensitive.

Commissions represent remuneration to travel agents for booking rooms. Since these charges are usually based on a percentage of rooms revenue, they are highly occupancy- and rate-sensitive. Similarly, reservation expenses normally reflect the cost of a franchise reservation system, which typically charges a percentage of rooms revenue.

Other rooms expenses, such as laundry, linen, supplies, and uniforms, are also affected by volume and are therefore slightly or very slightly occupancy-sensitive.

TABLE 5.9 Rooms Expenses

Category	Percent of Category	Fixed Expenses	Variable Expenses		
			Occupancy Sensitive	Rate Sensitive	Food and Beverage Sensitive
Salaries and wages	50–70%	–	Moderately	–	–
Employee benefits	5–15	–	Moderately	–	–
Cost of employee meals	1–4	–	Moderately	–	–
Cable/satellite television	1–5	–	Moderately	–	–
Commissions	0–3	–	Highly	Highly	–
Complimentary guest services	1–5	–	Moderately	–	–
Contract cleaning	1–3	Moderately	–	–	–
Guest relocation	1–4	–	Moderately	–	–
Guest transportation	1–4	–	Moderately	–	–
Laundry and dry cleaning	7–12	–	Slightly	–	–
Linen	3–8	–	Very slightly	–	–
Operating supplies	1–4	–	Very slightly	–	–
Other operating expenses	1–4	–	Very slightly	–	–
Reservation expenses	0–8	–	Highly	Highly	–
Telecommunications	1–4	–	Moderately	–	–
Training	1–4	–	Moderately	–	–
Uniforms	1–3	–	Very slightly	–	–

Because room expenses are influenced by changes in occupancy and average room rates, the applicable unit of comparison would be either a percentage of rooms revenue or an amount per occupied room.

The comparable statement of income and expense shows the following data, which can be used to project the base rooms expense for the proposed Sheraton.

Total rooms expense	$2,444,000
Rooms expense per available room	$8,428
Rooms expense per occupied room	$33.96
Ratio of rooms expense to rooms revenue	23.5%

The percentage of rooms expense to rooms revenue was selected as the appropriate unit of comparison for the appropriate proposed Sheraton. A fine-tuned adjustment is required because, as Table 5.5 indicates, the proposed Sheraton has an estimated average room rate of $148.56 in the base year, compared with the comparable property's current average rate of $144.50. This slight difference should enable the Sheraton to achieve a rooms expense ratio that is somewhat lower than the comparable property's. The amount of the downward adjustment can be based on the percentage relationship between the average room rates of the comparable and the Sheraton. The comparable's average room rate divided by the Sheraton's average room rate shows that the comparable property's rate is 97% of the Sheraton's. Multiplying this percentage by the comparable property's ratio of rooms expense to rooms revenue quantifies the downward adjustment.

$$0.235 \times 0.97 = 0.228, \text{ or } 22.8\%$$

In addition to this room rate modification, a slight upward adjustment should be made to reflect the fact that the comparable has 40 more rooms than the subject does. Based on this analysis, the comparable property's rooms expense ratio is adjusted to 23.0%. The base rooms expense is calculated by multiplying the subject's base rooms revenue by the rooms expense ratio.

$$\$9,218,000 \times 0.23 = \$2,120,000 \text{ (rounded)}$$

Food and Beverage Expense

The food and beverage department expense consists of costs incurred for the operation of a hotel's food, beverage, and banquet facilities. Although food revenue and beverage revenue are normally projected separately and each has its own categories on a hotel's income and expense statement, the expenses for these revenue sources are combined into a single expense category called food and beverage expense. Table 5.10 outlines the components of the food and beverage department expense category.

The costs of sales, salaries, and wages constitute the major portion of food and beverage expenses. These components are moderately to highly food and beverage-sensitive in that they vary directly with changes in food and beverage volume. Costs of operating supplies, other operating expenses, and uniforms tend to be very slightly food and beverage-sensitive. Based on this analysis, the appropriate unit of comparison is a percentage of food and beverage revenue. When using this unit of comparison, care must be taken to select comparable properties with similar ratios of beverage to food sales.

Since the profit margin from the sale of beverages is considerably higher than the profit from the sale of food, a hotel with a higher ratio of beverage to food sales should have a lower food and beverage departmental expense ratio. The expense ratio increases as the ratio of beverage to food sales declines.

To quantify the impact of different ratios of beverage to food sales, it is sometimes helpful to analyze the cost of food sold and the cost of beverages sold separately. The three cost components that make up the comparable

TABLE 5.10   Food and Beverage Expenses

Category	Percent of Category	Fixed Expenses	Variable Expenses — Occupancy Sensitive	Rate Sensitive	Food and Beverage Sensitive
Cost of food consumed	35–45%	–	–	–	Highly
Cost of employee meals	1–4	–	–	–	Moderately
Cost of beverage sales	20–30	–	–	–	Highly
Salaries and wages	25–35	–	–	–	Moderately
Employee benefits	2–9	–	–	–	Very slightly
Contract cleaning	0–3	Moderately	–	–	–
Kitchen fuel	1–2	Moderately	–	–	–
Laundry and dry cleaning	1–2	–	–	–	Slightly
Licenses	1–2	Moderately	–	–	–
Music and other entertainment	2–7	Moderately	–	–	–
Operating supplies	1–3	–	–	–	Very slightly
Other operating expenses	1–3	–	–	–	Very slightly
Uniforms	1–2	–	–	–	Very slightly

property's food and beverage expense category are shown below. This information can be obtained from the supporting schedules, which are normally part of a hotel's financial statements.

Cost of food sold	$1,565,000	33%*
Cost of beverages sold	271,000	18%**
All other food and beverage expenses	2,873,000	46%***
Total	$4,709,000	

*   Percent of food revenue
**   Percent of beverage revenue
*** Percent of total food and beverage revenue

The comparable data indicate a food cost of 33% of food revenue, a beverage cost of 18% of beverage revenue, and all other expenses totaling 46% of total food and beverage revenue.

The comparable hotel shows a ratio of beverage revenue to food revenue of approximately 33%, compared to the proposed Sheraton's base ratio of 27%. Because of this difference, one would expect the Sheraton's food and beverage department expense ratio to be higher than the comparable property's 75.0%. The comparable also has higher food and beverage volume on a per-room basis, indicating stronger banquet capture, which tends to increase food and beverage profits due to lower costs. (See Table 5.11.)

TABLE 5.11	Dollars per Available Room–Food and Beverage	
	Comparable	**Proposed Sheraton**
Food revenue	$16,325	$13,876
Beverage revenue	5,324	3,747

Based on this analysis, an upward adjustment to the comparable property's food and beverage expense ratios is warranted. Shown below are the adjusted expense ratios that will be used to project the base food and beverage expense for the proposed Sheraton Hotel.

Cost of food sold	34%
Cost of beverages sold	19%
All other food and beverage expenses	47%

The base food and beverage expense for the proposed Sheraton is calculated in Table 5.12.

TABLE 5.12	Food and Beverage Expense–Proposed Sheraton					
	Expense Ratios		**Projected Revenue**		**Food & Beverage Base Expense**	
Cost of food sold	0.34	×	$3,469,000	=	$1,179,000 (rounded)	
Cost of beverages sold	0.19	×	937,000	=	178,000 (rounded)	
All other food and beverage expenses	0.47	×	4,406,000	=	2,071,000 (rounded)	
Total					$3,428,000 (rounded)	

The ratio of the Sheraton's total food and beverage base expense to its total base food and beverage revenue ($4,406,000) is 78%, which appears to be well supported by the comparable data and data from other, similar hotels.

Telephone Expense

Telephone expenses consist of all costs associated with the operation of a hotel's telephone department. For smaller hotels with automated phone systems, the telephone department may be simply an additional responsibility for the front desk personnel. In most large properties the telephone department will have one or more full-time telephone operators to provide necessary phone service to guests.

Table 5.13 illustrates the various accounts that make up telephone expenses.

The bulk of the telephone expense is attributable to the cost of local and long-distance calls billed by the telephone companies providing this service. Since in-house guests make most of these calls, these expenses are moder-

TABLE 5.13 Telephone Expenses

Category	Percent of Category	Fixed Expenses	Variable Expenses		
			Occupancy Sensitive	Rate Sensitive	Food and Beverage Sensitive
Local calls	20–60%	—	Moderately	–	–
Long distance calls	20–60	—	Moderately	–	–
Rental of equipment	0–30	Moderately	–	–	–
Salaries and wages	0–10	Moderately	–	–	–
Employee benefits	0–4	Moderately	–	–	–
Equipment charges	0–10	Moderately	–	–	–
Other operating expenses	0–5	Moderately	–	–	–
Printing and stationary	0–5	Moderately	–	–	–
Uniforms	0–2	Moderately	–	–	–

ately occupancy-sensitive. Unless a particular department has unusually heavy telephone usage, normal telephone usage by hotel employees is also charged to this account. The remaining costs, such as salaries and wages, other expenses, and printing are all moderately fixed. Note that according to the Uniform System of Accounts for the Lodging Industry (USALI), the rental of telephone equipment is categorized as a fixed charge, under the rent, taxes, and insurance item. Care should be taken to determine exactly how the hotel accounts for telephone equipment rental or leasing.

Based on this analysis of the components of telephone expense and considering that the cost of telephone service is largely driven by in-house usage that generates telephone revenue, the appropriate unit of comparison would be a percentage of telephone revenue.

The comparable statement of income and expense provides the following data as a basis for projecting the base telephone expense for the proposed Sheraton:

Total telephone expense	$199,000
Telephone expense per available room	$687
Telephone expense per occupied room	$2.77
Ratio of telephone expense to telephone revenue	42.0%

Using the ratio of telephone expense to telephone revenue as the unit of comparison, a slight upward adjustment is needed because the comparable property's telephone department will probably generate more profit than the proposed Sheraton's will. This difference can be attributed to the comparable property's higher concentration of meeting and banquet space, which attracts more outside capture and therefore more telephone usage than is expected for the Sheraton. Greater telephone usage is indicated by the comparable property's telephone revenue per available room, which is $1,636, compared to the Sheraton's base of $1,612 (1.5% difference).

Based on this analysis, the comparable property's ratio of telephone expense to telephone revenue is adjusted upward very slightly from 42.0% to 43.4%. With this adjustment, the following base telephone expense is produced:

$$0.434 \times \$403,000 = \$175,000 \text{ (rounded)}$$

Other Income Expense

Other income expense covers all of the expenses associated with other income revenue. The extent of these expenses depends on the nature of the revenue. For example, if a hotel leases a gift shop to an operator (tenant), the hotel's expenses will be minimal, consisting only of items such as rental fees and commissions. If, on the other hand, the hotel operates the gift shop, both the revenue and expenses will be higher; the products sold will generate revenue and the cost of goods sold, payroll, and other expenses will be incurred. The appropriate unit of comparison is a percentage of other income (revenue).

The comparable statement of income and expense shows the following data, which provide a basis for projecting the base other income expense for the proposed Sheraton:

Total other income expense	$413,000
Other income expense per available room	$1,425
Other income expense per occupied room	$5.74
Ratio of other income expense to other income revenue	47.5%

Using the ratio of other income expense to other income revenue as a unit of comparison, an upward, fine-tuned adjustment is required to reflect the premium in the comparable property's other income revenue expressed on a per-available-room basis, relative to the subject property. (See Table 5.14.)

TABLE 5.14 Other Income Revenue per Available Room

Comparable	$3,000
Proposed Sheraton	2,948

Based on this analysis, the comparable property's ratio of other income expense to other income revenue is adjusted upward from 47.5% to 48.3%. This reflects an adjustment of approximately 1.8% and takes into account both the fixed and variable components of other income expense, which is generally 50% fixed and 50% variable. The following calculation shows the base other income expense for the proposed Sheraton:

$$0.483 \times \$737,000 = \$356,000 \text{ (rounded)}$$

Administrative and General Expense

A hotel's administrative and general expenses include all the managerial and operational expenses that cannot be attributed to a particular department. For example, the general manager might work part of the day solving a problem in the rooms department and spend the remainder of the day booking an important food and beverage function. It would be difficult to allocate the manager's salary to the individual departments served, so the category of administrative and general expense is used. Table 5.15 outlines the components of the administrative and general expenses category according to the *Uniform System of Accounts for the Lodging Industry.*

Most administrative and general expenses are moderately fixed. The exceptions include cash overages and shortages; credit card commissions; provisions for doubtful accounts that are moderately affected by the quantity of transactions or total revenue; and salaries, wages, benefits, and security, which are very slightly influenced by volume.

In recent years several new categories have been added to administrative and general expenses. The human resources account includes the cost of recruiting, relocating, and training employees. Security expenses cover the cost of contract security for the property and other related expenses. General insurance (also known as liability insurance) was recently moved out of the administrative and general expenses category into the insurance category. Insurance expenses previously consisted of only building and building contents insurance. The elements of the newly defined insurance expenses category will be detailed later in this section.

Considering the components of administrative and general expenses, the appropriate unit of comparison is the amount per available room, supported by the percentage of total revenue.

The following data from the comparable statement of income and expense provide a basis for projecting the base administrative and general expenses for the proposed Sheraton.

Total administrative and general expenses	$1,361,000
Administrative and general expenses per available room	$4,692
Administrative and general expenses per occupied room	$18.90
Ratio of administrative and general expenses to total revenue	7.5%

TABLE 5.15 Administrative and General Expenses

Category	Percent of Category	Fixed Expenses	Variable Expenses		
			Occupancy Sensitive	Rate Sensitive	Food and Beverage Sensitive
Salaries and wages	15–35%	–	Very slightly	–	Very slightly
Employee benefits	1–8	–	Very slightly	–	Very slightly
Bank charges	0–3	Moderately	Very slightly	–	Very slightly
Cash overages and shortages	0–3	–	Moderately	Moderately	Moderately
Communication systems	0–3	Moderately	–	–	–
Contract services	0–3	Moderately	–	–	–
Credit and collection	0–3	Moderately	Moderately	Moderately	–
Credit card commissions	3–10	–	Highly	Highly	Highly
Donations	0–2	Moderately	–	–	–
Dues and subscriptions	1–4	Moderately	–	–	–
Head office	3–10	Moderately	–	–	–
Human resources	3–10	–	–	–	–
Information systems	3–10	–	–	–	–
Internal audit	1–3	–	Moderately	–	–
Internal communications	0–2	–	Moderately	–	–
Loss and damage	0–1	–	Moderately	–	–
Meals and entertainment	3–10	–	Moderately	–	–
Operating supplies and equipment	3–10	–	Moderately	–	–
Postage	2–8	Moderately	–	–	–
Printing and stationary	3–10	Moderately	–	–	–
Professional fees	2–5	Moderately	–	–	–
Provision for doubtful accounts	1–3	–	Moderately	Moderately	Moderately
Security	3–10	–	Moderately	Moderately	Moderately
Telecommunications	3–10	–	Moderately	Moderately	Moderately
Training	3–10	–	Moderately	Moderately	Moderately
Transportation	3–10	–	Moderately	Moderately	Moderately
Travel	1–8	Moderately	–	–	–
Other	1–4	Moderately	–	–	Highly

Using the administrative and general expense per available room as a unit of comparison, with support from the ratio of administrative and general expenses to total revenue, several fine-tuned adjustments are needed to compensate for various differences between the comparable and the subject property.

As Table 5.16 indicates, the comparable hotel's total rooms, food and beverage, telephone, and other income revenue expressed in dollars per available room is 5.2% higher than that of the proposed Sheraton. The difference between the total revenue per available room of the Sheraton and the comparable is $62,150 – $59,056, or $3,094. Applying the comparable property's ratio of administrative and general expense to total revenue of 7.5%, the additional administrative and general expense incurred by the comparable is estimated to be $3,094 × .075 = $232. Since the administrative and general expense category is 70% fixed and 30% variable, only 30% of the $232 of administrative and general expense, or $70, would be deducted from the comparable property's per-room cost.

TABLE 5.16 **Dollars per Available Room—Administrative and General Expenses**

	Comparable	Proposed Sheraton
Rooms	$35,865	$36,872
Food	16,325	13,876
Beverage	5,324	3,748
Telephone	1,636	1,612
Other income	3,000	2,948
Total	$62,150	$59,056

Based on this analysis, the comparable property's administrative and general expense of $4,692 per available room is adjusted downward to $4,622. This adjustment of approximately 1.5% takes into account the fixed and variable components of this expense category. The following calculation shows the base administrative and general expense for the proposed Sheraton.

$$250 \times \$4,622 = \$1,156,000 \text{ (rounded)}$$

The base administrative and general expense estimated above equates to 7.8% of the Sheraton's total revenue. Relative to the comparable, this increase in the expense ratio appears to be normal and provides support for the previous per-available-room calculation.

Marketing Expense

Marketing expense includes all the expenses associated with the advertising, sales, and promotion of a lodging facility. These marketing activities are designed to obtain new customers and retain existing ones. Marketing efforts attempt to create an image for the hotel, develop customer awareness, and stimulate patronage for the property and its facilities. Unlike most expense categories, marketing is controlled almost completely by management. Most hotel operators develop annual marketing plans that detail the expenditures for the coming year. If such a budget is followed, total marketing expenses can be projected accurately.

In establishing a marketing budget, a hotel operator considers many factors. The results of marketing expenditures are not always realized immediately. Depending on the type of advertising and promotion used, the increased patronage generated may not be seen for several months or years. An advantage of this lag period is that the benefits of a successful marketing campaign tend to continue after the marketing program has ended.

Hotels have unique operating characteristics that must be considered in developing a marketing plan or reviewing the effectiveness of an established marketing effort. Some significant characteristics are outlined below.

- New hotels, especially those catering to the meeting and group segment, need a pre-opening marketing plan that begins before the hotel opens. Most groups book hotels months or years prior to their meetings. For business meetings and conferences, accommodations are typically arranged three to six months in advance; large national conventions may choose their sites as many as five years in advance. If a meeting-oriented hotel is not active in the marketplace in time to obtain this pre-booked business, it will lose out to established competition and suffer from low occupancy during its initial years of operation.

- Marketing efforts tend to be cumulative, so the initial marketing budget for a new hotel should allow for greater expenditures, which may be needed to generate the desired impact.

- If an existing property has neglected its marketing efforts for the past several years, a higher-than-normal marketing budget may be needed to maintain or increase current revenues. However, if an aggressive marketing program has been in effect, marketing expenses may be reduced without hurting revenues.

- The marketing budget should be tailored to the specific property and to the nature of the local supply and demand for transient accommodations. Characteristics such as location, visibility, chain affiliation, class, and the types of market segments served can affect the type and amount of marketing expenditures required. The local competitive environment can also influence the amount of money needed to capture the necessary market demand.

Table 5.17 shows the various accounts that make up marketing expense according to the *Uniform System of Accounts for the Lodging Industry.*

TABLE 5.17   Marketing Expenses

Category	Percent of Category	Fixed Expenses	Variable Expenses		
			Occupancy Sensitive	Rate Sensitive	Food and Beverage Sensitive
Salaries and wages	10–60%	Budgeted	–	–	–
Employee benefits	2–10	Budgeted	–	–	–
Sales	20–60	Budgeted	–	–	–
Advertising	20–60	Budgeted	–	–	–
Merchandising	5–40	Budgeted	–	–	–
Public relations and publicity	5–30	Budgeted	–	–	–
Research	0–15	Budgeted	–	–	–
Fees and commissions	0–50	–	Highly	Highly	Highly
Other selling and promotion	5–20	Budgeted	–	–	–

Marketing expenses can be divided into five subcategories: sales; reservations; advertising and merchandising; other marketing activities; and fees and commissions. Together these activities describe the property's entire marketing effort, incorporating both internal staff and outside operators.

Costs related to the marketing of guest rooms—e.g., reservations, travel agency fees, commissions—have traditionally been charged to rooms department expense. *The Uniform System of Accounts for the Lodging Industry* states: "There is a growing recognition that these costs are elements of the overall marketing activity. . .and hotels which recognize these functions as marketing responsibilities should charge these expenses to marketing."

Table 5.17 shows that all categories are budgeted as fixed expenses except fees and commissions, which are occupancy- and rate-sensitive because they are generally based on a percentage of rooms revenue.

Considering the components of marketing expenses, it appears that the appropriate unit of comparison is the amount per available room. Note that in most cases (and in the presentation of this case study), franchise fee costs are calculated separately. These costs are generally 100% variable and dependent on rooms revenue.

The proposed Sheraton is expected to implement an extensive pre-opening marketing effort focusing on meetings and convention patrons who typically book their functions in advance.

The comparable property's marketing expenditures are currently $2,095 per available room, or approximately 3.4% of total revenue. Since the comparable property's total revenue per available room is approximately 5.2%

higher than the projected base total revenue per available room of the proposed subject property, it is logical to assume that the marketing budget for the subject will be somewhat lower than the comparable property's $2,095 per available room. Based on this consideration, the appraisers have adjusted the comparable expense ratio downward by 5.2%. The calculations for the comparable property's base marketing expense are

$$\$2,095 \times 0.948 = \$1,986$$
$$\$1,986 \times 250 \text{ rooms} = \$497,000 \text{ (rounded)}$$

A $497,000 base marketing expense budget, which equates to 3.4% of base total revenue, should suffice for this type of hotel.

A new hotel often requires a larger marketing budget during its initial years of operation to penetrate the market effectively, capture its market share, and build occupancy. In the case of the subject property, this particular competitive market is approaching a point of saturation and, in this competitive environment, an intense marketing effort will be required to capture a sufficient level of patronage. This adjustment will be addressed later in the case study.

Franchise Fee

A number of fees are commonly charged as part of a given hotel's affiliation with a hotel chain. Reservation fees, marketing assessments, and royalties are the most common ongoing expenses. Reservation fees are categorized as a rooms department expense, while the marketing assessment is categorized as a marketing department expense. The royalty portion of the franchise expense represents the fees paid for the use of the company's name, trademarks, and service marks. The royalty is typically considered the equivalent of the franchise fee and is charged as a percentage of rooms revenue. In the Sheraton case, current royalty rates equate to 5.0% of rooms revenue. The base year franchise fee is therefore calculated as follows:

$$\$9,218,000 \times 0.05 = \$461,000 \text{ (rounded)}$$

Property Operations and Maintenance Expense

Property operations and maintenance (PO&M), formerly known as repair and maintenance, is another expense largely controlled by management. Except for essential repairs needed to keep the facility open and prevent damage, most maintenance items can be deferred for varying lengths of time. Maintenance is an accumulating expense, meaning if a necessary repair is postponed, it does not go away; rather, it becomes deferred maintenance, which ultimately must be cured at a later date. When an appraiser projects an existing lodging facility's income and expenses, the property operations and maintenance expenses over the past several years should be investigated to determine if adequate expenditures were made to maintain the facilities. This investigation should be conducted in conjunction with the physical inspection of the property to ensure that the funds spent took care of the required repairs.

Several factors influence the level of maintenance required for a lodging facility:

- *The hotel's age.* Most new hotels are protected for several years by the manufacturer's warranties on new equipment, which reduce PO&M costs during the initial years of operation. As hotels age, maintenance costs tend to escalate rapidly.

- *Use of a preventive maintenance system.* Some hotel operators adopt preventive maintenance programs, periodically checking and maintaining all of the lodging facility's important components. Preventive maintenance allows management to anticipate possible maintenance problems and correct them early with minor repairs rather than having to do a major overhaul later.

- *Quality of facilities.* The quality and type of the initial construction can directly impact future maintenance requirements. The use of quality building materials and sound construction methods will reduce maintenance costs over the long term. During the inspection, the appraiser should investigate the physical condition and quality of the hotel's original construction.

Property operations and maintenance are considered operating expenses and, as such, must only contain components that can be expensed rather than capitalized under IRS regulations. For example, if a table leg breaks, repairing the leg would be considered an expense chargeable to property operations and maintenance. If the table is replaced, it becomes a capital expenditure that would not fall into the property operations and maintenance category. Appraisers account for the capital replacement of items such as furniture and equipment in the reserve for replacement account, which will be discussed later in this chapter.

Table 5.18 outlines the components of the property operations and maintenance expense category. The items in the property operations and maintenance category are either moderately fixed or very slightly influenced by changes in occupancy and food and beverage usage. Because PO&M is mostly fixed, the appropriate unit of comparison for this expense category is the amount per available room supported by the percentage of total revenue.

The property operations and maintenance expense for the comparable is currently $2,724 per available room. A downward adjustment to the comparable property's per-room PO&M unit of comparison is needed to reflect the 5.2%

Category	Percent of Category	Fixed Expenses	Variable Expenses Occupancy Sensitive	Rate Sensitive	Food and Beverage Sensitive
Salaries and wages	20–40%	–	Very slightly	–	Very slightly
Employee benefits	3–10	–	Very slightly	–	Very slightly
Building supplies	3–10	–	Very slightly	–	Very slightly
Contract services					
Curtains and draperies	1–7	–	Very slightly	–	Very slightly
Electrical and mechanical equipment	5–25	–	Very slightly	–	Very slightly
Elevators	0–5	Moderately	–	–	–
Engineering supplies	2–7	–	Very slightly	–	Very slightly
Floor covering	1–10	–	Very slightly	–	Very slightly
Furniture	1–20	–	Very slightly	–	Very slightly
Grounds and landscaping	1–10	Budgeted	–	–	–
Heating, ventilation, and air-conditioning equipment	1–5	Moderately	–	–	–
Kitchen equipment	1–5	Moderately	–	–	–
Laundry equipment	1–5	Moderately	–	–	–
Life/safety	1–5	Moderately	–	–	–
Light bulbs	0–3	–	Very slightly	–	Very slightly
Locks and keys	0–4	–	Very slightly	–	Very slightly
Operating supplies	1–10	–	Very slightly	–	Very slightly
Painting and decorating	4–25	–	Very slightly	–	Very slightly
Removal of waste matter	2–8	Moderately	–	–	–
Swimming pool	1–5	Moderately	–	–	–
Telecommunications	1–5	Moderately	–	–	–
Training	0–5	Moderately	Very slightly	–	Very slightly
Uniforms	0–5	Moderately	Very slightly	–	Very slightly
Vehicle maintenance	0–5	Moderately	Very slightly	–	Very slightly
Other	2–8	Moderately	Very slightly	–	Very slightly

TABLE 5.18 Property Operation and Maintenance Expenses

higher total revenue per available room of the comparable, relative to the base year projections for the proposed Sheraton. As with previous per-available-room adjustments, the variable component must be factored into the calculation.

First, the $2,724 per room PO&M expense of the comparable is multiplied by the 5.2% difference in revenue ($2,724 × 0.052 = $142). The resulting figure is then multiplied by 30%, which represents the portion of the PO&M expense category that is considered variable ($142 \times .30 = \$43$). This amount is deducted from the comparable property's per-room PO&M expense to produce the subject's per room base ($2,724 − $43 = $2,681). The total base property operation and maintenance expense for the proposed Sheraton is calculated as follows:

$$\$2,681 \times 250 \text{ rooms} = \$670,000 \text{ (rounded)}$$

As with the marketing expense, an adjustment is warranted in the initial years of a maintenance expense forecast for a new hotel. Because wear and tear happens gradually and a new hotel has the benefit of warranties for the first one to three years of operation, maintenance expense tends to require a discount in the first two to three projection years. The basis for this adjustment is set forth later in the case study.

Energy Cost

Energy consumption within a lodging facility typically adopts several forms: water and space heating, air conditioning, lighting, cooking fuel, and other miscellaneous power requirements. Electricity, natural gas, oil, and steam are the most common sources of hotel energy. The energy cost account also includes water and sewer costs.

Table 5.19 illustrates the various accounts that constitute energy expenses according to the *Uniform System of Accounts for the Lodging Industry.* The total energy cost varies with the source and quantity of fuel used. Electricity

TABLE 5.19 Energy Expenses

			Variable Expenses		
Category	Percent of Category	Fixed Expenses	Occupancy Sensitive	Rate Sensitive	Food and Beverage Sensitive
Electric current	–	–	Very slightly	–	Very slightly
Fuel	–	–	Very slightly	–	Very slightly
Steam	–	–	Very slightly	–	Very slightly
Water	–	–	Very slightly	–	Very slightly

tends to be the most expensive energy source, followed by oil and gas. Although hotels consume a sizable amount of electrical energy, most properties supplement less expensive sources, such as gas and oil, for heating and cooking.

The cost of electrical energy is a function of the amount of energy consumed and the size of the peak demand. The unit of electrical consumption is the kilowatt hour (kwh), which is measured with a watt-hour meter. To calculate the monthly electric bill, the utility company reads the electric meter and determines the number of kilowatt hours of electricity consumed since the last reading. This amount is multiplied by the appropriate rate schedule to determine the usage charge. The peak demand charge reflects the highest number of kilowatts the property requires during a specific, short period. The demand is also read monthly from the utility meter, with the additional charge added to the electric bill based on a demand rate schedule.

Utility charges for other energy sources such as gas and oil often are calculated based entirely on usage, with no additional expense for demand. The unit for gas consumption is the therm, which is measured by a gas meter. Oil is delivered to the property and stored in tanks. Bills are rendered upon delivery, and the gallon is the unit of measurement.

Much of a hotel's energy consumption is fixed and varies little with changes in occupancy. Restaurants, kitchens, public areas, and corridors must be continually lighted and heated or air-conditioned, whether the hotel is full or nearly empty. The energy costs of an additional occupied room (i.e., the cost of a few hours of light, television, heat, or air-conditioning) are minimal.

To forecast the energy costs of a hotel or motel, total energy consumption, the sources of energy used, and utility rates must be estimated.

The amount of energy consumed in heating, air-conditioning, and operating a lodging facility is measured in British thermal units (BTUs). By estimating the number of BTUs a hotel or motel will use in a year and multiplying that amount by a cost factor based on local utility charges, an energy cost forecast can be developed.

Electricity tends to be the most expensive energy source. Much of a hotel's energy consumption, for lighting, heat systems, and air-conditioning, is used by facilities in a hotel's public space and depends little on changes in occupancy.

A survey performed by The Hospitality, Lodging and Travel Research Foundation, Inc., provides information on the annual BTU energy requirements of hotels in various regions on a square-foot basis. The foundation surveyed 268 properties with 100,281 guestrooms. Table 5.20 shows the results of this survey. If the hotel's approximate square footage is known, this table can be used to estimate its total annual energy consumption.

TABLE 5.20   Hotel Energy Consumption by Region

Region	Number of Hotels Surveyed	BTUs/Sq. Ft./Year
Hawaii	3	106,431
Alaska	1	175,046
Southwest	50	122,139
Northwest	9	129,500
Mountain	4	153,123
Upper Midwest	26	163,035
Midwest	36	143,016
South Central	31	135,333
Southeast	63	132,936
Mid-Atlantic	19	139,941
Northeast	26	161,807

To estimate the amount of fuel consumed, a factor is applied to convert the unit of consumption (kilowatt hour, therm or gallon) into the specific number of BTUs. Table 5.21 shows the conversion factors for electricity, gas, and oil.

Hotels and motels always consume electricity, but electricity is sometimes supplemented with gas or oil when they are available and cost-effective. According to another survey performed by The Hospitality, Lodging and Travel Research Foundation, Inc., electrical energy accounts for roughly 50% of the total BTU consumption for a typical lodging facility. The supplemental fuels represent the remainder.

Once the total units of consumption are calculated, the utility company and fuel oil dealer can be contacted to determine rates and costs. Utility companies are usually helpful in providing the information needed to estimate a lodging facility's energy costs.

The comparable hotel used in developing the base for the proposed Sheraton is located in the Northeast United States. So is the subject, but they are not served by the same utility company. Therefore, the energy expense,

TABLE 5.21	Conversion Factors	
Energy Source	Unit of Consumption	BTUs Per Unit of Consumption
Electricity	kwh	3,413
Oil	gallon	140,000
Gas	therm	100,000

particularly the comparable's electricity charges, may not be appropriate for projecting the Sheraton's base. The data presented in tables 5.20 and 5.21 will be used to estimate the specific components of energy consumption, taking into account the rates actually charged within the market area.

Table 5.20 indicates that a hotel like the proposed Sheraton located in the Northeast would consume approximately 161,807 BTUs per square foot annually. According to the facility recommendations for the subject property, the total building area will be approximately 168,750 square feet (675 square feet per room). Multiplying the number of BTUs per square foot per year by the hotel's total area results in the estimated annual BTU consumption.

$$161,807 \times 168,750 = 27,304,931,250 \text{ BTUs/year}$$

Assuming that half of the subject property's energy will come from electricity and half from oil, the calculations in Table 5.22 show the projected kilowatt hours of electricity and the gallons of oil that will be required during the hotel's stabilized year of operation.

TABLE 5.22	Energy Consumption of Proposed Sheraton	
	Electricity	Oil
Total BTUs per year	27,304,931,250	27,304,931,250
× Usage allocation	0.50	0.50
Energy consumption	13,652,465,625	13,652,465,625
÷ Conversion factor	3,413	140,000
Quantity consumed	4,000,136 kwh	97,518 gallons (rounded)

The current electric rate quoted by the local utility company is $0.0868 per kilowatt hour, including normal demands charges, seasonal fuel adjustments, and quantity discounts. Oil prices are currently $1.20 per gallon, including delivery charges and appropriate quantity discounts. Water charges were estimated at $112,000. The total base energy expense for the proposed Sheraton can be calculated as shown on the following page.

Electricity:	4,000,136 kwh × $0.0868	$347,212 (rounded)
Oil:	97,518 gallons × $1.20	117,022 (rounded)
Water:		112,000
		$576,234
Total base energy expense (rounded)		$576,000

The total base energy expense for the proposed Sheraton Hotel is estimated to be $2,300 per available room, which agrees with the comparable property's energy expense of $2,483 per available room.

Management Fee

The management fee expense category covers the basic fee paid to the type of hotel management company that is anticipated to operate the subject property. Some hotel management companies provide management services only, while others offer both management services and a brand-name affiliation. When a management company has no brand affiliation, the property owner can often acquire a franchise. Doing so will ideally provide the company with the image and recognition it needs to be successful. Although most hotel management companies use a fee structure that includes both a basic fee (usually a percentage of total revenue) and an incentive fee (usually a percentage of a defined profit), the incentive portion is generally subordinated to debt service and does not appear in a forecast of net income before debt service. Although the incentive fee does not reduce the cash flow available for debt service, it does reduce the potential cash flow to equity and therefore must be considered in the valuation process.

The most appropriate way to account for an incentive fee's impact on an investment's equity component is to use the net income forecast before debt service and incentive fee, but adjust the equity dividend or yield rate upward to reflect this added cost of management.

Basic hotel management fees are almost always based on a percentage of total revenue, which means that they are 100% variable. The proper unit of comparison is therefore a percentage of total revenue.

The HVS Hotel Group, an independent hotel operating company experienced in managing similar hotels, will operate the proposed Sheraton. The hotel will have a Sheraton franchise affiliation for brand name identification and a reservation system. The group has agreed to operate the subject property for a basic management fee of 3.0%, which is considered typical for this type of operator.

Applying this management fee structure to the base total revenue for the proposed Sheraton Hotel produces the following base management fee estimate:

$$0.03 \times \$14,764,000 = \$443,000 \text{ (rounded)}$$

Property Taxes

Property taxes are the taxes paid to local municipalities for government services such as highways, schools, parks, and sanitation services. They are used to allocate the municipal tax burden on the basis of property value. The higher the property value, the larger the tax burden the owner must assume. The legal term for property tax is *ad valorem* tax, or a tax "in proportion to value." Depending on the municipality's tax policy, property taxes may be based on the value of the real property alone (real estate tax) or may also include the value of the personal property (personal property tax.)

To properly allocate the tax burden, municipalities employ assessors, who assess, or value, all of the taxable real estate within their jurisdictions. Theoretically the assessment bears a definite relationship to market value, so properties with similar market values will have similar assessments and properties with higher or lower values will have proportionately larger or smaller assessments.

Projecting property taxes for an existing hotel is relatively simple. The assessed value is normally a matter of public record and can be obtained by contacting the local taxing authority. Multiplying the assessed value by the anticipated tax rate produces the estimated property tax. However, care must be taken to determine whether the assessed value may increase in the future due to increasing real estate values in the local market or a new assessment of the subject property triggered by a recent sales transaction.

Projecting property taxes for a proposed lodging facility is more difficult. Since the property assessor must maintain a specific value relationship among all of the properties in a taxing jurisdiction, the best way to estimate a proposed hotel's assessed value is to use the actual assessed values of comparable hotels. This procedure is similar to the sales comparison approach. The subject property's assessed value is estimated by comparing it with the assessed values of similar hotels in the market area. The estimate is then adjusted to reflect dissimilarities between the comparable data and the subject.

It is advisable to compare and adjust the assessed values of property improvements only and not the combined value of the land and improvements. Taxing jurisdictions provide separate assessed values for land and improvements. The combination of the two equates to the total property value, which forms the basis for calculating the real estate tax burden.

The land's assessed value is developed from actual land sales within the jurisdiction. Based on these known land sales, the assessor forms a grid of land values in the jurisdiction indicating the locations of the best parcels with the highest values. Values decline as one moves away from this prime area toward less desirable sites. Since each parcel is assessed based on its desirability relative to the surrounding parcels, assessors are reluctant to change one land assessment; doing so could alter the assessment grid for all of the other parcels in the jurisdiction. Consequently, when estimating a proposed hotel's assessed value, the actual assessed value of the land should be considered unchangeable; only the value of the improvements should be compared and adjusted.

Since only the value of the improvements is to be adjusted, any location-specific advantages or disadvantages of the property should be disregarded, because they have theoretically been accounted for in the land assessment. Moreover, the value of hotel improvements also does not include consideration of non-real estate components such as decor, management, franchise, and business value.

If the local taxing jurisdiction uses a personal property assessment, the appraiser must also estimate the value of the facility's furniture and equipment. Since personal property assessment procedures vary widely, assistance from an assessor is often helpful. In many instances the assessed value of furniture and equipment is based on their actual cost minus the depreciation specified by a mandated depreciation schedule. It is important to have a clear definition of what is considered personal property and what is considered real property.

The taxing jurisdiction in which the proposed Sheraton is located assesses only real property. The current land assessment for the subject property is $2,800,000, or $11,200 per room for the 250-room hotel. Information on the assessed values of competitive hotels in the subject's taxing jurisdiction is presented in Table 5.23.

TABLE 5.23 **Assessed Values of Competition**

Name of Hotel	Number of Rooms	Assessed Value Land	Improvements	Value Per Room Land	Improvements
Embassy Suites	200	$3,200,000	$14,700,500	$16,000	$73,503
Hilton Hotel	275	2,900,000	15,300,350	10,545	55,638
Radisson	250	1,800,000	12,800,500	7,200	51,202
Holiday Inn	175	2,000,000	8,530,900	11,429	48,748
Courtyard	124	(partial assessment only)			
Ramada Inn	150	1,500,000	6,650,700	10,000	44,338
Island Inn	135	1,700,000	5,775,000	12,593	42,778
Quality Inn	175	1,800,000	6,999,700	10,286	39,998
Days Inn	120	1,400,000	4,800,700	11,667	40,006

In the above table, the unit of comparison is the assessed value per room, the key variable tracked by hotel investors and consultants. Depending on the taxing jurisdiction, some assessors' office personnel use value per square foot as the basis for comparison. In either case, the findings rely on the same basic notion of comparison and would likely result in similar findings.

The facilities at the Hilton Hotel, which has an improvements assessment of $55,638 per available room, are most comparable to those of the proposed Sheraton. The proposed Sheraton will be newer than the Hilton and feature a more modern design. Based on this comparison, an improvements assessment of $60,000 per available room will be used for the proposed Sheraton. This per-room assessed value equates to a total improvements assessment for the proposed Sheraton of $15,000,000 ($60,000 x 250). Thus, the total base year assessment for the proposed Sheraton, assuming it is fully constructed and operational, is estimated as follows:

Land	$2,800,000
Improvements	15,000,000
Total	$17,800,000

The current tax rate is $24.72 per $1,000 of assessed value. Based on this rate, the base property tax for the proposed Sheraton would be

$$\$17,800,000 \div \$1,000 = \$17,800.00$$
$$\$17,800.00 \times \$24.72 = \$440,000 \text{ (rounded)}$$

These estimated base property taxes for the proposed Sheraton equate to $1,760 per available room. Any comparison of the Sheraton's property tax burden with that of the comparable is not appropriate because the comparable is located in another taxing jurisdiction.

Insurance Expense

The insurance expense category consists of the cost of insuring the hotel and its contents against damage or destruction from fire, weather, sprinkler leakage, boiler explosion, plate glass breakage, and other accidents. Furthermore, as of the latest revision of the USALI, it also includes general (or liability) coverage.

Insurance rates for contents insurance are based on many factors, including building design and construction, fire detection and extinguishing equipment, the fire district, distance from a firehouse, and the area's fire experience. Sometimes an estimate of insurance cost can be obtained from a local insurance agent familiar with the project and area insurance rates. If this is not possible, the appraiser should use insurance expenses derived from comparable lodging facilities expressed on a per-available-room basis.

General (or liability) insurance covers third-party actions involving bodily injury and personal property and is typically based on rooms receipts, meeting and banquet revenue, and food and beverage revenue. Factors that can affect a hotel's liability insurance expense include the size of the meeting, banquet, or restaurant facility, the amount of alcohol served as a percentage of total food and beverage sales, and the presence of a dance floor in the lounge. Factors that can increase a hotel's liability insurance expense include a high-rise structure, a swimming pool, life safety support systems, and any transportation services the hotel provides.

The comparable statement of income and expense shows an insurance expense of $650 per available room. A slight downward adjustment is appropriate to reflect that the proposed Sheraton will have a somewhat smaller array of public facilities. Based on this analysis, the comparable hotel's insurance expense, expressed as a dollar amount per available room, is adjusted downward to $600 per room. The following calculation shows the base insurance expense for the proposed Sheraton.

$$\$600 \times 250 \text{ rooms} = \$150,000$$

Reserve for Replacement Expense

Furniture, fixtures, and equipment are essential to operating a lodging facility, and their quality often influences a property's class. Included in the reserve for replacement expense category are all non-real estate items that are normally capitalized, not expensed.

Hotel furniture, fixtures, and equipment are exposed to heavy use and must be replaced regularly. The useful lives of these items is determined by their quality, their durability, and the amount of guest traffic and use.

Periodic replacement of furniture, fixtures, and equipment is essential to maintaining a lodging facility's quality, image, and income. Capitalized expenditures are not included in the operating statement, but they do affect an owner's cash flow. Therefore, an appraisal should reflect these expenses in an appropriate reserve for replacement.

Based on industry experience, a reserve for replacement ranging from 3% to 5% of total revenue is generally sufficient to provide for the timely replacement of furniture, fixtures, and equipment.

A reserve for replacement equal to 4% of total revenue was determined to be sufficient to provide for the periodic replacement of the furniture, fixtures, and equipment of the proposed Sheraton. The following calculation shows the base reserve for replacement expense.

$$\$14,764,000 \times 0.04 = \$591,000 \text{ (rounded)}$$

Base Statement of Income and Expense

Table 5.24 shows two statements of income and expense. The first is the comparable statement that was selected through the financial comparable

TABLE 5.24 Proposed Sheraton and Comparable Property—Base Year Statement of Income and Expense

	Comparable Property				Proposed Sheraton			
Number of rooms:	290				250			
Occupancy rate:	68%				68%			
Occupied rooms:	71,978				62,050			
Average rate:	$144.50				$148.56			
	Total $ (in thousands)	Percent of Gross	Per Available Room (PAR)	Per Occupied Room (POR)	Total $ (in thousands)	Percent of Gross	Per Available Room (PAR)	Per Occupied Room (POR)
Revenue								
Rooms	$10,401	57.7%	$35,865	$144.50	$9,218	62.4%	$36,872	$148.56
Food	4,734	26.3	16,325	65.77	3,469	23.5	13,876	55.91
Beverage	1,544	8.6	5,324	21.45	937	6.3	3,748	15.10
Telephone	474	2.6	1,636	6.59	403	2.7	1,612	6.49
Other income	870	4.8	3,000	12.09	737	5.0	2,948	11.88
Total revenue	$18,023	100.0%	$62,150	$250.40	$14,764	100.0%	$59,056	$237.94
Departmental Expenses*								
Rooms	$2,444	23.5%	$8,428	$33.96	$2,120	23.0%	$8,480	$34.17
Food & beverage	4,709	75.0	16,237	65.42	3,437	78.0	13,748	55.39
Telephone	199	42.0	687	2.77	175	43.4	700	2.82
Other income	413	47.5	1,425	5.74	356	48.3	1,424	5.74
Total departmental expenses	$7,765	43.1%	$26,777	$107.89	$6,088	41.2%	$24,352	$98.12
Departmental Income	$10,258	56.9%	$35,373	$142.51	$8,676	58.8%	$34,704	$139.82
Undistributed Operating Expenses (UDOE)								
Administrative & general	$1,361	7.5%	$4,692	$18.90	$1,155	7.8%	$4,620	$18.61
Marketing	608	3.4	2,095	8.44	497	3.4	1,988	8.01
Franchise fee	551	3.1	1,900	7.66	461	3.1	1,844	743
Property operation & maintenance	790	4.4	2,724	10.98	670	4.5	2,680	10.80
Energy	720	4.0	2,483	10.00	575	3.9	2,300	9.27
Total UDOE	$4,030	22.4%	$13,894	$55.98	$3,358	22.7%	$13,432	$54.12
Income Before Fixed Charges	$6,228	34.5%	$21,479	$86.53	$5,318	36.1%	$21,272	$85.71
Fixed Charges								
Management fee	$586	3.3%	$2,021	$8.14	$443	3.0%	$1,772	$7.14
Property taxes	560	3.1	1,951	7.78	440	3.0	1,760	7.09
Insurance	189	1.0	650	2.62	150	1.0	600	2.42
Reserve for replacement	503	2.8	1,734	6.99	591	4.0	2,364	9.52
Total fixed charges	$1,838	10.2%	$6,336	$25.53	$1,624	11.0%	$6,496	$26.17
Net Income	$4,390	24.3%	$15,143	$61.00	$3,694	25.1%	$14,776	$59.54
Ratios								
Food revenue to rooms revenue	45.5%				37.7%			
Food and beverage revenue to rooms revenue	60.4				47.8			
Telephone revenue to rooms revenue	4.6				4.3			
Other income to rooms revenue	8.4				8.0			
Beverage revenue to food revenue	32.6				27.0			

* Departmental expenses expressed as a ratio to departmental revenues

Hotels and Motels—Valuations and Market Studies

selection order. (These figures were shown in Table 5.4.) The second is the base statement of income and expense for the proposed Sheraton, which has been developed in this case study through category-by-category analysis. This one-year base financial statement uses the subject's stabilized average room rate, deflated to current base year dollars, and income and expense ratios that reflect the level of occupancy actually experienced by the comparable. This profit and loss statement provides the basis for the fixed and variable component relationships developed in the subsequent steps of the analysis.

Step 3. Revise the base

The base revenue and expense categories must be revised to reflect current dollars for each forecast year and the anticipated rate fluctuations resulting from other, non-financial variables (general inflation).

Step 3 is intended to adjust the comparable operating data that make up the subject property's base so that it will reflect forecasted costs stated in the current dollars anticipated for each particular year. To compute the fixed and variable operating data and forecast relationships for each projected year, an assumed rate (or rates) of inflation is (are) applied to each operating category.

Each revenue and expense category can be affected by different factors that increase or decrease associated costs. For example, future changes in the average room rate are largely influenced by local supply and demand conditions, which may modify general inflation assumptions. Energy costs are usually tied to fuel prices, which often fluctuate erratically. Changes in property taxes are often correlated to changes in the local tax base, which means that the rate assumption may be negative in an area experiencing rapid new development. Labor costs can change radically if a new union contract is implemented.

The appraiser should look at each revenue and expense category and project an individualized assumption that reflects the market's current view of pricing for the components within the stated category or the category as a whole. Often it is appropriate to apply a single inflation factor to all categories of revenue and expense data, particularly for the years projected after the property reaches a stabilized level of occupancy. This assumes that all other cost-influencing variables remain stable.

CASE STUDY

Revising the Base

After analyzing the local market for the proposed Sheraton, the appraiser has developed the following change assumptions:

- *Energy costs.* The local utility company has had difficulty meeting the energy needs of this growing market area. As a result, energy costs have been increasing faster than the area's general rate of inflation has. With the recent opening of a new generating plant and the introduction of several efficiency measures, future energy costs should increase at a slower rate. Table 5.25 shows the anticipated future growth in energy costs.

- *Property taxes.* The market area has recently experienced rapid growth in new commercial and residential development, which has significantly increased the local tax base. Assuming efficient government spending, property taxes are expected to increase, as shown in Table 5.26.

- *All other categories.* An overall inflation assumption of 3% per year will be used to project other categories of revenue and expense. In practice, such an assumption should be supported with adequate market data. (Note that the rooms revenue forecast already reflects the above-inflation growth rates applied to average rates in the first three projection years. The stabilized average rate projected for the sixth projection year was deflated back to base year dollars using the underlying 3.0% inflation rate. Thus, the application of the base inflation rate through the projection period essentially inflates the average rate to the level projected earlier in the case study.)

Table 5.27 shows the subject property's base year income and expenses projected out at the rate of inflation forecast for each revenue and expense category. After the stabilized year, all revenue and expenses are assumed to increase at an annual rate of 3%.

TABLE 5.25 Energy Cost Projection

Projection Year	Percent Change from Previous Year
Base	—
1	8.0%
2	6.0
3	5.0
4 and beyond	3.0

TABLE 5.26 Property Tax Projection

Projection Year	Percent Change from Previous Year
Base	—
1	1.0%
2	2.0
3	2.0
4 and beyond	3.0

TABLE 5.27 Projection of Base Year Revenue and Expense

	Base Year	Inflation	Year 1	Inflation	Year 2	Inflation	Year 3	Inflation	Year 4	Inflation	Stabilized
Revenue											
Rooms	$9,218	3.0%	$9,495	3.0%	$9,780	3.0%	$10,073	3.0%	$10,375	3.0%	$10,686
Food	3,469	3.0	3,573	3.0	3,680	3.0	3,791	3.0	3,904	3.0	4,022
Beverage	937	3.0	965	3.0	994	3.0	1,023	3.0	1,054	3.0	1,086
Telephone	403	3.0	415	3.0	428	3.0	441	3.0	454	3.0	468
Other income	737	3.0	759	3.0	782	3.0	806	3.0	830	3.0	855
Total revenue	$14,764		$15,207		$15,664		$16,134		$16,617		$17,117
Expenses											
Rooms	$2,120	3.0%	$2,184	3.0%	$2,249	3.0%	$2,317	3.0%	$2,386	3.0%	$2,458
Food & beverage	3,437	3.0	3,540	3.0	3,646	3.0	3,756	3.0	3,868	3.0	3,984
Telephone	175	3.0	180	3.0	186	3.0	191	3.0	197	3.0	203
Other income	356	3.0	367	3.0	378	3.0	389	3.0	401	3.0	413
Administrative & general	1,156	3.0	1,190	3.0	1,226	3.0	1,263	3.0	1,301	3.0	1,340
Marketing	497	3.0	512	3.0	527	3.0	543	3.0	559	3.0	576
Franchise fee	461	3.0	475	3.0	489	3.0	504	3.0	519	3.0	534
Property oper. & maint.	671	3.0	691	3.0	711	3.0	733	3.0	755	3.0	777
Energy	575	8.0	621	6.0	658	5.0	691	3.0	712	3.0	733
Management fee	443	3.0	456	3.0	470	3.0	484	3.0	499	3.0	513
Property taxes	440	1.0	444	2.0	453	2.0	462	3.0	476	3.0	491
Insurance	150	3.0	155	3.0	159	3.0	164	3.0	169	3.0	174
Reserve for replacement	591	3.0	608	3.0	627	3.0	645	3.0	665	3.0	685

Step 4. Estimate fixed and variable percentages for each revenue and expense category

As discussed previously, each category of revenue and expense has a component that is fixed and one that varies directly with occupancy and facility usage. To apply the fixed and variable component approach to forecasting, the fixed and variable percentage of each revenue and expense category must be determined. The ranges of fixed and variable percentages for each revenue and expense category presented in Table 5.3 and subsequent descriptions of each category's composition can be used as general parameters. Specific fixed and variable percentages are developed by evaluating the subject property's operating characteristics. The fixed and variable components of each category should total 100.

CASE STUDY

Estimating Fixed and Variable Percentages

Table 5.28 shows the fixed and variable percentages selected for each revenue and expense category of the proposed Sheraton Hotel.

TABLE 5.28 Fixed and Variable Percentages

	Proposed Sheraton	
Category	Fixed	Variable
Revenue		
Food	30%	70%
Beverage	0	100
Telephone	10	90
Other income	50	50
Expense		
Rooms	60%	40%
Food & beverage	55	45
Telephone	60	40
Other income	50	50
Administrative and general	70	30
Marketing	70	30
Franchise fee	0	100
Property operation & maintenance	70	30
Energy	90	10
Management fee	0	100
Property taxes	100	0
Insurance	100	0
Reserve for replacement	0	100

The fixed food revenue percentage for the proposed Sheraton was set at 30%. This portion of food revenue is composed of non-guest business, which includes local banquets and restaurant customers. All fixed and variable percentages have been selected to be in line with the established ranges.

Steps 5 through 9: Final forecast of revenue and expense

The actual projection of each revenue and expense category using the fixed and variable calculations is accomplished in Steps 5 through 9. The elements of each step are outlined below.

- *Step 5.* The fixed component is estimated by multiplying the appropriate fixed percentage by the base revenue or expense category.

- *Step 6.* The amount of variable change is quantified based on the appropriate index of variability.

- *Step 7.* The unadjusted variable component is calculated by multiplying the appropriate base revenue or expense category by the variable percentage.

- *Step 8.* The unadjusted variable component calculated in Step 7 is multiplied by the amount of variable change calculated in Step 6 to produce the adjusted variable component.

- *Step 9.* The fixed component calculated in Step 5 is added to the adjusted variable component calculated in Step 6 to yield the forecast for the revenue or expense category.

CASE STUDY

Final Forecast of Revenue and Expense—Proposed Sheraton Hotel

The process outlined in Steps 5 to 9 will be applied to forecast the revenue and expense of the proposed Sheraton Hotel. Each revenue and expense category will be illustrated separately. The projection of revenue and expense for the existing Embassy Suites will also be presented following the completion of the Sheraton forecast.

Food Revenue

The fixed component of the food revenue is calculated by multiplying the base food revenue in each projected year by the 30% fixed percentage of food revenue. (Table 5.29).

Food revenue is occupancy-variable in that any revenue above the fixed component is largely dependent on changes in occupancy. The variable

TABLE 5.29 Food Revenue–Fixed Component (in thousands)

	Year 3	Year 4	Year 5 (Stab.)
Base food revenue	$3,791	$3,904	$4,022
Percent fixed	× 30%	× 30%	× 30%
Food revenue–fixed component	$1,137	$1,171	$1,207

change for each projected year is calculated by dividing the projected occupancy by the base occupancy (Table 5.30).

TABLE 5.30 Variable Change

	Year 3	Year 4	Year 5 (Stab.)
Projected occupancy	60.0%	67.0%	71.0%
÷ Base occupancy	68.0	68.0	68.0
Variable percentage change	88.2%	98.5%	104.4%

The unadjusted variable component is calculated by multiplying the base food revenue in each projected year by the 70% variable percentage (Table 5.31).

TABLE 5.31 Food Revenue–Unadjusted Variable Component (in thousands)

	Year 3	Year 4	Year 5 (Stab.)
Base food revenue	$3,791	$3,904	$4,022
Percent variable	× 70.0%	× 70.0%	× 70.0%
Unadjusted variable component	$2,654	$2,733	$2,815

Multiplying the unadjusted variable component by the variable percentage of change attributed to different occupancy levels produces the adjusted variable component of food revenue (Table 5.32).

TABLE 5.32 Food Revenue–Adjusted Variable Component (in thousands)

	Year 3	Year 4	Year 5 (Stab.)
Unadjusted variable component	$2,654	$2,733	$2,815
Variable percentage change	× 88.2%	× 98.5%	× 104.4%
Adjusted variable component	$2,341	$2,692	$2,939

The fixed and adjusted variable components of food revenue for each projected year are totaled to estimate total food revenue (Table 5.33). Table 5.34 shows several pertinent units of comparison.

TABLE 5.33 Total Food Revenue (in thousands)

	Year 3	Year 4	Year 5 (Stab.)
Food revenue–fixed component	$1,137	$1,171	$1,206
Food revenue–variable component	+ 2,341	+ 2,693	+ 2,939
Total food revenue	$3,478	$3,864	$4,145

TABLE 5.34 Units of Comparison

	Year 3	Year 4	Year 5 (Stab.)
Percent of total revenue	25.6%	24.3%	23.3%
Per available room	$13,916	$15,456	$16,584
Per occupied room	$63.54	$63.20	$63.99

Beverage Revenue

Beverage revenue is assumed to be 100% variable and directly tied to changes in food revenue. The ratio of beverage to food revenue is 27%. Table 5.35 shows the beverage revenue projection.

TABLE 5.35 Beverage Revenue (in thousands)

	Year 3	Year 4	Year 5 (Stab.)
Total food revenue	$3,479	$3,864	$4,146
Percent of food revenue	× 27.0%	× 27.0%	× 27.0%
Total beverage revenue	$939	$1,043	$1,119

Telephone Revenue

Telephone revenue is projected much like food revenue is (Table 5.36). The variable percentage change is based on occupancy.

Other Income

Other income is projected in Table 5.37.

Total Revenue

The total of all revenue sources is shown in Table 5.38.

Rooms Expense

The rooms expense for the proposed Sheraton is calculated in Table 5.39.

Variable Percent Change for Expense Categories

The variable percent change for expense categories is based on the change in corresponding revenue levels. Table 5.40 shows the bases for calculating the variable percent change for various expense categories.

TABLE 5.36 Telephone Revenue (in thousands)

	Year 3	Year 4	Year 5 (Stab.)
Base telephone revenue	$441	$454	$468
Percent fixed	× 10.0%	× 10.0%	× 10.0%
Fixed component	$44	$45	$47
Base telephone revenue	$441	$454	$468
Percent variable	× 90.0%	× 90.0%	× 90.0%
Unadjusted variable component	$397	$409	$421
Unadjusted variable component	$397	$409	$421
Variable percentage change	× 88.2%	× 98.5%	× 104.4%
Adjusted variable component	$350	$403	$440
Fixed component	$44	$45	$47
Variable component	+ 350	+ 403	+ 439
Total telephone revenue	$394	$448	$486
Percent of total revenue	2.9%	2.8%	2.7%
Per available room	$1,576	$1,792	$1,944
Per occupied room	$7.20	$7.33	$7.50

TABLE 5.37 Other Income (in thousands)

	Year 3	Year 4	Year 5 (Stab.)
Base other income	$806	$830	$855
Percent fixed	× 50.0%	× 50.0%	× 50.0%
Fixed component	$403	$415	$428
Base other income	$806	$830	$855
Percent variable	× 50.0%	× 50.0%	× 50.0%
Unadjusted variable component	$403	$415	$428
Unadjusted variable component	$403	$415	$428
Variable percentage change	× 88.2%	× 98.5%	× 104.4%
Adjusted variable component	$355	$409	$447
Fixed component	$403	$415	$428
Variable component	+ 355	+ 409	+ 447
Total other income	$758	$824	$875
Percent of total revenue	5.6%	5.2%	4.9%
Per available room	$3,032	$3,296	$3,492
Per occupied room	$13.84	$13.48	$13.47

TABLE 5.38   Total Revenue (in thousands)

	Year 3	Year 4	Year 5 (Stab.)
Rooms*	$8,022	$9,719	$11,158
Food	3,479	3,864	4,146
Beverage	939	1,043	1,119
Telephone	394	448	486
Other income	758	824	873
Total revenue	$13,592	$15,898	$17,782

* Rooms revenue for the proposed Sheraton was calculated in Table 5.1 at the beginning of this chapter.

TABLE 5.39   Rooms Expense (in thousands)—Proposed Sheraton

	Year 3	Year 4	Year 5 (Stab.)
Base rooms expense	$2,317	$2,386	$2,458
Percent fixed	× 60.0%	× 60.0%	× 60.0%
Fixed component	$1,390	$1,432	$1,475
Base rooms expense	$2,317	$2,386	$2,458
Percent variable	× 40.0%	× 40.0%	× 40.0%
Unadjusted variable component	$927	$954	$983
Unadjusted variable component	$927	$954	$983
Variable percentage change	× 88.2%	× 98.5%	× 104.4%
Adjusted variable component	$818	$940	$1,026
Fixed component	$1,390	$1,432	$1,475
Variable component	+ 818	+ 940	+ 1,027
Total rooms expense	$2,208	$2,372	$2,502
Percent of rooms revenue	27.5%	24.4%	22.4%
Per available room	$8,832	$9,488	$10,004
Per occupied room	$40.33	$38.80	$38.60

TABLE 5.40   Variable Percent Change Bases

Expense Category	Basis for Calculating Variable Percent Change
Food & beverage	Food & beverage revenue
Telephone	Telephone revenue
Other income	Other income
Administrative & general	Total revenue
Marketing	Total revenue
Property operation & maintenance	Total revenue
Energy	Total revenue

In Table 5.41, the variable percent change for each expense category is calculated. The subsequent tables show the estimated expenses for the proposed Sheraton. (See Tables 5.42 through 5.53.)

TABLE 5.41 Projected Variable Change (in thousands)

	Year 3	Year 4	Year 5 (Stab.)
Food & beverage expense			
Projected food & beverage revenue	$4,418	$4,907	$5,265
÷ Base food & beverage revenue	4,814	4,959	5,107
Variable percentage change	91.8%	99.0%	103.1%
Telephone expense			
Projected telephone revenue	$394	$448	$486
÷ Base telephone revenue	441	454	468
Variable percentage change	89.4%	98.7%	103.9%
Other income expense			
Projected other income	$758	$824	$873
÷ Base other income	806	830	855
Variable percentage change	94.1%	99.3%	102.2%
All other expenses			
Projected total revenue	$13,592	$15,898	$17,782
÷ Base total revenue	15,152	16,106	17,116
Variable percentage change	89.7%	98.7%	103.9%

TABLE 5.42 Food and Beverage Expense—Proposed Sheraton (in thousands)

	Year 3	Year 4	Year 5 (Stab.)
Base food & beverage expense	$3,756	$3,868	$3,984
Percent fixed	× 55.0%	× 55.0%	× 55.0%
Fixed component	$2,066	$2,127	$2,191
Base food & beverage expense	$3,756	$3,868	$3,984
Percent variable	× 45.0%	× 45.0%	× 45.0%
Unadjusted variable component	$1,690	$1,741	$1,793
Unadjusted variable component	$1,690	$1,741	$1,793
Variable percentage change	× 91.8%	× 99.0%	× 103.1%
Adjusted variable component	$1,551	$1,724	$1,849
Fixed component	$2,066	$2,128	$2,191
Variable component	+ 1,551	+ 1,723	+ 1,848
Total food & beverage expense	$3,617	$3,851	$4,039
Percent of food & beverage revenue	81.9%	78.5%	76.7%
Per available room	$14,468	$15,400	$16,160
Per occupied room	$66.06	$62.97	$62.36

TABLE 5.43 Telephone Expense–Proposed Sheraton (in thousands)

	Year 3	Year 4	Year 5 (Stab.)
Base telephone expense	$191	$197	$203
Percent fixed	× 60.0%	× 60.0%	× 60.0%
Fixed component	$115	$118	$122
Base telephone expense	$191	$197	$203
Percent variable	× 40.0%	× 40.0%	× 40.0%
Unadjusted variable component	$76	$79	$81
Unadjusted variable component	$76	$79	$81
Variable percentage change	× 89.4%	× 98.7%	× 103.9%
Adjusted variable component	$68	$78	$84
Fixed component	$115	$118	$122
Variable component	+ 68	+ 78	+ 84
Total telephone expense	$183	$196	$206
Percent of telephone revenue	46.4%	43.8%	42.4%
Per available room	$732	$784	$824
Per occupied room	$3.34	$3.21	$3.18

TABLE 5.44 Other Income Expense–Proposed Sheraton (in thousands)

	Year 3	Year 4	Year 5 (Stab.)
Base other income expense	$389	$401	$413
Percent fixed	× 50.0%	× 50.0%	× 50.0%
Fixed component	$195	$201	$207
Base other income expense	$389	$401	$413
Percent variable	× 50.0%	× 50.0%	× 50.0%
Unadjusted variable component	$195	$201	$207
Unadjusted variable component	$195	$201	$207
Variable percentage change	× 94.1%	× 99.3%	× 102.2%
Adjusted variable component	$183	$200	$212
Fixed component	$195	$201	$207
Variable component	+ 183	+ 200	+ 212
Total other income expense	$378	$401	$419
Percent of other income revenue	49.9%	48.4%	47.8%
Per available room	$1,512	$1,596	$1,668
Per occupied room	$6.90	$6.53	$6.44

TABLE 5.45 **Administrative & General Expense–Proposed Sheraton (in thousands)**

	Year 3	Year 4	Year 5 (Stab.)
Base adm. & general expense	$1,263	$1,301	$1,340
Percent fixed	× 70.0%	× 70.0%	× 70.0%
Fixed component	$884	$911	$938
Base adm. & general expense	$1,263	$1,301	$1,340
Percent variable	× 30.0%	× 30.0%	× 30.0%
Unadjusted variable component	$379	$390	$402
Unadjusted variable component	$379	$390	$402
Variable percentage change	× 89.7%	× 98.7%	× 103.9%
Adjusted variable component	$340	$385	$418
Fixed component	$884	$911	$938
Variable component	+ 340	+ 385	+ 418
Total adm. & general expense	$1,224	$1,296	$1,356
Percent of total revenue	9.0%	8.1%	7.6%
Per available room	$4,896	$5,180	$5,420
Per occupied room	$22.36	$21.18	$20.91

TABLE 5.46 **Marketing Expense–Proposed Sheraton (in thousands)**

	Year 3	Year 4	Year 5 (Stab.)
Base marketing expense	$543	$559	$576
Percent fixed	× 70.0%	× 70.0%	× 70.0%
Fixed component	$380	$391	$403
Base marketing expense	$543	$559	$576
Percent variable	× 30.0%	× 30.0%	× 30.0%
Unadjusted variable component	$163	$168	$173
Unadjusted variable component	$163	$168	$173
Variable percentage change	× 89.7%	× 98.7%	× 103.9%
Adjusted variable component	$146	$166	$180
Fixed component	$380	$391	$403
Variable component	+ 146	+ 166	+ 180
Total	$526	$557	$583
Initial year's premium factor	× 1.21	× 1.10	× 1.00
Total marketing expense	$631	$613	$583
Percent of total revenue	4.6%	3.9%	3.3%
Per available room	$2,525	$2,455	$2,332
Per occupied room	$11.53	$10.04	$9.00

TABLE 5.47 Franchise Fees—Proposed Sheraton (in thousands)

	Year 3	Year 4	Year 5 (Stab.)
Rooms revenue	$8,022	$9,719	$11,158
Franchise fee ratio	× 5.0%	× 5.0%	× 5.0%
Franchise fees	$401	$486	$558
Percent of total revenue	3.0%	3.1%	3.1%
Per available room	$1,604	$1,944	$2,232
Per occupied room	$7.32	$7.95	$8.61

TABLE 5.48 Property Operation & Maintenance Expense—Proposed Sheraton (in thousands)

	Year 3	Year 4	Year 5 (Stab.)
Base property op. & maint. expense	$733	$755	$777
Percent fixed	× 70.0%	× 70.0%	× 70.0%
Fixed component	$513	$529	$544
Base property op. & maint. expense	$733	$755	$777
Percent variable	× 30.0%	× 30.0%	× 30.0%
Unadjusted variable component	$220	$227	$233
Unadjusted variable component	$220	$227	$233
Variable percentage change	× 89.7%	× 98.7%	× 103.9%
Adjusted variable component	$197	$224	$242
Fixed component	$513	$529	$544
Variable component	+ 197	+ 224	+ 242
Total	$710	$753	$786
Discount for new facilities	× 80.0%	× 90.0%	× 100.0%
Total property op. & maint. expense	$568	$678	$786
Percent of total revenue	4.2%	4.3%	4.4%
Per available room	$2,272	$2,707	$3,144
Per occupied room	$10.37	$11.07	$12.13

TABLE 5.49 Energy Expense–Proposed Sheraton (in thousands)

	Year 3	Year 4	Year 5 (Stab.)
Base energy expense	$692	$713	$735
Percent fixed	× 90.0%	× 90.0%	× 90.0%
Fixed component	$623	$642	$662
Base energy expense	$692	$713	$735
Percent variable	× 10.0%	× 10.0%	× 10.0%
Unadjusted variable component	$69	$71	$74
Unadjusted variable component	$69	$71	$74
Variable percentage change	× 89.7%	× 98.7%	× 103.9%
Adjusted variable component	$62	$70	$77
Fixed component	$623	$642	$662
Variable component	+ 62	+ 70	+ 77
Total energy expense	$685	$712	$739
Percent of total revenue	5.0%	4.5%	4.1%
Per available room	$2,740	$2,848	$2,948
Per occupied room	$12.51	$11.65	$11.38

TABLE 5.50 Management Fees–Proposed Sheraton (in thousands)

	Year 3	Year 4	Year 5 (Stab.)
Total revenue	$13,592	$15,898	$17,782
Management fee ratio	× 3.0%	× 3.0%	× 3.0%
Management fees	$408	$477	$533
Per available room	$1,632	$1,908	$2,132
Per occupied room	$7.45	$7.80	$8.23

TABLE 5.51 Property Taxes–Proposed Sheraton (in thousands)

	Year 3	Year 4	Year 5 (Stab.)
Property taxes	$462	$476	$491
Percent of total revenue	3.4%	3.0%	2.8%
Per available room	$1,848	$1,904	$1,964
Per occupied room	$8.44	$7.79	$7.58

TABLE 5.52 Insurance Expense–Proposed Sheraton (in thousands)

	Year 3	Year 4	Year 5 (Stab.)
Insurance	$164	$169	$174
Percent of total revenue	1.2%	1.1%	1.0%
Per available room	$656	$676	$696
Per occupied room	$3.00	$2.76	$2.69

TABLE 5.53 Reserve for Replacement–Proposed Sheraton (in thousands)

	Year 3	Year 4	Year 5 (Stab.)
Total revenue	$13,592	$15,898	$17,782
Reserve for replacement ratio	× 4.0%	× 4.0%	× 4.0%
Reserve for replacement	$544	$636	$711
Per available room	$2,176	$2,544	$2,844
Per occupied room	$9.94	$10.40	$10.97

Marketing Expense

The proposed Sheraton Hotel will be new when it opens in Year 3 of the projection. As a result, an upward adjustment to the market expense is warranted in the first two projection years in order to reflect the costs of establishing a new hotel's market position. In the first projection year a premium factor of 1.20 is applied, (reflecting an upward adjustment of 20%). In Year 2, the premium factor is estimated at 1.10. In Year 3, the expense is assumed to stabilize with no premium factor. Table 5.46 identifies the associated calculations.

Property Operation and Maintenance Expense

Because the proposed Sheraton Hotel will be new when it opens in Year 3 of the projection, its property operation and maintenance expense during the initial years should be less than the comparable expenses used to develop the base. These savings are reflected by adjusting downward the property operation and maintenance expense for the first two years of operation— when downward adjustments of 20% and 10%, respectively, will be applied. No adjustments will be made after the fourth projection year. Table 5.48 identifies the associated calculations.

Table 5.54 shows the results of the individual fixed and variable calculations for each item of income and expense. The forecast of income and expenses for the proposed Sheraton Hotel covers the first two years of operation as well as the stabilized year.

TABLE 5.54	Forecast of Income and Expense—Proposed Sheraton					
Calendar year end:	——— Year 3 ———		——— Year 4 ———		— Year 5 (Stab.) —	
Number of rooms:	250		250		250	
Occupancy:	60%		67%		71%	
Occupied rooms:	54,750		61,138		64,788	
Average rate:	$146.52		$158.97		$172.22	
Revenue		% of Gross		% of Gross		% of Gross
Rooms	$8,022	59.0%	$9,719	61.1%	$11,158	62.7%
Food	3,479	25.6	3,864	24.3	4,146	23.3
Beverage	939	6.9	1,043	6.6	1,119	6.3
Telephone	394	2.9	448	2.8	486	2.7
Other income	758	5.6	824	5.2	873	4.9
Total revenue	$13,592	100.0%	$15,898	100.0%	$17,782	100.0%
Departmental Expenses*						
Rooms	$2,208	27.5%	$2,372	24.4%	$2,501	22.4%
Food & beverage	3,617	81.9	3,850	78.5	4,040	76.7
Telephone	183	46.4	196	43.8	206	42.4
Other income	378	49.9	399	48.4	417	47.8
Total departmental expenses	$6,386	47.0%	$6,817	42.9%	$7,164	40.3%
Departmental Income	$7,206	53.0%	$9,081	57.1%	$10,618	59.7%
Undistributed Operating Expenses (UDOE)						
Administrative & general	$1,224	9.0%	$1,295	8.1%	$1,355	7.6 %
Marketing	631	4.6	614	3.9	583	3.3
Franchise fee	401	3.0	486	3.1	558	3.1
Property operation & maintenance	568	4.2	677	4.3	786	4.4
Energy	685	5.0	712	4.5	737	4.1
Total UDOE	$3,509	25.8%	$3,784	23.9%	$4,019	22.5%
Income Before Fixed Charges	$3,697	27.2%	$5,297	33.2%	$6,599	37.2%
Fixed Charges						
Management fee	$408	3.0%	$477	3.0%	$533	3.0 %
Property taxes	462	3.4	476	3.0	491	2.8
Insurance	164	1.2	169	1.1	174	1.0
Reserve for replacement	544	4.0	636	4.0	711	4.0
Total fixed charges	$1,578	11.6%	$1,758	11.1%	$1,909	10.8%
Net Income	$2,119	15.6%	$3,539	22.1%	$4,691	26.4%

* Departmental expenses expressed as a ratio to departmental revenues

Forecast of Revenue and Expense–Embassy Suites

The methodology associated with the projection of income and expense for an existing hotel is less complex than that associated with a proposed hotel, particularly if the hotel is established and operates at its stabilized level. In the case of the existing Embassy Suites, the subject property's historical income and expense levels are identified in Table 5.55.

Table 5.56 identifies the inflation factors applied to each of the revenue and expense items, from the base year through the third projection year.

Table 5.57 identifies the fixed and variable percentages selected for each revenue and expense category of the existing Embassy Suites.

After applying the fixed and variable calculations detailed in the case of the proposed Sheraton Hotel, the forecast of income and expense for the Embassy Suites through the stabilized year results. Table 5.58 sets forth the results of the calculations.

As indicated, the Embassy Suites' overall level of operating efficiency is expected to decline from the first projection year through the third projection year then improve slightly in the stabilized year. These shifts are a function of the hotel's occupancy rate decline, a dynamic that is itself a function of increased supply.

TABLE 5.55	**Historical Statement of Income and Expense–Embassy Suites–Base Year**			

Number of rooms:	200			
Occupancy rate:	78%			
Occupied rooms:	56,940			
Average rate:	$151.00			
	Total $ (in thousands)	Percent of Gross	Per Available Room (PAR)	Per Occupied Room (POR)
Revenue				
Rooms	$8,598	68.5%	$42,990	$151.00
Food	2,425	19.3	12,125	42.59
Beverage	970	7.7	4,850	17.04
Telephone	346	2.8	1,730	6.08
Other income	208	1.7	1,040	3.65
Total revenue	$12,547	100.0%	$62,735	$220.36
Departmental Expenses*				
Rooms	$1,819	21.2%	$9,095	$31.95
Food & beverage	2,716	80.0	13,580	47.70
Telephone	208	60.1	1,040	3.65
Other income	166	79.8	830	2.92
Total departmental expenses	$4,909	39.1%	$24,545	$86.22
Departmental Income	$7,638	60.9%	$38,190	$134.14
Undistributed Operating Expenses (UDOE)				
Administrative & general	$975	7.8%	$4,875	$17.12
Marketing	650	5.2	3,250	11.42
Franchise fee	430	3.4	2,149	7.55
Property operation & maintenance	520	4.1	2,600	9.13
Energy	390	3.1	1,950	6.85
Total UDOE	$2,965	23.6%	$14,824	$52.07
Income Before Fixed Charges	$4,673	37.3%	$23,366	$82.07
Fixed Charges				
Management fee	$147	1.2%	$736	$2.59
Property taxes	279	2.2	1,395	4.90
Insurance	156	1.2	780	2.74
Reserve for replacement	196	1.6	982	3.45
Total fixed charges	$778	6.2%	$3,893	$13.68
Net Income	$3,895	31.1%	$19,473	$68.39
Ratios				
Food revenue to rooms revenue	28.2%			
Food and beverage revenue to rooms revenue	39.5			
Telephone to rooms	4.0			
Other income to rooms revenue	2.4			
Beverage revenue to food revenue	40.0			

* Departmental expenses expressed as a ratio to departmental revenues

	Base Year	Inflation	Year 1	Inflation	Year 2	Inflation	Year 3	Inflation	Stabilized
TABLE 5.56 Projection of Base Year Revenue and Expense—Embassy Suites									
Revenue									
Rooms	$8,598	6.0%	$9,114	5.0%	$9,570	4.0%	$9,952	3.0%	$10,251
Food	2,425	3.0	2,498	3.0	2,573	3.0	2,650	3.0	2,729
Beverage	970	3.0	999	3.0	1,029	3.0	1,060	3.0	1,092
Telephone	346	3.0	356	3.0	367	3.0	378	3.0	389
Other income	+ 208	3.0	+ 214	3.0	+ 221	3.0	+ 227	3.0	+ 234
Total revenue	$12,547		$13,181		$13,760		$14,267		$14,695
Expenses									
Rooms	$1,819	3.0%	$1,874	3.0%	$1,930	3.0%	$1,988	3.0%	$2,047
Food & beverage	2,716	3.0	2,797	3.0	2,881	3.0	2,968	3.0	3,057
Telephone	208	3.0	214	3.0	221	3.0	227	3.0	234
Other income	166	3.0	171	3.0	176	3.0	181	3.0	187
Administrative & General	$975	3.0%	$1,004	3.0%	$1,034	3.0%	$1,065	3.0%	$1,097
Marketing	650	3.0	670	3.0	690	3.0	710	3.0	732
Franchise fee	430	3.0	443	3.0	456	3.0	470	3.0	484
Property Oper. & Maint.	$520	3.0%	$536	3.0%	$552	3.0%	$568	3.0%	$585
Energy	390	8.0	421	6.0	446	5.0	469	3.0	483
Management fee	376	3.0	388	3.0	399	3.0	411	3.0	424
Property taxes	279	1.0	282	2.0	287	2.0	293	3.0	302
Insurance	156	3.0	161	3.0	166	3.0	170	3.0	176
Reserve for Replacement	$502	3.0%	$517	3.0%	$532	3.0%	$548	3.0%	$565

TABLE 5.57   **Fixed and Variable Percentages—Embassy Suites**

Category	Embassy Suites	
	Fixed	**Variable**
Revenue		
Food	10%	90%
Beverage	10	90
Telephone	10	90
Other income	50	50
Expense		
Rooms	60	40
Food & beverage	55	45
Telephone	60	40
Other income	50	50
Administrative and general	70	30
Marketing	70	30
Franchise fee	0	100
Property operation & maintenance	70	30
Energy	90	10
Management fee	0	100
Property taxes	100	0
Insurance	100	0
Reserve for replacement	0	100

TABLE 5.58 Forecast of Income and Expense—Existing Embassy Suites

Calendar year end:	Year 1		Year 2		Year 3		Year 4 (Stab.)	
Number of rooms:	200		200		200		200	
Occupancy:	82%		75%		70%		72%	
Occupied rooms:	59,860		54,750		51,100		52,560	
Average rate:	$160.06		$168.06		$174.79		$180.03	
Revenue		% of Gross		% of Gross		% of Gross		% of Gross
Rooms	$9,581	69.3%	$9,201	69.4%	$8,932	69.4%	$9,462	69.5%
Food	2,613	18.9	2,484	18.7	2,405	18.7	2,540	18.7
Beverage	1,041	7.5	997	7.5	972	7.6	1,024	7.5
Telephone	373	2.7	354	2.7	343	2.7	362	2.7
Other income	220	1.6	216	1.6	216	1.7	225	1.7
Total revenue	$13,828	100.0%	$13,252	100.0%	$12,868	100.0%	$13,613	100.0%
Departmental Expenses*								
Rooms	$1,912	20.0%	$1,900	20.6%	$1,906	21.3%	$1,984	21.0%
Food & beverage	2,854	78.1	2,838	81.5	2,848	84.3	2,964	83.2
Telephone	218	58.4	218	61.6	219	63.8	228	63.0
Other income	173	78.6	174	80.6	177	81.9	183	81.3
Total departmental expenses	$5,157	37.3%	$5,130	38.7%	$5,150	40.0%	$5,359	39.4%
Departmental Income	$8,671	62.7%	$8,122	61.3%	$7,718	60.0%	$8,254	60.6%
Undistributed Operating Expenses (UDOE)								
Administrative & general	$1,019	7.4%	$1,023	7.7%	$1,034	8.0%	$1,073	7.9%
Marketing	679	4.9	682	5.1	689	5.4	715	5.3
Franchise fee	479	3.5	460	3.5	447	3.5	473	3.5
Property operation & maintenance	543	3.9	546	4.1	551	4.3	572	4.2
Energy	423	3.1	445	3.4	464	3.6	479	3.5
Total UDOE	$3,143	22.8%	$3,156	23.8%	$3,185	24.8%	$3,312	24.4%
Income Before Fixed Charges	$5,528	39.9%	$4,966	37.5%	$4,533	35.2%	$4,942	36.2%
Fixed Charges								
Management fee	$415	3.0%	$398	3.0%	$386	3.0%	$408	3.0%
Property taxes	282	2.0	287	2.2	293	2.3	302	2.2
Insurance	161	1.2	166	1.3	170	1.3	176	1.3
Reserve for replacement	553	4.0	530	4.0	515	4.0	545	4.0
Total fixed charges	$1,411	10.2%	$1,381	10.5%	$1,364	10.6%	$1,431	10.5%
Net Income	$4,117	29.7%	$3,585	27.0%	$3,169	24.6%	$3,511	25.7%

* Departmental expenses expressed as a ratio to departmental revenues

Market Value and the Valuation Process

CHAPTER 6

Hotels and motels are income-producing, investment properties that are periodically bought, sold, financed, refinanced, condemned, assessed, and bequeathed. All of these activities usually require a professional appraisal.

The various authorities and entities involved in the practice of appraisal have formed numerous definitions of market value. Most market value definitions contain common elements. One widely accepted definition is

> The most probable price that a specified interest in real property is likely to bring under all the following conditions:
>
> 1. Consummation of a sale occurs as of a specified date.
> 2. An open and competitive market exists for the property interest appraised.
> 3. The buyer and seller are each acting prudently and knowledgeably.
> 4. The price is not affected by an undue stimulus.
> 5. The buyer and seller are typically motivated.
> 6. Both parties are acting in what they consider their best interest.
> 7. Marketing efforts were adequate and a reasonable amount of time was allowed for exposure in the open market.
> 8. Payment was made in cash in U.S. dollars or in terms of financial arrangements comparable thereto.
> 9. The price represents the normal consideration for the property sold, unaffected by special or creative financing or sales concessions granted by anyone associated with the sale.[1]

The Uniform Standards of Professional Appraisal Practice (USPAP) of The Appraisal Foundation require that certain items be included in every appraisal

---

1. *The Appraisal of Real Estate,* 12th ed. (Chicago: Appraisal Institute, 2001), 24.

report. Among these items, the following are directly related to the definition of market value:

1. Identification of the specific property rights to be appraised.
2. Statement of the effective date of the value opinion.
3. Specification of whether cash, terms equivalent to cash, or other precisely described financing terms are assumed as the basis of the appraisal.
4. If the appraisal is conditioned upon financing or other terms, specification as to whether the financing or terms are at, below or above market interest rates and/or contain unusual conditions or incentives. The terms of above- or below-market interest rates and/or other special incentives must be clearly set forth; their contribution to, or negative influence on, value must be described and estimated; and the market data supporting the opinion of value must be described and explained.[2]

The following definition has been agreed upon by the agencies that regulate federal financial institutions in the United States:

> The most probable price which a property should bring in a competitive and open market under all conditions requisite to a fair sale, the buyer and seller each acting prudently and knowledgeably, and assuming the price is not affected by undue stimulus. Implicit in this definition is the consummation of a sale as of a specified date and the passing of title from seller to buyer under conditions whereby
>
> 1. Buyer and seller are typically motivated;
> 2. Both parties are well informed or well advised and acting in what they consider their own best interests;
> 3. A reasonable time is allowed for exposure in the open market;
> 4. Payment is made in terms of cash in U.S. dollars or in terms of financial arrangements comparable thereto; and
> 5. The price represents the normal consideration for the property sold unaffected by special or creative financing or sales concessions granted by anyone associated with the sale.[3]

The market value of a lodging facility may include the value of its various components, which consist of land; improvements (buildings); furniture, fixtures, and equipment; inventories; working capital; and any business value. Market value is estimated by applying the valuation process, and the opinion of value is usually communicated in a written appraisal report.

In arriving at the market value of real estate, the appraiser considers three approaches:

---

2. Ibid., 22.
3. *Federal Register,* Vol. 55, No. 165, August 22, 1990: 34228 and 34229.

1. The cost approach
2. The sales comparison approach
3. The income capitalization approach

Cost Approach

The cost approach is based on the assumption that an informed purchaser will pay no more for a property than the cost of producing a substitute property with equal utility. When the cost approach is applied, an opinion of market value is developed by calculating the current cost of replacing the subject improvements and subtracting an appropriate amount for depreciation.

The cost of replacing a property is estimated on a square-foot basis using figures from a construction cost manual published by a recognized cost reporting service. The value of the land as if vacant and available for development is then added to the depreciated replacement cost estimate to yield the estimate of value.

Depreciation is defined as a loss in value caused by one or more of the following factors:

- Physical deterioration—the physical wearing out of the property
- Functional obsolescence—a lack of desirability in the layout, style, and design of the property as compared to a new property serving the same function
- External obsolescence—a loss in value from causes outside the property itself

Appraisal literature recommends using the cost approach for new properties, which have not been affected by the various forms of depreciation, and for unique or specialized improvements such as schools and libraries that have no comparable market or income potential.

The cost approach is seldom used to value existing hotels and motels because lodging facilities are particularly vulnerable to physical deterioration, functional changes, and uncontrollable external factors. Sometimes a hotel can suffer from functional and external obsolescence before its construction is completed. As the building and other improvements age and depreciate, the resulting loss in value becomes difficult to quantify. Estimating the impact of even minor forms of obsolescence may require unsubstantiated judgments that undermine the credibility of the cost approach.

The cost approach is not applied to hotels and motels because its underlying assumptions do not reflect the investment rationale of typical hostelry buyers. Lodging facilities are income-producing properties that are purchased to realize future profits. Replacement or reproduction cost has little bearing on an investment decision when the buyer is primarily concerned with the potential return on equity.

The cost approach can be useful, however, in determining the feasibility of a proposed hotel. When applied in conjunction with the income capitalization approach, the cost approach can verify a project's economic feasibility. If the value obtained by applying the income capitalization approach is equal to or greater than the replacement cost plus the land value, the project is usually considered economically feasible. If, however, the value estimated by the income capitalization approach is less than the value derived by the cost approach, the investors should scrap the project, reduce capital costs, or lower their desired return. Moreover, if this is the case, an additional equity investment may be needed to secure sufficient financing. The data used to estimate the replacement cost of property improvements should come from a qualified source such as an experienced contractor, architect, or engineer, or from a construction cost manual. Land value is established by analyzing sales of comparable parcels or by capitalizing the ground rental.

Table 6.1 shows ranges of typical replacement costs, land values, and soft costs for luxury, standard, and economy accommodations for 1985 through 1999.

Estimating Hotel Land Values

Hotel appraisers are sometimes asked to estimate the value of a total property and then calculate a separate land value. To calculate land value the appraiser investigates the market to find recent transfers of vacant parcels with similar acreage, street frontage, location, and zoning. Any differences between the comparable property and the subject are then adjusted on a grid. In practice, this process can be difficult due to the lack of sufficiently comparable vacant land sales data and the complexity of estimating the necessary adjustments. An alternative approach is the comparable ground lease method, based on the premise that the value of land is tied directly to its capacity to generate income at its highest and best use.

Each year a number of hotel transactions are structured using ground leases. Typical rental terms vary from simple flat payments with escalation adjustments to formulae based entirely on gross revenues. To quantify the income attributed to the land alone, the net rental using a percentage of gross revenue is the logical choice.

TABLE 6.1   Hotel Development Costs (in dollars per available room)

Year	Category	Improvements	Furniture, Fixtures & Equipment	Land	Pre-Opening	Operating Capital	Total	Percent Change
1985	Luxury	$60,000–$115,000	$13,400–$30,000	$11,000–$26,500	$3,000–$5,000	$2,100–$3,100	$89,500–$179,600	—
	Standard	38,000–57,000	9,500–16,500	5,500–14,700	1,900–3,600	1,500–2,500	56,400–94,300	—
	Economy	20,000–36,000	5,000–8,800	3,300–9,500	1,000–1,700	1,000–1,500	30,300–57,500	—
1986	Luxury	62,000–120,000	13,700–30,600	11,500–27,800	3,100–5,200	2,300–3,100	92,600–186,700	1.2–1.3
	Standard	39,000–60,000	9,700–16,800	5,800–15,400	2,000–3,800	1,500–2,600	58,000–98,600	0.9–1.5
	Economy	21,000–37,000	5,100–9,000	3,500–10,000	1,000–1,800	1,100–1,500	31,700–59,300	1.5–1.0
1987	Luxury	63,000–122,000	13,800–30,900	11,900–28,600	3,300–5,500	2,300–3,200	94,300–190,200	0.9–0.9
	Standard	40,000–61,000	9,800–16,800	6,000–15,900	2,100–3,900	1,500–2,600	59,400–100,200	1.2–0.8
	Economy	21,000–39,000	5,200–9,100	3,600–10,200	1,100–1,800	1,100–1,500	32,000–61,600	0.5–1.9
1988	Luxury	65,000–125,000	14,000–31,000	11,900–28,600	3,300–5,500	2,300–3,200	96,500–193,300	1.2–0.8
	Standard	41,000–63,000	10,000–17,100	6,000–15,900	2,100–3,900	1,500–2,600	60,600–102,500	1.0–1.1
	Economy	22,000–40,000	5,200–9,100	3,600–10,200	1,100–1,800	1,100–1,500	33,000–62,600	1.6–0.8
1989	Luxury	66,000–126,000	15,000–32,000	11,900–28,600	3,300–5,500	2,300–3,200	98,500–195,300	1.0–0.5
	Standard	41,000–64,000	10,500–18,000	6,000–15,900	2,100–3,900	1,500–2,600	61,100–104,400	0.4–0.9
	Economy	22,000–40,000	5,500–9,700	3,600–10,200	1,100–1,800	1,100–1,500	33,300–63,200	0.5–0.5
1990	Luxury	67,000–128,000	15,400–33,000	10,700–25,800	3,500–5,700	2,500–3,500	99,100–196,000	0.6–0.4
	Standard	42,000–65,000	10,800–18,500	5,400–14,300	2,200–4,000	1,600–2,800	62,000–104,600	1.5–0.2
	Economy	22,500–41,000	5,600–10,000	3,200–9,200	1,200–1,800	1,200–1,600	33,700–63,600	1.2–0.6
1991	Luxury	65,000–122,000	14,500–31,500	10,200–24,000	3,700–5,900	2,600–3,600	96,000–187,000	(3.1)–(4.6)
	Standard	40,000–63,000	10,000–17,800	5,100–13,500	2,300–4,200	1,700–2,900	59,100–101,400	(4.7)–(3.1)
	Economy	21,000–39,000	5,000–9,500	3,000–8,600	1,300–2,000	1,300–1,700	31,600–60,800	(6.2)–(4.4)
1992	Luxury	64,000–120,000	14,200–30,900	9,200–21,600	3,800–6,100	2,700–3,700	93,900–182,300	(2.2)–(2.5)
	Standard	39,000–62,000	9,800–17,400	4,600–12,300	2,300–4,400	1,800–3,000	57,500–99,100	(2.7)–(2.3)
	Economy	21,000–38,000	4,900–9,300	2,800–7,900	1,400–2,100	1,300–1,800	31,400–59,100	(0.6)–(2.8)
1993	Luxury	63,000–119,000	14,000–30,500	8,700–20,500	3,900–6,200	2,800–3,800	92,400–180,000	(1.6)–(1.3)
	Standard	39,000–61,000	9,700–17,200	4,400–11,800	2,300–4,500	1,800–3,000	57,200–97,500	(0.5)–(1.6)
	Economy	21,000–38,000	4,900–9,200	2,700–7,700	1,400–2,100	1,300–1,800	31,300–58,800	(0.3)–(0.5)

TABLE 6.1 Hotel Development Costs (in dollars per available room) *(continued)*

		Improvements	Furniture, Fixtures & Equipment	Land	Pre-Opening	Operating Capital	Total	Percent Change
1994	Luxury	64,000–121,000	14,300–31,100	8,900–20,900	3,900–6,200	2,800–3,800	93,900–183,000	1.6–1.7
	Standard	40,000–63,000	10,000–17,600	4,500–12,300	2,400–4,600	1,800–3,000	58,700–100,500	2.6–3.1
	Economy	22,000–40,000	5,100–9,500	2,800–8,000	1,500–2,200	1,300–1,800	32,700–61,500	4.5–4.6
1995	Luxury	65,000–124,000	14,800–32,300	9,200–21,700	4,100–6,400	2,900–4,000	96,000–188,400	2.2–3.0
	Standard	41,000–65,000	10,400–18,300	4,700–12,800	2,500–4,800	1,900–3,100	60,500–104,000	3.1–3.5
	Economy	23,000–42,000	5,400–9,900	3,000–8,400	1,600–2,300	1,300–1,800	34,300–64,400	4.9–4.7
1996	Luxury	66,000–126,000	15,000–34,200	10,500–23,800	4,300–6,500	2,900–4,100	98,700–194,600	2.8–3.3
	Standard	42,000–67,000	10,500–18,500	4,900–13,300	2,500–4,900	1,900–3,100	61,800–106,800	2.1–2.7
	Economy	23,000–43,000	5,600–9,900	3,000–9,200	1,600–2,300	1,300–1,800	34,500–66,200	0.6–2.8
1997	Luxury	68,000–131,500	15,000–36,000	11,000–30,200	4,500–6,800	3,000–4,300	101,500–208,800	2.8–7.3
	Standard	43,000–69,500	10,500–19,000	5,000–14,500	2,800–5,000	2,000–3,100	63,300–111,100	2.4–4.0
	Economy	24,000–47,000	5,600–10,000	3,000–9,400	1,750–2,500	1,500–2,000	35,850–70,900	3.9–7.1
1998	Luxury	70,000–139,400	15,300–37,800	11,000–32,300	4,600–7,100	3,100–4,400	104,000–221,000	2.5–5.8
	Standard	43,900–71,200	10,600–19,600	5,000–14,900	2,900–5,100	2,000–3,200	64,400–114,000	1.7–2.6
	Economy	24,500–48,600	5,700–10,100	3,000–9,600	1,800–2,600	1,500–2,000	36,500–72,900	1.8–2.8
1999	Luxury	73,900–149,200	15,800–39,700	11,300–33,900	4,700–7,500	3,200–4,500	108,900–234,800	4.7–6.2
	Standard	45,700–75,500	10,800–20,600	5,000–14,900	2,900–5,100	2,000–3,200	66,400–119,300	3.1–4.6
	Economy	25,200–50,500	5,900–10,600	3,000–9,800	1,900–2,700	1,500–2,000	37,500–75,600	2.7–3.7

Average Annual Compounded Percent Change:

1985–1999:	Luxury	1.4%–1.9%		1992–1999:	Luxury		2.1%–3.7%
	Standard	1.2%–1.7%			Standard		2.1%–2.7%
	Economy	1.5%–2.0%			Economy		2.6%–3.6%

Source: HVS International

Hotels and Motels—Valuations and Market Studies

Land Value Estimation

In the following example, the comparable ground lease procedure is used to estimate the land value of a hotel in its third year of operation. The following data are given:

Projected rooms revenue	$11,158,000
Projected food revenue	$4,146,000
Projected beverage revenue	$1,119,000

Ground leases for eight hotels similar to the subject were found; their rental formulae are set forth in Table 6.2. The estimated ground rental for the subject is calculated using the comparable formulae and the subject's projected revenues.

TABLE 6.2 Hotel Ground Rental Formulae

Comparable	Percentage of Gross Rooms Revenue	Food Revenue	Beverage Revenue	Estimated Ground Rent
1	3.0%	1.0%	1.0%	$387,390
2	3.0	–	–	334,740
3	7.0	–	–	781,060
4	4.0	2.0	–	529,240
5	2.0	1.0	1.0	275,810
6	5.0	–	3.0	591,470
7	4.0	1.0	1.0	498,970
8	5.0	–	–	557,900
Average estimated ground rental				$494,573*

* Note that in evaluating data, averaging is not appropriate unless the data are similar and homgenous, such as the ground rentals set forth above. When information from dissimilar sources is used, the appraiser should select data that are most comparable to the characteristics of the subject property.

If all the comparable formulae are assumed to be equally similar to the subject, the average ground rent of $494,573 would be a supportable estimate of the income attributed to the land. The land's value can then be calculated by capitalizing the subject's estimated ground rent by an appropriate land capitalization rate.

Ground Rent		Capitalization Rate		Land Value
$494,573	÷	0.085	=	$5,818,506
				rounded $5,800,000

This land value estimate is approximately 17% of the total value estimate for the proposed Sheraton and is within the 10% to 20% range considered normal for a hotel.

The ground lease approach assumes that the hotel represents the land's highest and best use.

For a more detailed explanation of cost approach methodologies, the reader is directed to the most recent edition of *The Appraisal of Real Estate,* published by the Appraisal Institute. This text devotes a chapter to the valuation of real estate via the cost approach. The methods for estimating the forms of depreciation described in this text apply to hotels.

Sales Comparison Approach

The sales comparison approach is based on the assumption that an informed purchaser will pay no more for a property than the cost of acquiring an existing property with equal utility. When this approach is applied, market value is estimated by comparing the sale prices in recent transactions involving properties similar to the property being appraised. Dissimilarities are resolved with appropriate adjustments. These differences may pertain to transaction characteristics such as property rights conveyed, financing terms, conditions of sale, and market conditions, as well as property characteristics such as location, physical condition, scope of facilities, and market orientation.

The reliability of the sales comparison approach depends on three factors:

- Availability of timely, comparable sales data
- Verification of sales data
- Degree of comparability, i.e., the extent of adjustment needed to account for the differences between the subject and the comparable property.

The sales comparison approach often provides highly supportable value estimates for homogeneous properties such as vacant land and single-family homes when the adjustments are few and relatively simple to compute. For larger, more complex properties such as office buildings, shopping centers, and hotels, the required adjustments are often numerous and difficult to estimate.

For example, assume an appraiser is valuing a motel property by comparing it with a similar motel across the street that was sold last year. In this case the subject differs from the comparable in the following ways:

- Seller will take back purchase-money financing
- Different franchise affiliation

- Better visibility
- More parking facilities
- Larger restaurant and smaller lounge
- Enclosed swimming pool
- Higher-grade furnishings
- Two vanity sinks per guest room

These are just a few of the many potential differences for which adjustments will be needed to make the comparable's indicated sale price reflect the subject's market value. In appraising lodging facilities, the adjustment process is often difficult and unsubstantiated by market data. The market-derived capitalization rates that appraisers occasionally use are susceptible to the same shortcomings of the sales comparison approach. In fact, the income capitalization approach's reliability can be substantially reduced when capitalization rates obtained from unsupported market data are used. This practice not only weakens the final estimate of value, it also ignores the typical investment analysis procedures hotel buyers employ.

Although the sales comparison approach seldom is given substantial weight in a hotel appraisal, it can be used to bracket a value or to check the value derived by the income capitalization approach. For example, assume an appraiser is valuing a mid-rate commercial hotel. The appraiser has researched the market and discovered two recent sales. One sale involved a first-class hotel with a value of $120,000 per room. The other sale was of a mid-rate hotel that was less attractive than the property being appraised; it had a value of $85,000 per room.

Although a value estimate based on these data would be difficult to support, a range of values within which the final estimate should fall has been established. If the income capitalization approach results in a value indication that is outside this range, the appraiser knows that the data must be re-evaluated. Occasionally appraisers may apply a gross income multiplier or rooms revenue multiplier in the sales comparison approach. If this practice reflects the market's actions, it can be considered in an appraisal.

Lodging DataBank by HVS International

As in all appraisals, the market must be researched to locate comparable sales with which to support the market value estimate. To help appraisers identify comparable sales of hotels and motels, HVS International has established the Lodging DataBank (LDB), a central clearinghouse of information relating to hotel and motel transactions. The LDB is developed to house facilities information, sales transactions, and development statistics along with market information and company research pertaining to the hospitality industry. The LDB has compiled data on thousands of hotel sales throughout the United States. The data are categorized by property name, city, and state, and include pertinent information relating to each transaction.

To provide a measure of lodging sales activity, HVS International publishes the Hotel Transactions Survey each year. This survey tracks the sales of hotels that sold for more than $10 million throughout the United States. Table 6.3 identifies the major hotel sales activity in the United States during the 1990s.

	TABLE 6.3	Major Hotel Sales				
Year	Number of Transactions	Percent Change	Number of Rooms	Percent Change	Average Price Per Room	Percent Change
1990	130	–	40,053	–	$136,000	–
1991	56	(56.9)%	16,489	(58.8)%	96,000	(29.4)%
1992	70	25.0	26,751	62.2	82,000	(14.6)
1993	53	(24.3)	20,026	(25.1)	93,000	13.4
1994	108	103.8	38,759	93.5	81,000	(12.9)
1995	147	36.1	48,619	25.4	80,000	(1.2)
1996	227	54.4	77,916	60.3	106,000	32.5
1997	280	23.3	82,867	6.4	117,000	10.4
1998	241	(13.9)	78,865	(4.8)	136,000	16.2
1999	118	(51.0)	33,107	(58.0)	142,000	4.4
Avg. annual % change, 1990–1999:	(1.1)%			(2.1)%		0.5 %
Source: Lodging DataBank						

In 1990 the number of transactions and the average price per room were both strong. During the recession of the early 1990s, the number of major hotel transactions declined. Debt and equity financing was unavailable; owners were reluctant to sell at deflated values; and large, full-service hotels were out of favor when compared to more profitable, limited-service properties. The picture changed radically in 1994, when the number of transactions more than doubled from the previous year. Full-service hotels were in demand again, and buyers were attracted to the upside potential of acquiring hotels priced at discounts to their replacement costs. By 1998 the average sale price per room returned to $136,000. In 1999, while hotel sales activity dropped by more than 50% from the previous year, the average price per room continued to climb, peaking at $142,000 per room, the highest point of the decade.

The decline in the number of major hotel sales was caused by several factors in the marketplace. During the buying rush between 1995 and 1998, real estate investment trusts (REITs) dominated the acquisitions market. However, with new legislation and waning stock prices, the buying power of REITs has decreased considerably. Moreover, lenders have become more hesitant about financing the purchase of lodging facilities. The diminishing RevPAR growth, along with new supply outpacing demand growth, has caused lending institutions to be more cautious in their due diligence processes. Furthermore, whereas buyers are currently available, the prices being offered by sellers often make deals prohibitive. While there are instances where buyers are willing to pay a premium to gain a key asset in a major market, this is not typically the case.

Hospitality Valuation Services has also developed a sophisticated valuation benchmark known as the hospitality valuation index (HVI). The HVI, which HVS International initiated in 1986, reflects trends in value. The index is intended to represent HVS International's opinion and may not represent actual value trends.

Income Capitalization Approach

The income capitalization approach converts the anticipated future benefits of property ownership (dollar income) into an estimate of present value. In hotel-motel valuation, this approach typically involves a discounting procedure.

The income capitalization approach is generally the preferred technique for appraising income-producing properties because it closely simulates the investment rationale and strategies of knowledgeable buyers. The approach relates to most hotel and motel properties, which involve relatively high risks and are bought for investment purposes only. Most of the data used in the income capitalization approach is derived from the market, which reduces the need for unsubstantiated, subjective judgments.

The income capitalization approach is applied in three steps.

- Forecast net income for a specified number of years.
- Select an appropriate discount factor or capitalization rate.
- Apply the proper discounting and/or capitalization procedure.

Each of these steps will be discussed in detail.

Forecasting Net Income

Many terms are used to describe the net income that is capitalized into an estimate of value: *net income before recapture, net income before depreciation,* or *net operating income.* All of these terms may be defined as the *annual net income before financial charges* (e.g., the recapture of debt service) are deducted. In this book the concept is referred to as *net income before debt service* (after a reserve for replacement).

In the income capitalization approach, the forecast of net income before debt service is based on two assumptions: the income and expenses forecast are expressed in changing dollars and management is competent.

When a predecessor to this book was published in 1978, the use of constant dollars in all hotel projections was recommended. As inflation became a more important consideration to both hotel lenders and investors, however, it became apparent that interest, discount, and capitalization rates were being adjusted upward for inflation. Hotel investors now base their purchases on the property's expected future benefits with inflation built in, so inflation is also built into the other investment parameters.

Income and expense forecasts are usually based on competent management because the quality of management plays an important role in a lodging facility's profit potential. The appraiser must equalize the effects of varying managerial expertise by assuming that the property being appraised will be managed competently. In reality, management quality may be poor, competent, or superior. If the property is poorly managed, the appraiser is justified in projecting improved operating results based on competent management. If, on the other hand, the subject has superior management, the income and expenses used to estimate market value should reflect less managerial skill—i.e., lower revenue and/or higher expenses. No such assumption is needed if management is fixed by a long-term contract and would not change in the event of a sale, or if the appraiser is estimating investment value rather than market value. Investment value is the value to a particular investor based on individual financial and managerial requirements. It differs from market value in that market value must represent the actions of typical buyers and reflect average, competent management.

The procedure for forecasting income before interest and depreciation has already been described. The appraiser defines the market area, locates and quantifies the demand, and allocates the room nights among the competitive facilities. This procedure provides the information needed to estimate occupancy and average rate. Based on these data, rooms revenue and other sources of income, such as food and beverage sales and telephone income, can be computed. Expense data can be obtained from actual operating statements if the subject is an existing property, or from comparable properties and national averages if the subject is a proposed facility.

Hotel-Motel Life Cycle
The expected flow of net income before debt service must be assessed to select the appropriate discounting procedure. All real estate investments have specific life cycles that show the rise and fall of net income over the property's economic life. Most income-producing properties reach their full economic potential relatively quickly. This level may then be maintained for a number of years and then gradually decline as various forms of depreciation erode the property's income.

It usually takes time for lodging facilities to achieve their maximum level of income. A typical hotel will experience rising occupancy in its first two to four years of operation; often net income does not cover normal debt service during this period. A stabilized level of income usually is reached sometime between the second and fifth years of operation; this stabilized level represents the property's discounted average net income. The income before debt service will usually rise above the stabilized level for a few years and then gradually start to decline between the seventh and twelfth years due to physical deterioration and/or functional and external obsolescence. This decline continues over the property's remaining economic life. A lodging facility's life cycle is not predetermined, however. It can be lengthened or shortened depending on how much maintenance and periodic upgrading the owner is willing to do.

Table 6.4 shows net income figures for a hotel over its 40-year life cycle, where a sale of the property is assumed to occur at the end of the 40th year. The income from the 40th year includes both the net income and sale proceeds.

TABLE 6.4	Hotel Life Cycle					
	— Net Income Before Debt Service —			— Net Income Before Debt Service —		
Year	Inflated Dollars	Constant Dollars	Year	Inflated Dollars	Constant Dollars
1	$1,634,000	$1,634,000	21	$9,700,400	$3,656,000
2	3,322,200	3,164,000	22	9,725,736	3,491,000
3	4,306,365	3,906,000	23	9,729,355	3,326,000
4	5,195,125	4,488,000	24	9,709,021	3,161,000
5	6,060,980	4,987,000	25	9,662,331	2,996,000
6	6,841,331	5,361,000	26	9,586,699	2,831,000
7	7,545,223	5,631,000	27	9,479,348	2,666,000
8	8,162,560	5,801,000	28	9,337,295	2,501,000
9	8,326,907	5,636,000	29	9,157,338	2,336,000
10	8,487,284	5,471,000	30	8,936,043	2,171,000
11	8,642,880	5,306,000	31	8,669,724	2,006,000
12	8,792,818	5,141,000	32	8,354,434	1,841,000
13	8,936,143	4,976,000	33	7,895,941	1,676,000
14	9,071,818	4,811,000	34	7,559,711	1,511,000
15	9,198,720	4,646,000	35	7,070,895	1,346,000
16	9,315,633	4,481,000	36	6,514,297	1,181,000
17	9,421,240	4,316,000	37	5,884,362	1,016,000
18	9,514,119	4,151,000	38	5,175,148	851,000
19	9,592,733	3,986,000	39	4,380,302	686,000
20	9,655,423	3,821,000	40	26,550,815	3,960,000

Proposed hotels and motels are appraised at the beginning of their life cycles, but existing lodging facilities may be appraised at any point in the cycle. By estimating a property's position in the life cycle the appraiser can project future net income before debt service (if adequate market data are available) and select an appropriate discounting procedure.

Selecting Appropriate Capitalization Rates and Discount Factors

Capitalization rates and discount factors are used to convert expected future income into an indication of value. These rates and factors have an interest component, which reflects the return on capital, and a recapture component, which provides for a return of capital.

Theoretically, the interest component can be derived through risk and investment analysis. Starting with a base rate that represents the minimal risk of a safe investment such as a federally insured savings account, the analyst makes a series of upward adjustments to reflect different elements of risk and the investment burden. For example, adjustments might be made for the following factors:

	%
Safe rate (minimum risk)	X
Add for general hostelry risk	1_1
Add for management burden	1_2
Add for food and beverage risk	1_3
Add for rapid functional obsolescence	1_4
Add for lack of liquidity	1_5
Add for other elements	$\underline{1_6}$
	Final interest rate

In practice, estimating the magnitude of each upward adjustment is too subjective a process to provide a supportable interest rate. Utilizing the analytical expertise of the hundreds of money managers who serve the nation's lending institutions can produce a more reliable rate.

A hotel investment often consists of a large amount of mortgage money (55%–75% of the total investment) and a smaller amount of equity capital (25%–45%). Thus, 55% to 75% of a hotel project's cost of capital is based on the mortgage interest rate, which implies that 60% to 75% of the capitalization or discount rate is determined by the cost of the mortgage financing. The lender, who considers all possible risks, establishes the interest rate on a hotel mortgage. The mortgagee is in a more secure position than the equity investor is but, in the event of a foreclosure, the lender may be forced to assume the equity position.

To develop a capitalization rate, the appraiser first researches the cost of the investment's debt component by evaluating recent hotel financing transactions. To simplify the calculations for appraisal purposes, the interest rate is generally assumed to be fixed rather than variable. Although variable-rate mortgages are used to finance some hotel projects, it is often possible to have another lending entity fix the interest rate at a specific level, which effectively converts the variable payments into fixed payments. For the purpose of illustration, a fixed-payment mortgage will be used.

Among mortgage provisions, the mortgage interest rate has the greatest economic impact on an investment. To assess the cost of mortgage capital, hotel appraisers must know the current lending rates for hotel mortgage loans. To provide appraisers with a reference point from which to estimate the cost of mortgage financing, there is a critical need for reliable, timely estimates of hotel mortgage interest rates.

One procedure for accumulating mortgage rate information is to survey lenders actively making hotel loans. This approach will often yield results, but the data may not be accurate for the following reasons:

- It may be difficult to find lenders who are actively lending on hotel projects.

- Even lenders who are active in the hotel lending market do not regularly make hotel loans. Therefore, any information obtained for these sources may be dated, particularly in a fast-changing money market.

- Not all lenders are willing to provide data relative to the loans they have made.

- A lender who responds to an interest rate survey may provide information that represents the "asking price" for a hotel loan, rather than the final terms negotiated.

A more reliable approach is for the appraiser to obtain accurate information on hotel loans actually originated by lenders. The American Council of Life Insurance is the best source for this type of data. The council, which represents most major life insurance companies, publishes quarterly reports about the hotel mortgages originated by their member companies. Relevant data available to subscribers include the number of loans made, the total dollar amounts loaned, the interest rates, the loan-to-value ratios, and the terms of the loans.

The drawback, however, is that the data published by the American Council of Life Insurance is generally four to six months old by the time they are accumulated and distributed. Thus, appraisers need to find a way to update the data continuously. Ideally, appraisers can use as an indicator some type of money market instrument with a rate of return (yield) that can be obtained on a daily basis. If the movement of this rate shows a high correlation with hotel mortgage interest rates, then a regression equation can be developed to estimate current hotel mortgage interest rates using the known money market instrument.

HVS International developed such a procedure by running a series of regression analyses. Quarterly mortgage interest rate data supplied by the American Council of Life Insurance were compared with numerous, widely reported money market instruments. Included in this analysis were the prime rate, the federal funds rate, several stock market rates, different types of bond yields, and a variety of similar indexes. As a result of this research, a close mathematical relationship was found between the average interest rate of a hotel mortgage and the concurrent yield on an average A corporate bond, as reported daily in *Moody's Bond Record.*

Table 6.5 shows the annual rates for several of the money market instruments that were evaluated. The first column shows the interest rates for hotel mortgages as reported by the American Council of Life Insurance. The other columns contain the comparative rates, including the yields on federal funds, the prime rate, FHA-

TABLE 6.5 Annual Rates for Money Market Instruments

Year	Period	Hotel Interest Rates (ACLI)	Federal Funds	Prime Rate	FHA Ins. Home Mort.	S&P 500 Composite	US Treasury Notes and Bonds					Treasury Bills—Auction Avg.		U.S. Govt. Securities Composite—LT (Over 10 Years)
							3-Year	5-Year	7-Year	10-Year	30-Year	3-Month	6-Month	
1973	Ann. Avg.	9.02%	8.73%	8.02%	8.08%	4.08%	6.95%	6.85%	N.A.	7.05%	7.20%	7.02%	7.16%	6.31%
1974	Ann. Avg.	9.69	10.50	10.80	9.18	5.97	7.82	7.80	7.71%	7.56	7.80	7.87	7.91	6.98
1975	Ann. Avg.	10.31	5.82	7.86	9.19	4.31	7.49	7.77	7.90	7.99	8.35	5.82	6.11	7.00
1976	Ann. Avg.	10.08	5.05	6.84	8.84	3.77	6.77	7.18	7.42	7.61	8.30	5.00	5.28	6.78
1977	Ann. Avg.	9.79	5.54	7.07	8.68	4.62	6.69	6.99	7.23	7.42	7.74	5.27	5.51	7.06
1978	Ann. Avg.	9.94	7.93	9.06	9.65	5.28	8.29	8.32	8.36	8.41	8.49	7.22	7.57	7.89
1979	Ann. Avg.	10.78	11.20	12.67	10.98	5.47	9.71	9.52	9.48	9.44	9.29	10.04	10.02	8.74
1980	Ann. Avg.	12.63	13.36	15.27	13.44	5.26	11.51	11.45	11.40	11.43	11.27	11.61	11.47	10.81
1981	Ann. Avg.	14.63	16.38	18.87	16.31	5.20	14.44	14.24	14.06	13.91	13.44	14.08	13.81	12.87
1982	Ann. Avg.	15.73	12.26	14.86	15.31	5.81	12.92	13.01	13.06	13.00	12.76	10.72	11.11	12.23
1983	Ann. Avg.	12.97	9.09	10.80	13.11	4.40	10.45	10.80	11.02	11.10	11.18	8.62	8.74	10.84
1984	Ann. Avg.	13.29	10.23	12.04	13.82	4.64	11.89	12.24	12.42	12.44	12.41	9.57	9.80	11.99
1985	Ann. Avg.	12.24	8.10	9.94	12.24	4.25	9.64	10.12	10.50	10.62	10.79	7.49	7.66	10.75
1986	Ann. Avg.	9.95	6.81	8.33	9.91	3.49	7.06	7.30	7.54	7.67	7.78	5.97	6.02	8.14
1987	Ann. Avg.	9.91	6.66	8.21	10.12	3.08	7.68	7.94	8.23	8.39	8.59	5.83	6.06	8.63
1988	Ann. Avg.	10.27	7.57	9.32	10.49	3.64	8.26	8.47	8.71	8.85	8.96	6.67	6.91	8.98
1989	Ann. Avg.	10.11	9.22	10.88	10.24	3.53	8.55	8.50	8.52	8.49	8.45	8.11	8.04	8.59
1990	Ann. Avg.	10.53	8.10	10.01	10.17	3.61	8.26	8.37	8.52	8.55	8.61	7.51	7.47	8.73
1991	Ann. Avg.	10.42	5.69	8.47	9.25	3.24	6.82	7.37	7.68	7.86	8.14	5.41	5.47	8.16
1992	Ann. Avg.	9.73	3.52	6.25	5.58	2.99	5.30	6.19	6.63	7.01	7.67	3.48	3.59	7.53
1993	Ann. Avg.	9.06	3.02	6.00	7.50	2.78	4.44	5.14	5.54	5.87	6.59	3.02	3.14	6.46
1994	Ann. Avg.	9.51	4.20	7.14	8.68	2.82	6.27	6.69	6.91	7.09	7.37	4.27	4.65	7.41
1995	Ann. Avg.	8.86	5.84	8.83	8.18	2.56	6.25	6.38	6.50	6.57	6.88	5.51	5.60	6.94
1996	1st Quarter	7.79	5.36	8.33	7.59	NA	5.38	5.57	5.79	5.91	6.30	4.95	4.91	6.36
Coefficient of correlation (R) (year)			74.4%	80.2%	92.9%	58.4%	92.6%	95.2%	96.0%	96.6%	97.3%	79.7%	81.4%	94.4%
Coefficient of correlation (R) (qtr)			68.4%	76.7%	93.0%	67.8%	Quarterly rates unavailable					73.2%	76.4%	91.3%

TABLE 6.6 Annual Rates for Corporate Bonds

							Moody's Corporate Bond Yield Averages						
Year	Period	Avg. Corporate	Avg. Aaa	Avg. Aa	Avg. A	Avg. Baa	Avg. Public Utility	Aaa Public Utility	Aa Public Utility	A Public Utility	Avg. Industrial	Aa Industrial	A Industrial
1973	Ann. Avg.	7.80%	7.44%	7.66%	7.84%	8.24%	7.83%	7.67%	7.72%	7.84%	7.60%	7.40%	7.63%
1974	Ann. Avg.	9.03	8.57	8.84	9.20	9.50	9.27	9.01	9.04	9.50	8.78	8.64	8.90
1975	Ann. Avg.	9.57	8.83	9.17	9.65	10.61	9.88	9.17	9.44	10.09	9.25	8.90	9.21
1976	Ann. Avg.	9.01	8.43	8.75	9.09	9.75	9.17	8.46	8.92	9.29	8.84	8.59	8.88
1977	Ann. Avg.	8.43	8.02	8.24	8.49	8.97	8.58	8.12	8.43	8.61	8.28	8.04	8.36
1978	Ann. Avg.	9.07	8.73	8.92	9.12	9.45	9.22	8.90	9.10	9.29	8.90	8.74	8.94
1979	Ann. Avg.	10.12	9.63	9.94	10.20	10.69	10.39	9.92	10.22	10.49	9.85	9.65	9.91
1980	Ann. Avg.	12.75	11.94	12.50	12.89	13.67	13.15	12.68	13.00	13.34	12.35	11.99	12.44
1981	Ann. Avg.	15.06	14.17	14.75	15.29	16.04	15.62	15.65	15.30	15.95	14.50	14.19	14.62
1982	Ann. Avg.	14.94	13.79	14.41	15.43	16.11	15.33	14.71	14.79	15.86	14.54	14.03	15.03
1983	Ann. Avg.	12.78	12.04	12.42	13.10	13.55	13.31	12.25	12.83	13.66	12.25	12.00	12.53
1984	Ann. Avg.	13.49	12.71	13.31	13.74	14.19	13.90	13.40	10.20	14.03	13.21	12.95	13.27
1985	Ann. Avg.	12.05	11.37	11.82	12.28	12.72	12.29	11.67	12.06	12.49	11.80	11.57	12.09
1986	Ann. Avg.	9.71	9.02	9.47	9.95	10.39	9.46	9.09	9.30	9.58	9.96	9.63	10.30
1987	Ann. Avg.	9.91	9.38	9.68	9.99	10.58	9.99	9.52	9.77	10.10	9.83	9.59	9.88
1988	Ann. Avg.	10.18	9.71	9.94	10.24	10.83	10.49	10.05	10.27	10.49	9.91	9.62	10.04
1989	Ann. Avg.	9.66	9.26	9.46	9.74	10.18	9.66	9.32	9.56	9.77	9.66	9.36	9.71
1990	Ann. Avg.	9.77	9.32	9.56	9.82	10.36	9.83	9.45	9.75	9.86	9.77	9.45	9.79
1991	Ann. Avg.	9.23	8.77	9.05	9.30	9.80	9.14	8.85	9.04	9.36	9.25	9.00	9.19
1992	Ann. Avg.	8.55	8.14	8.46	8.62	8.98	8.58	8.19	8.55	8.69	8.52	8.37	8.54
1993	Ann. Avg.	7.54	7.22	7.40	7.58	7.93	7.40	7.29	7.44	7.59	7.51	7.37	7.42
1994	Ann. Avg.	8.26	7.97	8.15	8.28	8.63	8.39	8.06	8.21	8.30	8.21	8.09	8.32
1995	Ann. Avg.	7.83	7.59	7.72	7.83	8.20	7.75	7.68	7.77	7.89	7.77	7.67	7.77
1996	1st Quarter	7.34	7.05	7.22	7.37	7.71	7.43	7.16	7.26	7.44	7.43	7.19	7.30
Coefficient of correlation (R) (year)		97.9%	97.6%	97.6%	98.0%	97.9%	97.7%	97.2%	97.6%	98.0%	97.5%	97.4%	97.5%
Coefficient of correlation (R) (qtr)		95.8%	94.9%	95.3%	96.4%	96.1%	95.5%	94.8%	95.0%	94.1%	95.6%	95.2%	95.7%

insured home mortgages sold in the secondary market, the Standard & Poors composite index of 500 stocks, and treasury notes, bonds, and bills of various terms. Table 6.6 shows the annual rates for various corporate bonds. Each table also shows the coefficient of correlation, R, which is derived from the regression analysis used to compare the rates for each money market instrument with the hotel mortgage interest rate. The instrument exhibiting the highest coefficient of correlation (R) provides the most accurate basis for estimating hotel lending rates.

Table 6.6 shows that Average A corporate bond yields have the highest coefficient of correlation, so this instrument is used to develop the hotel interest rate regression equation. To best reflect the ever-changing money market climate, a more comprehensive regression analysis was run using the A corporate bond

TABLE 6.7   **Corporate Bond Yields and Hotel Interest Rates**

Period	Average Interest Rate	Average A Corporate Bond Yield	Period	Average Interest Rate	Average A Corporate Bond Yield
3rd Quarter 1999	8.19%	7.78%	4th Quarter 1992	9.43	8.48
2nd Quarter 1999	8.05	7.41	3rd Quarter 1992	9.99	8.38
1st Quarter 1999	7.86	6.98	2nd Quarter 1992	9.47	8.79
4th Quarter 1998	7.47	6.87	1st Quarter 1992	10.02	8.81
3rd Quarter 1998	7.12	6.87	4th Quarter 1991	10.49	8.97
2nd Quarter 1998	7.44	6.98	3rd Quarter 1991	10.03	9.29
1st Quarter 1998	7.26	7.00	2nd Quarter 1991	10.75	9.45
4th Quarter 1997	7.65	7.46	3rd Quarter 1990	10.47	9.89
3rd Quarter 1997	8.44	7.42	2nd Quarter 1990	10.58	9.83
2nd Quarter 1997	8.85	7.84	4th Quarter 1989	9.96	9.42
1st Quarter 1997	8.25	7.71	3rd Quarter 1989	9.55	9.46
4th Quarter 1996	9.49	7.54	2nd Quarter 1989	10.54	9.93
3rd Quarter 1996	8.96	7.90	1st Quarter 1989	10.39	10.16
2nd Quarter 1996	8.82	7.93	4th Quarter 1988	10.07	10.03
1st Quarter 1996	7.79	7.37	3rd Quarter 1988	10.66	10.51
4th Quarter 1995	8.44	7.28	2nd Quarter 1988	10.09	10.33
3rd Quarter 1995	8.61	7.67	4th Quarter 1987	10.41	10.45
2nd Quarter 1995	9.25	7.87	3rd Quarter 1987	10.00	9.95
1st Quarter 1995	9.14	8.50	2nd Quarter 1987	9.81	9.46
3rd Quarter 1994	9.64	8.48	1st Quarter 1987	9.43	9.19
2nd Quarter 1994	9.38	8.28	4th Quarter 1986	9.44	9.55
4th Quarter 1993	9.38	7.80	3rd Quarter 1986	9.56	9.71
3rd Quarter 1993	8.41	7.28	2nd Quarter 1986	9.80	9.91
2nd Quarter 1993	10.53	9.65	1st Quarter 1986	10.99	10.62

Sources: American Council of Life Insurance; Moody's Bond Record
Note: Some quarterly data were unavailable.

Hotels and Motels—Valuations and Market Studies

yields over an extended period. Table 6.7 sets forth hotel mortgage interest rates and corresponding Average A corporate bond yields on a quarterly basis from 1986 until the third quarter of 1999.

Using the regression command from a computer-based spreadsheet, the following regression output was obtained:

Constant	2.4232
Coefficient of correlation	0.8094

This regression output can be used in the following equation, which calculates the mortgage interest rate *(Y)* based on the actual yield on an A corporate bond *(X):*

$$Y = 2.4232 + 0.8094X$$

On December 10, 1999, the yield on an A corporate bond was 7.86%. Substituting this yield for X and solving for Y generates an estimated mortgage interest rate of 8.79%.

Appraisers using this regression approach to update hotel mortgage interest rates should rerun the regression analysis each quarter when the American Council of Life Insurance releases its latest data on hotel mortgage interest rates.

The real strength of a mortgage-equity analysis for real estate investment is the fact that the discount rate's mortgage component can be readily supported by current, accurate interest rate data. Most investors would agree that it is far better to have 55% to 75% of the mortgage-equity discount rate fully supported than to rely on a totally subjective (and usually outdated) overall discount rate.

Other sources of lending information include local banks and insurance companies, real estate investment trusts, mortgage brokers, and regulatory agencies. By comparing the rates derived from several sources, an appraiser can estimate the mortgage interest components with relative accuracy.

The mortgage recapture component, which represents the return of the investment, is expressed in the rate of amortization. According to the American Council of Life Insurance, hostelry loans have typically been structured to be repaid over a 20- to 30-year term. The recapture component plus the interest component equals the yearly mortgage constant. The annual debt service is calculated by multiplying the mortgage constant by the original loan amount.

Equity money constitutes the remaining 25% to 45% of a hotel investment. Like common stock, which entitles the owner to the residual earnings after all expenses, including debt service, have been paid, real estate equity investments normally provide overall returns that are higher than those the mortgage component demands. The short-term equity return—which appraisers call the *equity dividend rate* and hotel investors call the *cash-on-cash return*—represents the annual net income after debt service divided by the value of the equity.

The rate of return that an equity investor expects over a 10-year holding period (the long-term return) is called *equity yield.* Unlike the equity dividend—a short-term rate of return—the equity yield specifically considers a long holding period (generally 10 years), annual cash flows impacted by inflation, property appreciation, mortgage amortization, and proceeds from a sale at the end of the holding period.

Accurate data relating to equity return expectations are not always obtainable. However, since the equity return component represents only 25% to 45% of the discount rate (depending on the loan-to-value ratio), the negative impact of any error is reduced. Hotel appraisers typically rely on two sources of equity data: investor interviews and past appraisals.

To obtain data through investor interviews an appraiser surveys actual or potential hotel investors who have recently made or contemplated an equity investment in a lodging facility. Depending on the type of property being appraised, the appraiser should survey either institutional investors or individual investors. The key to obtaining reliable information from investor interviews is to explain carefully the terms *equity dividend* and *equity yield* before conducting the survey. Many hotel investors may not understand the exact meaning of terms such as *overall rate, capitalization rate, or total property yield.* Misunderstandings can distort the appraiser's findings and invalidate the survey. Unless the equity investor clearly understands *equity dividend* or *equity yield,* it is best not to include his or her responses in that particular survey's results.

A broad cross section of active buyers must be surveyed because each is influenced by a variety of factors. The results of a limited sample can produce misleading assumptions. For example, an investor in a high tax bracket may settle for a lower-than-market equity return if the investment's tax shelter benefits are particularly attractive. Similarly, the opportunity to resell a property after several years for a higher price may cause a buyer to accept a lower equity dividend. Because owning a hotel has a certain amount of status, some buyers may be willing to accept a lower equity return. An active hotel-motel broker, such as a member of the Hotel Motel Brokers Association, can often provide insight into the equity rates of return demanded in the current market. Useful sources of equity information include typical hotel buyers and investors, lenders seeking equity participation and joint ventures, and hotel management companies.

A second source of equity return information is readily available to appraisal firms that regularly perform hotel valuations. These appraisers can derive equity dividend and equity yield rates from actual sales of hotels they have recently appraised. This approach differs from deriving an overall rate from the market in that the appraiser uses the actual forecast of income and expense that was developed in the appraisal immediately preceding the sale. An illustration of this procedure follows.

Over the past year the hotel appraisal firm HVS International has appraised more than 1,000 hotels in most major market areas. In each of these appraisals, a similar mortgage-equity technique was used to forecast income into the future and discount it back to present value at rates that reflect the cost of both debt and equity capital. In instances where hotels were actually sold subsequent to the appraisal, equity dividend and equity yield rates were derived from the

TABLE 6.8 **Hotel Equity Yield Rates**

Hotel	Location	Number of Rooms	Date of Sale	Equity Yield
Westin St. Francis	San Francisco, CA	1,192	Apr-00	13.0%
Embassy Suites	Pleasant Hill, CA	249	Apr-00	21.1
Loews Coronado Bay Resort	Coronado, CA	440	Jan-00	21.1
Sheraton Miramar	Santa Monica, CA	300	Sep-99	21.7
Executive Inn	Sacramento, CA	190	Aug-99	21.8
Hyatt Regency	La Jolla, CA	419	Jul-99	17.6
Hilton Garden Inn	Sacramento, CA	153	Jun-99	25.0
Residence Inn	San Diego, CA	121	Jun-99	19.0
Clift Hotel	San Francisco, CA	362	May-99	15.2
Donatello Hotel	San Francisco, CA	94	Apr-99	24.8
Semiahmoo Inn	Blaine, WA	198	Mar-99	27.3
Grand Wailea Resort	Maui, HI	761	Dec-98	20.3
Best Western Palmer Inn	Princeton, NJ	106	Nov-98	24.7
Hotel Rex	San Francisco, CA	94	Nov-98	17.4
Ritz-Carlton Hotel	San Francisco, CA	336	Sep-98	17.2
ANA Hotel	Washington, DC	415	Sep-98	17.6
ANA Hotel	San Francisco, CA	667	Sep-98	11.4
Renaissance Hotel	Beverly Hills, CA	139	Aug-98	14.0
Executive Tower Inn	Denver, CO	425	Jul-98	30.7
The Stoneleigh Hotel	Dallas, TX	153	Jul-98	30.6
Radisson Hotel Central	Dallas, TX	288	Jul-98	22.8
Olympus Hotel	Salt Lake City, UT	393	Jun-98	24.4
Richelieu Hotel	San Francisco, CA	157	Jun-98	17.4
Loews Santa Monica	Santa Monica, CA	343	Mar-98	4.5
Best Western Pheasant Inn	Willows, CA	104	Mar-98	38.5
Ramada Inn	Tallahassee, FL	200	Feb-98	24.1
Sheraton Fisherman's Wharf	San Francisco, CA	524	Feb-98	17.2
Bell Rock Inn	Sedona, AZ	96	Feb-98	9.3
Crowne Plaza St. Anthony Hotel	San Antonio, TX	352	Jan-98	25.7
Hyatt Regency	Rochester, NY	335	Jan-98	21.0
Crowne Plaza Branson	Branson, MO	500	Jan-98	28.5
Holiday Inn	Beachwood, OH	174	Jan-98	14.9
Hyatt Regency Savannah	Savannah, GA	346	Jan-98	18.5
Harrisburg Marriott	Harrisburg, PA	348	Jan-98	22.7
Residence Inn Bellevue	Bellevue, WA	120	Jan-98	10.9
Residence Inn So. Seattle	Tukwila, WA	144	Jan-98	6.7
Residence Inn	San Diego, CA	144	Jan-98	24.0
Residence Inn	Sacramento, CA	126	Jan-98	20.5
Hilton Suites	Romulus, MI	151	Dec-97	14.3
Chateau Inn	Fresno, CA	78	Dec-97	5.7
Picadilly Inn University	Fresno, CA	190	Dec-97	16.6
Picadilly Inn Airport	Fresno, CA	185	Dec-97	5.7

projection of income and expense by excluding any incentive management fees and then inserting the projection into the valuation model. The appraised value was adjusted to reflect the actual sale price merely by modifying the return assumptions. Table 6.8 shows a representative sample of hotel sales that were evaluated in this manner and their calculated equity yield rates.

In addition to quantifying the equity dividend and equity yield, the appraiser sometimes needs to estimate a terminal capitalization rate. When a 10-year forecast is utilized, the terminal, or going-out, capitalization rate is used to capitalize the net income in Year 11 into a reversionary value. It is basically an overall rate that can be estimated with a simple mortgage-equity band of investment using an equity dividend. Note that this rate is applied to the net income before debt service 11 years after the date of value; thus it should be adjusted upward somewhat to reflect the fact that the hotel will probably be closer to the end of its economic life.

Applying the Proper Capitalization or Discounting Procedure

Several procedures can be used to combine mortgage and equity data into a discount factor or capitalization rate that will transform a projected net income estimate into an indication of value. The selection of discount factors and capitalization rates depends on many factors, including the length of the income projection period, the age of the property and its stage in its life cycle, the nature of the mortgage financing, and the sophistication of equity investors. The following discussion describes the various methods for developing discount factors and their proper application in the valuation process.

Discount Each Year's Income Over the Full Life Cycle

The simplest form of valuation begins with a projection of the property's net income before debt service for each year over the full life of the improvements. Each year's net income is then multiplied by the proper present value of a reversion of one factor and all these discounted net income figures are totaled to produce the overall property value.

Capitalize One Stabilized Year's Income

Instead of projecting net income over the entire life of the property, a single, stabilized estimate of net income can be capitalized at an appropriate rate. The stabilized net income relates to a representative year or, more technically, it is the discounted average net income over the property's economic life. In estimating stabilized earnings, more weight is given to the income expected during the investment's early years because this income is less affected by discounting.

Capitalizing Stabilized Income

The forecast of income and expense developed for the proposed Sheraton indicates that the hotel is expected to stabilize in its third year of operation. The net income before debt service as of the stabilized year is forecast to be $4,691,000. (Note that this is only one method for estimating stabilized net income. The appraiser should ultimately try to reflect the actions of typical buyers and sellers for the type of hotel in question.)

Now the appraiser must develop a rate to capitalize the stabilized net income. *The band-of-investment* (weighted cost of capital) technique is one procedure for developing a capitalization rate. Combining the weighted average of the return demanded by the mortgage position of the investment with the dividend required by the equity component results in a capitalization rate that reflects the hotel investment's basic financial composition.

Using the previously described mortgage interest rate regression formula and a survey of hotel equity investors, the following mortgage and equity terms were established as appropriate.

Mortgage finance terms:	
Interest rate	9.75%
Amortization	25 years
Mortgage constant	10.694%
Loan-to-value ratio	65%
Equity dividend rate	10.0%

The band-of-investment technique is used to develop a capitalization rate that is the weighted average of the mortgage constant and equity yield rate:

	Portion	Rate	Weighted Rate
Mortgage	0.65	×0.10694 =	0.06951
Equity	0.35	×0.10000 =	0.03500
Overall capitalization rate =			0.10451

The stabilized net income is divided by the capitalization rate to produce the capitalized value as of the stabilized year:

$4,691,000 ÷ 0.10451 = $44,885,000 (rounded)

The value can be mathematically proven through the following calculations:

65% Mortgage	$29,175,000 × 0.10694 =	$3,120,000
35% Equity	$15,710,000 × 0.10000 =	$1,571,000
	$44,885,000	$4,691,000

These calculations show that the $44,885,000 value can be divided into a mortgage portion of $29,175,000 and an equity portion of $15,710,000. The yearly mortgage payment, consisting of interest and amortization, is calculated by multiplying the original mortgage balance ($29,175,000) by the constant (0.10694), which results in an annual debt service of $3,120,000. The equity dividend is established by multiplying the equity investment ($15,710,000) by the anticipated equity return (0.10), which yields $1,571,000. The annual debt service plus the equity dividend equals the stabilized net income before debt service.

Essentially, the band-of-investment technique works backward, using the projected stabilized net income to calculate the value that will meet the demands of both the mortgage and equity investors. The components that form the band of investment (mortgage terms and equity requirements) can be well documented and supported. However, the stabilized net income used in this approach does not always reflect the potential for low income during the investment's early years. To get a better indication of a property's net income in the early years, the analyst should project several years of income and expenses.

Analyzing the terms and conditions of actual market sales is another way to derive a capitalization rate. For example, assume an investor has recently purchased a motel for $3,000,000. An income analysis indicates that the property has a stabilized income before interest and depreciation of $359,700. The market-derived overall capitalization rate for this sale is

$$\frac{\$359,700}{\$3,000,000} = 11.99\%$$

To apply this or any other market-related procedure, the appraiser needs to understand the transaction and the motivations of the parties involved. Adjustments must be made for any unusual factors so that the capitalization rate derived represents normal market conditions. Some questions that the appraiser might ask are:

- Is the stated selling price the market value or has unusual existing or purchase-money financing affected the transaction price?
- Is the price based on existing or anticipated income?
- Is the buyer motivated by special factors such as tax shelter or referral benefits?
- Does the property suffer from deferred maintenance that the buyer must correct?

- Did the transaction involve a willing buyer and a willing seller, both with full knowledge of all circumstances?
- Is the comparable property somewhat similar to the property being appraised with respect to size, location, market, and condition?
- Does the comparable's income statement contain a reserve for replacement? If it does not, the subject property's projected income before debt service should also exclude a reserve for replacement.

An appraiser is seldom able to obtain enough data on the sale of a comparable hotel to derive a meaningful capitalization rate based on the current market. Understanding the buyer's and seller's motives requires more than a casual observation of the transaction.

10-Year Forecast Using an Equity Yield Rate

To eliminate some uncertainties associated with excessively long-term net income projections and to show the normal occupancy build-up for new hotels, most appraisers use projection periods of three to 10 years.

A 10-year projection using an equity yield rate is similar to an Ellwood valuation approach, in which the yearly income to equity plus an equity reversion is discounted at an equity yield rate, and the income to the mortgagee is discounted at a mortgage yield rate. The sum of the equity and mortgage values is the total property value.

The benefits to the equity position include equity dividends from the net income remaining after debt service during the 10-year projection period and the gain or loss realized from the property's assumed resale. The resale or reversionary benefits include the gain or loss caused by value appreciation or depreciation plus any mortgage amortization. The benefits to the mortgage position are interest and amortization plus repayment of the remaining mortgage balance at the end of 10 years.

Valuation using a 10-year income projection and an equity yield rate is performed in four steps.

1. The terms of typical hotel financing are set forth, including the interest rate, amortization term, and loan-to-value ratio.
2. An equity yield rate of return and terminal capitalization rate are established.
3. The equity component's value is calculated and added to the initial mortgage amount to produce the overall property value.
4. The value estimate is allocated between the mortgage and equity components.

Researching and analyzing typical financing terms has been discussed in detail, so the next step is to establish an equity yield rate of return. Currently a number of hotel buyers base their equity investments on a 10-year equity yield rate projection that considers the benefits of ownership such as periodic cash flow distributions, residual sale or refinancing distributions that return any property appreciation and mortgage amortization, income tax benefits, and nonfinancial considerations such as status and prestige. In addition, the appraiser must estimate a terminal capitalization rate, which will be used to capitalize the Year 11 net income into a reversionary value.

Next, the value of the equity component is calculated by deducting the yearly debt service from the forecasted income, which leaves the net income to equity for each year of the forecast. The net income as of Year 11 is capitalized into a reversionary value. After deducting the mortgage balance as of the end of the 10th year as well as normal legal and selling costs, the equity residual is discounted to the date of value at the equity yield rate. Then the net income to equity for each of the 10 projection years is also discounted. The sum of these discounted values equals the value of the equity component. Adding the equity component to the initial mortgage balance yields the overall property value.

Because the amount of the mortgage and the debt service are unknown but the loan-to-value ratio is determined in Step 1, the calculation can be solved either through an iterative process using a computer or with an algebraic equation that computes the total property value.

A complex algebraic equation that solves for the total property value using the 10-year mortgage-equity technique was developed by Suzanne R. Mellen, MAI. This equation is known as the *simultaneous valuation formula.* A complete discussion of this technique is contained in Mellen's article "Simultaneous Valuation: A New Capitalization Technique for Hotel and Other Income Properties," which appeared in the April 1983 issue of *The Appraisal Journal.* Material from this article has been incorporated into this chapter.

Finally, the value estimate is proven by allocating the total property value between the mortgage and equity components and verifying that the rates of returns set forth in steps 1 and 2 can be precisely met through the forecasted net income.

The process will be illustrated using the case study example.

Step 1. Determine the appropriate mortgage debt financing terms.

CASE STUDY

Determining Financing Terms

The mortgage interest regression formula indicates a current interest rate of 9.29%. Since the mortgage data reported by the American Council of Life Insurance generally represents investment-grade hotel properties, the appraiser may want to adjust this rate for the location, type of hotel, age and condition of the property, operating history, local supply and demand trends, management expertise and affiliation, and interest being appraised.

It is assumed that the proposed Sheraton Hotel will have new facilities, proper management, and a recognized affiliation. Offsetting these positive attributes is the projected downward trend in area occupancies as additional rooms open in the market and become more competitive. In addition to increased competition, the Sheraton will need to survive the normal buildup of occupancy that all new hotels experience; many lenders account for this risk factor. Based on the appraiser's analysis, the following mortgage terms would probably be available for the proposed Sheraton.

Interest rate	9.75%
Amortization schedule	25 years
Payments per year	Monthly
Mortgage constant	0.10694
Mortgage term	10 years
Loan-to-value ratio	65%

Step 2. Estimate an appropriate equity yield and a terminal capitalization rate.

CASE STUDY

Estimating Equity Yield and Terminal Capitalization Rates

A survey of hotel investors was conducted to determine their current equity yield requirements. In addition, the appraiser reviewed recent appraisals of hotels that sold proximate to the date of value. The range of equity yields for hotels comparable to the proposed Sheraton is 18% to 22%.

Using the same investment criteria employed to determine the mortgage interest rate, a 21% equity yield rate was selected for the proposed Sheraton. The terminal capitalization rate can be estimated with the mortgage-equity band of investment utilizing an equity dividend rate. The factors that were considered are set forth on pages 329 and 330.

	Portion	Rate	Weighted Rate
Mortgage	0.65	× 0.10694 =	0.06951
Equity	0.35	× 0.10000 =	0.03500
Overall Capitalization Rate		=	0.10451

Adjusting the rates to reflect the 10th year terminal capitalization rate produces a going-out rate of 11% for the proposed Sheraton.

Step 3. Estimate overall property value by valuing equity component and adding initial mortgage balance.

By this point in the analysis, the appraiser has made all the necessary subjective and objective decisions. The remainder of the process is purely mathematical. The appraiser must solve an algebraic equation that calculates the exact amount of debt and equity that the hotel will be able to support based on the anticipated cash flow derived from the forecast of income and expense and the specific return requirements that the mortgage lender (interest) and the equity investor (equity yield) demand.

Step 4. Allocate value between mortgage and equity components

To solve for the value of the mortgage and equity components, the appraiser first deducts the yearly debt service from the forecast of income before debt service; the remainder is the net income to equity for each year in the forecast. The net income as of Year 11 is capitalized into a reversionary value using the terminal capitalization rate. The equity residual—the total reversionary value minus the mortgage balance at that time and any broker and legal cost associated with the sale—is discounted to the date of value at the equity yield rate. The net income to equity for each of the forecast years is also discounted. The sum of these discounted values equates to the value of the equity component. Since the equity component represents a specific percentage of the total value, the value of the mortgage and the total property value can be easily computed.

The process described above can be expressed in two algebraic equations, which set forth the mathematical relationships between known and unknown variables. The symbols used to represent these variables are listed below.

NI Net income available for debt service

V Value

M Loan-to-value ratio

F Annual debt service constant

N Number of years in projection period

d_e Annual cash available to equity

d_r Residual equity value

b Brokerage and legal cost percentage

P^* Fraction of loan paid off in projection period

Fp Annual constant required to amortize the entire loan during the projection period

R_r Overall terminal capitalization rate applied to net income to calculate total property reversion (sale price at end of the projection period)

$1/S_n$ Current worth of $1 (discount factor) at the equity yield rate

Using these symbols a series of formulas can be derived to express some of the components involved in this mortgage-equity valuation process.

$$*P = (f - i) \div (fp - i) \text{ where } i = \text{the interest rate of the mortgage}$$

Debt service. To calculate a property's debt service, the appraiser first determines the amount of the mortgage, which is the total property value (V) multiplied by the loan-to-value ratio (M). Then the amount of the mortgage is multiplied by the annual debt service constant (f) using the following formula:

$$f \times M \times V = \text{debt service}$$

Net income to equity (equity dividend). The net income to equity (d_e) is the property's net income before debt service (NI) minus the debt service. The following formula represents net income to equity:

$$NI - (F \times M \times V) = d_e$$

Reversionary value. The hotel's value at the end of Year 10 is calculated by dividing the net income in Year 11 before debt service (NI^{11}) by the terminal capitalization rate (R_r). The following formula calculates the property's reversionary value in Year 10:

$$NI^{11}/R_r = \text{reversionary value}$$

Broker and legal costs. When a hotel is sold, costs associated with the transaction usually include a broker's commission and attorneys' fees. For a hotel transaction, broker and legal costs typically range from 1% to 4% of the sale price. Because these expenses reduce the proceeds to the seller, they are usually deducted from the reversionary value in mortgage-equity analysis. Broker and legal costs (b) expressed as a percentage of the reversionary value (NI^{11}/R_r) can be calculated by using the following formula:

$$(b(NI^{11}/R_r)) = \text{broker and legal costs}$$

Ending mortgage balance. The balance of the mortgage at the end of Year 10 must be deducted from the total reversionary value (debt and equity) to isolate the equity residual. A financial formula is used to calculate the fraction of the loan paid off, which is expressed as a percentage of the original loan balance at a particular time. The mortgage interest rate (i) is deducted from the annual debt service constant of the loan over the entire amortization period (f). The result is divided by the annual constant required to amortize the entire loan over the projection period (sub p) minus the mortgage interest rate. The formula is

$$(f - i) / (f_p - i) = P$$

If the fraction of the loan paid off expressed as a percentage of the initial loan balance is P, then the percentage of the loan remaining can be expressed as $1 - P$. Thus, the ending mortgage balance is the fraction of the loan remaining $(1 - P)$ multiplied by the amount of the initial loan $(M \times V)$. The formula is

$$(1 - P) \times M \times V = \text{ending mortgage balance}$$

Equity residual value. The equity's value when the property is sold at the end of the projection period (d) is the reversionary value minus broker and legal costs and the ending mortgage balance. The following formula represents the equity residual value:

$$(NI^{11}/R_r) - (b(NI^{11}/R_r)) - ((1 - P) \times M \times V)) = d_r$$

Annual cash flow to equity. The annual cash flow to equity consists of the equity dividend for each of the 10 projection years plus the equity residual at the end of Year 10. The following formulae represent the annual cash flow to equity:

$$NI^1 - (F \times M \times V) = d_e^1$$
$$NI^2 - (F \times M \times V) = d_e^2 \ldots$$
$$NI^{10} - (F \times M \times V) = d_e^{10}$$
$$(NI^{11}/R_r) - (b(NI^{11}/R_r)) - ((1 - P) \times M \times V)) \, d_r$$

Value of the equity. If the mortgage's initial amount is calculated by multiplying the loan-to-value ratio *(M)* by the value of the property *(V)*, then the equity value will be 1 minus the loan-to-value ratio times the property value. The formula is

$$(1 - M) \, V$$

Discounting the cash flow to equity to present value. The cash flow to equity for each of the projection years is discounted to present value at the equity yield rate $(1/S^n)$. The sum of all these cash flows is the value of the equity $(1 - M)V$. The following formula calculates equity as the sum of the discounted cash flows:

$$(d_e^1 \times 1/S^1) + (d_e^2 \times 1/S^2) + \ldots + (d_e^{10} \times 1/S^{10}) + (d_r \times 1/S^{10}) = (1 - M)V$$

Combining equations: annual cash flow to equity and cash flow to equity discounted to present value. The final step in the process is to make one, overall equation that shows that the annual cash flow to equity plus the yearly cash flows discounted to present value equal to the value of the equity.

$$((N^1 - (f \times M \times V)) \, 1/S^1) + \ldots ((NI^2 - (f \times M \times V)) \, 1/S^2) + \ldots + ((NI^{10} -$$
$$(f \times M \times V)) \, 1/S^{10}) + \ldots + (NI^{11}/R_r) - (b(NI^{11}/R_r)) - ((1 - P) \times M \times V) \, 1/S^{10}) = (1 - M)V$$

Since the only unknown is the property value *(V)*, this equation is easy to solve.

CASE STUDY

Applying the 10-Year Discounted Cash Flow Valuation Formula—Proposed Sheraton
Generally the net income before debt service is projected beyond the stabilized year at an assumed rate of change. By increasing a property's revenue and expenses at the same rate of inflation, the net income expressed as a percentage of total revenue will remain constant and the dollar amount of net income will escalate each year at the rate of change. When a category of

revenue or expense is expected to increase at a different rate, the appraiser should reflect this aberration in that year's income and expense forecast. This situation is likely to be the result of contractual changes in a ground rent expense, use of an escalating reserve for replacement percentage, or an expected change in the property tax expense.

The appraiser finds that hotel investors are using inflation rates of approximately 3%. Table 6.9 shows the net income of the proposed Sheraton Hotel projected beyond the stabilized year at a 3% rate of inflation.

Solving for Value Using the Simultaneous Valuation Formula

In the case of the subject property, the following variables are known:

Annual net income	NI	See Table 6.9
Loan-to-value ratio	M	65%
Debt service constant	f	0.10694
Equity yield	Y_e	21%
Brokerage and legal fees	b	3%
Annual constant required to amortize the loan in 10 years	f_p	0.156924
Terminal capitalization rate	R_r	11%

TABLE 6.9   Net Income Forecast—Proposed Sheraton

Year of Operation	Net Income
1	$2,120,000
2	3,541,000
3	4,691,000
4	4,832,000
5	4,975,000
6	5,125,000
7	5,278,000
8	5,437,000
9	5,600,000
10	5,768,000
11	5,941,000

Table 6.10 shows the present value of $1 factor at the 21% equity yield rate. Intermediary calculations must be made using these known variables before the simultaneous valuation formula can be applied.

TABLE 6.10	Present Value of $1 at 21% Equity Yield Rate	
	Year of Operation	$1/S_n$
	1	0.8264
	2	0.6830
	3	0.5645
	4	0.4665
	5	0.3855
	6	0.3186
	7	0.2633
	8	0.2176
	9	0.1799
	10	0.1486

The fraction of the loan paid off during the projection period is calculated as follows:

$$P = (0.10694 - 0.0975) \div (0.156924 - 0.0975) = 0.158799$$

The annual debt service is calculated as $f \times M \times V$.

$$0.10694 \times 0.65 \times V = 0.069509V$$

Next, the formula is expressed in terms of V.

$$(2,120,000 - 0.0695V) \times 0.826446$$
$$+ (3,541,000 - 0.0695V) \times 0.683013$$
$$+ (4,691,000 - 0.0695V) \times 0.564474$$
$$+ (4,832,000 - 0.0695V) \times 0.466507$$
$$+ (4,977,000 - 0.0695V) \times 0.385543$$
$$+ (5,126,000 - 0.0695V) \times 0.318631$$
$$+ (5,280,000 - 0.0695V) \times 0.263331$$
$$+ (5,438,000 - 0.0695V) \times 0.217629$$
$$+ (5,601,000 - 0.0695V) \times 0.179859$$
$$+ (5,769,000 - 0.0695V) \times 0.148644$$
$$+ (((5,942,000 \div 0.11)$$
$$- (0.03 \times (5,942,000 \div 0.11))$$
$$- ((1 - 0.158799) \times 0.65 \times V)) \times 0.148644) = (1 - 0.65) \times V$$

Then, like terms are combined.

$$\$24,852,044 - 0.363069 \, V = (1 - 0.65) \, V$$
$$\$24,852,044 = 0.71307 \, V$$
$$V = \$24,852,044 \div 0.71307$$
$$V = \$34,852,000 \text{ (rounded)}$$

Proof of Value

Calculating the yields to the mortgage and equity components over the projection period mathematically proves the value. If the mortgagee receives its 9.75% yield and the equity yields 21%, then $34,852,000 is the correct value estimate derived by the income capitalization approach.

The indicated market value is allocated as follows:

Mortgage component	0.65	$22,654,000
Equity component	0.35	12,198,000
		$34,852,000

Calculation of annual debt service:

Mortgage component	$22,654,000
Mortgage constant	× 0.106936
Annual debt service	$2,423,000 (rounded)

Net income to equity is forecast in Table 6.11.

TABLE 6.11 **Forecast of Net Income to Equity**

Year of Operation	Net Income Available for Debt Service		Debt Service		Net Income to Equity
1	$2,120,000	–	$2,423,000	=	$(303,000)
2	3,541,000	–	2,423,000	=	1,118,000
3	4,691,000	–	2,423,000	=	2,268,000
4	4,832,000	–	2,423,000	=	2,409,000
5	4,975,000	–	2,423,000	=	2,552,000
6	5,125,000	–	2,423,000	=	2,702,000
7	5,278,000	–	2,423,000	=	2,855,000
8	5,437,000	–	2,423,000	=	3,014,000
9	5,600,000	–	2,423,000	=	3,177,000
10	5,768,000	–	2,423,000	=	3,345,000

The residual value to equity at the end of Year 10 is calculated by capitalizing the Year 11 net income as follows:

$5,942,000 ÷ 0.11 =	$54,018,000 (rounded)
Sales proceeds	$54,018,000
Less:	
Broker & legal fees	1,621,000
Mortgage balance	19,057,000
Net sales proceeds to equity	$33,340,000

The annual cash flow to equity plus the residual equity value is discounted to present value at the equity yield rate of 21% in Table 6.12.

TABLE 6.12	Equity Component Yield (*IRR* of 21%)				
Year of Operation	Net Income to Equity		Present Value Factor @ 21%		Discounted Cash Flow
1	$(303,000)	×	0.8264	=	$(250,000)
2	1,118,000	×	0.6830	=	764,000
3	2,268,000	×	0.5645	=	1,280,000
4	2,409,000	×	0.4665	=	1,124,000
5	2,552,000	×	0.3855	=	984,000
6	2,702,000	×	0.3186	=	861,000
7	2,855,000	×	0.2633	=	752,000
8	3,014,000	×	0.2176	=	656,000
9	3,177,000	×	0.1799	=	571,000
10	36,686,000*	×	0.1486	=	5,453,000
Value of equity component					$12,195,000

* Year 10 net income to equity	$3,345,000
Plus net sales proceeds to equity	33,341,000
Total Year 10 *NI* to equity	$36,686,000
Note: Totals are rounded.	

The table demonstrates that the equity investor will receive a 21% yield on the equity component if the annual cash flow and reversion take place as projected. Since the debt service factored into the calculations is based on an interest rate of 9.75%, the required yield for the lender will also be achieved. In addition to the yield to the equity investor, Tables 6.13 and 6.14 show the property yield (15.0%) and the mortgage yield (9.68%).

As indicated in Table 6.14, the mathematically correct yield to the mortgagee calculates to 9.68%. Whereas the mortgage constant and value are calculated based on monthly mortgage payments, the mortgage yield in this proof assumes single annual payments. As a result, the proof's derived yield may be slightly less than the stipulated investment parameter.

Applying the 10-Year Discounted Cash Flow Valuation Formula–Embassy Suites

The methodology just applied to the proposed Sheraton can also be applied to the existing Embassy Suites. Table 6.15 shows the net income of the Embassy Suites, projected beyond the stabilized year at a 3% rate of inflation.

TABLE 6.13 Total Property Yield (*IRR* of 15.0%)

Year of Operation	Net Income Before Debt Service		Present Value Factor @ 15.0%		Discounted Cash Flow
1	$2,120,000	×	0.8698	=	$1,844,000
2	3,541,000	×	0.7565	=	2,679,000
3	4,691,000	×	0.6580	=	3,087,000
4	4,832,000	×	0.5724	=	2,766,000
5	4,975,000	×	0.4978	=	2,477,000
6	5,125,000	×	0.4330	=	2,219,000
7	5,278,000	×	0.3766	=	1,988,000
8	5,437,000	×	0.3276	=	1,781,000
9	5,600,000	×	0.2849	=	1,595,000
10	58,166,000*	×	0.2478	=	14,414,000
Total property value					$34,850,000

* Year 10 net income before debt service $5,768,000
  Plus net sales proceeds   52,398,000
  Total Year 10 *NI* before debt service $58,166,000
Note: Totals are rounded.

TABLE 6.14 Mortgage Component Yield (*IRR* of 9.68%)

Year of Operation	Debt Service		Present Value Factor @ 9.68%		Discounted Cash Flow
1	$2,423,000	×	0.9117	=	$2,209,000
2	2,423,000	×	0.8312	=	2,014,000
3	2,423,000	×	0.7579	=	1,836,000
4	2,423,000	×	0.6910	=	1,674,000
5	2,423,000	×	0.6300	=	1,526,000
6	2,423,000	×	0.5744	=	1,392,000
7	2,423,000	×	0.5237	=	1,269,000
8	2,423,000	×	0.4774	=	1,157,000
9	2,423,000	×	0.4353	=	1,055,000
10	21,480,000*	×	0.3969	=	8,525,000
Value of mortgage component					$22,657,000

* Year 10 debt service $2,423,000
  Plus outstanding mortgage balance   19,057,000
  Total Year 10 *NI* to equity $21,480,000
Note: Totals are rounded.

Solving for Value Using the Simultaneous Valuation Formula

Because the Embassy Suites is an existing hotel with an established operating history, it is subject to slightly less risk than the proposed Sheraton. As such, we have applied slightly different investment parameters for this portion of the case study. Specifically, we have applied an interest rate of 9.5% and an equity yield rate of 20%. Otherwise, the same variables used in the valuation of the proposed Sheraton are considered to be appropriate for the existing Embassy Suites:

Annual net income	NI	See Table 6.15
Loan-to-value ratio	M	65%
Debt service constant	f	0.104844
Equity yield	Y_e	20%
Brokerage and legal fees	b	3%
Annual constant required to amortize the loan in 10 years	f_p	0.15527
Terminal capitalization rate	R_r	11%

TABLE 6.15   Net Income Forecast—Embassy Suites

Year of Operation	Net Income
1	$4,117,000
2	3,585,000
3	3,169,000
4	3,511,000
5	3,616,000
6	3,724,000
7	3,836,000
8	3,951,000
9	4,070,000
10	4,192,000
11	4,318,000

Intermediary calculations must be made using these known variables before the simultaneous valuation formula can be applied. The fraction of the loan paid off during the projection period is calculated as follows:

$$P = (0.104844 - 0.095) \div (0.15527 - 0.095) = 0.163306$$

The annual debt service is calculated as $f \times M \times V$.

$$0.104844 \times 0.65 \times V = 0.0681V$$

Next, the formula is expressed in terms of V.

$$(4,117,000 - 0.0681V) \times 0.8333$$
$$+ (3,585,000 - 0.0681V) \times 0.6944$$
$$+ (3,169,000 - 0.0681V) \times 0.5787$$
$$+ (3,511,000 - 0.0681V) \times 0.4823$$
$$+ (3,616,000 - 0.0681V) \times 0.4019$$
$$+ (3,724,000 - 0.0681V) \times 0.3349$$
$$+ (3,836,000 - 0.0681V) \times 0.2791$$
$$+ (3,951,000 - 0.0681V) \times 0.2326$$
$$+ (4,070,000 - 0.0681V) \times 0.1938$$
$$+ (4,192,000 - 0.0681V) \times 0.1615$$
$$+ (((4,318,000 \div 0.11)$$
$$- (0.03 \times (4,318,000 \div 0.11))$$
$$- ((1 - 0.163306) \times 0.65 \times V)) \times 0.161506) = (1 - 0.65) \times V$$

Then, like terms are combined.

$$\$21,752,760 - 0.373545\ V = (1 - 0.65)\ V$$
$$\$21,752,760 = 0.72355\ V$$
$$V = \$21,752,760 \div 0.72355$$
$$V = \$30,064,000 \text{ (rounded)}$$

Proof of Value

The value is mathematically proven by calculating the yields to the mortgage and equity components over the projection period. If the mortgagee receives its 9.5% yield and the equity yields 20%, then $30,064,000 is the correct value estimate derived by the income capitalization approach.

The indicated market value is allocated as follows:

Mortgage component	0.65	$19,542,000
Equity component	0.35	10,522,000
		$30,064,000

Calculation of annual debt service:

Mortgage component	$19,542,000
Mortgage constant	× 0.104844
Annual debt service	$2,049,000 (rounded)

Net income to equity is forecast in Table 6.16.

TABLE 6.16	Forecast of Net Income to Equity					
Year of Operation	Net Income Available for Debt Service		Debt Service		Net Income to Equity
1	$4,117,000	−	$2,049,000	=	$2,068,000
2	3,585,000	−	2,049,000	=	1,536,000
3	3,169,000	−	2,049,000	=	1,120,000
4	3,511,000	−	2,049,000	=	1,462,000
5	3,616,000	−	2,049,000	=	1,567,000
6	3,724,000	−	2,049,000	=	1,675,000
7	3,836,000	−	2,049,000	=	1,787,000
8	3,951,000	−	2,049,000	=	1,902,000
9	4,070,000	−	2,049,000	=	2,021,000
10	4,192,000	−	2,049,000	=	2,143,000

The residual value to equity at the end of Year 10 is calculated by capitalizing the Year 11 net income as follows:

$4,318,000 ÷ 0.11 =	$39,255,000 (rounded)
Sales proceeds	$39,255,000
Less:	
Broker and legal fees	1,178,000
Mortgage balance	16,350,000
Net sales proceeds	$21,727,000

The annual cash flow to equity plus the residual equity value is discounted to present value at the equity yield rate of 20% (see Table 6.17).

The table demonstrates that the equity investor will receive a 20% yield on the $10,522,000 investment if the annual cash flow and reversion take place as projected. Since the debt service factored into the calculations is based on an interest rate of 9.5%, the required yield for the lender will also be achieved. In addition to the yield to the equity investor, Tables 6.18 and 6.19 show the property yield (13.8%) and the mortgage yield (9.4%).

TABLE 6.17 Equity Component Yield (*IRR* of 20.0%)

Year of Operation	Net Income to Equity		Present Value Factor @ 20%		Discounted Cash Flow
1	$2,068,000	×	0.8333	=	$1,723,000
2	1,536,000	×	0.6944	=	1,067,000
3	1,120,000	×	0.5787	=	648,000
4	1,462,000	×	0.4823	=	705,000
5	1,567,000	×	0.4019	=	630,000
6	1,675,000	×	0.3349	=	561,000
7	1,787,000	×	0.2791	=	499,000
8	1,902,000	×	0.2326	=	442,000
9	2,021,000	×	0.1938	=	392,000
10	23,869,000*	×	0.1615	=	3,855,000
Value of equity component					$10,522,000

* Year 10 net income to equity	$2,143,000
Plus net sales proceeds to equity	21,726,000
Total Year 10 *NI* to equity	$23,869,000

Note: Totals are rounded.

TABLE 6.18 Total Property Yield (*IRR* of 13.8%)

Year of Operation	Net Income Before Debt Service		Present Value Factor @ 13.8%		Discounted Cash Flow
1	$4,117,000	×	0.878705	=	$3,618,000
2	3,585,000	×	0.772122	=	2,768,000
3	3,169,000	×	0.678467	=	2,150,000
4	3,511,000	×	0.596172	=	2,093,000
5	3,616,000	×	0.523859	=	1,894,000
6	3,724,000	×	0.460317	=	1,714,000
7	3,836,000	×	0.404483	=	1,552,000
8	3,951,000	×	0.355421	=	1,404,000
9	4,070,000	×	0.312310	=	1,271,000
10	42,269,000*	×	0.274428	=	11,600,000
Total property value					$30,064,000

* Year 10 net income before debt service	$4,192,000
Plus net sales proceeds	38,077,000
Total Year 10 *NI* before debt service	$42,269,000

Note: Totals are rounded.

TABLE 6.19	Mortgage Component Yield (*IRR* of 9.4%)				
Year of Operation	Debt Service		Present Value Factor @ 9.4%		Discounted Cash Flow
1	$2,049,000	×	0.913808	=	$1,872,000
2	2,049,000	×	0.835044	=	1,711,000
3	2,049,000	×	0.763070	=	1,564,000
4	2,049,000	×	0.697299	=	1,429,000
5	2,049,000	×	0.637197	=	1,306,000
6	2,049,000	×	0.582276	=	1,193,000
7	2,049,000	×	0.532088	=	1,090,000
8	2,049,000	×	0.486226	=	996,000
9	2,049,000	×	0.444317	=	910,000
10	18,399,000*	×	0.406020	=	7,470,000
Value of mortgage component					$19,541,000

* Year 10 debt service	$2,049,000
Plus outstanding mortgage balance	16,350,000
Total Year 10 *NI* to equity	$18,399,000

Note: Totals are rounded.

One advantage of valuing a hotel with a 10-year forecast using an equity yield rate is that the projection period can specifically show the build-up of net income over the assumed holding period most investors use. Another benefit is that the mortgage component's value can be easily substantiated in the market by analyzing current and comparable mortgage terms for similar lodging facilities; assuming a 65% loan-to-value ratio, 65% of the property's market value can be supported.

Using this approach, however, it is difficult to estimate the proper equity yield rate. Although many hotel owners have become more sophisticated, they do not always understand the meaning of equity yield from an appraiser's point of view. Some still think in terms of cash on cash or equity dividend and hold that the reversionary benefits of property appreciation and mortgage amortization are inherently considered in an equity dividend, rather than specifically incorporated into a yield calculation. Consequently, care must be taken in obtaining yield rates from investors to ensure that their responses represent yields, not dividends.

Even with sufficient data and support, estimating a hotel equity yield rate is a subjective process based largely on an appraiser's judgment. On the other hand, the estimate of a hotel mortgage interest rate can be well documented using published life insurance industry data and the interest rate regression formula described previously. Although a degree of subjectivity remains in this process, the mortgage component's value is largely objective. Thus, the capitalization technique produces results that are approximately 65% objective and 35% subjective. In contrast, a 10-year forecast using a discount rate produces results that must be considered largely subjective and do not reflect the investment analysis procedures typical hotel buyers currently use.

10-Year Forecast Using a Discount Rate

Some large institutional investors who purchase hotels on an unleveraged basis (with no debt capital) will apply an overall discount rate to the 10-year forecast of net income before debt service. To this discounted cash flow they add the discounted value of the property at the end of the tenth year, which is derived by capitalizing the net income in Year 11 at the terminal capitalization rate.

CASE STUDY

Applying a Discount Rate to the 10-Year Forecast

In the following example, data associated with the proposed Sheraton portion of the case study is used to illustrate 10-year forecasting using a discount rate. Table 6.20 sets forth the associated data and assumptions.

TABLE 6.20 Data and Assumptions

Year of Operation	Net Income Before Debt Service
1	$2,120,000
2	3,541,000
3	4,691,000
4	4,832,000
5	4,975,000
6	5,125,000
7	5,278,000
8	5,437,000
9	5,600,000
10	5,768,000
11	5,941,000
Terminal capitalization rate	11.0%
Discount rate	15.0
Broker & legal fees	3.0

The reversionary value is calculated by capitalizing the net income before debt service in Year 11 at the terminal capitalization rate.

$5,941,000 \div 0.11 =$				$54,009,091
Sales proceeds				$54,009,091
Less: brokerage and legal				1,620,273
Net sales proceeds				$52,388,818

The net income before debt service for each year plus the reversionary value (net sales proceeds) is discounted to present value at the 15% discount rate. (See Table 6.21.)

TABLE 6.21 **Calculation of Discounted Cash Flow**

Year of Operation	Net Income Before Debt Service		Present Value Factor @ 15%		Discounted Cash Flow
1	$2,120,000	×	0.8696	=	$1,844,000
2	3,541,000	×	0.7561	=	2,677,000
3	4,691,000	×	0.6575	=	3,084,000
4	4,832,000	×	0.5718	=	2,763,000
5	4,975,000	×	0.4972	=	2,473,000
6	5,125,000	×	0.4323	=	2,216,000
7	5,278,000	×	0.3759	=	1,984,000
8	5,437,000	×	0.3269	=	1,777,000
9	5,600,000	×	0.2843	=	1,592,000
10	58,156,818*	×	0.2472	=	14,376,000
Total property value					$34,786,000

* Year 10 *NI* before debt service $5,768,000
    Plus net sales proceeds   52,388,818
    Total Year 10 *NI* to equity $58,156,818
Note: Totals are rounded.

The 10-year forecast using a discount rate does not consider the impact of mortgage debt, leverage, and the specific equity demands of typical hotel investors. Furthermore, it requires a subjective estimate of the entire discount rate, not just the equity portion as in the equity yield approach. Since few hotel investors purchase lodging facilities on an unleveraged basis, documented support for the discount rate is usually unavailable or inconclusive.

10-Year Forecast Using a Debt Coverage Ratio

The 10-year discounted cash flow valuation formula assumes a mortgage-equity relationship and a fixed loan-to-value ratio. The 10-year forecast using a debt coverage ratio also assumes a mortgage equity relationship but utilizes a specific debt coverage ratio as of a certain year.

The debt coverage ratio is the ratio of the net income available for debt service as of a specified year divided by the debt service. Thus, if a hotel's net income as of the third year is projected to be $280 and the debt service is $187, the debt coverage ratio is:

$$\$280/\$187 = 1.5$$

This debt coverage ratio assumption forms the basis for valuing the hotel's mortgage component. Once the value of the mortgage component has been estimated, the value of the equity component can be quantified. The overall property value is therefore the value of the mortgage component plus the value of the equity component.

The initial mortgage balance can be obtained by multiplying the debt coverage ratio by the mortgage constant and dividing this number into the net income before debt service. Assuming a 9% mortgage with a 25-year amortization schedule produces an annual mortgage constant of 0.1007. The initial mortgage balance or the value of the mortgage component can be calculated as follows:

$$\$280/(1.5 \times 0.1007) = \$1,854$$

The next step is to value the equity component. Equity value equals the annual cash flows to equity (equity dividends) plus the equity residual discounted to the present value by the equity yield rate.

The annual cash flow to equity is the net income available for debt service minus the annual debt service. The annual debt service is calculated by multiplying the initial mortgage balance by the mortgage constant:

$$\$1,854 \times 0.1007 = \$187 \text{ (rounded)}$$

The annual cash flow to equity is calculated in Table 6.22.

TABLE 6.22	Calculation of Cash Flow to Equity		
Year	Net Income Available for Debt Service	Debt Service	Cash Flow to Equity
1	$75	$187	$(112)
2	175	187	(12)
3	280	187	93
4	291	187	105
5	303	187	116
6	315	187	128
7	328	187	141
8	341	187	154
9	354	187	168
10	368	187	182

The present value of the cash flows to equity is the cash flow to equity multiplied by the appropriate present value factor. Table 6.23 identifies this calculation, using an 18% discount rate (equity yield).

TABLE 6.23	Discounted Cash Flow		
Year	Cash Flow to Equity	Present Value Factor @ 18%	Discounted Cash Flow
1	$(112)	0.847458	$(95)
2	(12)	0.718184	(8)
3	93	0.608631	57
4	105	0.515789	54
5	116	0.437109	51
6	128	0.370432	48
7	141	0.313925	44
8	154	0.266038	41
9	168	0.225456	38
10	182	0.191064	35
PV cash flow to equity			$265

The equity residual is the reversionary value less the ending mortgage balance. The reversionary value is calculated by taking the projected Year 11 net income before debt service and capitalizing it by the terminal capitalization rate. From that capitalized value the selling expenses such as brokerage and legal fees are deducted. In this example, an 11% terminal capitalization rate is used with selling expenses equal to 2% of the capitalized value. Table 6.24 shows these calculations.

TABLE 6.24	Reversionary Value	
	Year 11 net income	$383*
	Terminal capitalization rate	0.11
	Capitalized value	$3,484
	Less: selling expenses	$70
	Reversionary value	$3,414

* Rounded

The equity residual can then be determined by deducting the ending mortgage balance, which in this example works out to be $1,534. Table 6.25 shows this calculation.

The present value of the equity residual is calculated by multiplying the equity residual by the appropriate present value factor. Table 6.26 shows this calculation.

The value of the equity component is the present value of the cash flows to equity plus the present value of the equity residual as shown in Table 6.27.

TABLE 6.25	Equity Residual	
	Reversionary value	$3,414
	Less: ending mortgage balance	$1,534
	Equity residual	$1,880

TABLE 6.26	Present Value of Equity Residual	
	Equity residual	$1,880
	PV factor @ 18%	× 0.191064
	PV equity residual	$359

TABLE 6.27	Present Value of Equity Component	
	PV cash flow to equity	$265
	PV equity residual	$359
	PV equity component	$624

The overall property value is the value of the mortgage component plus the value of the equity component. Table 6.28 shows this calculation.

TABLE 6.28	Overall Property Value	
	Value of the mortgage component	$1,854
	Value of the equity component	$624
	Overall property value	$2,478

Many lenders base their mortgages on a predetermined debt coverage level as of a certain year. This valuation approach works well for those types of investment decisions.

CASE STUDY

Applying a Debt Coverage Ratio to the 10-Year Forecast

In the following example, data associated with the proposed Sheraton portion of the case study is used to illustrate 10-year forecasting using a debt coverage ratio, assuming the mortgage lender for the proposed Sheraton wants to base the amount of the mortgage on a debt coverage ratio of 1.46 as of the second year of operation. Based on this assumption, the initial mortgage balance can be obtained by multiplying the debt coverage ratio by the mortgage constant and dividing this number into the net income before debt service. Assuming a 9.75% mortgage and a 25-year amortization schedule produces an annual mortgage constant of 0.106936. Using the second year's net income available for debt service, the initial mortgage balance, or the value of the mortgage component, can be calculated as follows:

$$\$3,541/(1.46 \times 0.106936) = \$22,680$$

The next step is valuing the equity component. Equity value equals the annual cash flows to equity (equity dividends) plus the equity residual discounted to present value by the equity yield rate.

The annual cash flow to equity is the net income available for debt service minus the annual debt service. The annual debt service is calculated by multiplying the initial mortgage balance by the mortgage constant.

$$\$22,680 \times 0.106936 = \$2,425$$

Table 6.29 identifies how the annual cash flows to equity are calculated.

TABLE 6.29 Cash Flow to Equity

Year	Net Income Available for Debt Service	Debt Service	Cash Flow to Equity
1	$2,120	$2,425	$(305)
2	3,541	2,425	1,116
3	4,691	2,425	2,266
4	4,832	2,425	2,407
5	4,977	2,425	2,552
6	5,126	2,425	2,701
7	5,280	2,425	2,855
8	5,438	2,425	3,013
9	5,601	2,425	3,176
10	5,769	2,425	3,344

The present value of the cash flows to equity is the cash flow to equity multiplied by the appropriate present value factor. Table 6.30 assumes a 21% discount rate (equity yield).

The equity residual is the reversionary value less the ending mortgage balance. The reversionary value is calculated by taking the projected Year 11 net income before debt service and capitalizing it by the terminal capitalization rate. From that capitalized value, selling expenses such as brokerage and legal fees are deducted. In this example, an 11% terminal capitalization is used with selling expenses equal to 3% of the capitalized value. Table 6.31 shows these calculations.

TABLE 6.30 Discounted Cash Flow

Year	Cash Flow to Equity	PV Factor @ 21%	Discounted Cash Flow
1	$(305)	0.826446	$(252)
2	1,116	0.683013	762
3	2,266	0.564474	1,279
4	2,407	0.466507	1,123
5	2,552	0.385543	984
6	2,701	0.318631	861
7	2,855	0.263331	752
8	3,013	0.217629	656
9	3,176	0.179859	571
10	3,344	0.148644	497
PV cash flow to equity			$7,233

TABLE 6.31 Reversionary Value

Year 11 net income	$5,942
Terminal capitalization rate	11%
Capitalized value	$54,018
Less: selling expenses	$1,621
Reversionary value	$52,398

The equity residual can then be determined by deducting the ending mortgage balance, which in this example works out to $19,079. Table 6.32 shows this calculation.

TABLE 6.32 Equity Residual

Reversionary value	$52,398
Less: ending mortgage balance	$19,079
Equity residual	$33,319

The present value of the equity residual is calculated by multiplying the equity residual by the appropriate present value factor. Table 6.33 shows this calculation.

The equity component's value is the present value of the cash flows to equity plus the present value of the equity residual, as shown in Table 6.34.

TABLE 6.33	Present Value of the Equity Residual	
	Equity residual	$33,319
	PV factor @ 21%	× 0.148644
	PV equity residual	$4,953

TABLE 6.34	Present Value Equity Component	
	PV cash flow to equity	$7,232
	PV equity residual	$4,953
	PV equity component	$12,185

The overall property value is the value of the mortgage component plus the value of the equity component. Table 6.35 shows this calculation.

TABLE 6.35	Overall Property Value	
	Value of the mortgage component	$22,680
	Value of the equity component	$12,185
	Overall property value	$34,865

Conclusion

Of the three valuation approaches available to the appraiser, the income capitalization approach generally provides the most persuasive and supportable conclusions when valuing a lodging facility.

To select a discounting or capitalization procedure, the appraiser considers the market and the techniques hotel buyers and sellers use in making investment decisions. In the past, hotel investors have used various procedures. Their selections have usually been based on factors such as the quality and reliability of the available data, economic conditions, inflation, the availability of financing, and risk. A brief summary of each technique follows.

- *Discounting each year's income over the investment's full life cycle.* This technique is rarely used because a 40-year forecast of income and expenses is unreasonably long and there is no comparable or support data to derive a 40-year discount rate.

- *Capitalizing one stabilized year's income.* This simple technique works well for an established property that is expected to maintain a stable level of occupancy and net income in the future. It is difficult, however, to establish an appropriate stabilized net income for hotels with increasing or decreasing occupancies.

- *Developing a 10-year forecast using an equity yield rate.* Although this technique is complicated, it most accurately reflects the actions of typical hotel buyers, who purchase properties based on their leveraged discounted cash flows. Often the mortgage component can be fully supported by recent market transactions, so 55% to 75% of the discount rate can be substantiated.

- *Developing a 10-year forecast using a discount rate.* This technique is simple but less reliable because the derivation of the discount rate has little support. Moreover, it is difficult to adjust the discount rate for changes in the cost of capital.

Regardless of the technique applied, the estimate of market value should represent the actions of hotel investors and provide a basis for comparing investment alternatives.

Developing capitalization rates and applying the proper discounting procedures are crucial to the income capitalization approach. Appraisers should always try to mirror the rationale and actions of typical buyers and sellers in the current market. Although some capitalization and discounting procedures described in this chapter have been criticized for being overly subjective and inconsistent with present investment thinking, the analyst should remember the axiom of change. The discounting procedure hotel buyers favor this year may not be suited to market and investment conditions next year. Appraisers must constantly re-evaluate and update their appraisal procedures to reach supportable estimates of market value.

CHAPTER 7

Hotels and Motels as Investments

Like most real estate investments, hotels and motels consist of land and improvements (e.g., buildings, permanent equipment, parking areas, swimming pools). Commercial land value generally represents 10% to 20% of total property value. Hotels and motels are unique real estate investments because they contain elements not typically found in income-producing properties. These characteristics affect the risks and the benefits associated with hotel investments and demonstrate the specialized nature of this type of real estate.

Unique Investment Elements

A hotel derives value from certain unique characteristics.

1. *Furniture, fixtures, and equipment.* This category includes guestroom, dining room, and lounge furnishings; kitchen equipment; front office and administrative equipment; and decorative items. Together these elements can account for up to 25% of total property value.

2. *Retail business.* Hotels require specialized, highly trained management. Because they are labor-intensive, employee wages and benefits may consume as much as 40% of gross revenues.

3. *Inventories and working capital.* Lodging facilities may have large inventories of expendable items such as linen, paper supplies, cleaning materials, food, and beverages. Working capital is used for house banks and a petty cash fund and to finance accounts receivable.

When valuing a hotel or motel, the appraiser must accurately define the elements to be included in the final value. For example, if the appraisal is supposed to estimate the value of the real estate alone, appropriate adjustments must be made to separate the value of the furniture, fixtures, and equipment, the business value, and the cost of the inventories and working capital. All of these elements influence the risks, benefits, and value of a hotel investment.

Furniture, Fixtures, and Equipment

Furniture, fixtures, and equipment, or FF&E, are essential to the operation of a lodging facility. Their quality often influences a property's class. Included in this category are all non-real estate items that are normally capitalized, not treated as expenses.

A hotel's furniture, fixtures, and equipment are exposed to heavy use and must be replaced regularly. The useful lives of these items are determined by their quality, durability, and amount of use. (See Table 7.1.)

TABLE 7.1	Typical Useful Lives for Various Items of FF&E
Item	Useful Life in Years
Furnishings	5–12
Lobby	5–12
Restaurant	
Guest rooms	
Case pieces	8–15
Mattresses	5–8
Carpet	
Lobby	3–6
Corridor	2–4
Guestrooms	4–8
Drapes	4–8
Bedspreads	3–6
Kitchen equipment	8–25

Periodic replacement of furniture, fixtures, and equipment is essential to maintaining a lodging facility's quality, image, and income. Capitalized expenditures are not included in the hotel's operating statement, but since they affect an owner's cash flow an appraisal should account for these expenses with an appropriate reserve for replacement.

A reserve for replacement allowance can be estimated on a straight-line basis or as a percentage of the gross revenue. To estimate a reserve with the straight-line method, the estimated future replacement cost of the item is divided by its weighted-average useful life (usually eight to 10 years). Alternatively, a replacement reserve of 4% to 5% of the gross revenue can be used to reflect both the quality of the facilities (average rate) and the amount of use they receive (occupancy level).

In some appraisals, the FF&E's value must be separated from the real estate's value.[1] This separation is required in condemnation proceedings and property tax assessments and in situations where a lender is unable to use chattel as mortgage security. In this process, the income attributed to the personal property is deducted from the hotel's overall net income by multiplying either the current value or the replacement cost of the FF&E by factors that represent returns on and of the FF&E. A return *on* the FF&E reflects the owner's cost of capital and is used with the current market value of the FF&E in place. A return *of* the FF&E is the same as a reserve for replacement and is based on the replacement cost of the items and their estimated useful lives.

Retail Business Value

A lodging facility is a labor-intensive retail business that depends on customer acceptance and highly specialized management skills. Apartment or office building tenants sign leases for one or more years, but a hotel experiences a complete turnover of patronage every two to four days. News of a hotel's poor reputation spreads rapidly and can impact its occupancy levels immediately.

Separating the value of a hotel's business from the value of its real estate is controversial. Determining exactly where the income attributed to the business stops and the income from the real estate begins is difficult. In an appraisal assignment in which the market value encompasses the entire property, the business is part of the going-concern value and is not separated from the real estate. However, some insurance laws, condemnation proceedings, and property tax assessments require a "pure" real estate value, which necessitates treating business value as a separate entity.

Methodologies associated with the separation of business value from total property value have been evolving over time, and many theories exist. For further information about the separation of business value, the reader is directed to recent Appraisal Institute publications.

Inventories and Working Capital

In most instances, inventories and working capital are not included in an estimate of a lodging facility's market value. At the time of closing, any inventory on hand is normally "purchased" by the buyer on a dollar-for-dollar basis, just as fuel oil, taxes, and insurance are adjusted. Working capital is withdrawn by the seller and replaced by the buyer. This process is repeated when the property changes hands again. The result is full recovery of all monies invested in working capital.

If an appraiser wishes to include inventories and working capital in the property value, an appropriate amount must be added to the capitalized net income.

---

1. Members and affiliates of the Appraisal Institute should adhere to Standards Rule 1-2(e), which pertains to the consideration of FF&E in an appraisal. In certain cases, departures from the standards are permitted. Separate valuation of such items may be required when they are significant to the overall value or necessary to fulfill the purpose of the appraisal.

General Risks and Benefits

This chapter has described three unique hotel characteristics and their potential effects on value. To develop an appropriate equity return rate, however, the appraiser must also consider several general factors related to hotel investments. A hotel investment has potential disadvantages, including the possibility of incompetent management, long start-up periods, food and beverage risks, rapid functional obsolescence, susceptibility to external obsolescence, and a lack of liquidity.

- *Competency of management.* The quality of a lodging facility's on-site management directly affects the property's economic viability and value. Competent hotel management can be measured by a manager's ability to maximize long-term revenues while minimizing long-term expenses. Any variance from this definition may noticeably impact the hotel's projected operating results.

- *Long start-up periods.* Lodging facilities usually experience a one- to four-year start-up period before they reach an income level that can support normal financing and equity requirements. Usually hotel investors are advised to budget an adequate cash reserve to carry the property until its occupancy and room rates are sufficient enough to generate a profit.

- *Food and beverage risks.* The food and beverage department carries high risk, yields low profits, and is a source of constant aggravation for most operators. Opening early for breakfast, providing room service, and extending coffee shop hours are essential for competitive reasons, but these practices erode profits for many hotels. Most operators see the food and beverage department not as a profit center, but as a necessary service provided strictly for guests' convenience. Except for a few, high-volume banquet operations, most hotels and motels lose money on food and beverages when all expenses (administrative and general, marketing, energy costs, and property operations and maintenance) are properly allocated. This potential income loss constitutes a major risk and can reduce a hotel's market value.

- *Rapid functional obsolescence.* Lodging facilities' optimal layout, design, construction materials, and amenities change constantly. Over the past 30 years industry standards have changed from exterior corridors to interior hallways, black-and-white televisions to color televisions (often with in-room movies), outdoor pools to enclosed health spas, live entertainment to sports bars, large ballrooms to conference centers, and hand accounting to sophisticated property management systems. With each innovation, existing properties must either alter their facilities or suffer functional obsolescence. Often, correcting functional deficiencies is not economically justified, and the property gradually becomes less competitive. The proliferation of new lodging products and segmentation within the market area tends to amplify the functional obsolescence of older properties. The resulting decline in competitive standing makes hotel investments risky.

- *Susceptibility to external obsolescence.* The events of the late 1980s and early 1990s demonstrated how external factors can hurt the lodging industry. Overbuilding and economic recession caused area occupancies to decline. While capacity increased, businesses curtailed commercial travel and individuals had less disposable income available for leisure travel. The increased use of air transportation, more sophisticated communication systems, and competition from new forms of accommodations (such as time share condominiums and corporate housing) are all examples of macro factors that can cause economic obsolescence.

On a micro level, many motels constructed during the 1950s were forced out of business by the changeover from highways to interstates. The deterioration of downtown areas through the 1970s and 1980s prompted many restaurants, lounges, and other places of entertainment to move to the suburbs. Uncontrollable factors such as these are constant risks for lodging facilities. In most cases external obsolescence cannot be cured and the affected property's value declines immediately.

- *Lack of liquidity.* The sale of a lodging facility is specialized. Because the market is limited to comparatively few potential buyers, generating interest may take three months or longer. Once a prospective buyer is found, many time-consuming details must be worked out. Financing and the transfer of licenses, leases, service contracts, and franchise agreements must be arranged, equity and tax shelter programs must be structured, and appraisals and surveys must be performed. Often the seller is forced to maintain an interest in the property by taking back purchase money financing.

There are, however, aspects of hotel investments that help offset their negative features. The two most important advantages of such investments are favorable tax treatment and the potential for large profits.

- *Favorable tax treatment.* Much of the personal property within a hotel can depreciate within a short time. As a result, hotels and motels generate tax shelter benefits and are therefore well suited for syndication.

- *Potential for large profits.* Once the income from a lodging facility breaks even, profits tend to increase rapidly. As this text has indicated, many hotel expenses are fixed and do not vary significantly with occupancy. Thus, profits increase with occupancy.

The financial returns from a hotel investment are derived from the annual cash flow after debt service (equity dividend), mortgage amortization, and the potential value appreciation realized when the property is sold. Over the past decade, the perceived equity returns demanded by hostelry investors have ranged from a high of 20% to 25% to a low of 12% to 20%. Equity returns are influenced by a variety of circumstances, including the market's condition, general real estate and hotel-motel risk factors, individual property risk factors, supply and demand ratios, the availability and cost of financing, and tax benefits.

Equity build-up through mortgage amortization and value appreciation are also important investment considerations. Together they form the basis of the Ellwood method of valuation, which employs the concept of equity yield. Today's hotel investors are increasingly sophisticated, and discounted cash flow analysis, before- and after-tax equity yield calculations, and other computer techniques have become well-established procedures.

In this century, the valuation and analysis of hotel investments are bound to change as evaluation techniques become more sophisticated and data become more abundant. Appraisers are hopeful that their ability to forecast future economic results will also be enhanced and help to reduce the risks of investing in lodging facilities.

Index

based on an analysis of lodging activity, 105–128, 197, 202
business value, 359, 361

C

Cahners Travel Group, 95
capitalization rates
    and actual market sales, 317–319
    applying, 330–333
    selecting, 321–330, 332–333
    terminal, 335
cash-on-cash return, 327
cash flow to equity, 338
casino hotels, 163
center city hotels, 13, 167
chains, 164, 168–187
    defined, 168
    expansion of, 12, 21, 168
    future of, 187
    history of, 9–10
    and image, 170
    and internal expansion, 186
    and management contracts, 168, 170
    origin of, 6, 8
    See also franchising
classification, of lodging facilities, 155–168
class rankings, 164–165
coefficient of correlation, 326–327
commercial property, 159–160
communications, 23
community-financed hotels, 4
comparable base, 246, 247, 256
comparable financial statements, 248–251
    adjusting, 252–287
comparable sales, 317
competition, 112–114
    analysis of, 37, 56–57
    case study, 115–116
    defined, 187
    primary, 113–114, 188
    secondary, 113–114, 188
competitive positioning method of forecasting rates, 231–232
conference center, 162–163
constant and current dollars, 64, 66
construction
    cost data, 69–70
    trends, 4, 6, 12–13, 16
Consumer Price Index (CPI), 64, 66, 102–103
Consumer Price Index for all Urban Consumers (CPI-U), 103, 148
contacts, as data sources, 36–38
contract business, 37
convention center and visitor bureau, 55
convention hotels, 13, 160, 168
corporate bond yields, 326
corridors and elevator lobbies, 43–44
cost approach, 311–312
customer preference items, 197–201

D

data
    area-specific, 49–52
    assignment-specific, 30–31
    categories, 77–79
    client-supplied, 34
    comparable financial, adjusting, 256–289
    economic and demographic, 52–60, 62–66, 139

    field, 32, 36–38
    in-house, 32, 35–36
    local sources of, 58–59
    mortgage rate, 69
    occupancy and average rate, 67–68
    property-specific, 29–30
    sources of, 32, 65
    types of, 29–31
data analysis, 27
data collection, 26–27, 31–60
    checklist, 32–33
    techniques, 60–76
data of last resort, 69
date of value, 30
debt coverage ratio
    applying with 10-year forecast, 350–356
debt service, 327, 336–337
demand
    accommodatable, 124
    induced, 124–125
    latent, 122–127
    macro, 77–104, 141
    micro, 104–105
    temporary induced, 125
    total accommodatable latent, 190
    total usable latent, 188, 190–196
    unaccommodatable latent, 190–195
    unaccommodated, 122–124
    See also build-up approach; generators of transient visitation; room night demand
demand allocation, 202
demand generators
    case study, 134–139
    identifucation of, 37
    list of, 37, 54–55, 131
demand levels, 149
demand projections, 139
Department of Commerce, 91
depreciation, 311
deterioration, 311, 321
development costs, 313–314
directories of lodging facilities, 66–67
discounted cash flow valuation formula, 338–348
discount factors, 238, 330
    applying with 10-year forecast, 349–350
    selecting, 321–330

E

economic and demographic data, 53–60, 62–66, 139
economic development agencies, 53
economy,
    affect on lodging industry, 13–19
Educational Institute of the American Hotel and Motel Association, 241
elevators, 46–47
employment, hotel, 87–89
energy consumption
    by region, 279
    conversion factors, 280
energy expense, 277–281
    calculating, 279–281
energy management systems, 48
Engineering Economics Foundation, 5
entertainment facilities, 48, 243
equity capital, 18
equity data
    investor interviews, 328
    sources, 328

equity dividend rate, 327–329
equity investment, 327
equity residual value, 338, 353
equity return, 328
equity yield rates, 327–330
    applying with 10-year forecast, 333–349
estimate of occupancy, 201
European Plan, 160
excess land, 30, 38
existing vs. proposed facility, 239–240
expansion of economy, 15–22
extended-stay facility
    characteristics of, 19–20, 161–162
external obsolescence, 363

F

facilities
    comparison of, 249
fair share, 202, 203–204
fair share factors, 120, 213
feasibility studies, 25
Federal Aviation Administration (FAA), 64
fill nights, 123
finance, insurance, and real estate (FIRE) sector, 95
financial comparable selection procedure, 249–252
financial statements, 240, 248–250
    adjusting, 252–287
financial structure of property, 31
financing, 318, 322–323
    historical, 5, 6, 7, 12, 13–14, 19, 24
    terms, 334–335
FIRE. *See* finance, insurance, and real estate sector
first-tier management company, 181–183, 185
fixed component, estimating, 248
fixed and variable component approach to forecasting, 245–307
fixed and variable income and expense forecasting model, 27
    case study, 290–291
    steps in, 246–291
    theoretical basis of, 245–246
fixed and variable percentages
    of revenues and expenses, 247
food and beverage
    risk, 322, 362
    service described, 44
food and beverage expense. *See* beverage expense; food expense
food and beverage revenue. *See* beverage revenue; food revenue
food expense, 242
    characteristics of, 264–266
    components of, 265
    dollars per available room, 266
food revenue
    characteristics of, 257–259
    fixed and variable component calculation of, 291–292
    percentage of, 255
    projecting, 258
    total, 293
forecast of revenue and expense, 243–244
    existing vs. proposed facility, 239–243
    See also income and expenses
franchising, 12, 170–187, 281
    and benefits to chain, 180
    and benefits to owner, 170–171
    and costs to chain, 180

    and costs to owner, 171
    fees, 171–178, 274
    and liability of owner, 180
    long-term strategies of, 178–180
    and management contracts, 180–182
    origins of, 8–9
    reservations from, 38
    and segmentation, 178–179
    See also chains
franchise reports, 35
furniture, fixtures, and equipment (FF&E), 285, 359–361
F.W. Dodge, 188

G

generators of transient visitation
    identifying, 129–130
    survey of selected, 130–133
geographic location, 250
globalization, 13, 22, 23, 91
ground leases, 312, 315–316
guest room
    description, 43
    supply, 188–195

H

hard budget hotel, 19, 20, 23
health spas, 4, 164
heating, ventilation, and air-conditioning, 47–48
highway department, 52
highway lodging facility, 23, 167
historic average room count (HARC), 114
Hospitality, Lodging, and Travel Research Foundation, 279
hospitality valuation index (HVI), 319
Hospitality Valuation Services, 319
Hotel Association of New York City, 240
hotel associations, 57
Hotel Motel Brokers Association, 328
hotel-motel life cycle, 320–321
hotel-motel industry. *See* lodging industry
Hotel Management
    See Hotel and Motel Management
Hotel and Motel Management, 5
hotels
    See lodging facilities
hotel survey boilerplate, 74–75
Hotel Transactions Survey, 318
Hotel and Travel Index, 67
hotel unit, 117
housekeeping, 44–45
house profit, 241

I

improvements, 41–49
incentive management fee, 183–184
income capitalization approach, 317, 319–357
    assumptions of, 319–320
    application methods, 319
    and forecasts, 239
income and expenses
    forecasting, 69, 239–302, 320, 328
    ratios, 249
    revising the base, 287–289
    statements of, 241–243, 250–251, 256, 258–259, 285–289
    and variable change calculation, 292
    See also administrative and general expenses; beverage expense; beverage revenue; energy expense; food expense; food revenue; marketing

financing, 322
  interest rates, 322
  types, 322
mortage-equity analysis, 322–327
mortgage-equity technique, 69, 329
mortgage-equity valuation model, 27
mortgage interest rates, 327
  and money market instruments, 323–327
mortgage rate data, 69, 323
mortgage recapture, 327
motel
  origin and characteristics, 7–9
motor hotel, 8

N

national parks, 99–100
  traveler characteristics, 99, 101
national park service, 99
neighborhood characteristics, 49–50
net income, 242
net income to equity, 337, 341–342, 346
net income forecast, 319–353

O

obsolescence, 3, 9, 23
  external, 311, 321, 363
  functional, 311, 321–322, 362–363
occupancy
  cycles, 224–225
  estimating, 117–122, 226–227
  forecast of, 218
  historical trends, 4, 6, 13, 15, 19
  levels by location, 152, 155
  levels by property type, 153, 155
  levels by state, 148, 151, 154
  market-wide levels, 196, 230
  maximum, 224
  projections, 221–222, 226–227, 248
  property-specific, 223
  rate, 68, 150, 218, 221, 222
  stabilized, 223–227
Official Meeting Facilities Guide, 67
operating departments, 241
operating expenses
  undistributed, 241
operating statistics, 68–69
  and ratios, national averages, 240
other income, 260–262, 293, 294
  characteristics of, 262, 268–269
  expense, 268–269
overall rate, 328
overbuilding, 6, 12, 15, 17, 24
over-hoteling, 5

P

Patriot American Hospitality, 21
payroll employment, 87, 89
penetration factor, 202–212
  analyzing, 197
  assigning, 206
  case study, 120–122, 205–212
  converting, 211–213
  defined, 120
  overall, 218
  projecting, 206
  by segment, 211–212
person-trips, 79–80, 83–85
  See also trips
photographs, 59

pleasure travel, 1, 2, 6
  future of, 23–24
Plog Research, 95, 98
population growth, 140–141
present values, 340–353
primary market area, 36
profits, 363–364
property operations and maintenance expense
(PO&M), 243, 273–277, 301
  categories of, 276
property rights appraised, 30
property size, 250
property-specific information, 38–49
property taxes. *See* taxes
property yield, 328
proposed vs. existing facility, 239–240

Q

questionnaires, 132

R

rate of change, 139, 142–145
rate
  data, 68
  resistance, 38
  strategy, 38
real estate bonds, 4–5
real estate investments, 4
real estate investment trusts (REITs), 12, 16, 18, 318–319
recapture, 321–322, 327
recession, 15–22, 148, 318
request for proposals (RFP), 29
reserve for replacement, 285
Resolution Trust Corporation (RTC), 16
resort hotels, 4, 23
  all-inclusive, 160
  characteristics of, 160–161, 168
  and occupancy levels, 160–161
Restaurant Activity Index (RAI), 64
Restaurant Business, 64
restaurants and lounges, 57–58
reversionary value, 337, 352, 355
revising the base, 287–289
  case study, 287–289
  revenue and expense categories, 287–289
RevPAR data, 148, 150, 155, 318
  by location, 159
  by property type, 159
  by state, 158
risk analysis, 322
risk and benefits
  of food and beverage service, 362
  of hotel investment, 362–364
room, 117
rooming houses, 4, 23
room night, 62, 64, 104, 130
room night analysis, 27
room night capture, 218
  case study, 218–222
  conversion of, 219
  by segment, 219–220
room night demand, 104–105
  accommodated, 119–120
  case study, 142–145
  forecasting, 139–145
  quantifying, 133–134
  total, 105, 128

room rates
    average rate per occupied room, 227–238, 249
    by brand, 166
    case study, 233–238
    classifications, 249
    commercial rate, 228
    contract rate, 228
    discounts, 233–238
    published rate, 228
    rack rate, 228
room rates, macro, 102
rooms expense, 242, 262–264, 293, 295
rooms revenue, 256–257
    calculating, 244, 256
    case study, 244
room supply, 7
royalty, 172, 274
rule-of-thumb method of forecasting rates, 232–233

S
safety systems, 48–49
sales comparison approach, 70, 316–319
sales data, 70
sales of major hotels, 318
sampling, 133–139
savings and loans, 14–16
seasonality, 37, 160
second-tier management company, 181–183, 185
security system, 49
seers, 132
simultaneous valuation formula, 339–340, 344–345
Smith Travel Research, 67, 68, 81, 139, 147–148
stabilized income
    capitalizing, 331–332
stabilized occupancy, 223–227
Standard & Poors composite index, 326
start-up period, 362
suburban hotel, 167–168
supply, 16, 19, 103–104
    historical levels by state, 151
    macro, 147–155
    micro, 187–227
surveys, 60, 72–75

T
taxes
    personal property, 50–51, 363
    real estate, 14–16, 50–51, 282–284
    room, bed, or occupancy, 57
telephone
    expense, 266–268
    revenue, 259–260, 293, 294
    system, 48
temporary induced demand, 125
terminal capitalization rate, 330
termination provisions, 184–185
Texas Rooms Tax, 68
total accommodatable latent demand, 190
total income before fixed charges, 242
total revenue calculations, 262
total usable latent demand, 188, 190–196
traffic counts, 65
transient visitation, 107, 129–130

transportation, 22–23, 85, 89–91
    changes in, 7, 104
    modes of, 37
    patterns of, 167
    vertical systems of, 46–47
travel
    agent commissions, 38
    airline, 89–91
    business, 81, 85, 86, 94–95
    by car, 13, 89–91, 167
    characteristics of, 87
    commercial, 94–95
    data on prices, 102–104
    international, 91–94
    leisure, 1–5, 23–24, 81, 85, 86, 99–101
    meeting and group, 95–99
    month of, 87, 88
    trends, 87
Travel Industry Association of America (TIA), 78–79, 102
travel price data, 102
Travel Price Index (TPI), 102–104
trends
    economic and demographic, 52–53
trips, 79–86
    categories of, 80–81
    characteristics of, 82–86
    purpose of, 80–81, 86

U
unaccommodatable latent demand, 190–195
unaccommodated demand, 38, 122–124
undistributed operating expenses, 241
Uniform Franchising Offering Circular (UFOC), 173
Uniform Standards of Professional Appraisal Practice (USPAP), 309–310
Uniform System of Accounts for Hotels, 227
Uniform System of Accounts for the Lodging Industry (USALI), 240–242, 257, 259, 262, 267, 269, 272, 273, 277, 284
unions, 38
units of comparison, 252–253, 293
U.S. Travel Data Center, 78–82, 87–89, 91, 94
utilities, 40–41

V
valuation
    applying a discounted cash flow formula, 338–348
    applying a discount rate, 349–350
    by capitalizing stabilized income, 331–332
    using a debt coverage ratio, 350–356
    using an equity yield rate, 333–348
variable component
    estimating, 248
variable percent change, 293, 295–296
visiblity, 40

W
weighting factor, 114
Woods & Poole data, 64

Z
zoning, 51–52
    manuals, 61–62
    and planning, 52, 62